BRANDISHING THE FIRST AMENDMENT

Brandishing the First Amendment

Commercial Expression in America

TAMARA R. PIETY

THE UNIVERSITY OF MICHIGAN PRESS

ANN ARBOR

Published in the United States of America by
The University of Michigan Press
Manufactured in the United States of America
⊗ Printed on acid-free paper

2015   2014   2013   2012   4   3   2   1

A CIP catalog record for this book is available from the British Library.

Library of Congress Cataloging-in-Publication Data

Piety, Tamara R.
Brandishing the First Amendment : commercial expression in America /
  Tamara R. Piety.
       p.   cm.
  Includes bibliographical references and index.
  ISBN 978-0-472-11792-5 (cloth : alk. paper) — ISBN 978-0-472-02772-9
(e-book)
    1. Corporate speech—United States.   2. Freedom of speech—United
States.   3. Advertising law—United States.   I. Title.
KF4772.P54   2012

342.7308'53—dc23

2011043629

To Gerald

Contents

Acknowledgments

This book is the result of many years of research, writing, talking, and thinking about its topic. Some of the arguments and some of the text throughout the book have appeared previously, in a somewhat different form, in my article "Against Freedom of Commercial Expression," 29 *Cardozo L. Rev.* 2583 (2008).

Although I have written extensively on the topic of commercial and corporate speech, the process of generating a book on the subject at times seemed too much for me. It is a very large subject and a more sustained exploration of some aspects of the problem had to be sacrificed in the interest of keeping this book to a manageable length. For those interested in the subject the bibliography offers a wealth of resources for further reading, including my earlier articles.

This book could not have been written without the continuous and enthusiastic support of Gerald Torres. It was he and Jim Reische, my first editor at the University of Michigan Press, who urged me to consider writing a book and Gerald who was unflagging in his support and encouragement when I became discouraged and overwhelmed. I cannot thank them enough. I also thank my subsequent editor at the Press, Melody Herr, who was helpful and supportive through what often seemed like an endless process, particularly when the *Citizens United* decision required a substantial last minute rewrite. Special thanks are also due to Ron Collins and David Skover, who were early champions of my work and who invited me to present my works in progress at many conferences that helped me to develop and refine the ideas in this book. Similarly, I want to thank those with whom I have debated: Martin Redish, at a panel sponsored by the Federal Trade Commission pursuant to an invitation from its director of consumer protection, David Vladeck; Calvin Massey, at a debate organized by Charles Knapp and Evan Lee at the University of California, Hastings; and Bradley A. Smith, at a Federalist Society debate sponsored by the University of Tulsa Chapter of the Federalist Society.

I also thank my colleagues at the University of Tulsa College of Law, Florida State University, and elsewhere as well as friends and family members who have read and commented on multiple drafts of the book or earlier, related articles or on presentations given at various conferences: Kate Adams, Gary Allison, Tom Arnold, Ed Baker, Ann Bartow, Marianne Blair, Curtis Bridgeman, Barbara Bucholtz, Russell Christopher, Robin Craig, Reza Dibaji, Garrett Epps, Maggie Epps, Michael Fischl, Catherine Fisk, Brian Foley, Paul Finkelman, Brian Galle, Eric Goldman, Kent Greenfield, Dan Greenwood, Sam Halabi, Jon Hanson, Paul Horwitz, Robert Jensen, Charles Knapp, Doug Kysar, Linda Lacey, Sanford Levinson, Dan Markel, Tom McGarity, Lawrence Mitchell, Jeremy Paul, M. G. Piety, Steven Shiffrin, Gordon Smith, Robert Spoo, Fernando Tesón, Rebecca Tushnet, Jim Rossi, Mark Seidenfeld, Michael Siedebecker, Faith Stevelman, Manuel Utset, David Vladeck, Kate Waits, Cynthia Williams, Jan Doolittle Wilson, and Hannah Wiseman. Apologies to anyone I've inadvertently left out. Special thanks go to Jami Fullerton, professor of advertising at Oklahoma State University, for helping me to get the advertising part right; anything I got wrong is my fault. Special thanks are also due to my mother, Patricia R. Piety, who freely gave me the benefit of her professional editing skills at several critical junctures. Thanks go to the University of Tulsa College of Law and to Dean Janet Levit and to former dean Robert Butkin for supporting this work with research grants through several successive years and to Dean Don Weidner at Florida State University for inviting me to spend a sabbatical semester there to work on the book. Thanks also go to the students in my commercial speech seminars at Florida State University and at the University of Tulsa and to my many research assistants over the years who have assisted in this work: Andrei Alkhou, Emily Cipra, John Hawkins, Stephanie Landolt, John Olson,

Kelly O'Neill, John Williamson, Linda Smith, Derek Weinbrenner, and Philip Davis for work on the bibliography. Thanks to Maridel Allinder for proofreading the final draft. Finally, my thanks go to University of Tulsa librarians Melanie Nelson and Courtney Selby for all their assistance. It is a source of profound sorrow that my friends and colleagues Linda Lacey and C. Edwin Baker both passed away before I was able to finish this book. I like to think they both would have approved of it.

The Problem of Commercial Expression

[P]rotection of commercial speech, particularly in robust form,
is a recent occurrence.
—Lawrence O. Gostin,
Public Health Law: Power, Duty, Restraint

In 2009 *Advertising Age* reported that advertising and marketing were taking a "beating" in Washington.[1] Several legislative proposals that would either directly or indirectly threaten to put more limits on the industry were receiving serious attention in Washington. Marketing folk opposed these proposals because they wanted "an unencumbered advertising and marketing environment."[2] Despite this new interest in regulation, the marketing environment is likely to remain relatively unencumbered for some time to come because efforts to restrain it are likely to encounter a formidable obstacle in the courts—the First Amendment. Although the situation is little known outside of the litigation circles involved, industry has been engaged for the last forty years or so in strategic litigation raising First Amendment challenges to governmental attempts to regulate commercial speech. These efforts have met with some success because, although they did not always result in a win in a particular case, cumulatively they have successfully changed judicial and public attitudes toward governmental regulation of commercial speech.

Although for the first 200 years or so of this country's existence most observers took it for granted that the government could regulate commercial speech as a function of its power to regulate commerce, by the mid-1970s this was no longer obviously the case. Regulation had gotten a bad name, and the marketplace was increasingly trusted to take care of many problems formerly thought to be the preserve of government.

After the events of the last couple of decades however, regulation is starting to look good again. We have seen the spectacular failure of some of the world's largest companies (e.g., Enron and AIG); the discovery of widespread corruption and incompetence of private contractors like Halliburton and Blackwater in the conduct of two wars; repeated shocks in the financial and credit markets; the mining accidents and the explosion of the Deepwater Horizon oil drilling rig in which inadequate regulatory oversight is alleged to have played a role; and a seemingly endless stream of news about recalled cars, tainted food, children's toys contaminated with lead, poisoned dog food, and heavily advertised drugs removed from the market after widespread use revealed more dangers than their manufacturers disclosed.

All these events have prompted calls for regulatory reform. However, the foundation laid by industry through strategic litigation during the period of relative regulatory inertia may make it very difficult for government to reassert control. This litigation around commercial speech and the rights of businesses to engage in protected expression have made an argument seem natural and inevitable that only fifty years or so ago would have seem absurd—that commercial speech is entitled to full First Amendment protection.

Beginning in 1976 and then accelerating into the early part of the new century, courts have been increasingly willing to entertain arguments that governmental attempts to regulate commercial speech violate the First Amendment. This is a disturbing development, because if the government cannot regulate commercial speech, it cannot regulate commerce—period.[3]

Marketing is big business, perhaps one of the biggest businesses in the United States. According to one estimate, it generates an annual $6 trillion in economic activity.[4] But all this economic activity may come at a steep price. Marketing has been implicated in virtually every major news story of the past few years—spiraling health care costs, spectacular corporate meltdowns like Enron and AIG, financial reform, the mortgage crisis, tainted foods, environmental safety, global warming, increasing childhood obesity, and many others. Sometimes it has played a central role in creating or exacerbating a crisis, sometimes only a supporting one. But it is always a part of the problem. Although marketing practices are regulated in a number of ways, enforcement has often been uneven. It is becoming obvious that plugging gaps and greater oversight are long overdue.

The realization that more regulation is in order is at odds with the increased willingness of the courts to grant commercial speech (and commercial speakers) greater First Amendment protection from regulation. That judicial willingness is the product of several decades during which industry has engaged in strategic litigation, brandishing the First Amendment as a means of fending off regulatory efforts of all types—for cigarette labels, the marketing of junk food to children, disclosure rules on financial instruments, do-not-call registries, pharmaceutical advertising, and many other regulations. This is extremely significant because the First Amendment can be a legal trump card. Ever since the Supreme Court proclaimed in *Marbury v. Madison*[5] that courts have the power to overturn acts of Congress or of the executive branch on the grounds that they are unconstitutional, a constitutional defense has become a potential game ender, particularly in the hands of a wealthy and powerful litigant. Any renewed efforts by Congress or by federal agencies to regulate commercial expression could be struck down by a Supreme Court sympathetic to calls for an "unencumbered" marketing environment.

This is not idle speculation. Several individual members of the Supreme Court have already signaled their belief that commercial speech ought to enjoy more protection than it currently does.[6] In 2010 the Court as a body rendered a decision in *Citizens United v. Federal Election Commission*[7] that strongly suggests that the majority of the Court favors fewer restrictions on commercial speech. In one of the most aggressive examples of judicial activism in recent times, the Court affirmatively reached out to decide the *Citizens United* case and overruled earlier precedents that limited expenditures by corporations in elections.[8] Central to the reasoning in the majority opinion in *Citizens United* is the rhetorical framing of corporations as "citizens" whose participation in political speech should not be limited because of their corporate status.

Citizens United was greeted with widespread public criticism.[9] It may well have the pernicious effects on elections that its critics predict,[10] but its most serious and far-reaching implications are more likely to be its effect on the regulation of commercial speech.[11] At present the commercial speech that most affects the public welfare is, by and large, issued by large, multinational corporations. *Citizens United,* by framing such corporations as citizens with distinct rights of expression, provides ammunition to collapse the distinction between commercial speech, which currently only has limited constitutional protection, and protected political or artistic expression, which enjoys heightened protection. Such a collapse would imperil existing consumer protection legislation and strangle in their infancy any efforts to assert greater regulatory supervision over critical industries like banking, pharmaceuticals, insurance, and many others. The connections between the *Citizens United* case and more First Amendment protection for commercial speech may not be obvious. To better understand why *Citizens United* may prove threatening to our ability to regulate commerce, not just to limit corporate participation in politics, we must go back a few years to another case, one that, like *Citizens United,* the Supreme Court reached out for but that, unlike *Citizens United,* the Court ultimately did not decide: *Nike v. Kasky.*

In 1996, Phil Knight, CEO of Nike, faced a problem. His company had been the undisputed leader in the athletic apparel market, with annual revenues in the billions. Hundreds of professional and college athletes wore Nike clothing and gear under exclusive endorsement contracts. Yet all was not well. The company had been the subject of a series of exposés about its labor practices. Various groups charged that workers making Nike products in factories in Southeast Asia were working brutal hours for wages of approximately $40 a month. They alleged that Nike's workers were exposed to unsafe levels of toxic chemicals like toluene and subjected to regular physical, psychological, and sexual abuse. In 1997, Bob Herbert of the *New York Times* wrote a column criticizing Nike for what he called its "abusive" labor practices.[12]

These charges hurt Nike's public image, endangering not only its sales but also its stock price. As some student groups began calling for boycotts of Nike on college campuses, analysts speculated about how these developments would affect the company's endorsement deals and its market share. Nike responded to the crisis with a concerted public relations effort. Its representatives sent letters to the editors of major newspapers defending Nike's labor practices. It also sent letters to organizations like the YWCA and to college presidents and athletic directors. It issued press releases about the issue and posted them on its website. At a public event, CEO Knight claimed that the air in the factories of many of Nike's contractors was cleaner than that in Los Angeles. Nike even funded a "fact-finding tour" of its own overseas operations. The tour was put together by a PR firm and led by former UN ambassador Andrew Young. At a press conference afterward, Young reported that although Nike could still do better, it was basically doing a good job with improving the conditions for the workers who made its products. In many of these communications, Nike made specific, factual claims about its labor practices (e.g., that workers received free lunches)—claims that could be checked. Apparently, some of these claims were not true.

Marc Kasky, a California consumer activist, read Nike's claims and got angry. He believed that many of Nike's statements were misleading (at best) and maybe knowingly false. So, although Kasky admitted he had never purchased a pair of Nike shoes himself, he sued Nike in a California court for violations of California's unfair trade practices and unfair competition laws, as well as for fraud and deceit. Kasky claimed he was suing on behalf of the consumers of California. He could do this because, at the time, California law allowed any citizen to sue as a private attorney general—in other words, to sue on behalf of all of the citizens of California—for an injury to the public.[13]

Nike responded to Kasky's suit with a demurrer, the legal equivalent of saying "So what?" By filing a demurrer, Nike was arguing that even if everything Kasky said was true—including his claim that Nike had engaged in fraud and deceit—those statements could not be the basis of a legal claim for relief, because the allegedly false statements were protected by the First Amendment. It is worth repeating this defense to underscore its audacity: *Nike argued that Kasky's claim for fraud and deceit did not state a cause of action because the speech was protected by the First Amendment.*

This is a bold assertion—that the First Amendment insulates fraud. It is important to highlight this aspect of the suit because supporters of more protection for commercial speech, when faced with objections that such protection might insulate more fraud, respond that "of course" the First Amendment does not protect fraud. Nike's response to Kasky's lawsuit illustrates the emptiness of those reassurances.

However, what was arguably more shocking than Nike's claim of a First Amendment defense was that the trial court agreed with Nike and dismissed Kasky's suit. A California court of appeals affirmed. Only when the case reached the California Supreme Court was Nike's argument subjected to closer scrutiny and rejected. The California Supreme Court found that some of Nike's statements appeared to be commercial speech and, as such, were not entitled to full First Amendment protection in the first place, let alone insulation from a fraud claim.

Pursuant to the commercial speech doctrine, commercial speech is not entitled to any protection at all unless it is true. Therefore, if any of Nike's contested statements were "commercial speech," then their truth or falsity mattered. Kasky claimed that some of Nike's statements were false and that Nike's management knew they were false. Pursuant to the doctrine, the First Amendment does not protect false commercial speech. Since the case had been dismissed prior to any discovery, it was possible, the majority wrote, that evidence produced through discovery would prove Kasky's claims had merit. Over some vigorous dissents, the majority held that, because some of the speech at issue in the case appeared to be commercial speech, the lower courts had erred in dismissing the case and that Kasky was entitled to go forward with discovery. This was bad news for Nike because it meant the company would have to turn over some of its internal documents about the conditions in its factories to Kasky. Anything produced to Kasky through discovery was likely to become a matter of public knowledge and possibly lead to more public relations problems.

Rather than submit to discovery, Nike chose to ask the Supreme Court of the United States to review its case. It wanted the Court to reinstate the trial court's dismissal. The Supreme Court accepted the case for review and heard oral argument. It was one of the most closely watched cases of that term, because Nike argued for more than just a resolution of its dispute with Kasky. It sought a definitive opinion from the Supreme Court that statements such as those it had made in defense of its labor practices were fully protected speech under the First Amendment.

At stake was whether a company could be held legally accountable for the accuracy of its statements about its labor, environmental, or other practices. If the Court's answer was that corporations could not be held accountable for these statements, it would be a green light for major corporations to continue their carefully massaged public relations campaigns regarding social responsibility practices, without fear of having those campaigns later be a basis for liability if some part of them turned out to be untrue. If Nike could get a ruling that all such speech was entitled to a constitutional shield, it would

ensure that the advertising and marketing environment would remain "unencumbered." The commercial benefits of being free to engage in promotional activities unfettered by any accountability for the accuracy of those
representations are obvious. What Nike tried to obtain was the freedom to issue whatever speech it deemed was in its best interest, even if some of its
statements were false and even if the company (or some of its employees)
knew they were false.[14] If, however, the Court ruled in favor of Kasky, companies issuing corporate social responsibility reports—press releases about issues like their labor, environmental, and human rights practices—could no
longer leave the content of such statements to the marketing and public relations departments. Instead, they would have to make sure their statements
were accurate, or they would face the possibility of legal liability.

Thus, in its appeal to the Supreme Court, Nike argued that none of the
speech in question was commercial speech, rather, it was all speech fully protected by the First Amendment. Because Nike's statements about its labor
practices had been issued in a public relations format and contained arguments (or, more accurately, references to arguments) about globalization,
Nike argued that these statements constituted speech about matters of public
concern and therefore ought to be protected from fraud claims to the same
extent as political speech, which is largely not regulatable for its truth or falsity. Nike claimed it should be entitled to contribute what it characterized as
valuable information to the debate about globalization, a matter of public
concern. (Note that Justice Kennedy's majority opinion in *Citizens United*
made this same argument with respect to his assertion that corporations
ought to be able to contribute to the political debates of the day on an equal
basis.) Of course, arguing that knowing falsehoods ought to be protected by
the First Amendment is not a terribly attractive position.

Perhaps with the fraud issue in mind, Nike had a fallback position. The
company's lawyers argued in the alternative that even if some of its statements were commercial speech and thus testable for their truth, judicial review of those statements should be subject to strict scrutiny review under the
actual malice standard of *New York Times v. Sullivan*.[15] Under the *Sullivan*
test, plaintiffs like Kasky must show that a speaker's false statements were
made with actual malice.[16] This standard was adopted to prevent the "chilling" of debate thought to result from the specter of liability for even honest
mistakes. Nike argued that this specter of liability would lead it to refuse to

issue corporate social responsibility statements or to offer its opinion on issues of public concern, thereby impoverishing the public debate. It asserted that the actual malice standard was necessary to ensure "balance" in debate on matters of public concern.[17] The company claimed that Kasky's complaint had not alleged facts or claims sufficient to meet the *Sullivan* standard and therefore that the case should be dismissed as inadequately pleaded. These arguments turned out to be entirely without merit. There was little evidence that the case had chilled Nike's public relations efforts or social responsibility reporting except to the extent that it was posturing for the pending case. More important, since so many of Kasky's claims were later corroborated by some of Nike's own statements, it is hard to argue that Nike had contributed much to the public debate beyond obfuscation.[18]

Had the Court accepted this argument, it would have presented Kasky with an interesting challenge on remand. It might be easy to prove that certain statements were false, but how would Kasky prove that these statements, promotional statements that Nike made about itself and that were intended to enhance its own image and bottom line, were made with "actual malice"?[19] The argument did not make sense. The *New York Times* test did not fit Kasky's case, because it was designed for the situation where a defendant makes false statements about someone else, statements that the defendant knows to be false and that are made with the intent to harm. Nike's statements—whether false or not—were intended to rehabilitate Nike's public image, not to harm it. So Nike's argument is best understood as a request for the Court to limit liability to knowing misstatements—in other words, to intentional torts. And notwithstanding Nike's suggestion to the contrary, Kasky had already pleaded an intentional tort when he included a count for fraud and deceit.[20]

As it turned out however, Kasky and the lower courts were spared the legal gymnastics of attempting to apply the *Sullivan* standard to his case. To the surprise of all and the dismay of many,[21] the Court abruptly dismissed *Nike,* announcing that certiorari had been "improvidently granted." Some observers had thought that the *Nike* case would break new ground in the commercial speech doctrine. Perhaps the Court would even, as some had urged, set the doctrine aside altogether and require that commercial speech be protected to the same extent as political speech.[22] But it was not to be. The dismissal meant that the California court's decision would be reinstated and that the case would be sent back to the trial court to proceed to discovery. Facing the prospect of protracted discovery and the potential for more public relations nightmares, Nike settled.

The Court's about-face was disappointing to many supporters of commercial speech. They had had reason to be optimistic that the issue would be decided in their favor. But even though the dismissal itself was a disappointment for commercial speech's supporters, the opinions issued with the dismissal contained reasons for optimism. The order dismissing *Nike* included dissenting and concurring opinions, all of which appeared to accept many of Nike's characterizations of the commercial speech issues. This suggested that the Court was indeed poised to expand First Amendment protection for commercial expression—just not with this case. So the issues raised by the case remained unsettled.

Scope of Corporations' First Amendment Rights

One of those issues was whether a corporation enjoys the same First Amendment rights as a human being. Nike had argued that the corporation was, for First Amendment purposes, a speaker just like any other speaker and therefore entitled to defend itself against criticism. Nike framed the dispute as one of simple fairness. Without protection, it would be left to the mercy of its critics, with no way to respond, and an important "perspective"—Nike's perspective—on a matter of public concern would be lost to the public. If Nike were just a person on a soapbox in the public square, this claim might have some force. However, this argument overlooked some important facts.

Nike was not powerless to air its views. Indeed, until the controversy over its labor practices had erupted, Nike had largely controlled its public image through spending millions, if not billions, of dollars to mold public opinion about the company and its products. The negative reports were only a small portion of the speech available to the public about Nike. Moreover, the corporation's critics did not have millions to spend to investigate Nike or to publicize the results. Nor did they have a profit motive directly related to pursuing investigation of Nike. The scales seemed already weighted heavily in Nike's favor. In addition, "balance" in the discussion of public concerns hardly seems to require insulation from liability for false statements, particularly false statements made in connection with commerce.[23]

Then came *Citizens United*. In *Citizens United*, the Supreme Court appeared to suggest that speech by a corporation is entitled to the same protection as speech by a human being and that distinctions between speakers on the basis of corporate status are untenable. If the Court extends this position to commercial speech, it would imperil the constitutional status of a great deal of regulation of commerce.

Commercial speech has enormous and often deleterious effects on the public welfare. It involves costs that are likely to increase if governmental efforts at control are further limited. It ought to be fairly uncontroversial that false advertising is capable of causing widespread social harms and that protecting the public against such harms is a legitimate role of the government. Yet Nike, like most proponents of freedom for commercial expression, seemed to feel that all this promotional activity is self-evidently valuable to the public—so valuable that any harm that might arise from false speech would be trivial in comparison to the violence done to the principles of freedom for expression if it is regulated. This is a deeply troubling line of argument, because a great deal of the regulation of commerce could be framed as "speech" and much of government's power to regulate any number of social issues flows through the constitutional power granted to Congress in the Commerce clause.[24] Although the Supreme Court thought in 1978 that it was obvious that the government could regulate a variety of commercial communications "without offending the First Amendment"[25] and that "the State does not lose its power to regulate commercial activity deemed harmful to the public simply because speech is a component of that activity,"[26] it is not clear that the Roberts Court would come to the same conclusion.

The corporate misconduct of the last few decades suggests that there is little reason to be sanguine about the benefits of unencumbered commercial expression and a good deal of reason to be concerned. If there are social harms attributable to commercial speech, the ability to marshal governmental resources to combat those harms through the regulation of false commercial speech is critical. Expansive protection for commercial speech is likely to be bad for consumers, bad for the press, bad for the economy, and ultimately, perhaps, bad for democracy.

The role of commercial expression in society has continued to grow. Some of the world's most powerful and (it is worth noting) global entities are making arguments similar to Nike's, and they are doing so in a variety of contexts. Global corporations (e.g., BP, Altria, Pfizer, and Microsoft), industry trade groups (e.g., the Business Roundtable and the Association of American Advertisers), and think tanks supported by industry have been engaged in a campaign to convince the courts that commercial expression should be afforded more protection under the First Amendment.[27] If influence and resources are reliable predictors of outcomes, they will probably get it.

Often, the arguments in favor of protecting commercial speech sound as if they are premised on some idea that it ought to be protected because of the speaker's interest in speaking. That is indeed the conventional understanding of who and what is protected by the First Amendment—the speaker on a soapbox, the artist, the dissident, the person who wants to express him- or herself. But what is distinctive about the First Amendment protection extended to commercial speech in the creation of the commercial speech doctrine is that it was created in order to protect the *listener's*—that is to say consumer's—interests. Protecting commercial speech in order to protect the commercial speaker's right to speak would turn the doctrine on its head. It would also entail treating large corporations as if they were entities with interests in self-expression. In other words, it means treating corporations as if they were human beings. (Although individuals, sole proprietorships, partnerships, and other forms of business organization can also engage in commercial speech, the principal source of commercial communication today is the corporation.)

The push to treat corporations like human beings for purposes of freedom of expression is a global trend.[28] This is not surprising, since many of the world's largest companies, such as Unilever, operate globally. They would like an "unencumbered" marketing environment worldwide. In the European Union, for example, corporations have argued, sometimes successfully, that restrictions on advertising violate the right of freedom of expression set forth in Article 10 of the Convention for the Protection of Human Rights and Fundamental Freedoms.[29] Given that many European countries presently have laws regulating commercial advertising that are significantly more restrictive than those in the United States,[30] if this trend continues, it will eventually pose a threat to the continued viability of those laws.

The question is this: if freedom of expression is a *human* right, why should corporations have human rights? Treating for-profit corporations as if they were natural persons undermines the notion that human beings are ends in themselves.[31] Nevertheless, claiming that a corporation is a "citizen" with expressive rights is a move with enormous rhetorical power. By claiming expressive rights, corporations invoke cherished notions of autonomy, freedom, and fair play, which, if applied without consideration of the real rather than the metaphorical context, could undermine the very basis for extending special protection to persons in the first place—the notion that human beings are entitled to unique moral consideration.

While it is by no means a foregone conclusion that the public interest and corporate interests will always be at odds, determining when there is a convergence should be in the hands of the electorate and the legislature, not the boards of directors and managers of the world's largest corporations. By their sheer size, these corporations are capable of having an immense impact on public welfare. Yet the public does not elect their boards or have any legal right of input or oversight of their actions. Unless we decline the invitation to offer full First Amendment protection to their speech, that power will be difficult to restrain.

What follows is an in-depth look at marketing practices in America and industry's use of the First Amendment as a legal weapon. I offer close-up inspection of what advertising does, how it works, what marketing researchers are doing and what they hope to accomplish, why knowledge of advertising's manipulative effects is not an effective protection against it, why the corporation is not a person just like any other, and how the ethos of marketing and public relations has infiltrated the communications and political environment to the detriment of our ability to obtain reliable information about everything from the most mundane consumer purchases to some of the most pressing issues of the day. It is a sustained argument for why the Supreme Court ought to reject arguments for full First Amendment protection for commercial speech.

This book's principal policy recommendation is a conservative one: do not extend strict scrutiny review to the commercial speech doctrine. In addition, I offer a rationale for expanding the definition of "commercial speech" to include everything that for-profit entities say, because no matter how it appears, no matter what communicative form it assumes, communications by for-profit entities are always and essentially promotional and hence "commercial," because for-profit corporations have no other purpose for being under the law (at least in the United States under current law). This analysis also provides a stronger base from which to argue that *Citizens United* is fundamentally misguided in reifying the corporate person and potentially dangerous in permitting expansive participation in our electoral processes by these profoundly undemocratic, unaccountable, and, in some cases, foreign entities. Pursuant to this second recommendation, I often use the term *commercial expression* to encompass a broader spectrum of speech than the commercial speech doctrine is understood to cover. However, when speaking of something other than the doctrine itself, I use the terms interchangeably. The Supreme Court's legitimacy is always most contested when it is acting in its countermajoritarian capacity to strike down legislation or to rule against an act of the executive branch on the grounds of unconstitutionality. That power seems an important and necessary corrective to the specter of an unconscionable tyranny of the majority over a minority.[32] But when it is invoked on behalf of the powerful, it undermines democracy and turns the Court into the "enforcer" for an unelected and unaccountable tyrant.

The book is organized into three parts. Part I deals with the applicable legal doctrines, offers a survey of the scope of commercial expression as broadly defined, and reviews the various interests the First Amendment is usually thought to protect. These interests break down into (roughly) four basic concerns: (1) advancing individual autonomy, dignity, or self-expression; (2) promoting truth; (3) protecting democratic values or processes; and (4) supporting social and political stability.

Although these concerns are interrelated, they do not perfectly overlap. As with all issues of constitutional law, protection of one value often seems to be in tension with the preservation of another value. Nevertheless, to better explore the impact of commercial expression and whether offering it more protection would further any of the interests served by the First Amendment, it is useful to break out each category. So the subsequent chapters, in parts II and III of the book, discuss the ways in which commercial expression affects these four groups of interests. Part II deals with protection of individual autonomy and truth, and examines why protecting commercial expression does not advance human beings' autonomy and shows that a corporation has no autonomy interests. Part III examines the concerns commercial expression raise with respect to the values of democracy and stability and argues that unfettered commercial expression both undermines democracy and contributes to social and economic instability.

Of course, it is not possible to answer every question or to anticipate every conceivable application of these suggestions. This is already an ambitious project, and I do not propose to expand its scope by attempting to anticipate every objection. As others have argued, commercial expression is not one problem but many. Those problems defy a unitary response. However, it seems that the time has come to reevaluate our stance on corporations and commercial expression. No doubt there will be difficult cases at the margins. And, to paraphrase Stewart Brand, the opinions stated here are "strongly stated and loosely held,"[33] and so I am prepared to revise them in light of more evidence. However, at present the evidence is against more protection for commercial expression. By attempting to define appropriate parameters for commercial expression, we may spur useful discussions about course corrections required to continue to protect other, noncommercial values and to do so in a manner consistent with democratic principles.

PART I

FOUNDATIONAL CONCEPTS

CHAPTER 1

Commercial and Corporate Speech

[T]he free flow of commercial information is indispensable.
—Supreme Court of the United States,
   Virginia Pharmacy (1976)

Prior to the twentieth century neither the courts nor most commentators appeared to believe the First Amendment had much bearing on commercial communications. Although, as legal historian David Rabban[1] has noted, there is substantial evidence of interest in the First Amendment prior to 1917, most conventional discussions of First Amendment doctrine and its meaning begin there. So, with respect to the commercial speaker, it is probably fair to say that if the First Amendment *itself* was not given much consideration prior to the twentieth century, it is axiomatic that little attention was paid to commercial speech specifically. Some have argued that the Framers had advertising in mind when they drafted the First Amendment because of the degree to which advertising supported the development of a free press at the time;[2] but there had been little direct evidence in the academic literature to support this reading. Given that the modern corporation and modern modes of communication were unknown to the Framers, they could have hardly had those practices in mind.

Thus, there is no venerable tradition supporting freedom of expression for the conduct of commerce[3]—at least not as a matter of constitutional law. To the contrary, at least until the latter part of the twentieth century, most observers thought it was self-evident that the government could regulate commercial speech with impunity. While there may have been titanic struggles about the scope of Congress's power to regulate commerce, those struggles were not framed as issues arising under the First Amendment. Indeed, in 1942 the Supreme Court dismissively declared there was "no such [First Amendment restriction] on government [ability to regulate] as respects purely commercial advertising."[4] The decisions creating First Amendment protection for commercial speech and for corporate political speech were not issued until the latter half of the twentieth century.

The Commercial Speech Doctrine

Most observers agree that the commercial speech doctrine was created in 1976 by the decision in the *Virginia Pharmacy* case.[5] The issue in *Virginia Pharmacy* was whether Virginia could forbid pharmacists to advertise drug prices.[6] A consumer group protested, arguing that by preventing pharmacies from advertising prices, the state unreasonably burdened their ability to find the cheapest drugs. In response, the state argued that price advertising would lead to pharmacy price wars and, in turn, to diminished professionalism, which, in the end, would hurt consumers.[7] Consumers countered that the state's rationale was excessively paternalistic, that the government ought not to be in the business of protecting the public from the truth.[8] The Supreme Court agreed and held that truthful commercial speech was protected by the First Amendment.[9] In so holding, the Court observed,

> So long as we preserve a predominately free enterprise economy, the allocation of our resources in large measure will be made through numerous private economic decisions. *It is a matter of public interest that those decisions, in the aggregate, be intelligent and well informed. To this end, the free flow of commercial information is indispensable.*[10]

The Court's holding, that truthful commercial speech ought to enjoy a measure of First Amendment protection, was a fairly novel interpretation of that amendment. Only a few years earlier, the Court had rejected out of hand the notion that advertising was protected by the First Amendment. It was also novel because it focused on the listeners' (consumers') right to hear rather than on the speakers' (pharmacies') right to speak, the usual focus in

First Amendment cases. It was so novel that apparently the Court felt that in order to find the consumer group had standing to raise the speech issue, it first had to find that the pharmacies had a First Amendment right to advertise, a right that the consumers were asserting derivatively.[11] With little discussion of this point, the Court held that they did have such a right. But the Court's key holding was that protection was necessary because the consumers had a First Amendment right to hear the price information.[12]

Had the Court been writing on a blank slate, these gyrations might not have been necessary. Indeed, it might not have been necessary to invoke the First Amendment at all. If you were looking simply at the language of the Constitution, you might have thought that the Commerce Clause was the provision applicable to a case about advertising. But because the Court's earlier decisions interpreting the Commerce Clause called for a fairly undemanding rational basis test for laws regulating commerce (a test that Virginia's rationale for its prohibition of price advertising for prescription drugs would have almost certainly passed), the consumers would not have gotten very far had they raised a Commerce Clause challenge. So they needed a different constitutional claim. What they hit on was the argument that consumers had a First Amendment right to hear this price information.[13] As noted, this was not a conventional reading of the First Amendment, but it was not unprecedented. The argument had been made in a law review article a few years earlier.

In 1971 a professor of law at Northwestern University, Martin Redish, published an article entitled "The First Amendment in the Marketplace,"[14] in which he argued that commercial speech was entitled to First Amendment protection because it was critical to market function, which was, in turn, an essential part of social welfare and self-actualization. He claimed that there was no intellectually respectable basis on which to distinguish between commercial and noncommercial speech for First Amendment purposes.[15] His argument placed the public's right to receive the information on the same plane as the speaker's interest in speaking. Moreover, he argued that as a category, commercial speech was as valuable as other types of protected speech, such as art or political speech. Of course, from the conventional perspective, the argument that information (speech) is critical to market function only applies to truthful information, at least if we are thinking of efficient markets.[16] Not surprisingly then, Redish argued that it was primarily truthful commercial speech that had this constitutional value. He did not claim that there was First Amendment value in false commercial speech, although he did argue that some false speech might need to be protected so as to avoid chilling valuable speech.

When the Virginia consumers group picked up this argument, it found a receptive audience in the Supreme Court. The Court's opinion in *Virginia Pharmacy* mirrored Redish's argument in virtually every respect, including his explanations for why commercial speech, unlike political speech, could be safely regulated for its truth. Regulation of commercial speech for its truth, Redish argued (and the Court later held), was not as troubling as similar regulation would be in the political sphere, because the economic motive for issuing it made commercial speech hardier; that is, because companies had a powerful motive (profit) to communicate, they would be unlikely to forgo speech altogether, even if it was regulated.[17] This claim made it possible to extend First Amendment protection to commercial speech while simultaneously leaving intact much consumer protection regulation that might otherwise seem inconsistent with the First Amendment.

After announcing the commercial speech doctrine in *Virginia Pharmacy,* the Court further clarified it four years later in *Central Hudson*.[18] There the Court set out the four-part test for commercial speech still applicable today. In order to receive First Amendment protection pursuant to the commercial speech doctrine, speech must meet four criteria: (1) it must concern a legal activity and not be misleading (i.e., it must be truthful speech about a legal activity); (2) if the government seeks to regulate speech, it must do so pursuant to a "substantial interest"; (3) such regulatory efforts must directly further the asserted substantial interest; and (4) the regulation must be no more expansive than necessary to advance that substantial interest (this is often described as the "fit" prong).[19]

What Makes Speech "Commercial"?

The *Central Hudson* opinion is clear that only truthful commercial speech receives First Amendment protection. It observed that because the whole justification for protecting some commercial expression was because of its informational function, this justification evaporated in the case of misleading speech. "The government," the Court said, "may ban forms of communication more likely to deceive the public than to inform it."[20]

This sets up something of a definitional problem. Pursuant to *Central Hudson,* if speech is commercial, it is protected only if it is truthful. But being truthful does not make speech "commercial." Unfortunately, the Court did not define what does makes speech "commercial." This is important because the government may not set up a truth test for most other sorts of protected speech (libel and defamation being exceptions). Redish himself argued that commercial speech was "communication concerned solely with promoting the sale of commercial services or products, which services or products are themselves not speech traditionally protected by the first amendment."[21] (Notice that this description neatly sidesteps the media problem.) The Supreme Court did not use this precise language in either *Virginia Pharmacy* or *Central Hudson,* leaving unclear what makes speech commercial. Typically, if clear definitions are not provided in a decision, lawyers will look at the facts of subsequent cases to see if a definition can be inferred from the pattern of decided cases. However, this is not easy to do with the commercial speech cases.

The Supreme Court has decided only a handful of commercial speech cases, yet they include a fairly broad range of factual circumstances. The *Virginia Pharmacy* case itself suggested an early definition: that by "commercial speech" the Supreme Court meant "advertising." Given that the Court used the terms *advertising* and *commercial speech* interchangeably in the *Virginia Pharmacy* opinion, this approach has some attraction.[22] However, the Court also suggested that speech is "commercial" when it does "no more than propose a commercial transaction."[23] This formulation remains one of those most often cited as a definition. However, it is not terribly helpful, since it could either simply be a restatement of the "commercial speech equals advertising" formulation or could be read much more broadly to encompass speech that is not synonymous with advertising. Moreover, in yet other cases, the Court appeared to explicitly reject the idea that commercial speech was nothing more than advertising. So the definition problem is still unresolved.

Although many cases the Court has decided involved advertising of the same sort of straightforward, factual information involved in *Virginia Pharmacy* (price),[24] others have involved communications that were not so clearly just advertising. One case, *Bolger v. Youngs Drug Products*,[25] involved a pamphlet with information about sexually transmitted diseases and their prevention. The pamphlet included references to its publisher's product, Trojan condoms. In another case, the question presented was whether a utility company could be required to include an insert about energy usage in every electricity customer's bill.[26] In *Posadas de Puerto Rico*,[27] the Court upheld a ban on advertising of casino gambling to the residents of Puerto Rico, a ban that included bans on certain kinds of promotional merchandise. Still other cases involved in-person solicitation or advertising or promotional bans supported by professional organizations, in particular the regulation of lawyer advertising.[28] Whatever the factual circumstances, the Court's decisions tended to focus not on the difficulty of defining commercial speech but, rather, on the power of the government to regulate it.

When the Court did address the definitional issue, as it did in *Youngs Drug*, the Court had no difficulty in concluding that the inclusion of some communications on a matter of public concern did not necessarily convert commercial speech into protected speech. The test the Court articulated in *Youngs Drug* for determining whether something is commercial speech is the test the California Supreme Court majority used to guide its decision in *Nike*: (1) whether the speech in question is an advertisement, (2) whether it is about a product, and (3) whether the speaker has an economic motivation for speaking.[29] Using this test, the California Supreme Court had no difficulty concluding that some of the speech in the *Nike* case could have easily been deemed commercial.[30] But by dismissing the *Nike* case, the Supreme Court of the United States did not make clear whether it agreed. To date, the definitional boundaries of commercial speech remain ambiguous. I argue that properly understood, commercial speech is much broader than the Court has suggested to date and ought to include any promotional speech by a corporation, perhaps even including speech that has been the subject of a separate line of cases—corporate political speech.

Corporate Speech

At the same time that the Court was crafting protection for commercial speech—based on the nature of the speech and the rights of the listener to receive the speech—it was confronted with claims by corporations that they had the right to expend resources on political ads. The Court did not analyze these claims as falling under the commercial speech doctrine, since political ads did not seem to obviously involve commerce (although, as I will argue later, it could have done so if the Court had considered the purpose for business participation in political speech). Instead, it analyzed these cases as ones involving quintessential protected speech and, in so doing, laid the foundation for the conclusion that for-profit corporations could be legitimate rights holders for purposes of the First Amendment. This conclusion would have spillover effect on commercial speech. Even though both individuals and corporations engage in commercial speech, it is the largest, multinational corporations that spend the most and contribute the most to commercial speech.

In *First National Bank of Boston v. Bellotti*,[31] the bank petitioner sought a declaratory judgment that it had a First Amendment right to take out ads urging voters not to approve a personal income tax proposal on the ballot.[32] Massachusetts law prohibited such expenditures by corporations (on pain of criminal sanctions) where such expenditures did not "materially affect" the property of the business. The Massachusetts attorney general had announced that he interpreted the law to prohibit the proposed ads and that he intended to enforce the law against the bank. The bank sought a declaratory judgment that it had as much right as any citizen to offer speech on a matter of public concern. That claim made its way to the Supreme Court.

Although the lower courts had framed the issue much the way the bank did—as whether a corporation had First Amendment rights that were the equivalent of a human being's—Justice Powell, writing for the majority, said this was "the wrong question."[33] "The proper question," he wrote in the opinion finding in favor of the bank, "is not whether corporations 'have' First Amendment rights and, if so, whether they are coextensive with those of natural persons. Instead, the question must be whether § 8 [the statute limiting corporate speech] abridges expression that the First Amendment was meant to protect. We hold that it does."[34]

By framing the issue this way, Powell dodged the question raised by the bank and lower courts and instead focused on the content of the speech to decide whether it was protected. These sorts of ads, urging voters to support or defeat a referendum on a tax question, were, he wrote, "at the heart of the First Amendment's protection." Reasoning this way, the conclusion was inescapable: the speech was protected, therefore so was the speaker. The speaker's identity was irrelevant: "The inherent worth of the speech in terms of its capacity for informing the public does not depend upon the identity of its source, whether corporation, association, union, or individual."[35] "If the speakers here were not corporations," Powell wrote, "no one would suggest that the State could silence their proposed speech."[36] This framing made it seem as if the issue were about the civil rights of a corporation—rather than about the regulation of commerce or limiting corporate influence in the political process. You can imagine this framing provoking what the late, great legal scholar Charles Black Jr. called "the sovereign prerogative of philosophers—that of laughter,"[37] if not outright derision, given how silly it sounds to suggest that powerful corporations could be victims of invidious discrimination. Nevertheless, this was not the reaction the opinion generated among the mainstream. Instead, it was treated by many as obviously correct.

That Justice Powell did not appear to feel it was a little ridiculous to imply that disparate treatment for corporate speech might constitute invidious discrimination may be a commentary on how thoroughly committed we are as a people to equality. Or perhaps it is just a testament to how easily people can be manipulated with language. Powell's framing is particularly troubling when we consider that the Court's power to declare a law unconstitutional is a countermajoritarian one. This power is sometimes controversial even when invoked to defend oppressed minorities who, because of their smaller number, cannot command the allegiance of the representatives elected by the majority; it is potentially tyrannical when invoked on behalf of the powerful. Major corporations are powerful. They command a great deal of attention to their needs from the legislature and the executive branch. There is little evidence that they require special protection from the courts as well. Casting the *Bellotti* issue as if it were one of civil rights, by focusing on the listeners' rights, avoids answering the question of whether a corporation could or should be a holder of First Amendment rights.

In the future, proponents of freedom for commercial expression would enthusiastically cite these passages from *Bellotti* in support of arguments that commercial speech should also not be "disfavored."

Justice Powell did not speak for the entire Court in his stirring defense of a corporation's contributions to political discourse. His argument that these contributions were no less valuable because of the speaker's corporate status—as if it were self-evidently true—actually had not been self-evident at all prior to *Bellotti*.[38] Fellow conservative Chief Justice Rehnquist, himself by no stretch of the imagination antibusiness, disagreed. In his dissent, Rehnquist wrote,

> Although the Court has never explicitly recognized a corporation's right of commercial speech, such a right *might be* considered necessarily incidental to the business of a commercial corporation. *It cannot be so readily concluded that the right of political expression is equally necessary to carry out the functions of a corporation organized for commercial purposes.*[39]

The other dissenters, led by Justice White, were concerned that the ruling in *Bellotti* would hamper the government's ability to limit the corrupting influence of corporate wealth on politics.

Only a little more than a decade after *Bellotti* was decided, it seemed the Court's majority was swinging back in the direction of the dissenters when the Court retreated significantly from *Bellotti*'s strong statement that corporate status was irrelevant to whether political speech could be regulated. In *Austin v. Michigan Chamber of Commerce*,[40] the Court, reviewing a Michigan statute that limited corporate political advertising, concluded that some distinctions between speakers could be justified on the basis of for-profit corporate status. Writing for the majority, Justice Marshall observed that because of corporations' ability to amass great wealth, an ability due in part to the special advantages of corporate status (particularly limited liability) conferred on them by the state, and because this great wealth could potentially become an instrument of corruption of the political process, give the appearance of corruption, or, at the very least, represent an antidemocratic influence, it was legitimate to treat corporations differently than persons and to distinguish between not-for-profit and for-profit entities on a close consideration of the specific facts:

> The resources in the treasury of a business corporation . . . are not an indication of popular support for the corporation's political ideas. They reflect instead the economically motivated decisions of investors and customers. The availability of these resources may make a corporation a for-

midable political presence, even though the power of the corporation may be no reflection of the power of its ideas."[41]

This position would not endure for long.[42]

Taken together, these two decisions, *Virginia Pharmacy* and *Bellotti*, created a strange, disembodied, denatured sort of First Amendment. Instead of protecting human beings' expressive interests or protecting human beings from retaliation by the government for expressing unpopular opinions, the First Amendment that emerges from these cases is one that protects the product, not the speaker, perhaps the reverse of common understanding of what protection for freedom of expression is for.

Streams Converge

These two strands of case law—the commercial speech doctrine and the corporate speech doctrine—developed separately. But they persisted in an uneasy and confusing coexistence. The timing of the *Bellotti* decision, occurring as it did in such close proximity to *Virginia Pharmacy*, suggests that the Supreme Court backed into the corporate speech formulation in *Bellotti* without fully considering the appropriateness of the corporate person as a rights holder under the First Amendment, its implications for the newly announced commercial speech doctrine, or the possibility that there might be valid reasons to distinguish between human beings engaging in commercial speech and entities such as corporations doing so.

This critical ruling in *Bellotti*, combined with the Court's holding in *Buckley v. Valeo*[43] that limitations on campaign expenditures constituted an unconstitutional limitation on speech, was to have far-reaching consequences, not just for political speech, but for commercial speech as well. *Bellotti* did not involve speech "proposing a commercial transaction." Nevertheless, *Bellotti* became a familiar part of the repertory for the defenders of commercial speech. They would use it as if the Court had answered in the affirmative what Powell said was "the wrong question"—do corporations enjoy the same First Amendment rights as natural persons?[44] Pro-commercial speech litigants used *Bellotti* to support the claim that there is no constitutional difference between corporate and human speakers or between a commercial and a political purpose.[45] Often they did so as if *Austin* had never been decided. By relying on this language in *Bellotti*, those arguing for expansive protection for commercial and corporate speech could frame their claims as ones seeking recognition of preexisting, self-evident rights, rather than as arguments for an extension or an expansion of rights. Now, with the *Citizens United* decision, which explicitly overruled *Austin*, those advocates have new ammunition in the form of another political speech case that, like *Bellotti*, is likely to make its way into the commercial speech doctrine.[46]

Citizens United

In *Citizens United*, the Supreme Court confronted a challenge to a portion of the Bipartisan Campaign Reform Act (BCRA), commonly known as the McCain-Feingold Act, that prohibited corporations and unions from using general treasury funds to make expenditures for "electioneering communication" within 30 days of a primary election.[47] Citizens United, a nonprofit corporation organized to engage in advocacy, had produced and was preparing to distribute a 90-minute documentary about then-candidate Hillary Clinton entitled *Hillary: The Movie*. The movie was clearly designed to persuade viewers that Hillary Clinton was unfit for the presidency, and as such, it arguably fell within the definition of electioneering speech in McCain-Feingold.

The film had been released in January 2008 and could be purchased on DVDs through the organization's website. However, the organization sought to distribute the movie through video-on-demand cable and had produced three ads promoting the video-on-demand purchases. It wanted to make the film available within the 30 days prior to the election. Fearing that the Federal Election Commission (FEC) would interpret McCain-Feingold restrictions to apply to these ads, it brought an action for a declaratory judgment and a preliminary injunction against the FEC. In this action, it raised both a facial and an as-applied challenge to the restriction under the First Amendment. The district court denied Citizens United's request and granted the FEC's motion for summary judgment, and Citizens United made a direct appeal to the Supreme Court. The Court accepted certiorari and heard oral argument in March 2009. Then, without warning, the Court announced that it would hear reargument in September 2009. In doing so, it specifically asked the parties to brief the question of whether *Austin* should be overruled.[48]

Not surprisingly, given the foreshadowing inherent in the question, the Court overruled *Austin* and found the statute's restriction on corporations unconstitutional. Justice Kennedy, writing for the majority, asserted, "By taking the right to speak from some and giving it to others, the Government *deprives the disadvantaged person or class* of the right to use speech to strive to establish worth, standing, and respect for the speaker's voice."[49] This sentence squarely situates the corporate speaker as "disadvantaged" by the BCRA, as if this were a self-evidently illegitimate aspect of the law, when the manifest purpose (or at least one of them) of the law was expressly to limit (i.e., "disadvantage") corporate participation in the electoral processes. That purpose is unremarkable if you think that there is an appropriate basis for treating corporations differently than individuals. It is only remarkable if you do not accept this distinction. If corporations qua corporations do not enjoy the same First Amendment protections as human beings do, there is no problem with "disadvantaging" them. Justice Kennedy wrote, however, "The Court has recognized that the First Amendment protection extends to corporations."[50] Although he did not say that the First Amendment protection that extended to corporations is identical to that extended to persons, this is strongly implied. Kennedy's use of words like *worth* and *voice* treats the metaphor of corporate personhood as if it were a material reality.

After a lengthy opinion rejecting all of both sides' arguments about why the case could be decided on narrower grounds and all of the arguments offered by the Court in *Austin* as grounds for distinguishing between corporate and noncorporate speakers, Kennedy concluded with the grand pronouncement that "the Government may not suppress political speech on the basis of the speaker's corporate identity" and declared *Austin* overruled.[51] The opinion is replete with rhetoric that characterizes the corporation as a "citizen"[52] whose voice is being "muffled"[53] or unfairly suppressed, which suppression stands in the way of letting people think for themselves, and he analogizes the McCain-Feingold Act to an attempt at thought control: "When Government seeks to use its full power, including the criminal law, to command where a person may get his or her information or what distrusted source he or she may not hear, it uses censorship to control thought. This is unlawful. The First Amendment confirms the freedom to think for ourselves."[54]

In writing this stirring defense of the value of corporate speech, Justice

Kennedy explicitly did not limit this protection to nonprofits like Citizens United; he extended it to for-profit and not-for-profit alike. If it is a bit much to claim that corporations are a "disadvantaged class," it might seem less of a stretch—barely—to claim that they are "citizens," especially given a corporation named "Citizens United." But by invoking the threat of the criminal law in particular, Justice Kennedy was pushing the anthropomorphizing further. He seemed to be trying to underscore the gravity of the encroachment on liberty that the criminal law suggests. Of course, a corporation cannot be thrown in jail; so this aspect of the criminal law that so markedly distinguishes it from civil sanctions when applied to a natural person is of far less significance when applied to a corporation. Whatever his intent, the *Citizens United* opinion appears to answer in the affirmative (although not explicitly) the question raised in *Bellotti* and only hinted at there: whether a corporation has First Amendment rights indistinguishable from those of a natural person.

What will *Citizens United* mean for the commercial speech doctrine? If a for-profit corporation's political speech should receive strict scrutiny and if a corporation is a "person" with First Amendment rights of no less dignity than a natural person, what standard should apply to what is surely the core expressive activity of a commercial enterprise: its commercial speech? *Citizens United* is silent on this point because the issue was not before the Court; but it is clear how the rhetoric in the decision will be used by proponents of stronger First Amendment protection for commercial speech. They will use it to bolster calls for increased protection for commercial speech in the form of strict scrutiny review, which most likely spells the end for much regulation of commercial speech (and maybe much regulation generally, since almost anything can be reframed as an issue of speech).

The *Virginia Pharmacy* and *Bellotti* decisions represented a watershed for the development of legal doctrines related to commercial participation in America. These cases replayed the political and legal struggles from the *Lochner*[55] era—an era in which the Court had resisted legislative attempts at progressive labor reform. In *Lochner* the Supreme Court set aside a state's attempt to regulate labor on the grounds that the regulation interfered with freedom of contract. With *Lochner,* as is so often the case (perhaps because reliance on precedent makes law essentially backward looking), the Court showed itself to be slow to accept what the public had already appeared to accept: a more active role for the government in the management of economic and social life.[56]

Eventually, *Lochner* was overruled, paving the way for the construction of the modern administrative state. But the struggle it represented reemerged in *Virginia Pharmacy* and *Bellotti*.[57] Business was back, this time brandishing claims to freedom of speech rather than freedom of contract as a weapon against governmental attempts at regulation. They were, in a sense, just the latest expression of an old struggle. There has always been a struggle for power in America between government and private economic interests. What was different about the struggle for power between government and business by 1976 was that the corporate form had grown—from a fairly small, little used, very circumscribed legal means of holding property and pooling capital, into *the* dominant form of business organization—and business had emerged as the dominant force in the creation of social life.

With the *Citizens United* decision, we may be seeing a replay of the *Lochner* drama and, like *Lochner* itself, *Citizens United* may later be seen as a mistake.[58] But later is not yet here, and between later and now lies a period in which we will discover whether the Court will extend the views expressed there, about the corporation as a speaker, into the commercial speech doctrine and if so, what a strict scrutiny standard for commercial speech will mean to the ability of the government to regulate in the public interest. In order to explore this question we must first look at the scope and penetration of commercial expression in American culture.

CHAPTER 2

The Scope of Commercial Expression

Under a free enterprise system commercial propaganda by any
and every means is absolutely indispensable.
—Aldous Huxley, *Brave New World Revisited*

The Supreme Court has never clearly defined "commercial speech," but if we
define it as all promotional or marketing speech by a for-profit entity, we find
that it takes many forms and is much larger than simply advertising. This
chapter provides an overview of the myriad forms that commercial expression can take, along with some observations about their social ramifications.
It is by no means an exhaustive review, however, since the creativity of marketing professionals appears to be truly inexhaustible, with new marketing
techniques dreamed up every day.

Marketing, the quintessential commercial expression, takes on a dizzying array of forms, but its two most important general categories are advertising and public relations. Although they are distinct industries, the communication they produce is less distinctively one or the other, and the chief
marketing officers of major corporations use all of the tools of both disci-
plines to promote their enterprises. The proliferation of devices by which
marketing can occur and the number of media platforms on which it can occur have given rise to the conviction that a firm's marketing will be more
successful if all of these efforts are coordinated. This practice is called *integrated marketing communications* (IMC). According to Terence Shimp, author of a popular textbook on IMC, "Current marketing philosophy holds

that *integration is absolutely imperative for success.*"[1] The significance of this comment for the commercial speech doctrine is that it emphasizes that the purpose of all commercial expression is promotion, including the sorts of press releases made by Nike about its labor practices. And it suggests that the format in which promotional speech is delivered does not affect its promotional character and therefore should be irrelevant for constitutional purposes.[2]

Advertising

Advertising is the most familiar form of commercial expression. It is what many people think of when they think of the commercial speech doctrine. Advertising has been defined as a "form of either mass communication or direct-to-consumer communication that is non-personal and is *paid for* by the various business firms, nonprofit organizations, and individuals who are in some way identified in the advertising message and who hope to inform or persuade members of a particular audience."[3] It can take many forms: billboards, print, television, radio, Internet, cable, direct mail, word of mouth (i.e., paid word of mouth), and others.

Although the *Virginia Pharmacy* Court described advertising as "information about who is producing and selling what product, for what reason, and at what price,"[4] anyone living in the modern world knows that, in practice, advertising contains both much more and often much less than simple information about who is selling what, where, and for how much. It creates an image for the product, often relying on emotional appeals, symbols, celebrity endorsements, music, and/or stirring visuals to do so. In addition, it is often intended to evoke responses that are not deliberative. Advertisers explicitly intend to create emotional reactions that will translate into sales. This is perhaps most true in the process of creating and then maintaining a brand identity. According to one author, "Just like people, brands even have their own unique personalities."[5] But since brands are not people, those "personalities" are created through commercial communication, which is not just about the product or service; it is about the brand—that ephemeral thing "imbued with an insane and spiraling amalgam of religious, mystical and even messianic possibilities."[6]

Brand and Image Advertising

As Shimp remarks, "We live in a world of brands."[7] Brands serve to differentiate (whether on a real or an illusory basis) among otherwise identical goods. Brands are or can be convenient symbols to convey information to consumers about the producer/manufacturer and, typically, to comment on the quality of the experience or product, thereby reducing what economists call "search costs."[8] Brands can help consumers save time and avoid unpleasant surprises. They are "a covenant with the consumer whereby the mere mention of the name triggers expectations about what the brand will deliver in terms of quality, convenience, status, and other critical buying considerations."[9] Of course, by sticking to familiar brands, consumers might also miss better options; but for many, it is simply more comfortable to choose the known quantity. This convenience in decision making is part of what makes brands work. As will be explored in more depth in chapter 5, the argument that brands reduce search costs is also actually an admission that search costs also apply to the efforts to defend against advertising with skepticism or investigation. Such costs negate some of the brand's supposed benefits, at least for the *consumer*. The combination of consumer exhaustion and confusion with strong brand marketing means that brands work very well for the seller.

There are tremendous advantages for the seller if its branding efforts are successful. This is why economists initially thought that money spent on brand advertising was anticompetitive, particularly where brands did not correlate with any distinctive material properties of the product and thus the brand (arguably) did not supply the consumer with useful information. Eventually, economists and then the courts were persuaded that branding was critical for businesses even if its benefits to the consumer were ambiguous.

It is precisely this possibility of detachment of the brand from the material properties of the product that makes branding so flexible and ultimately so valuable. It is possible to create a brand out of whole cloth. However, because brand value is so dependent on imagery built by communication efforts, it is, to some extent, always susceptible to sudden shifts in public perceptions. Such shifts may include total collapse of all brand value. So maintaining brand identity is a critical part of business strategy. Moreover, branding and brand identity depend (at least in the industry's eyes) on the activation of far more than just signaling mechanisms and the rational assessment of search costs. The accepted theory is that brands often trigger emotional associations and reactions, whether from past associations or present aspirations. And that is seen as the key to making them work. Creating those positive emotional associations is the main thrust of much advertising efforts.

Building those emotional ties creates what is known as *brand equity*—the value created through communications efforts. Brand equity involves both simple awareness of the brand and emotional associations with it. Shimp explains, "An *association* is simply the particular thoughts and feelings that a consumer has about a brand, much in the same fashion that we have thoughts and feelings about other people."[10] On the firm side, equity is measured by calculating market share and sales. On the consumer side, it is measured by testing brand recognition and collecting consumer perceptions. Brand equity permits a brand to serve as an umbrella from which an array of products can fan out. These offspring products are known as *brand extensions*. A significant portion of marketing research is devoted to finding out just how far a brand associated with a particular product can be pushed in the search to squeeze the maximum mileage out of it. Brands that support many extensions, that capture significant market share with robust sales figures, that have high recognition and retention numbers for their ads, and for which consumers show strong loyalty are considered very valuable.[11]

Although the brand is frequently the same as the company, it often is not. In fact, one company may be the holder of several brands. For example, Altria, the parent company of Philip Morris, at one point also owned Kraft Foods, which in turn holds multiple brands of food products, each of which may have a separate advertising strategy and identity. Advertising on behalf of these entities takes place at every level—from the specific product (e.g., Kraft Macaroni & Cheese), to the company (Kraft Foods), to the holding company (Altria). Such advertising efforts are directed sometimes at multiple audiences—not just to consumers, but also to investors and the general public—and sometimes at a single market segment, particularly as identified by demographic, psychographic, and geodemographic profiling.[12] However, because audiences regularly overlap, promoting or protecting the image of the company, not just the product that the company makes, is a part of an overall brand management strategy. Promoting the company promotes the brand. Advertising directed specifically at this goal is known as *image advertising*. Image advertising is intended to create an image or a brand personality.[13]

Issue Advertising and Political Advertising

In addition to protecting and promoting brands, for-profit companies often engage in *issue advertising*—that is, ads that take a position on some issue of public concern, such as breast cancer, land mines, global warming, labor practices, muscular dystrophy, aid to flood victims in New Orleans, or any number of political, social, or charitable causes. These messages do not appear to be promotional at all, but they are. They are calculated efforts to find an issue that will appear consistent with the brand personality. Such issue advertising may also generate positive press coverage because *the issue* is news, even if the brand is not, so the brand can piggyback off of the newsworthiness of the issue. Positive associations with a brand—such as "They donate to cancer research"—can then influence consumer decision making that, in turn, translates into sales. Or it can deflect regulatory impulses, if a company *appears* to be "responsible."

For-profit corporations may also, as we have seen in the introduction, engage (subject to some restrictions) in political advertising—either directly or indirectly through funded nonprofits or segregated funds. Election law is a complicated body of law, one made more complicated by the various attempts to restrict corporate participation through legislation like the McCain-Feingold Act. The role of corporations in campaign finance and electioneering has been the subject of highly contentious debate, as the *Citizens United, Bellotti,* and *Austin* cases illustrate. Suffice it to say here that, as with issue advertising, the purpose of corporate, political advertising—whether done by the company itself or through a nonprofit formed for that purpose or an industry trade group—is always, ultimately, to advance a commercial interest, because a corporation is an institution organized by law for a commercial purpose. A for-profit organization has no other legal reason for being. It may, as an ancillary matter, engage in activities that do not directly advance the corporation's economic interests. But such activities are virtually always authorized and defended to shareholders as supporting the long-term economic goals of the company. Speech by a for-profit entity is, therefore, by definition always commercial. Trade associations similarly are formed for the purpose of promoting the industries they represent and thus have the same narrow focus except it is the profitability of the industry in general.

For example, many in the pharmaceutical industry apparently concluded that health care reform was either in their companies' interest or inevitable and that it would be better to cooperate in the effort in order to wring some concessions from the plan for the industry than to fight it all out. Who made the initial approach is unclear, but it was reported that in exchange for some concessions in the legislation, the Pharmaceutical Research and Manufacturers of America (PhRMA) spent $100 million on "Harry and Louise" ads in support of health care reform.[14] This is the same fictional duo the industry had trotted out to *oppose* health care reform during the Clinton administration. This time around, Harry and Louise were stumping in favor of health care reform. It is hard to know how much these ads contributed to the eventual passage of the bill. But given how fiercely it was opposed, PhRMA's help was probably significant.

Interestingly, PhRMA representatives later expressed concern that the government was not planning to honor the bargain, suggesting that the commitment was never to the issue but to perceived economic advantages that might flow from supporting health care reform.[15] Should the fate of such important legislation rest in the hands of the very industry to be regulated? As the *Austin* Court observed, vast resources can produce vast influence. The Harry and Louise ads confirm this observation. But there is no necessary correlation between the vastness of the resources and the popularity of the ideas. The size of corporate treasuries is a function of the success of the business and the legal structures, including limited liability, which the law gives them, not their representativeness of the population. Ads like these come about because of the judgment of a few individuals that an issue is one of consequence to the economic welfare of the industry, not necessarily the welfare, economic or otherwise, of the public at large.

Ads like those run by PhRMA during the build up to the 2010 health care reform bill are both issue and political advertising, because while they were about an issue (health care), it was a contested political issue, not simply an exhortation on an uncontroversial topic like fighting breast cancer or promoting literacy. In the past, such advertising might represent the majority of the political advertising done by corporations. After *Citizens United,* we may be entering an era where we will see corporations like Exxon actually endorsing or opposing candidates. But probably not. *Citizens United* stirred up a fair amount of public opposition. In such a climate, an explicit corporate endorsement for a candidate would probably be counterproductive. However, that does not mean corporations will not be funding political ads. They will just not be doing it openly, if they can help it. Instead, they will be employing tactics drawn from the second major category of marketing —public relations. Public relations practice involves promotion by indirection. You might call it "free advertising."[16]

Public Relations

Public relations professionals claim that their activities cover far more than marketing, but it is hard to find a good definition of the field. Edward Bernays, often described as the father of public relations, described it as the practice of using "modern media of communications and the group formations of society" to bring "an idea to the consciousness of the public."[17] One scholar describes it as follows: "Advertising is publicity that a firm pays for; public relations seeks publicity that does not require payment to the media for time or space."[18] One standard academic text describes public relations practice as all those activities undertaken by an organization in an attempt to sell itself.[19]

As a field, PR is a product of the twentieth century. As a practice, it has been fully integrated into communications generally.[20] Today, not just all major industries but virtually any organization of any size, including most large-scale nonprofits, employ public relations professionals. Even universities and government agencies employ public relations or media specialists—sometimes in-house, sometimes hired from the outside, sometimes both. News media use press releases generated by PR firms. Many journalism graduates, even if they start their careers in a newsroom, find themselves working in public relations jobs instead of in journalism (just as many psychology majors find themselves doing marketing research instead of doing therapy or clinical research).

Public relations activities take so many forms that it is not possible to describe them all. At its most basic level, PR involves drafting press releases and preparing speeches for key personnel. Sometimes it involves staging events like concerts, parties, openings, groundbreakings, or other gatherings. (Bernays was not shy about employing tactics that were a bit more Barnumesque than the sober professional image he wished to convey.) Sometimes PR work is described as *corporate communications*. In this guise, PR professionals attempt to mold the public image of the company they represent by supplying the public with carefully crafted statements designed to show the client in the best light. Publicists perform the same function for individuals. This is a practice closely related to branding. PR professionals may also be retained to manage public perceptions after there has been a problem or accident.[21] This function is referred to as *crisis communications*. Although some people argue that not all PR work is promotional, a good deal of it is, even (or perhaps especially) crisis communications. However, marketing PR is often described as a separate category from PR generally.

Marketing PR (MPR) can be further divided into two categories: *proactive MPR* and *reactive MPR*. As the author of one textbook explains it, proactive MPR is simply promotion.

> Whereas advertising messages are paid for by identified sponsors and are regarded by consumers as direct attempts to influence their attitudes and behavior, MPR messages come across not as advertisements but as unbiased reports from journalists. An MPR message in comparison with an advertisement assumes a mantle of credibility. MPR messages also are considerably less expensive than advertisements because airtime or newspaper space is provided free of charge by the newspaper, magazine, radio, or television station that prints or airs the message.[22]

In contrast, reactive MPR

> describes the conduct of public relations in response to outside influences. It is undertaken because of external pressures and challenges brought by competitive actions, shifts in consumer attitudes, changes in government policy, or other external influences. Reactive MPR deals typically with changes that have negative consequences[23] for an organization. Reactive MPR attempts to repair a company's reputation, prevent market erosion, and regain lost sales.[24]

As is clear from this description, in the *Nike v. Kasky* case described in the Introduction, Nike was engaged in reactive MPR intended to repair its reputation, "prevent market erosion and regain lost sales."

The connection between these types of communication and marketing is worth looking at closely. According to Bernays, public relations professionals should be concerned not merely with how to communicate but with how to persuade—how to mold public opinion.[25] This is similar to the injunction in the IMC view that it is not enough to merely communicate and that "the goal is to *affect the behavior* of the communications audience."[26] The object of public relations, whether proactive or reactive, is, like advertising, to persuade.

Persuasion, in the view of Bernays, required the use of psychology.[27] Appealing directly to people's reason would, he claimed, be ineffective. Instead, the public relations person had to craft pitches to appeal to human emotions, prejudices, tastes, and unconscious associations in order to be effective. Accordingly, as Bernays put it, "the successful propagandist must understand the true motives and not be content to accept the reasons which men give for what they do."[28] It was clear to Bernays, approaching his practice from the point of view of the psychology of the listener, that one of the first challenges to molding public opinion was to overcome audience skepticism about a speaker's motives. Obviously, the most effective method for overcoming this skepticism is to not trigger it in the first place. As a result, disguising the identity of the messenger is the bedrock strategy on which much public relations practice is founded. Bernays gave this practice a name: the *third-party technique.*

The Third-Party Technique

In advertising, consumers (and other audiences) are aware that the speaker is trying to sell a product, and as a consequence (at least theoretically), they are on guard against it, at least to some extent. Opponents of advertising regulation regularly overemphasize the degree to which such skepticism actually shields consumers from advertising's influence. Marketing researchers, in contrast, know that consumer beliefs that "advertising doesn't work on me" are generally incorrect. But to get around these defenses, such as they are, and to enhance the credibility of the message, public relations professionals (and, increasingly, marketers generally) use Bernays's third-party technique. This technique involves getting some person or entity other than the seller to deliver the seller's message. Traditionally that third party was a newspaper, radio station, or television station. Today it includes all of these plus friends, neighbors, social media, product placement, blogs, academic journals—the list is limited only by the marketer's imagination. Stripped of its apparent partisan source, the message has more credibility. The benefit of free, undisclosed promotion is obvious: credibility. As marketing professionals Al and Laura Ries observed in *The Fall of Advertising and the Rise of PR,* "To get something going from nothing, you need the validity that only third-party endorsements can bring."[29] Advertising on someone else's dime is the ideal marketing strategy.

Not surprisingly, the nation's news organizations are, as a consequence, bombarded with press releases. "The nation's print and electronic media are increasingly filling news airtime and advertising space with video news releases [VNRs],[30] 'advertorials,' and other fake news generated by sophisticated public-relations and marketing firms,"[31] writes a former writer for the *Washington Post.* One academic text claims that *"upwards of 70%* of daily newspaper copy" emanates "from public relations–generated releases."[32] This material is "cleverly disguised as news and public-affairs journalism, precisely in order to enhance its credibility."[33]

One might think that this is not such a great deal for the newspaper or station that carries the material, because it might hurt their credibility. But credibility is lately taking a backseat. Most newspapers and many magazines are not moneymaking propositions, and many have fallen into bankruptcy or closed. Press release copy comes preproduced and ready to air or print. Several large firms, including the PR Newswire, exist to write and package "stories" for corporate clients. Those stories are then provided on a wire service to newspapers. This allows media organizations to reduce the number of staff dedicated to actually investigating, researching, and writing stories. In these days of mergers and declining revenues, papers are often short of personnel for these tasks, so press releases become a welcome source of filler for content.[34] What they may sacrifice in credibility and accuracy, though, may be another question. Arguably, when a newspaper runs a press release as given without disclosing that it is a press release, it is being deceptive. Many journalists condemn the practice as inconsistent with journalistic ethics.[35] Nevertheless, broadcasters and newspapers have at times argued that they should be free to run such content without disclaimers as a matter of editorial discretion.[36]

As media practices have changed, however, the gravy train of news placement has become more difficult to catch. Public relations professionals cost money, as do services like the PR Newswire. Apparently, desperate times call for even more desperate measures, paying for placement. In what may be a sign of the times, a 2006 survey by *PRWeek* magazine found that of 266 marketing executives asked if they had ever paid for broadcast or editorial news placement, 46 percent said they had.[37] The old wall that separated the editorial and the advertising sides of most media has eroded. However, it is one thing to offer your advertising content to a media outlet in the hopes they might run it as editorial content. It takes marketing to another level for an advertiser to pay a fee to the media producer to ensure that advertising is incorporated into the content. This practice, called *product placement,* is ubiquitous.

Product Placement

Product placement may be the ultimate product of integrated marketing communications. It is a blend of advertising (the message is being paid for) and PR (it is done under the radar). Product placement is the practice of paying a fee to have one's product featured prominently, perhaps even as a plot device, in entertainment. The classic example is the product placement of Reese's Pieces in *E.T.: The Extra-Terrestrial.*[38] With product placement, the television show or the movie acts as the third party to deliver the message, because the product's appearance in a movie or television show does not carry notice that it is a paid appearance.[39] Instead, it appears as if it might simply have been the spontaneous choice of the artists involved because the product was the best or the coolest or the most authentic for the character. Obviously, this is the impression the advertiser would like to create even though by now, most people are vaguely aware of the practice. However, its specific deployment often goes unnoticed.

For instance, in 2007 Nissan signed an agreement to launch a new sport-utility vehicle, the Rogue, in a complex multiplatform deal with NBC's then hit program *Heroes.*[40] The agreement included placement of the Rogue in the actual series; rights to *Heroes* artwork for use in its advertising and promotion; provision of five Rogues that cast members were to drive and "personalize," after which the company would give the vehicles away as sweepstakes prizes; and airing of episodes with limited commercial interruption with Nissan as the single sponsor.[41] Nissan took these steps because it found that its prior associations with the show had resulted in better consumer recall of Nissan ads, compared to other ads, and higher click-through rates on the NBC.com website.[42]

Such deals for the blending of advertising and entertainment content are routine practice in the industry. Whole television shows (particularly in the so-called reality programming) and some episodes of certain shows are created as vehicles to sell particular products. For example, the producers of the popular HBO program *Sex and the City* were paid by Absolut vodka to create an episode that featured Absolut.[43] Because the distinction between advertising and editorial or artistic content is increasingly hard to make, it is not always clear when obvious product references are intended as promotion or as irony—or maybe both. Usually you have to read trade publications to find out for sure, and the lines have gotten blurrier and blurrier.

Since product placement does not come with an announcement (which would defeat the purpose), one can never be sure if a product's presence is part of a placement effort. This lack of certainty cultivates a general skepticism and allows marketers and entertainment producers to leverage consumer awareness with a wink and a nod, as in the movie *Talladega Nights,* in which the brands Wonder Bread and KFC played a prominent role, but where it seems that their appearance was not a result of an explicit product placement agreement (although both Wonder Bread and KFC sponsored the movie after the fact). It is not clear whether the makers of the movie were hoping for such endorsement and promotional tie-ins or were intending to spoof the practice of product placement in the first place. Lady Gaga's video for the song "Telephone" included a number of product placements (including Diet Coke, Miracle Whip, and Wonder Bread), but not all of them were paid placements, which raises the question whether they were "placements" at all.[44]

Jason Reitman's feature film *Up In the Air*[45] is another example of a blending of art and promotion that leaves unclear how much of each it was. The film seemed like a feature-length promotional piece for American Airlines and Hilton Hotels, because both companies were portrayed in a promotional way, with beautiful lighting and spotless settings. The average viewer cannot know whether the director's intent was ironic or whether he entered into the agreement simply to get the use of the planes and locations at low or no cost.[46] Moreover, although product placement has mostly been confined to visual media (television and films), there is at least one documented case of a print author being paid to include a reference to a product in a novel.[47]

More Stealth Marketing Techniques

Product placement is only one way to get past consumers' awareness that they are being pitched. There are others. Ever more desperate to avoid consumer skepticism of conventional advertising, many marketers have taken to practicing what is known in the trade as *stealth marketing*. Stealth marketing takes many forms, but all are some sort of variation on the third-party technique. Sometimes companies may employ college students to talk up an airline, or they may pay actors to ride elevators in office buildings while discussing a product or service, to go to a bar and pose as a customer and tout a brand of vodka, or to pretend to be tourists and ask passersby to take their picture in order to have the opportunity to pitch a brand of camera.[48]

An actor may also be hired to pose as a "person in the street" to give a testimonial, a movie review, or other "interview" to a "reporter" who is also part of the PR team. (Actors who play the "man in the street" role are called "fake 'real people,'" in a superb example of the sort of utterly unself-conscious oxymoronic jargon PR generates.)[49] Sometimes a company has used its own employees to pose as customers in such testimonial ads, as when two employees of Sony posed as ordinary moviegoers in ads touting the Sony Pictures 2001 summer release *The Patriot*.[50] Whatever the product, this sort of marketing would almost surely be less effective if it were revealed that the participants were paid.

It is difficult to know just how many encounters like this we have every day. One suspects not as many as its proponents would like you to believe, since they often sound as if they are claiming more influence than they actually possess (a common problem with the profession). But stealth marketing takes place with more frequency than the general public seems to be aware of. Marketing communications devices are limited only by marketers' creativity. Some, like having a person shave a logo on his head, embedding a logo in the sand, skywriting, and other sensational techniques, seem destined

to be largely curiosities or occasional practices. Others, like product placement, have come into the mainstream and are a major part of marketing
practice. Of particular interest in the last decade are devices referred to variously as "word-of-mouth," "buzz," "guerrilla," or "viral" marketing.

Posting videos on YouTube (both videos that are overtly ads and some
that seem more like public service announcements) is a popular viral marketing method. Buzz marketing is often another attempt to circumvent whatever
skepticism consumers may have about advertising by relaying the seller's
messages through friends, coworkers, or even strangers. In many cases, buzz
marketing networks are built on groups put together in a way that probably
would have been impossible without the Internet and cell phones. Participants may be paid or not paid, trained by the company or not, but they are
selected to reflect the target market.[51] This is the *opinion leaders technique.*
It involves recruiting "opinion leaders" to adopt a product and then to promote it to their friends.[52]

The opinion leaders technique is particularly popular in marketing to
teens, since marketers are very eager to capture teen customers, on the theory
that brand loyalties adopted early in life will carry forward for a lifetime.
Teens are fairly sensitive to and skeptical about being pitched to, so the use
of peers to deliver the pitches helps decrease resistance to them.[53] Such promotional efforts may or may not include having the endorsers reveal that
they have received some compensation from the company. Where there is a
paid endorsement (e.g., free shoes to a teenager for serving as an opinion
leader), the payments are often so small as not to seriously undercut the value
of the endorsement in most people's eyes. Interestingly enough, in what may
represent a cultural shift, these marketing relationships are sometimes disclosed, because younger people do not seem to view promotional activity as
always suspicious, just when it is unmediated by a peer. The opinion leaders
technique often includes use of social networking media like Facebook or
MySpace to push products. Advertising in social media and on the Internet
generally through blogs is a fast-growing and popular type of promotion.[54]
Here, too, the third-party technique surfaces in the form of payment for posts
about products on blogs, Facebook, MySpace, and other social networking
sites.[55]

Although professionals in this sector of the business claim that paid endorsements that are not disclosed violate word-of-mouth marketing ethics,

we should not take these protestations seriously in light of the gospel of the third-party technique, which proclaims that it works *because* the speaker seems objective and unconnected to the seller. But perhaps people who have grown up in this sort of promotional environment do not find the fact that a friend receives a benefit from the seller a reason to discount the endorsement.

Of course, the product itself often bears an advertisement of sorts in the form of a logo, especially where the brand logo becomes a design element, as in the Louis Vuitton and Coach brands.[56] In these cases, the consumer is actually paying the seller for a product that then turns the buyer into a sort of walking billboard for the product. Many people do not even consider this marketing, but, of course, anything that contributes to brand identity is marketing.

Another third-party technique involves getting articles placed in academic publications. This practice is especially effective, because academic articles are often considered particularly respected sources. They are almost the paradigm of detached, objective, reliable informants. Yet when authors have undisclosed financial interests, it undermines the credibility of these articles. In some cases these articles may amount to nothing more than stealth marketing.[57] For example, in order to encourage physicians to prescribe its antidepressant Paxil to adolescents suffering from depression, GlaxoSmithKline allegedly enlisted doctors it identified as "key opinion leaders" to publish favorable reviews of a study of Paxil in the academic literature.[58] Company sales representatives would then get reprints of the articles to give to doctors to persuade them to prescribe Paxil. The most troubling aspect of this practice was that the manufacturer apparently engaged in this effort because the number of adverse incidents with the drug made it clear that it would be unlikely to receive FDA approval for prescription of Paxil to teenagers. Unfortunately, for some of the patients receiving the prescription, these commissioned articles did not clearly describe all of the risks.[59]

Front Groups and Astroturf Organizations

The most insidious and potentially destructive public relations practices are in the political arena and employ the third-party technique by *creating* the third party—a nonprofit organization, think tank, or other group that then can issue position papers on behalf of a company or industry. The paradigmatic example of this technique was the establishment of the Council for Tobacco Research (CTR), pursuant to advice from the PR firm Hill & Knowlton.[60] The tobacco companies pooled resources and formed the CTR. Its mission was to serve as a conduit for ostensibly neutral "information" on behalf of the tobacco companies that would counter the growing body of evidence of the negative health consequences of smoking and would have more credibility than if issued directly by the companies themselves.[61] The efforts of the CTR and similar organizations played an important role in minimizing the health dangers of smoking in the public's consciousness.[62] This was the role they were intended to play, and it worked very well for decades. According to some observers, it inspired similar efforts to create "a paralyzing fog of doubt around climate change"[63]—to perhaps even more devastating potential effect, since, unlike smoking, global climate change affects everyone.

Perhaps more insidious than a third-party think tank is the formation of what purports to be an organization of citizens. Such groups are known as "front groups" or "astroturf organizations"—the latter a play on the term *grassroots,* which is used to identify bottom-up social movements.[64] Astroturf groups are meant to appear as if they are a collection of concerned voters who have spontaneously formed to lobby for their own interests. In fact, they are created in the offices of public relations agencies in Washington and New York. The PR firm will establish a website and attract some attention, but it usually does not actually have "members" per se; it has resources. The group Working Families for Wal-Mart is an example of this strategy.

To respond to criticism of the company's labor practices, Wal-Mart, with the assistance of its public relations firm, set up an organization it called Working Families for Wal-Mart. The idea was to make it seem that there were working families across America who thought Wal-Mart's labor practices actually benefited them. The impression the organization's website conveyed was of an independent political organization.[65] Its website and blog contained what appeared to be positive testimonials from workers and customers.

Yet neither the Working Families for Wal-Mart organization nor its website clearly identified itself as sponsored by Wal-Mart.[66] Instead, the website explicitly said the organization was "giving voice to the millions of Americans who know Wal-Mart makes a real difference for their family and community."[67] At the "About Us" link, the organization identified its membership as made up of "leaders from a variety of backgrounds and communities all across America [and] customers, business leaders, activists, civic leaders, educators and many others with first-hand knowledge of Wal-Mart's positive contributions to communities."[68] It did not say that Wal-Mart had a role in creating the group.[69] After Wal-Mart's role in the website became known, Wal-Mart took the site down.

There are literally dozens of examples of such front groups or astroturf organizations. They are ubiquitous—so much so that other entities, such as SourceWatch, have sprung up to try to keep track of and unmask them.[70] This is difficult, however, because these organizations can be formed, taken on and off line, and moved or renamed almost at will. An organization interested in attracting members would never do this, for fear that people could not find it. For an organization that is not interested in attracting members, such moves do not matter, because they will not negatively affect recruiting. The purpose of these groups is to provide the appearance of a legitimate grassroots organization supporting the position that the corporation would like to promote but that would be less effective if the company did so openly.

For example, there were allegations that some of the protestors who disrupted town hall meetings on health care reform had been led there and coached by astroturf groups formed by those insurance companies opposing reform. In particular, a front group called FreedomWorks may have orchestrated many of these events.[71] Apparently the aim was to suggest to lawmakers that broad swathes of their constituents were opposed to health care reform.[72] Former congressman, now lobbyist, Dick Armey heads Freedom-Works. Another astroturf organization mobilizing against health care reform was 60 Plus Association.[73] The American Association of Retired Persons (AARP) exposed 60 Plus as a front group for the insurance lobby and accused it of taking positions counter to seniors' interests and lobbying with respect to issues with no discernible tie to senior citizen issues.[74] Groups such as FreedomWorks and 60 Plus continue to proliferate, blurring the lines between real and fake grassroots organizations. There is no doubt that at least some of the health care reform protestors were voicing genuine concerns. That these same protestors knew about the role or motives of the sponsoring organizations is doubtful.

Lobbying

Yet another form of public relations activity is lobbying. Because direct lobbying is subject to complex regulations of its own, lobbying groups are usually distinct units within public relations firms. Lobbyists' work is to attempt to influence and often even draft legislation favorable to their issues. For industry lobbyists, that means legislation favorable to industry. Because industry has more money, it has more lobbyists. For example, the banking industry played a key role in the revision of the bankruptcy laws to make personal bankruptcy harder to file by presenting the proposed change in the law as necessary to prevent irresponsible use of credit. It almost goes without saying that they did so without acknowledging the role banks themselves may have played in extending credit beyond reasonable limits and relentlessly promoting credit card use through techniques designed to obscure the true costs of credit.[75] As the world now knows, aggressive lending policies, through adjustable rate mortgages, balloon payments, home equity lines, and refinancing, were major contributors to the market volatility that began in 2007 and led to the economic crisis of 2008.

Lobbying and public relations efforts can also be directed at more global business interests, for example, tort reform. Several years of relentless public relations efforts by business lobbies have created the impression of a tort crisis by focusing on a few large verdicts that seem harmful and unfair to business, despite empirical research that demonstrates that business disputes, not tort cases, make up the majority of the courts' dockets. Research suggests that many of the so-called excessive verdicts reported in the press (perhaps directly from press releases) were not necessarily so excessive when seen in the context of what was at stake or of the facts in the case. Yet intensive lobbying by business has cemented in the public consciousness the notion that there is a "tort crisis" involving "excessive" verdicts.

Given the resources of large companies and their ability to employ media consultants and marketing professionals to advise them on how best to position a pitch, commercial interests seem to have a considerable advantage in the political arena over opponents who do not have generous resources and a commercial interest to protect. It is important to remember the aim of these kinds of advertising and lobbying efforts. All such activities are intended to enhance the economic value of the entity, no matter how far removed they may seem from the product. As such, they can all be described as "commercial expression." Seen from this vantage point, the volume of commercial expression would be difficult to overemphasize. It is all around us all the time. Its influence is literally inescapable in any industrialized society.

"Americans are swimming in a sea of messages"[76]

Advertising is a billion-dollar business. *Advertising Age* reported that advertising expenditures were $142 billion in 2008.[77] A study by the American Psychological Association, published in 2004, concluded that average adolescents in America were exposed to approximately 40,000 ads in the year 2000 and that the industry spent $12 billion on such ads.[78] According to another study, national advertisers spent $105 billion on traditional advertising in 2006.[79] That is only the tip of the iceberg. In 2005, the *Economist* reported that worldwide advertising expenditures for the previous year were $370 billion.[80] The *New York Times* reported that advertising spending for 2004 in the United States alone was in excess of $200 billion.[81]

Since 2006, advertising expenditures have tended to fluctuate along with the general health of the economy. One source forecast 1.7 percent growth to $152.3 billion in conventional advertising expenditures in the United States,[82] although expenditures in that year and 2007 were somewhat flatter than expected, reaching "only" $149 billion in 2007.[83] Such numbers do not include other marketing, public relations, and lobbying expenditures.

Some commentators have offered estimates, based on average viewing patterns and per capita spending, that the average American consumer is exposed to 237 television ads per day.[84] Television ads are just a small and perhaps the most obvious part of the promotional picture. "Advertising messages bombard us everywhere we go," say analysts Al and Laura Ries.[85] Virtually any available space, including people's bodies, can serve as a platform for an advertising message.[86] Whatever you think of advertising, it is impossible to escape. If an individual finds aspects of it antisocial, disturbing, unsavory, or contrary to his or her self-interest, there is very little he or she can do about it.

Once upon a time, it may have been possible to avoid marketing. You could buy only publications that did not carry advertising and watch only public television or no television at all. You could avoid malls, car dealerships, and any circumstances in which promotional pitches might be encountered. Now, short of moving to a cabin in the woods, this is no longer possible. We cannot avoid the visual clutter of billboards, or the promotional tie-ins to movies or other entertainment in stores, restaurants, and the culture at large. Even if it were possible for an individual to escape being the target of pitches, most of us interact with people who have not been so scrupulously shielding themselves, and we are thus influenced indirectly through our contacts. Thus, by virtue of human contact, we are forced to confront and negotiate the impacts of this tidal wave of communication. The problem is that marketing's volume and ubiquity are not the only factors that make it difficult to screen out. The bigger problem may be, as we have already seen, identifying it as marketing in the first place. It is advertising's very ubiquity that has generated consumer skepticism and indifference (at least at a superficial level), which has in turn led advertisers to try to disguise its source through the employment of the third-party technique and to leave no stone unturned in researching ways to influence us.

Playing with Our Minds

Clearly, the major commercial advertisers have a very powerful voice in the culture. To cast them as "disadvantaged" or lacking an adequate opportunity for a "voice" is risible. Commercial speakers are often entities with vast resources, far more than any comparable institution, except perhaps the U.S. government,[87] which itself uses many of these techniques.[88] So it stands to reason, because of both its scale and its ubiquity, that commercial expression has significant impacts on society, even if we cannot identify and measure those impacts with scientific precision. Moreover, large corporations play significant roles in shaping what constitutes news and the attitudes of the world around us, and that influence is exercised with what is perhaps unprecedented knowledge of human psychology and motivation.

Marketing research, with its goal of fine-tuning marketers' ability to engender positive reactions and thus improve return on investment in advertising, is a multibillion dollar business. It is reflected not only in the venerable focus group and surveys but also in the accumulation of massive amounts of data[89] through grocery store savings programs, rebate and warranty requests, census data,[90] functional magnetic resonance imaging, and other research and data collection efforts. Some of these efforts, were they conducted in a university setting (and sometimes commercial research *is* conducted under the auspices of corporate grants to universities),[91] would be subject to rigorous Internal Review Board (IRB) standards governing research on human subjects. IRB standards are intended to protect human subjects from experiments that may injure them in some way.[92] But there seems to be little or no protection for consumers from the vast experiment that commercial marketing represents.

The scale of such research efforts seems particularly troubling when it comes to targeting children, since we assume children are not as fully rational as adults. However unrealistic our view of adult rationality may be, it is fairly uncontroversial that children, because of their relative cognitive plasticity and limitations, are more vulnerable to manipulation than adults.[93] Given this fact, why should we permit children to be targeted by marketers in this way? With the unprecedented power that modern business now wields through a wide variety of commercial expression instruments comes a corresponding potential for harm on a large scale. So preventing harm to children by regulating some of these communication efforts is a legitimate governmental function. Should the First Amendment stand as an obstacle to government's ability to restrict the power of commercial expression to mold or mislead young children? This question cannot be answered, however, without considering the question of what values the First Amendment is meant to protect.

CHAPTER 3

Why Protect Speech? Four Fundamental Interests

[T]he problem of maintaining a system of freedom of expression in a
society is one of the most complex any society has to face.
—Thomas I. Emerson,
  Toward a General Theory of the First Amendment

The quest for a comprehensive theory to explain the First Amendment's
scope and purpose has been a popular activity of twentieth-century legal and
political thinkers. As soon as we begin talking about theories of the First
Amendment, it seems clear that we also need a theory of law identifying the
legitimate sources of legal authority and interpretation. Some say it is not
possible to come up with a single unifying theory of the First Amendment,
because it has been applied to too many disparate cases to be able to reconcile them under a single analytical framework.[1] But even if no single theory is
satisfactory, courts need some sort of method for deciding the cases brought
under the amendment. To this end, it is useful to consider what might be excluded under *any* theory. To do that, I needed to look to the theory with the
broadest scope: Thomas Emerson's *Toward a General Theory of the First
Amendment*[2] offers that scope.

Preliminary Matters

To understand why commercial expression should not be given full First
Amendment protection, we should examine why any speech ever gets it; what
does the First Amendment's prohibition that "Congress shall make no law . . .

abridging freedom of expression" really mean? Freedom of expression is never really totally "free." Protection for expression often costs someone something, even if it is only the discomfort of hearing disagreeable opinions.[3] So protection for freedom of expression starts with the possibility that sometimes it will mean protection of offensive or otherwise socially repugnant speech.[4] It could hardly be otherwise. Freedom of expression is not worth much if it is only the freedom to say what is already socially or politically acceptable.[5]

As much as, culturally, we often speak as if freedom of expression in the United States is wide-open and absolute, this is clearly not the case. Many disputes have speech components that we do not necessarily view as First Amendment cases. As freedom of speech comes into conflict with other values—like the right to be left alone, quiet enjoyment, autonomy, property, security, and so forth—the general public is often fairly sanguine about suppression of speech in aid of one of these other goals. For instance, we typically think parents not only have the right to control their children's expression but a duty to do so in some circumstances (like talking in church). We take it for granted that employers should be able to fire employees for insubordination or disloyalty or to control employees' self-expression with respect to dress, hairstyle, and the like.[6] Exercise of autonomy over one's business or property seems appropriate to most Americans.

Thus, perhaps not surprisingly, the Supreme Court has been relatively sparing in recognizing particular areas of speech as protected by the First Amendment. And it has done so without the benefit of a consistent theory about the scope and purpose of the amendment, even though, as noted, this has been the subject of decades of scholarly study and commentary. At the outset, courts' task in interpreting the First Amendment is complicated by its brevity and ambiguity. "Plain meaning" offers little help as an interpretive device, given that the meaning of the words "Congress shall make no law . . . abridging freedom of expression" is not very plain. Even at the most fundamental level, trying to define what constitutes "expression" turns out to be incredibly fraught.

A Limit on Government

Nevertheless, one of the most fundamental limitations on the interpretation of the First Amendment is its wording. The phrase "Congress shall make no law" is understood to act as a limitation on government rather than a reflection of a governmental duty to protect freedom of expression. The First Amendment does not provide an affirmative right to freedom of expression per se, as, for example, is found in Article 10 of the European Convention on Human Rights ("Everyone has the right to freedom of expression").[7] The difference is a very subtle one, to be sure, because Article 10 also indicates by its wording that the right to freedom of expression is protected against interference by a "public authority."[8] It is nevertheless a difference, because what usually triggers First Amendment scrutiny is a claim that a governmental enactment has violated the "make no law" injunction.

It turns out, however, that the law is not quite so straightforward. When a court allows a plaintiff to pursue a libel or defamation suit, it can be said that the government is acting to suppress the defendant's speech by providing the plaintiff with the legal means to impose a penalty on that speech.[9] This was the reason the Court in *New York Times v. Sullivan* created a very high evidentiary and procedural standard to be satisfied by plaintiffs wishing to bring a defamation action against public figures before their cases may go forward. Yet this principle, that providing legal remedies may violate the "make no law" provision in the First Amendment, is not uniformly applied. Many causes of action, in addition to libel or defamation, may involve the suppression of speech and are seen as acceptable limitations on freedom of speech, not violating the "make no law" injunction—for example, cases arising out of intellectual property law like copyright or trademark infringement. As a result, speech that the government may not directly suppress may be suppressed on behalf of a copyright or trademark holder against an infringer. Likewise, the refusal to provide a remedy for infringement on expressive interests—like employer control of employees' dress, hairstyles, piercings, tattoos, and so on—is not thought to raise a First Amendment issue in most cases.

The Speech/Act Distinction

One attempt to find the limits for First Amendment coverage has been to try to define the meaning of the word *expression* in the clause and to formulate a speech/act distinction. Under this theory, speech must be protected, but actions can be restrained. Thomas Emerson himself urged that a "fundamental distinction" existed between "belief, opinion and the communication of ideas on the one hand, and different forms of conduct on the other."[10] However, in practice, this distinction proved to be rather difficult to sustain, for several reasons.[11] In the first place, it is possible to reframe almost any action as "expression" of some sort. If every act we take (including, say, committing a robbery) is in some sense expressive, then no act could be prohibited, as the prohibition would represent an unlawful limitation of expression.

Moreover, the speech/act distinction proves unworkable for other reasons more fundamental to what most people probably feel the First Amendment *is* meant to cover. For example, much expressive activity is nonverbal: marches, silent vigils, armbands, dances, pantomimes, and so on. Most legal scholars agree that some or all of these activities should be protected, even if they are nonverbal and therefore are not literally "speech." Sometimes these sorts of actions are labeled "expressive activity" or "expressive conduct" in order to avoid the speech/act problem.[12] That label is not terribly helpful either, since it is unclear why wearing an armband is an expressive activity but running a business is not.

Conversely, speech itself can, in some circumstances, be an "act." When the participants in a marriage ceremony say, "I do," that is a speech act—that is, the recitation of the words constitutes the final action necessary to create some legal rights or commit a prohibited act. When an offeree to a contract says, "I accept," that is a speech act. If someone utters a defamatory falsehood about another, it is a speech act. An offer of a bribe is a criminal act committed through speech, as is perjury. In short, some nonspeech acts (armbands) are protected by the First Amendment as expressive, and some acts committed by speech (perjury) are not, and the speech/act distinction has failed to offer definitive guidance on when something falls into one or the other category.

Original Intent

Other theorists attempt to ground First Amendment interpretation on a historical foundation, limiting its protection to that which the Framers might have had in mind when writing it. From this perspective, the First Amendment might have been intended to guard against prior restraints (i.e., forbidding publication),[13] and the Framers might have been thinking of prior restraints primarily in the context of political speech.[14] It is hard to know. But we do know that the Constitution was drafted against the backdrop of the Enlightenment and that the Framers were influenced by specific political philosophers of that period and of earlier ones—Rousseau, Locke, and even Milton.[15] Of course, these philosophers did not draft the First Amendment. So while what they said is probably relevant to what the Framers intended, it is not dispositive—even if there was some way we could know precisely what the Framers understood (which we cannot) and if each of them had the same understanding (which they obviously did not).[16]

Original intent as an interpretive strategy, whatever its merits for constitutional interpretation elsewhere, seems particularly unsatisfying with respect to freedom of expression because of enormous changes in the means and forms of communication. And with respect to commercial speech, the development of complex organizational forms of doing business that did not exist at the time the First Amendment was drafted also gives pause for too much reliance on original intent in the absence of original context. Given how different the society was at that time, it is unclear that we could operate from a solely historical understanding and arrive at any satisfactory interpretation. In any event, the courts have clearly gone far beyond a strictly historical interpretation of the amendment's coverage. Instead, the courts have adopted a more gestalt, "as if" jurisprudence of the First Amendment, one that does not have a clear, single animating vision. As noted earlier, the person who came closest to articulating such a vision, one that would encompass much of the case law, was the late Yale law professor Thomas Emerson.

Thomas Emerson's General Theory

Emerson made a heroic attempt to explain all of the reasons why we do (or might want to) offer protection for freedom of expression. Many of the details of his theory, such as the distinction between action and speech, were not persuasive in the end. In his choice of sample cases—ones involving labor unions, obscenity, subversive organizations—it is clear that his theory was (not surprisingly) much influenced by the struggles of his day. Many of the specific solutions he proposes are not so persuasive in light of subsequent developments. Perhaps most interesting of all, he barely considered the question of commercial expression, apparently thinking it was largely and self-evidently outside the scope of First Amendment protection.[17] Nevertheless, in its basic architecture, Emerson's theory is the most comprehensive attempt to explain why any society might value freedom of expression. Although not everyone agrees that the First Amendment protects all of the interests Emerson identifies, virtually everyone agrees that it protects at least one of them.[18] So it is a useful lens through which to examine commercial speech to see if protection for commercial speech advances any, let alone all, of those interests.

Emerson's theory claimed the First Amendment protected four general interests, each of which serves as a sort of umbrella to encompass many similar interests: (1) individual self-fulfillment (also encompassing autonomy and right to self-expression or self-actualization), (2) attainment of truth, (3) participation in decision making (or democratic process), and (4) the maintenance of a balance between stability and change.[19] Emerson claimed that freedom of expression was a necessary part of self-expression and, thus, of personal fulfillment.[20] The second prong Emerson identified is that which is most resonant for many—that freedom of expression is thought to be the best method of ensuring discovery of truth.[21] This was the reasoning that convinced the *Virginia Pharmacy* Court to offer limited protection for commercial speech in the first place.[22] Next, Emerson argued that protection for freedom of expression was critical to democratic participation—not only in government, but also in the formation of all aspects of the culture.[23] Finally, he asserted that freedom of expression helped maintain a balance between societal impulses to change and those to stabilization.[24] Some scholars have argued that *all* of these considerations can be boiled down to speaker-centered justifications versus listener-centered justifications.[25] One could also reframe this as individual versus collective interests. Arguments in favor of greater protection for commercial speech have relied on arguments from all of these angles. However, on closer inspection of the evidence, protection for commercial expression does not advance some of these interests at all, and with respect to others, commercial expression produces more harms to these interests than benefits.[26]

Autonomy and Self-Expression

Emerson's first category contains elements that are overlapping but not entirely synonymous: autonomy (the freedom to make one's own choices) and freedom for self-expression (the freedom to speak one's mind, to create one's public persona through one's speech). Other terms, such as *self-actualization,* also capture these general ideas. Unlike Emerson's other three categories, which appear to speak to collective social goods, the interest in autonomy is an individual interest. As Vincent Blasi has explained, interpreting the First Amendment to advance individual interests is a relatively recent development.

> [T]he thrust of recent work on the First Amendment has been individual-centered, focused on such concepts as autonomy, individual flourishing, political consent, and personal character. Even arguments that are instrumental in form tend to invoke asserted causal relationships between free speech and certain capacities of individuals that in turn help those individuals to serve the collective good.[27]

Recent theories draw on the rich intellectual history of concern for the human being as a moral subject and thus as an end in oneself.[28]

In his famous concurrence in *Whitney v. California,*[29] Justice Brandeis reflected this concern, writing, "Those who won our independence believed that the final end of the State was to make men free to develop their faculties."[30] Thus, individual reflection, education, growth, development, and self-expression are all means to an end and goods in themselves. In this view human beings are entitled to a special dignity by virtue of their status as human beings. There is also an assumption that all people possess or can aspire to a sort of reflective rationality as a means for assessing and evaluating information, free of the taint of prejudice, bias, or emotional excesses. It "assumes that people approach the task of gaining knowledge individually rather than as socially constituted members of particular groups."[31]

This approach is not a good fit applied to corporations, which issue the bulk of commercial speech. Corporations are not human beings, so they lack the expressive interests related to self-actualization and freedom that human beings possess. Corporations are not moral subjects or ends in themselves. They are a means to an end. In the case of for-profit corporations, that end is—by virtue of the law governing their creation—profit. Although corporations have been granted the status of legal persons for some circumstances, that personhood does not support the conclusion that they have the same rights as natural persons. For example, corporations have no right against compulsory self-incrimination[32] and no right of privacy,[33] because these rights are said to be "purely personal."[34]

Freedom of expression as a function of autonomy, self-actualization, or self-determination seems similarly personal. As Emerson put it, the right to freedom of expression is necessary to human beings because

> expression is an integral part of the development of ideas, of mental exploration and of the affirmation of self. The power to realize his potentiality as a human being begins at this point and must extend at least this far if the whole nature of man is not to be thwarted.[35]

Corporations do not have a "self" to be actualized or affirmed.[36] Its employees may have them. Its shareholders may have them. But corporations themselves do not. Moreover, when a corporation's agents speak on its behalf, they are not expressing themselves; they are acting as agents to advance the corporation's ends. The corporation is the principal and management is its agent. If that corporation is a for-profit one, its ends are profit maximization (however management defines that goal).[37] According to Professor Daniel Greenwood,

> Corporate speech is coerced, not free. It is compelled, legally mandated speech, not the result of anyone's autonomous behavior. It does not reflect the views of shareholders, nor, if management is acting in good faith, those of managers or other corporate agents. Instead, corporate speech reflects the hypothetical interests of a creature given reality by the market and the law: the fictional shareholder.[38]

The corporation is a collective with no corporeal existence. Its shareholders (if they are people and not corporations themselves) are to some extent the embodiment of the corporation. But managing a company on the basis of the real preferences of real shareholders would probably be unduly cumbersome, and the law does not demand that of management. Instead, management's duty to maximize shareholder value actually is assessed with reference to a fictional shareholder who cares for nothing but profit. This fictional shareholder is a principle. Thus, a corporation's principal "is merely a principle, an abstraction, not a human being. Principles, unlike principals, do not have any autonomy rights to be respected."

Commercial expression does not represent the expression of the corporation's employees, even though it may feel that way for some employees, like those in advertising.[39] The expression belongs to the organization. The corporation owns employees' speech, and when they leave the job, it can do with that speech what it likes. In no sense does it belong to those who actually produce it. Moreover, however much employees' own creativity and interests may align with the corporation's, employees are, at the end of the day, agents speaking on the corporation's behalf—following orders. Greenwood explains, "[P]eople who are just following orders are neither full moral subjects nor appropriate participants in the difficult debates of the political forum."[40] Thus, if there is a justification for the protection for commercial speech, self-expression does not seem to be a part of that justification—at least not speaker self-expression.[41]

There is another possibility, however—listener self-expression. Commercial speech could contribute to the listeners' exercise of autonomy and thus provide a means of self-expression. This seems to be the approach adopted by the Court in *Virginia Pharmacy*. The Court emphasized the rights of the listeners, noting that "the function of self-rule is fostered by the receipt of information that enables the individual to make life-affecting decisions in a more informed fashion."[42] In other words, perhaps by giving corporations freedom to speak, more information (or at least social material, if not, strictly speaking, "information") is generated that, in turn, supports the goal of self-actualization or development for listeners. One might call this the argument of self-expression by proxy.

There may be something to this argument.[43] As columnist David Brooks observed, "Individuals don't build their lives from scratch. They absorb the patterns and norms of the world around them."[44] In this view, commercial expression creates material from which individuals can mold their statements about self.[45] There is no question that this is true to some degree. A highly developed consumer culture offers a dizzying array of material from which to craft a personal identity; particularly if you focus on the self-expression possible in the realm of consumer choices. However, that social reality is fairly relentlessly focused on the material. The billions of dollars spent on marketing face little competition from speakers on other issues: political, religious, spiritual, altruistic, or, most pointedly, antimaterialist.

Ideologically speaking, the array of choices that commercial expression offers is not very broad. It appears to be broad, in that it offers a wide array of choices about what to consume. But it offers few opportunities to reject consumption patterns in general or to conform one's consumption decisions with minority views about the appropriate conditions for the production of those choices (i.e., with respect to labor conditions, environmental impact, etc.). Comparatively little time is given in the commercial world to issues of labor, family, religion, altruism, or other noncommercial aspects of life, except insofar as they can be translated into something for sale. Nonprofit organizations must compete in a communications environment dominated by those with something to sell. Churches, schools, museums, environmental groups, labor organizations, and animal rights groups all find themselves under pressure to offer merchandise to sell their "brand" and carry their "message," even though such messages cannot really be reduced to a logo. So what appears, at first glance, to be a great deal of choice is actually a lot of choice within a relatively narrow spectrum.

Even if we assume that commercial expression offers very broad opportunities for the advancement of listeners' needs for autonomy and self-expression, what if there are significant social costs—for example, in environmental pollution or child labor—associated with the provision of that array of consumption choices? Are these social costs offset by the benefit of being able to use this speech as material for self-expression? It seems a bit much to say that we ought to put up with environmental degradation or child labor in order for us to have the freedom to express ourselves through the opportunity to choose from among many colors of shirts.

Moreover, in most cases, the informational function of advertising is very low. The *Virginia Pharmacy* Court dealt with advertising that was clearly informative—advertising of price. But very little in advertising is informative, and a great deal of it is misleading—the opposite of informative. It hardly seems to contribute to listeners' autonomy to mislead them. When a company imbues a brand with misleading social meaning, it also interferes with consumers' apparently expressive choices.

For example, if a maker of sportswear advertises and promotes its brand as "sweatshop free," it presumably does so in the hope that some consumers will base their purchasing decisions on such representations, in furtherance of the creation of an identity that includes, among other things, the consumer's desire to support fair labor practices.[46] However, if the company's actions are not consistent with those representations, how does that further the consumer's self-expression, if, instead of promoting their values with their purchases, they are actually contributing to the perpetuation of labor practices they intended to disavow? This miscommunication thwarts the consumer's attempt at self-expression. It violates, not vindicates, the justificatory principle of self-expression by proxy. This is precisely where it seems the government might justifiably intervene in furtherance of autonomy and rights to self-expression, to ensure that the products consumers buy in order to express themselves are truthfully labeled, promoted, described, and marketed so that consumers can accurately express their preferences.

Truth and the "Marketplace of Ideas"

Misleading information about a product brings us to Emerson's second category: the discovery, promotion, or preservation of truthful information. As Emerson and many others, notably John Stuart Mill, have argued, it may be necessary to protect freedom of expression, particularly that which is not popular, because "the unaccepted opinion may be true or partially true."[47] Mill wrote, "[T]he majority of the eminent men of every past generation held many opinions now known to be erroneous, and did or approved numerous things which no one will now justify."[48] In the absence of perfect knowledge, it is argued, tolerance for expression is the practice that both respects human dignity and furthers the search for truth.

Like Emerson, most scholars of the First Amendment have argued that the amendment has some sort of "protection for truth" dimension. Few have thought, however, that truth is the only interest the amendment protects.[49] Moreover, simply because an expression is truthful does not make it a particularly informative or valuable expression. Standing on a street corner reciting the names in a telephone book would involve truthful speech, but it is difficult to imagine any context in which it would be political, expressive, or even useful speech. Nevertheless, the idea that we must protect all speech to ensure that we receive truthful information is a common trope. And it is often advanced as a justification for protecting commercial expression. This is perhaps the least persuasive of the arguments for protecting commercial expression, since so little of it is truthful or informational in any conventional sense.

Truth for Truth's Sake

Truth is valuable for many reasons. It is valuable instrumentally, as a means to an end of achieving self-fulfillment and attempting to achieve correspondence between intentions and observed reality. In this way, it connects with interests in individual autonomy. Truth may also be valuable collectively, if society benefits from the dissemination of truth. Finally, it may be that we should seek to advance truth for its own sake, as a sort of Platonic ideal. All three of these ideas are reflected in discussions about why the First Amendment does or should protect truth.

By the same token, it is equally obvious that the dissemination of or acceptance of untruth is bad. It is bad for its own sake, bad for society, and often bad for the listener, because it may represent an obstacle to the development of his or her autonomy or self-expression. But respecting autonomy interests seems to preclude dictating truth, for just the reason Mill articulated—how can we be sure we are right? Freedom, so the argument goes, must include the freedom to be wrong. However, there are some serious social costs to the widespread adoption of some untruths. So the challenge in a free society is to achieve the correct balance between fraud and truth such that we have the minimum amount of fraud with the maximum amount of truth, what might be called "optimal fraud." The question is, what is the best method for preserving the maximum amount of truth and freedom?

The conventional answer is laissez-faire—minimal governmental regulation of truth. After all, as Justice Brennan noted in *New York Times v. Sullivan,* "erroneous statement is inevitable in free debate, and . . . must be protected if the freedoms of expression are to have the 'breathing space' that they need . . . to survive."[50] As John Stuart Mill observed, "Even a false statement may be deemed to make a valuable contribution to public debate, since it brings about 'the clearer perception and livelier impression of truth, produced by its collision with error.' "[51]

Proponents of a strong First Amendment right for commercial speakers say that this is precisely why government should not regulate commercial speech. Of course, this characterization sidesteps the issue of whether what is being said is truthful or in any sense informational. Proponents often act as if the truth-value of commercial expression was a given. They also often shift seamlessly between references to the market and to the "marketplace of ideas," as if they were the same thing.

Marketplace of ideas is a term commonly used in First Amendment cases. It is often identified with Justice Holmes's famous dissent in *Abrams*.

> [W]hen men have realized that time has upset many fighting faiths, they may come to believe even more than they believe the very foundations of their own conduct, that the ultimate good desired is better reached by free trade in ideas—that the best test of truth is the power of the thought to get itself accepted in the competition of the market, and that truth is the only ground upon which their wishes safely can be carried out. That at any rate is the theory of our Constitution.[52]

Proponents of freedom for commercial expression are fond of this quote, particularly the reference to the "market," which seems to put the issue on familiar commercial grounds. What they have not shown is that the extension of full First Amendment protection to commercial speech will increase the amount of truthful information in the "marketplace of ideas." To the contrary, if the present circumstances are any guide, the evidence suggests that a higher burden for governmental regulation of commercial expression would result in a great deal more fraud. Consider the following statements:

> Oxycontin poses a lower threat of abuse and addiction to patients than do traditional, shorter-acting pain killers.[53]

> Chemical tests have not found any substance in tobacco smoke known to cause human cancer or in concentrations sufficient to account for reported skin cancer in animals.[54]

> [T]he fibers of asbestos . . . are not injurious to the respiratory organs.[55]

All these statements are arguably commercial speech. All of them were false when they were made. Can it really be the case that the government is powerless to provide legal sanctions for false statements like these? The metaphor of the marketplace of ideas encourages us to think of freedom of expression in market terms. But markets are not always that good at producing truth, even if they are sometimes good at producing what people want.

Market influences actually provide structural amplification, not for truth, but for ideas that are already popular, palatable, or attractive, regardless of their truth. Because the access to means of communication is tied to financial means, commercial expression also inevitably results in amplification of the views congenial to the largest businesses, independent of whether these views are truthful or beneficial for society as a whole. This structural bias undermines the conventional assumption that less governmental regulation will result in more truth, let alone more freedom. Although Holmes used a marketplace analogy, which the notion of a "competition" does invoke, there is some evidence that he never meant to argue that the market would be a good arbiter of truth. Indeed, if we take the analogy literally, it would seem to point to the idea that truth is what most people believe. That was clearly not what Mill believed or what Holmes was arguing for.

The "marketplace of ideas" metaphor should not be used too literally as if it were synonymous with real markets. Even if it were a good analogy, it seems clear that real markets require some regulation to function optimally and to account for market failures.[56] More fundamentally, although some speech does equal commerce and is valuable for that reason, not *all* speech is valuable because it has a market value. We often value speech for reasons that have little or nothing to do with its cash value or its utility in any economic sense. The attempt to apply the marketplace of ideas metaphor too literally runs the risk of commercializing all speech or suggesting that speech's principal value is its market value.[57] While it is useful for illuminating some issues, the marketplace of ideas metaphor is inadequate to the task of providing appropriate boundaries for the regulation of commercial expression, even on its own terms, because it fails to capture, or maybe even transforms, important values that may not survive the translation to a market analogy.

It would be a mistake to confuse "the marketplace of ideas" with a literal market. As many others have observed, the popularity of an idea is not a reliable indicator of its truth. In particular, when it comes to commercial expression, which takes place in the context of enormous disparities of resources and incentives, it hardly seems plausible that unfettered commercial expression will produce a great deal of truth. To the contrary, experience suggests it will produce a great deal of fraud.

Truth, Balance, and Economic Inequality

Advocates of freedom of speech for corporations often claim that fairness requires that their "side" be heard. Dedication to principles of equality and nondiscrimination, they argue, require corporations to have their say.[58] This sort of "sauce for the goose" argument is very persuasive to many because it invokes commitments to fair play and equality. Moreover, it fits the legal fiction of the corporate "person"; its invocation makes the corporation appear more like a real person with a "viewpoint" that is being discriminated against. This is precisely the sort of rhetoric Justice Kennedy employed in *Citizens United*. However, the rhetoric obscures the degree to which the largest corporations already control much expression. Fair play would hardly seem to require giving them more.

Nevertheless, to the extent that there is an expressed commitment to the idea that debate on issues of public concern should be "uninhibited, robust, and wide-open,"[59] it is worth noting that if we fall short of that, corporations have a significant role in making it so, many times with the assistance of law. If expressive conduct is a sort of human right, an important aspect of selfhood and self-realization, as so many First Amendment scholars have argued (including those advocating for greater protection for commercial speech), it seems worth pausing to consider how much private suppression of that self-realization the law permits. It is a great deal.

Furthermore, much of the inequality of expression in society stems from inequality of resources. This does not just mean that the rich man is able to buy more speech than the poor man, a proposition with which many Americans have no quarrel. It also means that the rich man is better able to *invoke the legal tools for speech suppression* in some circumstances—for example, libel, defamation, unfair competition, violation of copyright or trademark and the like—because the vindication of such rights usually requires the financial resources to pursue a lawsuit. Lawsuits are extremely expensive. Few but the very wealthiest individuals have the means to pursue such lawsuits, particularly where there is no future profit at issue. These laws, which are often invoked by the same corporations that would like First Amendment protection for their speech, involve the suppression of the expression of others—not simply to drown them out, but to silence them altogether.

For example, in 2003, Sharper Image (which later went bankrupt) filed a lawsuit against Consumers Union (CU), a nonprofit organization that publishes the magazine *Consumer Reports,* alleging that various statements made in the magazine about its ionic air purifier were intentionally false and misleading and defamed the company.[60] The suit was ultimately dismissed, because the court found that Sharper Image was unlikely to prevail on the merits by showing CU's statements were false.[61] But this dismissal only came after more than a year of litigation that generated legal costs for CU. The fact that CU eventually prevailed is small comfort to more impecunious targets.

In another example, in what became known as the "McLibel" case,[62] McDonald's sued two members of London Greenpeace[63] for libel arising from their distribution of leaflets protesting a number of McDonald's business practices—primarily its environmental and labor practices and the low nutritional value of its foods. In response, McDonald's put the group under surveillance by private investigators for several months. The surveillance included infiltration of the group's meetings.[64] Then, armed with information gathered through this surveillance, McDonald's sued several members of the organization. It extracted apologies and retractions from three members of the group, who feared liability under Britain's very plaintiff-protective libel laws.[65] However, members Helen Steel and David Morris refused to apologize, so McDonald's pursued the case against them. Steel and Morris were too poor to hire lawyers, and they were clearly not economic competitors of McDonald's,[66] yet McDonald's saw fit to launch what became, at the time, the longest running trial in English history,[67] in order to suppress what its management felt were untruths about the company. As it turned out, much of what Steel and Morris said in the leaflets was true. So the vast expenditures in the case could also be said to have been spent to stop people from telling the truth. The case is an illustration that economic resources have profound effects on the realization of what the law may promise as well as on how those resources can be deployed to suppress speech through law.

But framing the issue as one of the rich man (or woman) versus the poor man (or woman) is, in general, misleading. More usually, it is an issue of the average person, not necessarily poor, versus a rich institution. Major corporations do not need a constitutional shield to engage in expressive activity. To the contrary, liability for false or misleading speech is one tool to restore balance to the grotesque imbalances that currently exist because of the funds available to these largest corporations. As noted earlier, big business spends staggering sums on advertising and marketing. Nike spent $1.7 billion on advertising in 2006.[68] Entities that spend this kind of money get a lot of airtime and face time in exchange for it.

Unless they are celebrities, individuals are also at a disadvantage to large institutions, because they are usually less newsworthy, so their opinions are seldom sought out by the media. Moreover, they typically do not have the resources to deploy to try to *appear* newsworthy, as large institutions may do through the use of public relations specialists. As one reporter observed, "parents, taxpayers, union members, students—don't have p.r. firms and they don't have time in their days set aside to field press inquiries."[69] Consequently, "large institutions, which already have so many ways to control the news, end up getting their positions heard, while the public gets pushed to the side."[70] All these observations are relevant to and intertwined with Emerson's third category of interests: the preservation of democratic processes.

Democratic Processes

Emerson argued that protection for freedom of expression was necessary to the proper functioning of a democracy. Perhaps the best-known other proponent of this position is the late Alexander Meiklejohn.[71] Meiklejohn considered the democracy-enhancing function to be the only real basis for protection for freedom of expression, and he argued that one way to distinguish between protected and unprotected speech was its content, with political content entitled to the greatest protection.[72] This view would provide for a fairly narrow range of protection for expression and has generally been rejected in favor of a more expansive vision.

While no one argues that political speech is not at least a part of what the First Amendment is meant to protect, many think, as Emerson did, that protection of democracy means protection not just of political speech but also of respect for democratic values in all spheres of society. Emerson wrote,

> [T]he right of all members of society to form their own beliefs and communicate them freely to others must be regarded as an essential principle of a democratically organized society. The growing pressures for democracy and equality reinforced the logical implications of the theory and demanded opportunity for all persons to share in making social decisions. This is, of course, especially true of political decisions. But the basic theory carried beyond the political realm. It embraced the right to participate

in the building of the whole culture, and included freedom of expression in religion, literature, art, science and all areas of human learning and knowledge.[73]

Until fairly recently, this theory would seem to have excluded corporations, the principal source of commercial expression (notwithstanding that corporations obviously contribute enormously to the building of the culture), because corporations were not considered citizens in their own right. After *Citizens United*, that line is not clear. There are also reasons to conclude that the process by which speech is produced in a corporation is not particularly democratic. In the first place, the corporation is run for the economic, not the expressive, interests of shareholders. Second, to the extent that shareholders vote, they vote on the basis of the number of shares (i.e., how much capital) they have, not on the basis of one shareholder, one vote. Third, as noted earlier, work produced in the corporation is work for hire and thus is not the product of individual expression. Finally and perhaps most fundamentally, the work environment is largely structured as private and thus as a sphere in which speech suppression is taken for granted.

Undemocratic Work

Perhaps the single biggest source of private suppression of speech in America is also the most basic and probably the least controversial—suppression of speech on the job. All over the country, most employees are not free to say whatever they like without fear of reprisal, because the employment-at-will doctrine permits employers to dismiss employees for any reason, including what might be considered a "bad" reason, like the exercise of an interest in self-expression.[74] Although it is by no means commonplace, there are many jurisdictions in the United States where you can be fired if the boss does not like the bumper sticker on your car. Employers can dictate that employees wear uniforms, and they can control (more or less) what employees say and do on the job, as well as some of what they may do outside of work.

For the most part, this sort of suppression goes unremarked and unchallenged—perhaps because it simply seems like "the way things are" or is unobjectionable to most people. Nevertheless, this significant suppression of expression (and thus autonomy) only escapes First Amendment scrutiny by being framed as "private," despite the fact that it owes its existence to a framework of law that permits the exercise of this discretion. As Bruce Barry, a professor of management and sociology at Vanderbilt, has argued,

> A toxic combination of law, conventional economic wisdom, and accepted managerial practice has created an American workplace where freedom of speech—that most crucial of civil liberties in a healthy democracy—is something you do after work, on your own time, and even then (for many) only if your employer approves.[75]

Because so much time is spent at work and because the lines between work and personal time are increasingly blurred, Barry argues that suppression of freedom of expression in the workplace is bad for democracy.

> Work is where most adults devote significant portions of their waking lives, and where many forge the personal ties with other adults through which they construct their civic selves. Yet work in America is a place where civil liberties, including but not limited to freedom of speech, are significantly constrained, even when the exercise of those liberties poses little or no threat to the genuine interests of the employer.[76]

Employer discretion to fire employees is largely a function of the employment-at-will doctrine, a development of the common law. In many cases, the employer's right to terminate at will has been enshrined in a statute passed by a legislature anxious to ensure that no exception to the rule, such as implied contracts, interferes with this discretion. Employers have also tended to want to see any exceptions to the at-will doctrine be strictly limited. This is not surprising, as the freedom to fire laborers gives the employer more flexibility and allows it to be more responsive to economic conditions.

Employer discretion is encroached on most notably in situations involving employment discrimination, sexual harassment, and protection for whistle-blowers. (Whistle-blower statutes protect employees from retaliation for reporting violations of the law.)[77] These exceptions are, however, notoriously narrow. Ironically, sometimes employers have objected to these restrictions on the freedom to fire as violating the *employer's* right to freedom of expression—as if the injunction that "Congress shall make no law" must shield the discretion to harass or to fire those who report the commission of crimes.[78] Concerns about deference to managers and economic efficiency are often persuasive counterarguments to broad enforcement of these exceptions to the at-will doctrine.[79] However, as others have already noted, these exceptions to the at-will doctrine were enacted for a public purpose that arguably will not be accomplished if enforcement is not vigorous: "Multiple recent examples of corporate heads who have failed to listen to dissenters and whistleblowers underscore the costly and disastrous consequences [of suppressing dissent in the workplace.]"[80] The largest commercial actors have not limited their interest in suppressing dissent to workplaces in the United States or even to the workplace in general but have been deeply implicated in the support for anti-democratic regimes in other countries.

Supporting Repressive Governmental Action

Ultimately, a business entity's management is concerned with securing an environment that is hospitable to earning a profit. Distressingly, in many cases, particularly when conducting business in foreign countries, this impulse has led large, multinational corporations to lend active support to repressive regimes engaging in egregious violations of human rights.[81] Such activity has led to a great deal of discussion about the obligations of corporations respecting human rights. It has been widely acknowledged that obtaining governmental cooperation to protect human rights is insufficient without similar undertakings by corporations.[82] It is yet unclear whether there is widespread agreement that corporations ought to have human rights obligations or, if so, how to make laws governing those obligations mandatory and enforceable. With respect to U.S. corporations, the Alien Tort Claims Act has provided one legal means of redress.[83] But it by no means provides complete coverage.

This growing concern about the role of corporations in violations of human rights has had particular resonance with respect to freedom of expression on the Internet. Thus, when the French government prohibited neo-Nazi websites,[84] many protested that this was inappropriate censorship, and some criticized the major search engines and Internet companies, like Google and Microsoft, for developing special software to comply with the French directives. In the protesters' view, the companies had the power to refuse to comply and ought to have used it to uphold free speech principles. Whatever you think about the appropriateness of regulation of hate speech, similar issues were raised with the claim that Google, Microsoft, Yahoo, and Cisco assisted the Chinese government in its efforts to suppress dissent, by monitoring e-mail and web searches and identifying dissidents to the Chinese government.[85] Assisting governmental efforts at suppression of dissent is a straightforward example of speech suppression.

Similarly, in the United States, when Internet and cell phone service providers were asked by the government to turn over customer lists in order to assist in terrorism investigations, many companies quickly acquiesced without requiring the government to produce a subpoena or a warrant. This reflected little concern on the part of management of these companies over the potential privacy concerns of their customers. Given the very large databases of information that many commercial entities are amassing through a variety of means, including social media, it is a little alarming to consider that they might respond with alacrity to such requests. It is not surprising, though, since they are institutions organized to engage in business, not to defend or uphold civil liberties. They can be expected to behave in a way that seems most likely to be either most profitable or least costly, not in a way that best preserves the rights of customers. For all these reasons and more that are developed in subsequent chapters, the evidence suggests that unfettered commercial expression and the failure to restrict participation of large commercial entities in the polity are deeply destructive of democratic principles.

Social Stability and Accommodating Change

Finally, Emerson and others have suggested that the protection of freedom of speech contributes to social stability: "The principle of open discussion is a method of achieving a more adaptable and at the same time more stable community, of maintaining the precarious balance between healthy cleavage and necessary consensus. . . . [W]here men have learned how to function within the law, an open society will be the stronger and more cohesive one."[86] The idea is that allowing dissent opens up a sort of safety valve for political pressure arising from social change. The state plays the role of both permitting free expression and regulating expression in the interest of the maintenance of stability.[87] This is particularly true in circumstances of imbalances of power, resources, or access to information, as previously described. Here is where Emerson parts company with more conventional understanding of the First Amendment. But the general assertion that the government may have a legitimate role under the First Amendment to regulate in order to provide better balance has been echoed by many others since,[88] though it remains a distinctly minority view.

However, it is not necessary to conclude that the First Amendment requires the government to affirmatively subsidize some speech in order to conclude, when looking at the facts, that the evidence is ambiguous as to whether freedom of commercial expression contributes to social stability. It may contribute to some sort of social cohesion through shared meaning, but most of that shared meaning is commercial, not political, spiritual, or ethical. While there is nothing wrong with the material or the commercial, not everything in the world can be reduced to that interest. Moreover, as discussed in the introduction and more fully explored in the remainder of this book, it appears that unbridled commercial speech may contribute significantly to social *in*stability or to consumption patterns that are deeply implicit in threats like global climate change. At the very least, it avowedly contributes to increased consumption, which is not always an unalloyed good.

Some supporters of commercial speech have argued that the failure to offer it First Amendment protection will have negative consequences with respect to corporate transparency and social responsibility reporting.[89] A failure to engage in such reporting, they argue, will have a negative impact on commercial relations with Europe to the extent that such transparency is required in order to do business there.[90] So far, though, this does not appear to be the case; Nike and other American companies continue to engage in corporate social responsibility reporting, undeterred by the fact that such reports do not enjoy First Amendment protection in Europe.

Proponents of freedom for commercial speech often appear to suggest that harms generated by commercial speech, while regrettable, are simply the price we must pay for a free society and that the political, social, and personal costs of suppressing some commercial speech outweigh any benefit to be obtained (although such proponents usually nominally agree that false commercial speech has no constitutional value). As I hope to show, this argument springs from a distortion of the values the First Amendment protects. As Justice Jackson noted, the Constitution is "not a suicide pact." Where speech causes widespread harm, loss of life, or a danger to the public health or to economic stability, the First Amendment does not require that the government stand idle. To the contrary, protecting the public from harm where it cannot protect itself is a legitimate function of government. My aim is to show how harmful unrestrained commercial speech can be and how necessary governmental intervention is to the protection of individuals in many instances.

Much of the existing freedom that commercial expression enjoys can be explained as a consequence of access to resources. Those resources and commercial motives promise that commercial expression will continue to flourish within whatever appropriate boundaries are set up to contain it. But like an invasive weed, those same incentives and resources suggest that expansive constitutional protection would increase the dominance of commercial institutions and commercial expression over human beings and nonpolitical expression in all spheres of the culture. Concern for genuine autonomy for individuals and for individual self-expression, collective interest in health and safety and welfare and in the promulgation of truthful information, and support for democratic participation and maintenance of social stability all argue against freedom for commercial expression. In the chapters that follow, I will examine in greater detail how commercial expression operates in practice and why it does not further any of the four interests Emerson identified. Because issues of truth, autonomy, and self-expression are intertwined, they are grouped together and are explored in more depth in part II, while part III discusses commercial speech as it affects interests in promoting democracy and social stability.

PART II

AUTONOMY AND TRUTH

CHAPTER 4

Autonomy as a Human Interest

Maintenance of a system of free expression is necessary [to]
assuring individual self-fulfillment.
—Thomas I. Emerson,
Toward a General Theory of the First Amendment

The first value Thomas Emerson thought the First Amendment should protect was what he called "self-fulfillment."[1] According to Emerson, "self-
fulfillment" encompassed many concepts that, while not synonymous, substantially overlap: autonomy, freedom, self-expression, and self-
actualization. Protection for self-fulfillment arose, he claimed, from "the
widely accepted premise of Western thought that the proper end of man is the
realization of his character and potentialities as a human being."[2] The right
to form one's own opinions was a part of self-fulfillment and necessarily entailed being able to express those opinions. "Otherwise," wrote Emerson,
"they are of little account."[3]

So described, self-fulfillment and autonomy take on a distinctly human
cast. Nonliving creatures do not "self-actualize." However, defense of protection for commercial expression usually proceeds on the theory that freedom
of commercial expression contributes to the self-fulfillment and autonomy of
the listeners rather than of the speakers. In the next several chapters, I will examine this claim from several angles. Because autonomy, freedom, self-expression, and self-actualization are related concepts, it is not possible to discuss them one at a time. Because claims for the self-actualizing, expressive, or
autonomy-enhancing aspect of commercial speech are also inextricably inter-

twined with assumptions about what constitutes information, truth, and the context in which commercial decision making takes place, these discussions will also involve exploring these aspects of commercial speech as they relate to the autonomy of the listeners and the net consequences for the quantum of information under circumstances of unfettered commercial expression.

I begin with the meaning of these related concepts—freedom, autonomy, and so on. For instance, having autonomy implies but does not absolutely require some freedom of action. We often assume that autonomy is only meaningful in the face of options. But freedom need not be (and rarely is) perfect in order to experience action as autonomous, and having options is not synonymous with freedom. At one or two choices, people may feel "free" because of the opportunity to choose. But when the number of choices expands upward, particularly if it seems important to gather information about the various choices, having more choices seems not freeing but oppressive.

Similarly, we typically consider autonomy and freedom most meaningful in the context of being able to exercise our rational faculties, whatever they may be. But decision making does not involve just rational thought; it also involves emotional and instinctive actions that are inextricably intertwined with rationality. Actions may be experienced as autonomous even if they are not experienced as deliberative. Autonomy might simply mean choosing under conditions free from restraint. However, in the idealized way in which autonomy appears in discussions of the First Amendment, it appears to be considered principally as it involves the application of deliberative intelligence and choices made from a synthesis of the complex components of human reasoning aimed at an individual's conception of what will be conducive to his or her flourishing.

Autonomy as a Distinctively Human Interest

Emerson's concept of self-fulfillment is related to human flourishing. Part of what makes human beings distinctive, he wrote, was the ability to engage in this self-development. He saw this position as arising from the intellectual foundations laid by Milton and Locke, whose thoughts had been influential in the development of American legal thought, both in 1791 and, later, from the writings of John Stuart Mill as the jurisprudence of the First Amendment developed across the next 200 years.

Emerson's conception of the importance of individual self-development also owes much to the philosopher Immanuel Kant, who asserted that human beings were moral ends in themselves and could not be treated as means to an end. The capacity for rational thought and autonomous action conferred this status. According to one legal scholar, Kant "equates autonomy and personhood."[4] In this view, autonomy is not simply freedom from restraint but entails corresponding responsibilities for self-development, of refraining from harming others or interfering likewise in the autonomy that others should enjoy. In this view, autonomy entails freedom and responsibility, power and constraint.

So neither autonomy nor freedom equals, in this view, the complete absence of restraints. A just society in which each human being recognizes the other's autonomy interests imposes some limits on the exercise of autonomy. The question is, which limitations are legitimate? Such a society obviously can no more endorse absolute freedom of speech than it would endorse absolute freedom of action. For example, if someone wants to be a suicide bomber in order to make a political statement, I think there is widespread consensus that governmental interference with that sort of authorship is entirely legitimate. But to make this observation is to come face-to-face with its circularity, if what you want to know is when limitations on freedom (or speech) are appropriate and when are they illegitimate.

If the autonomy interests that Emerson and many other First Amendment scholars are concerned with protecting are human interests, then it is not obvious why limitations on the freedom of expression of nonhuman organizations would be in any way illegitimate. Only human beings "self-actualize." Adopting the Kantian perspective, institutions and legal fictions are not moral ends in themselves; they are a means to an end. Ergo, it is not immediately apparent that expressive limitations on nonhuman speakers are in any way an interference with an autonomy interest that is entitled to special consideration. If these entities possess any autonomy interests at all, they have them by proxy, on behalf of their constituents, because the commercial *speaker's* "self-fulfillment" is not at interest in commercial speech. (Later, I will examine whether for-profit corporations can be said to be expressing the autonomy or self-fulfillment interests of any of their constituents. It should come as no surprise when I say that they do not, but the reasons are explored in more depth in chapter 8, on corporate personhood.)

But perhaps commercial expression contributes to the autonomy, freedom, and self-fulfillment rights of those human beings to whom it is directed—principally consumers—by protecting their right to hear the speech. This theory was advanced in the *Virginia Pharmacy* decision and has been propounded by defenders of commercial speech. The claim is that protection for commercial speech protects human autonomy indirectly, because commercial speech offers material with which and through which human beings may express themselves.[5] There is, no doubt, some truth to this claim. Defenders and critics alike readily concede that commercial speech helps create culture. The defenders of commercial speech celebrate this fact, arguing that it contributes to human happiness and self-fulfillment.[6] And so it might. Yet it is not an either-or proposition. Commercial expression may *both* contribute to and detract from human beings' struggles for autonomy and self-fulfillment.

It seems reasonable then to ask, what is commercial speech's *net* effect on listeners? Again, because institutions are not ends in themselves, we can dispense with claims that they are intrinsically entitled to freedom of speech. So if the claim for protection is based on the autonomy interests of the listeners, it is critical whether the net effect of commercial speech is to enhance listeners' self-fulfillment and autonomy interests. There is reason to think that it is not, which, in turn, offers support for the proposition that limitations on this speech do not violate interests that the First Amendment was intended to protect.

Defenders of commercial expression often seem reluctant to confront the myriad ways in which all this purported self-fulfillment arising from commercial expression also burdens autonomy, freedom, and so on, because it comes at a steep price—the necessity of fending off constant sales pitches; the ever-present danger that one will fall prey to some misleading pitch or false come-on; the emotional and psychological costs of constant vigilance; and perhaps the drain on psychological resources that occurs when it is necessary to work one's way back to some sort of emotional equilibrium after the repeated, daily attempts by advertisers to activate listeners' insecurities and fears.[7] These examples (and I can think of many others) represent some of the ways in which commercial expression may inhibit or interfere with self-fulfillment and autonomy.

The possibility that freedom of commercial expression might have substantial costs does not, of course, mean that we should not protect it. However, before we reinterpret the First Amendment to protect corporate and commercial speech, we should be very sure that the costs do not swamp the things we say we want to protect. With respect to self-fulfillment and autonomy interests, there is reason to believe that the costs exceed the benefits.

Ascriptive and Descriptive Autonomy

Autonomy is a complex concept that can be variously described. To be autonomous is not merely to be free of coercion by others. Rather, it encompasses some notion of a free mind as well as a free body, of self-possession. In the context of discussion of governmental regulation, the word *autonomy* is often used as if all it entailed was freedom from governmental restraint. But in its fuller sense, the term means to have "authorship of one's ends in action."[8]

If much commercial expression interferes with people's ability to have authorship of their actions, it seems fair to say that commercial speech contributes little to the autonomy interests of listeners. However, this is a question of autonomy as a merely descriptive matter. The First Amendment involves questions of both ascriptive (that is propositional) and descriptive (empirical) autonomy. Ascriptive autonomy, as Professor Richard Fallon of Harvard has put it, involves the question of inherent rights: what *should* be the case versus what is.[9] Descriptive autonomy, in contrast, refers to simply examining what is—whether someone's acts can, in fact, be described as autonomous.

A good deal of the argument around the issue of commercial communication involves the question of autonomy as an ascriptive matter but blurs the question of whose autonomy, as a propositional matter, is at issue—the commercial speaker's or the listener's? First Amendment autonomy concerns are typically framed from the speaker's standpoint. However, as noted, most defenders of commercial speech avoid claiming that the autonomy interest to be furthered by commercial speech is that of the speaker, probably because the idea that a legal fiction has expressive interests is hard to swallow and because large corporations (assuming that they have such interests) do not seem to suffer from a deficit of power.

Yet this evasion encourages the tendency to assume a unity between the speaker's and the listeners' autonomy interests, that is, that whatever the commercial speaker wants to say must necessarily advance the listeners' autonomy interests. This is an obvious fallacy. Many things that commercial speakers wish to say may cause listeners harm. And that harm is often not merely an abstraction. It is concrete, like the harm caused by smoking. That being the case, it is a mistake to assume that governmental action *necessarily* interferes with, rather than supports, individuals' capacity to exercise autonomy. Indeed, governmental regulation is often inspired precisely by the observation that some forms of commercial expression may interfere with the listeners' welfare and their ability to achieve self-fulfillment. This is particularly true when regulation involves a shield from promotional activities that the consumer would *like* to be free of or where it involves compelling the production of information the government assumes would be important to rational decision making.

To bolster the claim that, in the main, commercial speech furthers listeners' interests, its defenders argue that it enhances such interests because it provides "information" and "choice." However, this argument seems to depend on the production of real information, so that if it could be shown that commercial speech is not informative, the rationale for protecting it goes away as well. The next several chapters will demonstrate ample reason to conclude that a very great deal of commercial expression is not only not informative but the opposite—misleading. The importance of the information claim is its connection to rationality and what it means to exercise autonomy.

Information and the Assumption of Rationality

Emerson asserted that "[t]he achievement of self-realization commences with the development of the mind."[10] Freedom of expression is, he claimed, essential to the development of a human being's capacity to develop his or her nature and personality. If "the whole nature of man is not to be thwarted,"[11] Emerson argued that the receipt and exchange of ideas, information, beliefs and opinions needed to be protected. In other words, the First Amendment could be implicated from both speaking and listening perspectives. Again, this view is consistent with the *Virginia Pharmacy* Court's focus on listeners' interests. Emerson's quote reflects that he, like most theorists of the First Amendment, assumed that information and rational thought of some sort would play a part in his vision of self-realization, that an autonomous person would weigh information and would do so in a manner that is (at least in its ideal form) rational.

Justifications for freedom of expression as support for autonomy also tend to make this assumption of a hypothetical rational actor who chooses for himself or herself and who does so as a product of deliberation rather than of impulse or emotion. Much Western thought is deeply invested in this idealized notion of human cognition in which actions taken by impulse or under the influence of emotion are somehow corrupt or to be rejected in favor of deliberative actions. However, this understanding of human cognition does not appear to be supported by the most recent research.[12] This research suggests that human beings' capacity for rational behavior is subject to significant limitations, that we have bounded rationality.

There has been a great deal of research in the last few decades on the subject of human cognitive limitations. Some of these limitations are described by Daniel Kahneman and Amos Tversky in their cognitive psychology work on heuristics and biases.[13] Psychologist Cordelia Fine[14] has done related work, as have neurologists Antonio Damasio[15] and Robert Burton.[16] Moreover, research suggests that our emotions may be so intertwined with what we think of as rational thought that there is no easy way of dividing the two.[17] These facts are not inconsistent with autonomy or the experience of autonomy (which are not necessarily the same thing), but they have implications for what constitutes "information" or illegitimate interference with autonomy. There is evidence that marketers exploit those limitations.

Coping Strategies

Not all externally imposed limits on choice interfere with autonomy or are inherently illegitimate.[18] There are many instances in which people have time-inconsistent preferences—that is, instances where we might prefer one thing in the short run but something else in the long run.[19] Precommitment strategies, cooling-off periods, second opinions, and the like are various ways in which, despite bounded rationality, human beings are capable of leveraging their deliberative capacities toward the goal of self-fulfillment. Autonomous persons may decide, for example, to engage in precommitment devices to assist the exercise of their will in circumstances where they fear that their short-term preferences may be at odds with their long-term preferences.[20]

Withholding for taxes is a prime example of such a precommitment device. Everyone is aware that withholding amounts to an interest-free loan to the government in the event of an overpayment of taxes. From a purely rational standpoint, one should underwithhold as much as legally allowable (before incurring a penalty), in order to have the benefit of what amounts to an interest-free loan represented by the amount you owe in taxes at the end of the year. But most people do not try that. Instead, they ordinarily hope to have a refund, even though the larger their refund is, the more money they have loaned interest-free to the government. Why do so many people react this way? Most (not all) people know there is a substantial risk that without the withholding device, they will be unable to actually save enough to pay their taxes when they come due in April, because the accumulated effect, over time, of many small choices against savings and in favor of present consumption (which is usually more attractive for the same reason that the present value of a dollar a year from now is some amount less than a dollar) is likely to result in a shortfall at tax time.

Withholding is a precommitment device that permits people to bind their future selves in aid of a long-term goal in a way that is less painful than having to devote mental energy to assessing repeated choices over time to defer consumption in favor of savings. Governmentally imposed withholding is perhaps "paternalistic," in the sense that those who would prefer not to engage in this precommitment device may not opt out. But it is difficult not to conclude that tax collection would be severely undermined without it and that even many of those who think they would prefer to opt out of withholding might feel differently once they are confronted with a large tax liability they are unable to pay. Because people's preferences are often time-inconsistent, it is difficult to know such things. Precommitment strategies are just one of the many ways in which people may individually or collectively attempt to deal with their own cognitive and emotional limitations, in an attempt to maximize their happiness or satisfaction in the long run. Presumably maximizing happiness contributes to self-actualization.

Exploiting Bounded Rationality

Even if we were to assume that rationality is relatively unbounded, we should be reluctant to define as "information" material that takes advantage of cognitive limitations or that is intentionally designed to bypass deliberative decision making. Yet this is what many defenders of commercial speech do. They define advertising and marketing as "information" despite ample evidence that there is very little about it that is informational in the conventional sense. Most advertising is deliberately designed to bypass deliberative thought processes. Whether that is a good or a bad thing from an experiential or cultural standpoint, it hardly seems designed to contribute much to "the authorship of one's own ends." To the contrary, it is rather nakedly designed to bring the consumer's ends in line with the seller's—even where that end is antithetical to the consumer's health, well-being, or ideas about his or her own welfare.

Much marketing research explores the ways in which the limitations of human reasoning can be exploited in order to sell products. That research is not hypothetical. It is applied. Marketers are constantly applying the insights of marketing research to their actual practices in the field, retaining that which seems to produce results and discarding that which does not. In essence, they turn the whole market into a vast psychology experiment with consumers as the subjects.

While we are cautioned that it is simplistic to overestimate the generality of cognitive biases,[21] a fair reading of the related body of work produced by Kahneman and many others is that its significance stems from the observation that limitations are endemic to the human condition. It would not be much of a breakthrough to announce that some people do not reason clearly or that some people are irrational. By the same token, observing that all human reasoning is bounded clearly does not mean it is bounded to the same degree in all persons or in all cases. But it is just as clear that conventional notions of what it means to be rational are more fiction than fact. That marketers make use of the public's unwarranted optimism about their cognitive strengths seems obvious from observing marketing practices. Marketing overwhelmingly relies on techniques of manipulation; that they do not always work as planned does not mean they are not manipulative.

Autonomy and Freedom of Choice

There is another aspect to autonomy—the experience of autonomy. Sometimes, *feeling* free may be as important to the individual as actually being free. Marketers are exquisitely sensitive to this nuance. Sometimes it appears that proponents of freedom for commercial expression are really promoting the feeling of autonomy, not real autonomy. In America, "freedom" is often linked with freedom of choice; having choices is seen as an essential part of what it means to be free and autonomous. Perhaps this is why words like *freedom* and *choice* are used so frequently in advertising.

It is commonplace to assert that one of the advantages of a free market in contrast to a planned economy, is the greater array of choice in a market system, choices which cater to consumer desires, whereas a planned economy only offers governmentally approved choices. Wendy's famous ad featuring a "Soviet fashion show" reflected this idea.[22] The ad depicted a fashion show in which all the categories—day wear, evening wear, and swimwear—featured the same woman in the same gray dress. The tagline was that at Wendy's, not all burgers were "dressed the same." In other words, Wendy's offered you a choice.

The *Virginia Pharmacy* Court asserted that protection for truthful commercial information was important so that consumers' economic choices could be as informed as possible. But advertising does not convey much in the way of information. It also does not often convey much that could be tested for its truth. This leaves a good deal of that communication, the purpose of which seems largely to create artificial differences between products, to be described as "information" without being particularly informative.

In the advertising world, to be "informed" typically means to be informed of a brand choice. Consumer choice is often used as a slogan for what freedom of commercial expression would protect, except that in this context, "choice" often means a dizzying proliferation of essentially indistinguishable goods. There is no question that the availability of a wide variety of consumption choices may (in some circumstances) be pleasant or lead to an experience of freedom, or even improve subjective well-being;[23] but it hardly seems its apotheosis. In some cases it might not be that desirable to have too many choices.

We often assume that choices are an unalloyed good.[24] We are encouraged, in many ways, to think that freedom means the condition of having no limits, or having limitless choices. This may be a mistaken notion if limits are an unavoidable feature of the material world.[25] It is possible to imagine conditions under which freedom could mean no choice or few choices, because in a time-bounded and material world, infinite choice means corresponding limitless time devoted to trying to make informed choices. Where choices are further expanded to include the trivial as well as the substantive—choosing a deodorant or a particular color of laptop is not a choice of transcendent significance—the demands on one's time placed by exercising "choice" no longer appear to be so desirable.

Moreover, the assumption that infinite choice is desirable also seems predicated on the assumption that no external forces, like resource limits, will pose some limit to the ability to choose. Of course, they will for most people. Do we feel *more* or *less* self-fulfilled when we are constantly confronted with goods that we cannot afford? Moreover, the structures and habits necessary to sustain this boundless array of choices may be fairly costly to maintain. While resources are often so plentiful as to seem effectively limitless, global climate change prompts the uncomfortable realization that they perhaps are not. If freedom means freedom to consume at this level, what happens if the model of infinite growth on which the economy is based cannot be sustained?

It may be that we will have to make a choice between voluntarily deciding to limit our more trivial choices or continuing on the path we have been on the past hundred years or so and possibly passing some point of no return at which future generations will have fewer choices because of the choices we made now. Changing course and beginning to exercise restraint while retreating from the model of infinite choice would require some restrictions on promotional action or consumption. But surely it is less painful to restrict promotional activity, in the hopes of a corresponding decline in consumption, than to interfere directly in consumption.

There is no question that having freedom in some of the most important areas of our lives is no trivial thing, and maybe it is even important with respect to the trivial things. Maybe it *is* more important to feel as if one is free to choose even if one is not. This may be the function that the abundant choice in consumer goods performs—to give us the feeling of freedom while obscuring how much of our lives are unfree. Freedom risks being trivialized as a value, however, when freedom of choice in matters like the color of an appliance is celebrated as representing the apex of human freedom. The idea that freedom is good and is most accessibly and appropriately experienced through multiple consumer choices is so deeply embedded in the culture that it is unlikely to be discarded in the near future. It does seem worthwhile, however, to ask whether this is the sort of freedom the First Amendment is meant to protect. The next chapter examines in greater depth the concepts of branding and of the informational function of advertising.

CHAPTER 5

Brands, Information, and Consumer "Education"

[A]s any brand specialist knows, perception trumps reality every time.
—Claudia H. Deutsch, *New York Times,* November 7, 2007

We live in a world of brands. The brand has morphed from being a means to identify a specific source for goods to one of the dominant metaphors of the age.[1] We are encouraged to think of everything in terms of a brand—churches[2] and institutions of higher learning,[3] political[4] and music groups,[5] even self: "To be in business today, our most important job is to be head marketer for the brand called You."[6] Even rebellion and anticonsumerism movements seem to be inexorably colonized into the rhetoric of branding.[7] Some argue that the prominence of branding in the present economy is a function of the move from the emphasis on producing things to an emphasis on consuming things.[8] Whatever the reason for its prominence, the brand is a major factor in commercial expression.

If we agree with Emerson that one of the values the First Amendment is meant to protect is the production and exchange of truthful information, then very little marketing seems to qualify for protection, since little of it is informative. Indeed, much of it could be said to be *mis*information. Prominent psychologist Elizabeth Loftus has described advertising as "inherently misleading."[9] It is only in the parallel universe of marketing that advertising is "information." This is because of brands. When we examine one of the central organizing concepts of much commercial speech—the brand—it becomes clear that what claims for protection for commercial speech really involve is protection of property interests and the freedom to manipulate.

Ordinarily, when we say someone is "educated," we mean they have acquired useful or true information. Similarly, the word *learning* tends to refer to a process that is considered unequivocally good—again, oriented toward the acquisition of useful or true information. But what a marketer wants consumers to "learn" about a product is something more like indoctrination, and the material to be learned may be the view the marketer would like the consumer to have of the product or the feelings the marketer would like to conjure up, not any information about the concrete attributes or properties of the product. In a world dominated by brands, consumer education generally means developing a *brand meaning,* which, in turn, is "[n]othing we can measure or explain precisely. It's a fictional property, often illusory and evocative—the emperor's finest duds."[10] Branding communications can create economic value. That means they create "information" of a sort. It just is not clear whether the resources devoted to creating brand meaning might not be put to more productive use.[11]

What Is a Brand?

The brand is part of a product's "core meaning."[12] Branding is "the process of attaching an idea to a product."[13] Sometimes a brand is a product (although that may be increasingly rare these days, since confining the expression of a brand identity to one product rather than a line of products would seem to be a missed opportunity). More typically, a brand is a label associated with an identifiable line of products, often in the same general category of things (e.g., food), but not necessarily. For example, Starbucks is a brand primarily associated with coffee for sale in its retail stores, but it also sells tea, food, coffee-related appliances, and dishes. Its prepackaged coffee beans are available for sale in many grocery stores. In addition, Starbucks owns Hear Music, a venture producing CDs for sale in its stores; Ethos Water, a line of bottled water; and (most curiously of all, since it appears to be a competitor) Seattle's Best Coffee.[14]

Sometimes there are multiple layers of brand identity, as where a parent company holds many distinct brands or brand families for a particular type of product. Kraft Foods is an example of this kind of company. Kraft Foods owns Philadelphia brand, Oscar Mayer, Maxwell House, Nabisco, Oreo, and others.[15] Kraft itself is what might be called a master brand. It has its own identity that is related to but distinct from any particular product, for example, Kraft Macaroni & Cheese.

At other times, a parent or holding company is relatively unknown, or at least its separate corporate identity is less aggressively marketed. Unilever is an example of this kind of company. It owns brands with greater name recognition than its own; Dove, Axe, Wishbone, Hellman's, Knorr, and Slim-Fast are all Unilever brands.[16] Because Unilever is not really known on the consumer side as a brand in its own right, Unilever is not a brand. Conglomerates with varying levels of brand ownership often have brand or manufacturer recognition at each level of ownership. For example, Kellogg's is a manufacturer of cereal and has several brands under that umbrella (Frosted Flakes, Rice Krispies, Raisin Bran, etc.), but Kellogg's also owns Famous Amos, Cheez-It, Morningstar Farms, and Keebler. These are all separate brands.[17]

Although branding was initially a product concept, the idea has expanded to the corporation that holds the brands. The current marketing wisdom is that the corporation itself is or can be a brand and thus ought to have a carefully crafted corporate identity. A well-managed corporate identity reinforces the sale of the branded products. According to some marketers, "[C]orporate advertising is important to brand managers because consumers can develop knowledge from it that may influence their brand knowledge."[18] Legal scholar Jean Wegman Burns writes, "The design of a corporate brand is based on a coherent system of interrelated ideas that express corporate characteristics and thereby cause higher recall than a product brand." Corporate identity characteristics include things like the company's labor and environmental practices, the charities it supports, and a whole amalgam of loosely related "social responsibility" practices that supposedly go into informing the public what its brand "is all about." However, as the Nike case demonstrated, the connection between what the corporate advertising says and what the corporation actually does may be tenuous at best.

The Function of Brands

Initially, economists thought expenditures on advertising were not only wasteful but anticompetitive,[19] particularly where brands created the perception of a difference between products that did not actually differ in chemical composition. Somewhere in the mid-twentieth century, economists' opinion shifted, and they began to adopt the view reflected in business practices—that brand recognition and brand loyalty were things of real value and that advertising expenditures should not be characterized as invariably wasteful.[20] Instead, the argument went, branding offered consumers valuable information that reduced search costs. Brand value was built through trust that accumulated from experience. In large cities, where people no longer knew their butcher and their baker, the brand could stand in for those personal relationships.[21]

Economists' new views on the subject became the mainstream legal view as well: "[P]roducts that differ substantially in consumer regard are in a real sense different products and should be so considered in the eyes of the law."[22] What this quote means is that from a legal perspective, it does not really matter if people's preferences for Clorox bleach over a house brand that is chemically identical are "irrational." If consumers believe that Clorox is "better," then, in some sense, it is. The manufacturer's (or, perhaps more often, just the seller's) investment in the communications calculated to cultivate this perception creates something of economic value that the law should take cognizance of. Moreover, branding may not only create a perception; the perception may change the experience.

In one marketing study, children aged 3 to 5 "presented with identical foods—one in a McDonald's wrapper and the other without—overwhelmingly rated the branded one as tasting better."[23] A similar test in 1983 suggested that people would confirm that a soda was Coke or Pepsi depending on which they had indicated they preferred prior to the test, regardless of which beverage they were actually drinking. More recently, using functional magnetic resonance imaging, marketing researchers revisited the Coke/Pepsi challenge and discovered that telling subjects the brand name of a soda they tasted activated an additional portion of the brain compared to that activated when they participated in blind taste tests, leading the researchers to conclude that "the brand alone has value in the brain system."[24] Given brand preferences, brand advertising not only contains signaling information that reduces search costs relevant to these preferences; it also creates the satisfaction that consumers experience, because it creates the mental imagery, the "nebulous intangibles,"[25] that presumably are responsible for the feelings identified in these studies. So, in a way, advertising is "educational." But this "education" is not achieved by conveying "information" as we convention-ally understand the word. Advertising supplies information not from the ob-jective standpoint but as subjectively defined by the advertiser.

How Brands Are Created

Brand value is created largely through commercial communications, which are only sometimes mediated by experience. Those communications combine brand visuals with emotionally salient, vivid fantasies; aspirations and fears; and other emotional associations. Once established, these associations give the brand life, through both the sales generated and the legal protection that a brand's status as property gives it against piracy of trade name, trade dress, and the like.[26] This creates a feedback loop that makes it possible for rapid reproduction and amplification into reinforcing relationships.

For example, celebrity status can confer a complex set of marketing ad-vantages for the owner of the image that allows a Britney Spears, Martha Stewart, Jennifer Lopez, Donald Trump, or Kim Kardashian—the list is end-less—to leverage their fame into an opportunity to sell products. They are themselves persons, but they are also an industry. These celebrities are entre-preneurs of self, presiding over a vast network of product lines, licenses, and endorsements using their image to market the good in question. Celebrities may have quite a bit of input and control over the merchandise sold under their brand, or they may have little or none. It does not matter, because what they manufacture is the image, not the goods.

The development of the phenomena of the modern brand has meant that one of the principal things marketing speech informs consumers about is these ephemeral, completely self-constructed brand identities that are only imperfectly tethered to experience of the thing itself, rather than the thing in conjunction with the mental imagery created by the marketing. Over and over again in marketing research literature, authors use words like *learning* to refer to the process of building these associations. However, many of them are simply ephemera: "[T]here's no connection between joyful music or an exuberant dance, and a fabric softener sheet. The two are only connected through association."[27] Many of the associations, like the need for belonging or love, are also fairly abstract. As one advertising text puts it, "In this soci-ety probably more consumer goods are sold with appeals to this kind of need [for love] than on the basis of any other single category—in fact, maybe more than on the basis of all the others combined."[28]

Image, or the collective idea about a person or a company, if widely enough shared, can generate sales and higher profit margins. The trick is figuring out how best to do that. One tool for doing so is the Q rating system. The Q rating is a result of sampling consumer attitudes about celebrities to determine how many people recognize the individual and, if they recognize the person, whether their feelings are mostly positive or negative.[29] This generates a popularity rating. The popularity percentage is divided by the familiarity percentage to arrive at the Q rating. Q ratings determine public persons' desirability as endorsers for branded products.

Measures like Q ratings are important for a practice known as *brand extension* or *brand leveraging*. Brand leveraging is extremely profitable.[30] A brand extension is the development of a new product outside of the core production association of a familiar brand name. Brand extensions get the advantage of the name recognition of the brand for the new product. The creation of Virgin Atlantic Airways is an example of a brand extension of the Virgin record label into travel.[31] Theoretically, there is no limit to the number of directions a brand may be leveraged to sell other products; in practice, there are limits. Not all attempts at brand extensions work, but which extensions will work and which will not is difficult to predict.

Some brand extensions seem natural, as when Starbucks extends its coffee brand into other beverages like tea and into coffee-flavored ice cream. Others are not so natural, like the extension of the Virgin record label to an airline; nevertheless, this one worked. Generally, brand consistency—that is, the seeming congruence between the brand and the extension—is an important factor in being able to successfully develop a brand extension. For example, Caterpillar has been able to develop and sell a line of caps and tote bags because they seem consistent with the company's primary product— tractors.[32] It might not be able to sell coffee drinks or high-priced handbags, because such brand extensions would be highly incongruent.

Brand Personality

The creation of a brand personality is the sine qua non of marketing practice. As one advertising textbook puts it, "Just like people. Brands even have their own unique personalities."[33] Professor Susan Fournier of Harvard Business School has even proposed that consumers create relationships with brands: "Relationship principles have virtually replaced short-term exchange notions in both marketing thought and practice."[34] Fournier suggests that thinking of brands as relationship partners is a useful framework through which to analyze consumer responses to advertising and develop better, more congruent approaches to consumers: "Consumers' acceptance of advertisers' attempts to humanize brands and their tendencies to animate products of their own accord suggest a willingness to entertain brands as vital members of their relationship dyad."[35] In the language of marketing, brands have human characteristics and can stand for qualities like "playfulness" or "cheekiness."[36] In this parallel universe, a brand can be described, without irony or self-consciousness, as "trustworthy" or "loyal." Anthropomorphization of brands and of corporations is so successful that advertisers can talk about not only people's relationships with brands (or companies) but brands' relationships with each other.[37]

Perception *Is* Reality

Brand personality is meant to distinguish a company's product from its competitor's and to inspire a consumer to buy its product over a rival product or good, even though sometimes a rival product is identical in every way but the brand identity. In these circumstances, it is difficult to characterize communications intended to create brand personality as "informational," particularly if being "informational" means having some connection to the attributes of the product. As noted in the epigraph to this chapter, the belief in the advertising world is that "perception trumps reality every time."[38] Examples of this disconnect abound.

In a 2008 article for his "Consumed" column, former *New York Times* columnist Rob Walker reported that the supermarket chain Safeway had flipped an old concept of the house brand on its head by introducing two new "virtue-food" lines (O Organics and Eating Right) and giving them the sort of advertising resources usually reserved for name brands.[39] This was odd because the whole point of house brands has traditionally been to offer a generic version of a nationally advertised name brand, with the generic version being cheaper because house brands "don't need to waste money projecting a brand image via advertising to win the struggle for consumer attention and shelf space."[40] Because everyone knows that the seller does not actually manufacture the goods sold under the house brand label, the idea of attempting to build an image for a house brand would have probably been seen as quixotic in an earlier day. Today, however, these lines are increasingly blurred, since single suppliers sometimes contract to provide products under several name brands as well as house brands.[41]

Given this new reality, Safeway's decision to give their new house brands a traditional large-scale advertising campaign was not so odd. What was unusual was its goal for the campaign. Safeway developed the two lines in response to what it saw as an increased consumer desire for "more-healthful and less-processed food." Safeway did not, however, just want to add its own version of such "virtue-foods"; it wanted its house brands to become *the* dominant brand for such products. In other words, it wanted its house brand to become a name brand.

> [So Safeway] brought in executives from consumer-product giants like Procter & Gamble and Nestlé, gave the line a look that stands on its own (although the color choices may look familiar to anyone who knows the Whole Foods house brand) and hired the ad agency DDB in Chicago to create print and television advertising to help build the image of a full line of healthful, organic products in a wide range of categories.[42]

These efforts won Safeway the retailer of the year award from *Refrigerated and Frozen Foods Retailer.*

Conspicuously absent from this story is any mention of whether these foods are in fact organic, less processed, or particularly healthful. In his article, Walker makes liberal use of quotation marks and words like *feel* and *image,* suggesting he was consciously avoiding any statements about the brands' actual properties. Instead, he writes that "O Organics and Eating Right *feel* like an easily recognized 'solution' to the problem of at least trying to improve one's diet, a big part of the point of any 'name' brand."[43] Well sure, they *feel* like a solution; but *are* they a solution?

It is telling, though, that Walker apparently did not think the validity of the claims (that the products were organic or less processed) was sufficiently relevant to the story to discuss. This is typical of what I think of as "ad-speak." In the advertising world, the actual attributes of a product are often treated as an afterthought, if they are mentioned at all. Perhaps Walker simply was not permitted to discuss it because the whole piece was a PR piece. Or it may be that he thought most consumers take it for granted that brands are just images, so they would understand that this was a story about image creation, not about the actual qualities of the goods. If so, this is curious. It means Safeway develops these brands and markets them without regard to the actual properties of the product and that everyone knows this; that what Safeway is responding to is massive consumer denial—something like "Tell us this product is good for us. We won't believe you. But if you tell us that it is, it will make us feel better."

Maybe that *is* the implicit bargain; maybe no one really believes anything in advertising, but it works because it feeds the consumers' desire to avoid confrontation with reality. But it would seem to overstate the matter to think that no consumers really do want to know if a food is organic or better for you. If you are a consumer who wants to know, Safeway's campaign does not answer your need for information at all. In fact, it is just noise. If the products are not in fact organic or healthier, Safeway's attempt to suggest, with all these marketing activities, that they are actually interferes with your ability to make informed choices.

Branding often depends on creating associations that are unconnected to the physical properties of the product, because "[t]he more narrow the range of actual difference in commodity attributes, the more important it becomes to create a different kind of value—one that transcends the merely material."[44] In other words, if image is not tethered to material reality, it is much more flexible. This flexibility is what one industry spokesman claimed is the principal competitive advantage of American business.

> The future of this country, for better or worse, is going to be dependent on smart creative thinking. We can't compete in manufacturing terms with the cheaper labor and raw materials available in the rest of the world, *so we're going to have to fight to own the best intellectual property and brands,* and to be at the forefront of ideas and innovation. They're the value creators of America's future.[45]

What he means is that advertising creates value. Indeed, it creates economic value. The question from the First Amendment perspective is whether its production creates informational value.

Marketing as Conditioning

When advertisers speak of educating the consumer, they mean something more like classical conditioning—a process of associating one idea (the neutral response) with another (unconditioned response) through experience directed at creating the association—than what we usually think of as education. The most famous example of an exercise in classical conditioning is Pavlov's dogs. Pavlov trained the dogs to associate the sound of bell ringing with the appearance of food, so that when he rang the bell, the dogs salivated in anticipation of the food (a conditioned response) before any food actually appeared that would ordinarily engender salivation (the unconditioned response).[46]

Advertising may not be quite that powerful, although it is not for lack of trying. Marketing and advertising professionals, aided by psychologists, neurologists, economists, and others engaging in marketing research, have labored long in the service of marketing research attempting to discover the key to unlocking conditioned consumer responses. They want to find the "buy button" in the brain that would unerringly lead to the desired response.[47] So far, they have not been completely successful; but neither have they been unsuccessful.[48]

As the *Economist* reported, "The new marketing approach is to build a brand, not a product—to sell a lifestyle or a personality, to appeal to emotions"[49] and bring "warmth, familiarity, and trust."[50] People are said to love certain brands "beyond reason."[51] According to some researchers, "An ideal corporate brand creates a powerful corporate myth that is deeply anchored in the consumer's life-world, capable of turning ordinary consumption into a quasi-religious activity."[52] Consumers are encouraged to use the brand identity as a way of expressing their own identity: "A potent brand becomes a form of identity in shorthand."[53] Some brand loyalists, such as Mac users, are said to be "true believers." One marketer claims that brand loyalists are like members of cults, arguing that cult brands, like religious cults, offer their loyalists an opportunity to express themselves, to "belong," to "make meaning, feel secure, have order within chaos, and create identity."[54] Is this the sort of self-actualization that Emerson had in mind? Arguably not. However, it is possible that such conditioned responses serve larger social purposes.

Conditioning Consumption

One of the problems with the explosion of productive capacities in the wake of the Industrial Revolution and then accelerating after World War II was how to deal with excess productive capacity. Whether a product was an improvement on an older form or a wholly new invention, a market needed to be created for it. People needed to be encouraged to adopt practices that would incorporate the products available for sale and to adopt the habit of treating many products, like automobiles, as an object of fashion and thus susceptible to obsolescence rather than simple utility. As historian Susan Strasser has explained, "[P]eople who had never bought corn flakes were taught to need them; those formerly content to buy oats scooped from the grocer's bin were informed about why they should prefer Quaker Oats in a box."[55] Increased capacity and production would be of little use if there were no demand. So demand needed to be created or at least stoked. The marketing business was "based on the concept that a market was a malleable entity."[56]

Similarly, a number of holidays or rituals associated with life stages are now tied to consumption in some form. Some holidays appear to have been created out of whole cloth as a marketing opportunity: Valentine's Day, Mother's Day, Father's Day, and Secretary's Day, to name a few.[57] Other holidays have become an occasion around which sales are scheduled—the Fourth of July, Labor Day, Memorial Day, and (the granddaddy of them all) Black Friday (the day after Thanksgiving). Although it might be supposed that these shopping opportunities are the natural outgrowth of consumers' experiencing shopping as a pleasant activity (not a view universally held) and therefore that marketers are simply responding to consumer demand, it seems implausible that the marketers' desire to stimulate that demand has played no role in the construction of these various holidays as shopping moments. These are all ways that the needs of commercial enterprises have subtly and not-so-subtly shaped the culture. Nowhere is this more evident than in marketing to children.

Conditioning Children

We become the object of efforts to "educate" us about brands and what products we should want before we are old enough to talk. As one marketer observed, "If you don't realize your child is a consumer by three years old, you don't realize the impact the media are having."[58] Advertising is a potent source of the socialization of children into society generally, but particularly with respect to socializing them to be consumers.[59] One study observed, "Twenty-five years of consumer socialization research have yielded an impressive set of findings. Based on our review of these findings, there can be no doubt that children are avid consumers and become socialized into this role from an early age."[60]

It has been an article of faith in the advertising industry that brand loyalties created at an early age may well last a lifetime and that those sellers who manage to colonize the mental space of children first will end up virtually owning it by the time those children are grown up and able to command their own salaries.[61] Consider the following quotation from an advertising executive that appeared in 1957 in Vance Packard's exposé of the advertising industry, *The Hidden Persuaders.*

> [I]f you expect to be in business for any length of time, think of what it can mean to your firm in profits if you can condition a million or ten million children who will grow up into adults trained to buy your product as soldiers are trained to advance when they hear the trigger words "forward march."[62]

Packard reported that advertisers wanted to provide what they described as "educational" materials because, as stated in one ad, "[e]ager minds can be molded to want your products."[63] Not only are children "the buyers of tomorrow,"[64] according to this ad, but if advertisers sold these children on their brand, the children would "insist that their parents buy no other."[65] These statements were undoubtedly hyperbolic; no advertising technique has achieved the infallibility of response suggested by these quotes. Nevertheless, the basic idea that children should be marketed to early is well established in the industry.

So from at least the mid-twentieth century and accelerating to the present day, those with something to sell have been trying to educate us in consumption beginning at the earliest possible stage. There is some evidence that they have succeeded. One study indicates that children have fairly stable logo recognition as early as ages three through six.[66] This might not be too disturbing until you learn that one of the brands children reflected high recognition of was Joe Camel.[67]

One of the most potent sources of advertising's socialization of children is television: "Television advertising is a pervasive presence in the lives of most American children. Recent estimates suggest that children between the ages of 6 and 14 watch about 25 hours of television per week and are exposed to as many as 20,000 commercials in a single year."[68] This is part of the reason why there are so many commercial tie-ins—lunch boxes, clothing, fast foods, and many other products—to movies and television programming aimed at children. This is particularly true with movies, as a substantial number of them are made and marketed with kids, even toddlers,[69] in mind.[70] Advertising has also increasingly found its way into traditional educational environments—in other words, schools—with television programming like Channel One, product placement in textbooks, event sponsorships at schools, and exclusive contracts for food service and vending machines and to supply equipment to sports teams and the like.[71]

In addition, children are an enormous market in their own right: "[C]hildren spend, or cause to be spent, huge sums."[72] In 2002, one source reported that children aged 4–12 were directly responsible for $40 billion in spending. Those in the coveted "teen market" spent upwards of $155 billion during the same period. It is a small wonder, then, that many firms specialize in doing marketing research on children, particular tweens and teens. Some of these firms specifically engage in the practice of "cool hunting," trying to predict what teens will become attracted to so as to get in front of and direct those trends by making their brands part of what is cool. Media critic Douglas Rushkoff captured this process in his PBS *Frontline* documentary "The Persuaders," exploring how Sprite managed to position itself as the "cool beverage" for teens by promotional arrangements with MTV and rap groups.[73]

Of course, as children mature, they may lose their fondness for Transformers or Barbie dolls, so not all preferences established as children translate into future purchases. But some may, not to mention that when these children have their own children, they may naturally return to the toys, foods, and entertainment of their youth. In the meantime, marketers have also discovered that even though children do not earn the money in the household, they have considerable influence over how it is spent, even for those products that are not specifically aimed at them, such as cars and appliances. As one marketing professional puts it, "Advertisers know that children are a way to reach adults, too." Marketers of even big-ticket items such as cars attempt to pitch their product to interest children so as to influence their parents' purchase. This is particularly true where advertisers can inspire feelings of guilt or competition in parents to provide goods that "everyone else has."[74] The phenomenon of children's influence on adult purchasing has stimulated substantial research into what is known in the trade as the "nag factor." Marketers investigating the nag factor seek to discover how to leverage parents' love and concern for their children, their guilt about the limited time they have to spend with them, and their desire for peace or relief from nagging into a means for selling both products for children and other products.[75]

Since advertisers are speaking directly to children, they are only mildly responsive, if at all, to parental disapproval of marketing tactics. Rather, research and the advertising itself suggest that one of the most effective pitches for children, particularly teenagers, is to position a product as something their parents would disapprove of. An example of this strategy was an ad for the program *Gossip Girl*. The ad showed a picture of two of its teenaged characters naked in bed together, along with the caption "Mind-Blowingly Inappropriate."[76] The quote came from the Parents Television Council, an advocacy group that had criticized the show. The network's executive vice president of marketing said that the quote "fit hand in glove with the campaign and where we were going."[77] Where that might be is not clear. However, he said the network wanted to "talk to fans of the show in language that is relevant to them,"[78] which apparently entails suggesting, "If your parents don't think this is appropriate for you, it is exactly what you will want to watch!" These sorts of appeals trouble many observers.[79]

Those who promote freedom for commercial expression often respond to objections to this sort of marketing and entertainment content by saying that it is up to parents to control what their kids are exposed to. But the idea that parents could possibly shield their kids from these influences in the media is sheer fantasy. Even if you do not allow your kids to watch movies or TV, they will encounter other children who do and will probably be watching those programs at their friends' homes. Moreover, unless they are homeschooled and live in a cabin in the woods, shielded from all human contact, they will encounter billboards, advertising on the sides of buses, advertising in schools, and people who have been exposed to the undesired images.

Most significantly, viral marketing techniques, such as posting an ad on YouTube, allow an advertiser to reach children and teens through vehicles their parents will likely never see at all. For example, JCPenney was accused of using this tactic with a "viral video" that showed teens practicing speed dressing with, of course, JCPenney's clothing. The implicit message was that the teens in the ad were practicing speed dressing in order to have sex without getting caught by their parents. The ad won a Cannes Lions award (an international advertising award), but JCPenney subsequently denied responsibility for the ad and claimed that it had not been authorized.[80] It is hard to take this denial seriously, given that the "fool your parents" message seems popular with advertisers attempting to reach teen consumers.

It might seem that trying to increase viewers by suggesting that kids' parents will disapprove is just taking advantage of normal teenage rebellion and probably will not do them any harm. But how much of what we now take for granted as the normal attitude of children toward parents is really the product of several generations' immersion in advertising representing parents as the enemy, inept and out of touch? It is impossible to know. No one alive today who was born and lived continuously in the United States could say, because it has been this way for almost all of living memory. Perhaps we do need to just loosen up—except that when the "rebellion" being promoted is smoking or drinking or other practices that might put young people's lives in danger in a way they are not well placed to evaluate at this point, loosening up hardly seems appropriate.

For example, it is exhaustively well documented that the tobacco companies engaged in marketing to children with cartoon characters like Joe Camel, even as they claimed they were not doing so.[81] In an internal memo written in 1973 and entitled "Some Thoughts about New Brands of Cigarettes for the Youth Market," one R. J. Reynolds executive observed that "while 'pre-smokers' and 'learners' start smoking for psychological reasons (fitting in with the crowd, self-image, boredom relief), once the 'learning' period is over, the physical effects become of overriding importance and desirability to the confirmed smoker, and the psychological effects, except the ten-sion-relieving effect, largely wane in importance or disappear."[82] Tobacco companies' efforts included not only imagery aimed at "presmokers" but flavor additives that would make smoking more palatable to new smokers. One tobacco company memo noted, "It is a well known fact that teenagers like sweet products. Honey might be considered."[83] Representatives of the industry also sent brochures with "information" about "the smoking controversy" to schoolchildren, presumably in an attempt to deflect any negative information that might dissuade them from trying cigarettes.[84] When they sent these brochures, the tobacco companies knew that there was no foundation for claiming that the connection between smoking and negative health consequences was not established. Internal documents revealed that company employees were unmistakably engaged in attempting to preserve the stream of new smokers entering the market in order to be able to continue selling the product.

The movie[85] and video game industry does much the same kind of thing in marketing movies and video games with adult and R-rated content[86] to underage consumers. Manufacturers of alcohol have done the same with "al-copops." Indeed, in one study sponsored by Georgetown University's Center on Alcohol Marketing and Youth, researchers found that some publications with a majority of readers under 21 nevertheless carried advertising for both beer and distilled spirits.[87] The sellers of fast food, which is implicated in America's growing obesity crisis,[88] market openly to children by providing tie-ins to movies (often cartoons) and giving away toys with purchases. Such toy giveaways can *only* be directed at wooing children.

To be sure, the tobacco industry is something of a special case. It was faced with a particularly difficult problem as its management struggled with the implications of research that this legal product on which their companies' welfare was based was also potentially lethal. However, unless you are prepared to believe that everyone employed in the industry harbored a particular malevolence toward the public welfare, rather than just acting as they did because they saw their livelihoods endangered, one is forced to conclude there is no reason to believe that this kind of behavior would be confined to the tobacco industry. If this is the sort of behavior exhibited by those selling and marketing a product that the evidence increasingly and unmistakably showed had no safe level of use, what can we expect such incentive structures and processes to deliver when the connections between harm and the product are less clear-cut?

Indeed, even as this book goes to press, executives in the soft drink and junk food industries are behaving in a similar manner as the tobacco industry executives did.[89] This is not surprising, since these foods are of minimal nutritional value. It is troubling because of the link between junk food and the rising incidence of childhood obesity and diabetes. Numerous studies have documented the link between the marketing of, for instance, soda or sugary breakfast cereals and children's requests for the advertised brands and their eating habits. Marketing is intended to sell products, and the evidence is clear that it does so. Where those products are unhealthy and the marketing is aimed at children, it really does not seem that it ought to be controversial to restrict such advertising.

Yet there is very little regulatory oversight of these kinds of efforts, even as advertising and marketing efforts have infiltrated the educational setting (where children are a captive audience), in the form of Channel One, product placements in textbooks, exclusive contracts to sell beverages on school grounds or to use a particular brand of athletic wear for sports teams, and even nonprofit programming such as *Sesame Street*[90] and the PBS show *Teletubbies*.[91] An extensive study in 1978 by the Federal Trade Commission—its infamous "Kid Vid" investigation, which collected and reported on evidence that young children have a difficult time distinguishing between editorial and advertising content and between fantasy and reality—recommended a ban on advertising directed at children under the age of eight years old, yet such a ban has never been enacted.[92] The difficulty of distinguishing between commercials and program content is increasingly irrelevant, however, as so much marketing is embedded directly into the content, in the form of product placements.[93] In addition, much of the marketing in the teen market is through word-of-mouth and "viral videos," based on the sense, gleaned from marketing research, that kids are particularly sensitive to peer pressure and may be more likely to adopt a product or a practice because a peer does so than because of advertising efforts.[94]

In order to avoid regulation, certain industries have entered into agreements for voluntary restraints on advertising for some products like sugary cereals, candy, fast food, or sodas, usually in response to periodic flare-ups of public interest in the issue.[95] Some of these efforts may have been launched in the face of evidence of renewed government interest in the subject[96] or in response to lawsuits or threatened lawsuits.[97] A study by the American Psychological Association, produced by a task force formed to study advertising directed at children, came to similar conclusions as the FTC had in 1978. The APA task force's report, published in 2004, concluded that children at various ages lack either awareness of distinctions between commercials and programming or a full understanding of the nature of persuasive intent.[98] The conclusion was that this unprecedented level of advertising and marketing efforts directed at children contributed to various negative outcomes, including obesity, self-esteem issues, and increased levels of parent-child conflict.

When it comes to children, arguments made in support of freedom for commercial expression—for example, that consumers should be free to make their own decisions—do not seem very persuasive. How does making children the target (and *target* is the right word) of marketing for products, whose future implications they are poorly placed to evaluate, constitute a necessary component of freedom? Again, proponents of more freedom for commercial speech attempt to deflect these concerns by appeals to parental authority. Sometimes these arguments are dubious on their face, as when an editorial in the *St. Louis Post Dispatch* exhorted parents to "teach your children well"[99] about the dangers of credit, when it is so abundantly clear that many adults could use a refresher course. Others seem unrealistic. "Kids need to think critically to weed out unsavory marketing," proclaims columnist Larry Magid.[100]

This injunction seems in conflict with what we know about kids' powers of reasoning. One of the defining features of being a kid may be some difficulty with thinking critically. Calls for greater parental involvement or media literacy seem deeply misplaced when, particularly with respect to media literacy, those efforts must necessarily start many years after children have been targeted by marketing. As the APA task force reported,

> [A]n overreliance on media literacy as a key strategy for defending against advertising effects is misdirected and places too great a responsibility on children. All too often we see calls for interventions designed to "world proof" the child when we would be better off relying on strategies that offer protections for children, in this case from advertising deemed to be unfair and potentially harmful to children. An over-reliance on media literacy could, in this instance, be tantamount to blaming the victim.[101]

The APA task force made the preceding argument while focusing on the "unique" vulnerabilities of children to advertising. However, adults may not have it much better. Although most people seem to think they are not susceptible to advertising, the evidence suggests that we are more susceptible than we think we are. This vulnerability is explored further in the next chapter.

CHAPTER 6

Advertising and Manipulation

There is a group of people who know very well where the weapons
of automatic influence lie and who employ them regularly and
expertly to get what they want.

—Robert B. Cialdini, *Influence: The Psychology of Persuasion*

In the last chapter, I explored the question of the informational content of advertising and found that far from being informational, what advertisers mean by "information" is more like conditioning. I looked at the ways in which advertising and marketing are intended to create markets and begin to do so at the earliest stage possible, with children. Yet, when talking about advertising's capacity to mislead or manipulate adults, one usually encounters self-confident assertions such as "I just ignore advertising" or "No one pays any attention to advertising." Of course, advertisers are counting on the contrary, that millions will be moved by their efforts. In general, business writers and economists agree that advertising is an essential expenditure. So which is it—fluff or substance? Are we immune or not?

It would not seem like you could have it both ways. It turns out that most adults are far more susceptible to advertising than they like to think. Some of their susceptibility is located in aspects of the functioning of the human mind that have been the subject of intense study for the last several decades. Only recently has that research begun to make its way into the mainstream. But a great deal of it involved uncovering aspects of human cognition that were already well-known to marketers, and marketing professionals have been quick to exploit it where possible.

In *Nudge: Improving Decisions about Health, Wealth, and Happiness,*[1] economist Richard Thaler and law professor Cass Sunstein draw on this research to argue that there is an "architecture of choice" and that we can take what we know about human reasoning to "nudge" people toward better choices. This is not news to marketers. They have been in the business of choice architecture for decades. Some would say the techniques involved constitute a little more than "nudging." Sometimes it looks more like a shove or even a mugging. If the First Amendment is supposed to support and protect autonomy, persons' free choice, then the manipulation inherent in much commercial expression frustrates that goal.

The Architecture of Choice and the Architecture of Desire

In *Nudge,* Thaler and Sunstein review research by psychologists and economists that offers evidence of the fallibility of human judgment. This research has led to the establishment of a new school of economics—behavioral economics. Behavioral economists were inspired by the work of Daniel Kahneman and Amos Tversky[2] on bounded rationality. Kahneman and Tversky discovered that human beings reason in ways that will result in predictable failures of "rational" decision making. For example, the framing of questions matters so much that in response to a problem about whether to administer a vaccine where there will be a predictable number of deaths if the vaccine is administered and a predictable number of deaths if it is not, subjects recommend different actions depending on whether the question is framed as "lives saved" or "deaths caused." Or, in an example of something called the "anchoring and adjustment effect," test subjects asked what percentage of the members of the United Nations were African countries offered higher numbers after they had spun a roulette wheel rigged to stop on a high number than they offered when the wheel was stopped on a lower one. The roulette numbers caused subjects to "anchor" their estimates of the percentage of African countries in the UN, even though the numbers were obviously completely irrelevant to the question. Kahneman, Tversky, and many other researchers have identified many other such cognitive biases.

Thaler and Sunstein refer to the features of human reasoning revealed by this and other research as the "automatic system" of cognitive processes. In this automatic system, people are, as Dan Ariely, a behavioral economist at

Duke, puts it, "predictably irrational";[3] that is, they will predictably and systematically make logical errors of judgment. Human beings use rules of thumb, referred to as heuristics, to make decisions. These rules of thumb often lead to errors. For example, the "availability heuristic" describes a tendency to make decisions based on the information that is the most readily available or salient, like deciding whether to buy a particular make of car based on information gleaned from a friend at a cocktail party in preference to research on the subject. Even though the party recommendation is less meaningful statistically, it is liable to be more influential on the decision maker because it is salient and thus more compelling. In experimental conditions, many people will anchor a decision on the price they are willing to pay for something by reference to an irrelevant number merely because it was placed in proximity to the decision in question. Many subjects in other experiments also regularly have difficulty adding multiple percentage changes, so that they overestimate the savings from that "additional 20 percent off."[4] Most people tend to exhibit such an aversion to losses, even small ones, that framing something as a potential loss versus a potential cost engenders a different decision even where (rationally) participants should be indifferent to how the choice is framed. This is because of something called the "endowment effect," which leads us to value things more just because we own them.

People also tend to be overly optimistic. Virtually everyone believes they are "above average" in many important respects. Most healthy people underestimate their chances of getting divorced or of dying in an automobile accident. (Sadly, the clinically depressed are somewhat better at grasping the true odds of such unfavorable events. But who knows whether this is not part of their problem? It certainly does not seem to offer them an adaptive advantage.) Research suggests that human beings also have a tendency to assess new information through the lens of their existing beliefs (confirmation bias) and will display an irrational attachment to the status quo over change, even when the status quo is demonstrably unsatisfactory.

These are just a few of the kinds of errors explored by behavioral research. In a way, nothing here is really startlingly new. We have always known that some people are irrationally optimistic, that many people have difficulty imagining something bad will ever happen to them, and that some people can be stubborn and try to twist a fact to fit their hypothesis. But what makes this research noteworthy is its suggestion that these types of errors are sufficiently pervasive and robust that, even if they are not invariably present in every person at all times or in the same degree in every person, they seem to be an eradicable feature of the process of human cognition, not an anomaly or the preserve of the underdeveloped.[5] Even very educated people display these biases. For example, "[p]ercentage calculations have been shown to be difficult for children, college freshman, and even math teachers."[6] They are also fairly resistant, as a general matter, to debiasing efforts. In other words, knowing you are vulnerable to making these sorts of mistakes does not necessarily protect you from falling prey to them.

None of this is surprising either, because these choices often arise in circumstances where they are made fairly automatically, without a great deal of thought. Thaler and Sunstein propose that choices made by what they call the "automatic system" are not unthought, just unthought-out. But that distinction does not completely capture the problem. It is not merely a problem of consciousness or unconsciousness. Sometimes even when people think about a problem, they may predictably fail to make the right call ("right" being the call they intend to make or would have chosen if fully informed). One reason for this is because, as it turns out, human beings are not very good statisticians.

Consider what is known as the "Monty Hall problem." In the typical *Let's Make a Deal* scenario, a contestant is faced with three doors, behind one of which is a fabulous prize. Behind another door is a goat, and behind the third is a somewhat lesser prize (or another goat; it simplifies the problem to make it two goats, but the second-best prize is of sufficiently lesser value as to make it feel as though getting that prize is a "loss" if the object is to win the best prize). The contestant chooses a door. After this choice and before revealing what is behind the door the contestant has chosen, the host, Monty Hall, opens one of the other two doors to reveal a prize that is not the goat. The question then is, should the contestant switch doors? Or, put another way, does Hall's reveal of what is behind Door Number One change the odds of the likelihood that the contestant originally picked the right door? Most people, even really educated people, say that it does not. Most people are wrong.

When Monty Hall reveals what is behind one of the doors that the contestant has not picked and that prize is neither the goat nor the best prize, the odds that the contestant has picked the right door have changed, and the contestant should switch. But when Marilyn vos Savant, a syndicated columnist for *Parade* magazine gave this response in answer to a reader's posing of this scenario, she drew outraged responses from a number of PhDs, including mathematicians. They excoriated her. But she was right, and they were wrong. The reason she was right is the context. The contestant should change the original selection because, since Monty's selection is not random, the odds went up that the goat is behind the door originally picked. Monty knows which door has the goat, and that changes everything.

Why did so many people, including mathematicians, get it wrong? Well, according to a Harvard professor of probability, "Our brains are just not wired to do probability problems very well."[7] In addition, generally, when it comes to problems involving numbers, our reasoning may often be flawed in predictable ways—whether because of the way our brains work or because of widespread innumeracy (and this may make a difference in terms of social policy choices). Take your pick, but it is true, and telling people that they make these sorts of mistake is often not enough for people to be able to avoid them. Some of these limitations are not a problem of thinking. Indeed, there can be such a thing as "thinking too much." As Thaler and Sunstein observe, there are many cases in which we may do better by relying on our "guts."[8] So "conscious" does not invariably mean "better" or more "rational."

Feeling and Thinking

Psychologists[9] have done similar research tracking the ways in which cognitive limitations, perhaps neurologically based, contribute to our difficulties making decisions in the manner that economic theory or notions of rationality generally might predict that we would. We cling to theories that appear to explain the world in a way that we find congenial. We defer to authority rather than trust our own senses. For example, merely being primed with images of the elderly may make us walk more slowly.[10] We can be induced to have false "memories."[11]

You can tell people about these cognitive shortcomings, but it often does little to change their feelings or their decisions. For instance, one reason so many people are afraid of flying but not of driving a car is because of the salience of airplane crashes. When a plane crashes happens, it is news. Not every car crash is news. If a car crash does not happen to you, you usually do not know about it. You usually know about plane crashes. The news factor makes plane crashes salient and thus makes them seem more dangerous. However, your chances of dying in a car accident are far higher than your chances of dying in a plane crash. If you are frightened of flying, though, it is very likely that despite this information and despite thinking consciously about the issue, you will not be able to quell your fears once on an airplane. This is perhaps because the properties of air travel itself are different enough from your daily life that its novelty has an emotional effect on you, but it is perhaps also because the vividness of the newspaper stories have had an emotional effect not easy to dismiss.

Adaptive Irrationality

It may also be the case that emotional reactions are not easy to dismiss (despite evidence that they are unfounded) because, as some neurological research has suggested, some of our emotional responses are either hardwired or very nearly so. It appears that emotions may assist us to make a decision (of some kind) in circumstances of imperfect knowledge or where knowledge is irrelevant and where failing to make a decision is less adaptive than making a bad decision. As neurologists have documented, this connection between emotions and thoughts is such that with the parts of the brain that affect emotional responses destroyed, we may become paralyzed with indecision about ordinary things and cannot conform our behavior to social norms.[12] Things "feel right" or "feel wrong," and this feeling of certainty is not just driven by emotions, which are inextricably intertwined with our physiology.[13] Research into the role that emotions play in our decision making raises questions about the whole notion of the distinction between "rational" thought and "emotion" and about what it means to be "irrational."

What Marketers Know

Few of these insights about human beings' cognitive limitations—our tendency to anchor numbers to some other irrelevant number, our difficulty calculating percentages to see true costs, our tendency to respond to social cues and emotional connections more strongly than to information, the importance of salience to decision making and of repetition to memory—are news to marketers. They have been the subject of marketing research for a very long time. Marketing researchers have long been in the business of studying the quirks and cul-de-sacs of human cognition. As one writer put it, the goal of marketing is to encourage habit formation. "The goal of habit formation is to automate behavior so it doesn't need to be externally reinforced."[14] The key is to "[t]reat your customers like dogs."[15] Marketing researchers, most of whom are psychologists, have been studying methods of persuasion from every conceivable angle.

In his seminal work, *Influence: The Psychology of Persuasion*,[16] Robert Cialdini, an academic with joint appointments in marketing and psychology, describes six of what he calls "weapons of influence"—all techniques of manipulation that, in the main, rely on social norms to inspire cooperation rather than reflection. They are reciprocation, commitment and consistency, social proof, liking, authority, and scarcity.[17] Several of these techniques are basically the familiar tactics of the hard sell: asking people to make commitments before they know what they are committing to in order to take advantage of people's tendency to want to appear consistent, even to strangers; offering a free product or a gift in order to trigger social conventions about reciprocity; and gaining the endorsement of celebrities in order to activate the phenomena whereby social proof or authority figures ("four out of five doctors recommend") trigger acquiescence to authority (as in the infamous Milgram experiment). These techniques can be combined with specific marketing communications and practices to manipulate consumer behavior.

Another technique Cialdini describes is the creation of artificial scarcity to make a product more desirable. Cialdini tells the story of running into a friend by accident in a toy store in January to buy an expensive toy for his son, a toy that had been advertised prior to Christmas and that he had promised he would get but that had then been unavailable. Cialdini and his friend laughed at the "coincidence" of the two of them both being in the store on the same errand. A friend, formerly in the toy business, told them that their meeting was anything but coincidental. Rather, it was the result of a deliberate plan by the seller to inspire parental promises to children that could not be fulfilled.

Sellers heavily advertise a toy that they do not make available until after Christmas. Ads stoke demand by children. Sellers know that consumers like Cialdini and his friend will buy something for their children for Christmas.

But they also know that consumers like them will have very likely promised their children to buy the advertised toy. When it is not available, they will buy something else. But after Christmas, the parents, prompted by the children's desire, will feel that the promise still stands, despite the substitutes purchased for Christmas. Once the toy in question is available in stores, sellers expect that parents' sense of commitment to the earlier promise to buy the specific toy will get parents back in the store, thus generating two shopping trips rather than one.

If parents knew this, perhaps it would not work (although, since their kids have been exposed to the ads and would probably plead nonetheless, perhaps it would not make any difference). But this vignette illustrates a powerful truth about much of marketing practice: a great deal of that which may appear to the consumer to be merely happenstance or coincidence is actually the result of a great deal of study and is painstakingly choreographed. Of course, if consumers knew that, they might be taken aback. Efforts to inform them often meet with disbelief, however, because people dislike knowing they can be manipulated. Even when confronted with the evidence, they will often discount it because it is so disconcerting and uncomfortable. Marketing people know this, and it is one of the best protections against charges of manipulation culminating in regulatory restraints; people do not want to believe it.

The Irrational Commitment to Rationality

One of the most frustrating aspects of talking about commercial speech is the steadfastness with which most people, including those who should know better, cling to the view that the cacophony of marketing messages to which the average American is subjected does not affect them. The widespread commitment to the robustness of human rationality in the face of all these persuasion attempts is downright irrational. People argue that advertising is generally not very effective; that when it is, it is largely harmless; and that if it is not harmless, well, those who have been persuaded should not have been and are best left alone to suffer the consequences of their bad decisions. One often gets the sense that such observers are silently congratulating themselves on their own cleverness for avoiding the traps set for others.

The moral question of whether we should organize a society on a rule that works fine for clever people but will predictably fail the average Joe is a subject I will take up in the next chapter, but it is not clear that many of these folks are as smart as they think they are. If you think you are immune from marketing influence, it may be somewhat disconcerting to learn that everyone thinks that. According to professional marketers, everyone is wrong.

> Nobody wants to admit that they're in the least bit affected by advertising! They'll typically claim that they don't pay any attention to advertising, despite the fact that a glance at their pantry or closet, kitchen or garage reveals nothing but heavily advertised name-brand consumer goods.[18]

Advertisers, though, "play along, assuring us that we're tough to persuade."[19] They know that this belief comes in handy whenever advertising is blamed for any particular ill, because they can use it to claim that advertising is not really effective. Of course, this claim then begs the question, why is so much money spent on it?

A Lot of Nothing?

The conventional industry wisdom is that there is a high positive correlation between advertising spending and sales. The correlation is far from perfect, however. Even where advertising clearly stimulates sales, it is not always clear why.[20] Still, it is generally taken as a given that advertising drives sales. So, for example, when Proctor & Gamble's ad spending as a percentage of its sales appeared to decline in 2007, some investors expressed concern, leading P&G to reassure investors that the decrease was merely a function of an accounting change and that the company's expenditures for advertising as a percentage had not actually changed.[21] This same principle is why economists sometimes use expenditures on advertising as a measure of the health of the economy.[22] The same assumption led the *Virginia Pharmacy* Court to describe advertising as the sine qua non of business.

If you doubt that advertising drives sales, look around at your own cabinets and possessions. Look really hard. Do not just count the areas in which you have consciously made the choice to reject fashion or promotion. If you look closely, chances are really good that you, too, have far more brand-name purchases, far many more inexplicable decisions (like magazine subscriptions you keep meaning to cancel or extended warranties), than you might expect to find if you were not at all influenced by advertising. Do not feel too bad. You are not alone, and you have not made these decisions unassisted. As noted earlier, the fond belief that one is unmoved by advertising appeals is well known to marketing experts and researchers. The problem in this area is the same as that in any area of self-reporting or self-assessment where some answers would reflect on us less flatteringly. People are not spectacularly good at making accurate self-assessments. But they hate it when you suggest that they are biased or vulnerable. Consider the reception Vance Packard received when, over fifty years ago, he wrote a book, *The Hidden Persuaders*, reporting on advertising practices and suggested he found them alarming. Although his book was enormously popular, he was ridiculed as "paranoid" for suggesting that advertising might be as effective as its practitioners claimed it was through the use of manipulative appeals to the subconscious.

The defensive rejection of consumer manipulability that was reflected in the vociferous objections and criticisms of Vance Packard's seminal work of journalism continues to the present day. Over and over again, one is confronted with arguments to the effect that marketing or advertising does not change behavior but only influences brand choices or that anyone can or ought to be immune to "puffing." Yet when you consider the enormous volume of and expenditures on advertising, it defies credulity that businesses would spend this amount of money on something they knew did not work. Simply observing, as Rob Walker does, that we contribute to the meaning brands have does not mean marketing contributes nothing or that consumers are "in control," as advertisers like to claim. That position is little more than wishful thinking.

Marketers have invested staggering sums in research intended to identify what works. Most of the techniques Packard reported on continue to be used today. Some concepts, like market segmentation, have been developed and expanded beyond the wildest dreams of the people Packard interviewed. As Walker reports, "Today companies spend hundreds of millions of dollars studying our behavior—asking us questions, dispatching corporate ethnographers to scrutinize us in our kitchens."[23] We are sliced and diced into increasingly specialized groups by demographic data (e.g., age and race) supplied by official sources like the U.S. Census and by more personal information (e.g., purchasing habits, books read, and so on) that companies obtain by purchasing lists of data from other companies (credit card companies, Amazon, membership organizations, magazine subscriptions, alumni lists, and now social media like Facebook and Twitter).[24] If there is someone collecting names for a list, there is someone for whom that list is valuable.[25]

With all this information, marketers then can target pitches to market groups they believe will be receptive to them. This targeting goes very far beyond simply ensuring that information about arthritis drugs reaches a market segment over age 50. Marketing professionals have also come up with psychographic profiles that purport to capture consumer types under headings like "explorer" or "outlaw." The attributes of psychographic categories like these are fairly specific. They bear a great deal of resemblance to FBI offender profiles, although they may rely on equally questionable empirical foundations. Clotaire Rapaille, a psychologist whose work is almost exclusively marketing research, asserts that everything in a culture has an emotional "code" that, once decoded, can be used to successfully sell products. Moreover, much of the research in psychology, neurology, and other fields relating to cognition research has marketing implications.

The return on investment (ROI) of marketing and advertising expenditures is of critical importance to corporations and represents perhaps the principal obsession of chief marketing officers everywhere. But calculating ROI is very difficult. A very old joke in the industry states, "I know half of my advertising budget each year is wasted. I just don't know which half!" The joke obscures, however, how much is known by virtue of billions of dollars and decades of work. That knowledge is not trivial. Much of it is turned to account in structuring the layout of stores, the music playing in the background, and the lighting; coupons, logos, colors, displays, and the look of the product; precise word choice in ads; and a thousand other things—all of which are engineered to maximize public appeal. If its application does not always work, that is certainly not for lack of trying. Marketers do have a nuanced view of what works in advertising and marketing, even though perhaps the reason it works and thus the ability to predictably reproduce it often remain elusive. But with all this data and all these efforts, it seems counterintuitive—to say the least—to argue that the volume of advertising and marketing communication to which the average American is exposed has no effect, even if we do not know precisely what the effect is. Against this sort of investment, consumer awareness is a relatively puny weapon.

Is Knowledge Power?

Another common tack for those who claim that advertising's effect is trivial or negligible is to argue that even if advertising is sometimes effective, people who know some of the tricks can arm themselves with that knowledge to avoid being affected. This is a common assumption. Even observers who might favor some regulation of advertising claim that media literacy is connected to avoiding advertising's effects. So, for example, psychologist Timothy Wilson writes that "the failure to recognize the power of advertising makes us more susceptible to it . . . because we are likely to lower our guard while watching commercials or fail to avoid them altogether."[26] But even becoming aware of advertising's power may not be sufficient to avoid its effects. Advertising and other commercial expression draws on years of research and practice, on psychological experiments on methods of persuasion, and on appeals to authority and desire for acceptance; it relies on triggering fears and anxieties, makes appeals to suppressed desires or cravings, and uses emotional symbolism and manipulation of cognitive biases or blind spots. In the face of such a battery of manipulative techniques, knowledge of its power may not be sufficient to avoid its influence.

For the reasons already outlined, I am skeptical that knowledge is power when it comes to advertising. In the first place, compelling evidence points to the conclusion that none of us are as rational as we like to think we are and that our decision-making abilities are limited in predictable ways. Moreover, "recognition [that manipulation is going on] is not the same thing as immunity."[27] But perhaps most important, a good deal of what constitutes advertising today takes place in forms that do not trigger the skepticism that is supposed to protect you from putting too much credence on it. Given that marketing speech is ubiquitous, the proposition that people should "talk back" to it or educate their children about it in order to resist being affected seems akin to the proverbial finger in the dike. Such efforts are likely to be swamped by the sheer volume of ad speech.

Consumers as Targets

Advertisers view consumers as targets. Like big game, they are something to be bagged, not reasoned with. In 2007 the cable company Comcast was running business-to-business advertising spots touting its ability to reach the specific market that potential advertisers might want to reach, by showing a group of people walking down the street, apparently oblivious to the fact that one of them has a target on his chest. The target is suddenly, as if out of the blue, felled by some unidentified projectile hitting him. The commercial gave the impression of ducks in a carnival shooting gallery. Whether the imagery was accurate in its portrayal of Comcast's abilities to reach a specific target market, the imagery itself unmistakably reflects consumers as passive objects to be acted on. This representation stands in stark contradiction to the image of consumers as active participants, making choices on their own behalf.

This representation in Comcast's ad is not atypical. Marketing literature is replete with references to the ways in which the canny marketer gets around a consumer's defenses, skepticism, and indifference or even hostility toward being pitched. It regularly reflects the notion that consumers are targets to be acted on. Indeed, it would not overstate the case to say that a great deal of marketing research is devoted to precisely this subject: how to influence consumers' choices without the consumers being consciously aware of it. It might make one "feel like a lab rat."[28]

Some observers who defend the status quo based on research on bounded rationality urge caution about applying this research to law and warn that we should not discard existing theories about human behavior too readily. Belief in responsibility and free will means we can avoid governmental tyranny that would seek to impose on us what is good for us, not what we would choose for ourselves. But sometimes these arguments look fairly irrational themselves, as in the following quote: "[P]ersistently holding onto our own idiosyncratic theories, even past some ideal point of rational belief, may, in the long run, be the best way to develop a coherent body of knowledge that can improve public policy."[29] Can holding on to a theory without evidence that supports it and discarding evidence that undermines that theory really lead us to a body of "knowledge"?

It would seem that there is not much point in rationality if you are not prepared to alter your beliefs in accordance with the evidence. It may be that I am just looking at too general a level of applicability, but it seems to me that when (1) there is a multibillion-dollar business predicated on the notion that it is possible to inspire action by people through methods that do not rely on their conscious awareness, (2) the people who work in this industry act as if this is true and explicitly assert their intention to have these effects, and (3) there is widespread evidence (in the form of increased sales) that these things work, it is naked wishful thinking to suppose that advertising is not working. Yes, the success attributed to advertising could just be correlation and not causation. But the correlations are impressive, and when they are combined with research on cognitive limitations, it strains credulity to think that none of advertising is causal.

Moreover, isn't the present advertising environment one that is imposed on us without our consent? All things being equal, I would like to have no more direct mail sent to me, no more credit cards offers, no more spam e-mails, no more telephone solicitations. I would like to be able to zip through the ads on television and in other entertainment venues, and I would just as soon have less in the way of product placement, which I find cheesy and distracting. But it turns out that I probably do not know what is good for me; that despite my expressed preference to live in a world with less advertising, it is really in my best interest that I (and every other American) live in the 360-degree, 24-7 advertising environment; and that any attempt to restrict advertising is really just a paternalistic attempt to impose on us a "nanny state." In the next chapter, I identify this argument—that we must subject ourselves to unrestricted advertising despite our wishes to be free of it—as a "tough love" kind of paternalism.

CHAPTER 7

Tough Love Paternalism

In some departments of our daily life, in which we imagine ourselves free agents, we are ruled by dictators exercising great power.
—Edward L. Bernays, *Propaganda*

When it comes to restrictions on advertising designed to account for the exploitation of known cognitive limitations, even regulation's friends, such as Thaler and Sunstein, are likely to rather quickly concede that such interventions are "paternalistic."[1] Thaler and Sunstein attempt to offset the negative connotations of paternalism by describing their proposals as "libertarian paternalism." There is, however, another way to characterize such interventions—as not paternalistic at all, at least not any more so than is inherent in government. Perhaps they are simply democracy at work, government doing for us what we are unable to do for ourselves —in this case, to offer some insulation or a counterforce to the daily bombardment of professional persuasion efforts.

If, as Thaler and Sunstein argue, choice architecture is unavoidable, the question is, who gets to organize that architecture—the corporations with something to sell and an obvious interest or "we the people"? If sellers organize choice architecture in a manner that is inimical to the public health, why should the government not be able to reorganize or otherwise redistribute incentives? The answer is apparently that proponents of freedom for commercial expression view the unceasing bombardment of marketing pitches as good for us, whether we know it or not. When the refusal to regulate marketing or, indeed, to give consumers protection that they ask for is justified on this ground, we can see it for what it is—not antipaternalism but merely paternalism of a different sort, a sort of "tough love."

If a rule protects commercial speech even where that speech is demonstrably and intentionally false (which is what the strong version of First Amendment protection would do), however harsh the consequences, on the theory that any other rule would be too paternalistic, we simply have paternalism of a different stripe, tough love—hard paternalism rather than soft, protective paternalism. When one considers the relative advantages and incentives of each side in this struggle, regulation of commercial expression looks less like paternalism of any sort. We do not argue that criminalizing assault presents people with a moral hazard because it discourages them from staying fit or learning valuable self-defense skills. Marketing can be a form of assault. It is not paternalistic to forbid assaults.

Trying to Make the Great Escape

We live in an advertising blitz. You cannot get away from marketing even if you want to do so, and there is evidence that many people do want to. Consumers have indicated in various ways that they would like to avoid being pitched—at least sometimes—hence the popularity of TiVo, do-not-call registries,[2] software to block pop-up ads on the Internet and electronic cookies, and other attempts to short-circuit spam in our e-mail in-boxes. Yet when the government moves to try to limit the ways in which marketing can be conducted, to require disclosure, or to ban advertising for some products in some contexts, these efforts are often met with massive legal resistance by advertisers who argue that such restrictions on advertisers' speech is unconstitutional. If the First Amendment is meant to protect autonomy, as Emerson suggested, and if the people express a desire for a shield against some sorts of marketing, governmental limitations would appear to advance, not interfere, with autonomy interests.

However, commercial speech's supporters are mostly unmoved by the observation that many people wish to be free of advertising, perhaps because it is really the advertiser's autonomy they are concerned about. But advertisers' autonomy to conduct their businesses any way they like does not seem to be the sort of autonomy interest Emerson was talking about. Nor does it have much crowd appeal. It is far more attractive to argue that regulation interferes with consumers' autonomy. So even as many are struggling to escape advertising, the argument is made that governmental regulation of commercial expression interferes with listeners' autonomy interests and raises the specter of the dreaded "nanny state."

As one observer put it, "do you trust the government enough to appoint it your guardian?"[3] When the question is phrased this way, the answer is "Probably not." But the comment assumes that by not interfering, the government is protecting your freedom, when it actually is making a choice, purportedly on your behalf, that you might have made differently. The writer making this comment was responding to a proposal to tax sugar-sweetened beverages. These are beverages that have almost no nutritional value and that contribute significantly to national struggles with obesity and diabetes.[4] They are also among the most heavily advertised products.[5] A tax would be one way of attempting to alter incentive structures, presumably one that is less intrusive than banning the advertising of the product or the product itself. Arguably, such a tax might serve as a counterforce to all those advertising efforts. Why it is paternalistic to tinker with choice architecture in this way is not clear.

It is even less clear when the claim is made that the First Amendment prevents the government from mandating disclosures. If you are staking your argument for freedom of commercial expression on opposition to governmental paternalism, it is rather awkward to explain what is so paternalistic about requiring disclosure of the truth. Yet the First Amendment is also raised against disclosure rules for the sale of securities, the fat and calorie content of fast food, the health risks of smoking, or even the real identity of a speaker. So, for example, when the Federal Communications Commission proposed banner notices identifying product placements, advertisers and media entities cried foul, claiming that the First Amendment prohibited such disclosures. It is difficult to understand how providing truthful information—such as "the following products paid to be featured in this movie" or "this is a sponsored product"—represents governmental paternalism or in any way interferes with listeners' interests. Of course, once you know about the third-party technique, you know why advertisers object to these proposals. But it has nothing to do with listeners' freedom, autonomy, or choice and everything to do with the advertisers' freedom.

If government is supposed to be enacting laws for the benefit of the public, it is not at all self-evident that people would mostly choose a long, abstemious life over a short, more indulgent one. But neither is it absurd to suppose that in forming a government to act in our behalf to protect us from others, we might also want it to protect us against our own worst impulses and create incentives for actions in our long-run (versus short-run) best interest. Consumer support for interventions like the Federal Trade Commission's National Do Not Call Registry suggests that people sometimes do want governmental intervention. They tend to feel this way about product safety, truth in lending, truth in labeling, and a host of other regulations designed to save consumers from spending a great deal of time trying to verify product information or from potentially costly trial and error.

Paternalism and Autonomy

There is no question that many people would like to be free, in varying degrees, from marketing appeals. As it stands now, however, most people have little control over the amount of their exposure to advertising and often are not given the option to opt out of marketing. To the extent that notions of autonomy seem to be largely based on assumptions of conscious choice exercised in a condition of knowledge (perfect or otherwise), advertising and marketing speech does not seem to be a good candidate for protection on the grounds that it allows the exercise of freedom of choice. Opponents of advertising regulation claim that such regulation would interfere with people's choices. They argue that the choices in question may not necessarily be "rational," strictly speaking, but are nevertheless the people's own choices and that it is therefore unwarranted paternalism to interfere with those choices by imposing restrictions on advertising and marketing.

There is no question that within a consumerist society, promotional speech presents us with more choices of goods and services. It is surely an aspect of freedom that laptops come in more than one color. A world in which all computers were gray might be less stimulating, less satisfactory. But people want to express themselves and to experience freedom with respect to more than simply their consumption choices.[6] I do not mean to disparage the pleasures of consumption or the delights of having a dazzling array of choices of ways in which to spend one's money, but it trivializes notions of freedom to suggest that preserving these sorts of freedoms are a preeminent concern of the First Amendment. Surely, the First Amendment is intended to protect something a little more substantive than dozens of brands of breakfast cereals.

Moreover, as discussed in the last chapter, much marketing relies on manipulation of cognitive limitations or emotional responses. It is true that not everyone manifests these shortcomings to the same degree. But marketers depend on the notion that most of us have them. A casual glance at the professional literature makes this clear. Since much marketing is aimed at making the target feel special, it might make sense for someone to say they enjoy being manipulated (and it is often a pleasant feeling to be the object of a selling message) and still be consistent with notions of autonomy. In many cases, it may be similarly desirable and consistent with autonomy to remain uninformed. A certain amount of denial is probably crucial to good mental health. That does not mean we want to make a virtue of ignorance. Still, we often think that autonomy and freedom mean being free to go to the devil in our own way, thank you very much.

Governmental interference is particularly distasteful when it is intended to shield people from the truth. If there is anything that represents unwarranted paternalism, surely it is shielding people from the truth. This was precisely the argument the Supreme Court found compelling in deciding the *Virginia Pharmacy* case—that to keep people unaware of prescription drug prices out of fear that they would not be able to handle the information was unjustifiably paternalistic. However, from this observation that the government should not protect people from the truth, it does not follow that the government must protect the right to lie or to undermine people's efforts to exercise their autonomy in ways that allow them to avoid advertising, demand information, or shield themselves and their children from marketing. It is perfectly consistent with autonomy interests to declare you would like to avoid advertising.

Other People's Vulnerabilities

To press the case that regulation of marketing is paternalistic, proponents of freedom for commercial expression must trivialize the effects of marketing—and they do. This puts them in something of a bind. On the one hand, industry argues that advertising is critical to business interests. On the other, when confronted with claims that some of this advertising is harmful to its targets, industry often argues that it is mostly ineffective or trivial. How can it be simultaneously essential and trivial? It is a paradox.

What may explain this paradox is the unstated assumption by commercial speech's defenders that if advertising works on you, it is because you are not sufficiently savvy, and thus you deserve what you get for your credulity—never mind that this category includes virtually everyone. Put another way, the prey should have taken better care not to be prey. If most people thought that they were included in the category of prey, this argument would not be very convincing and would seem breathtakingly callous. The reason it works so well is that, as advertising professionals know, "[n]obody wants to admit they're in the least bit affected by advertising."[7]

Similarly, to preserve the advertiser's freedom to continue to engage in commercial speech, the antipaternalism argument relies on the (ironically) irrational attachment to rationality and on the felt desire to believe that one cannot be manipulated. Proponents appear to agree that advertising works on most people (otherwise, how could it be a business necessity?); they are just sure that they are not "most" people. They recognize that a lot of marketing is—to put it mildly—"puffing"; that is, it is made up of statements that, so the law says, no reasonable person should believe.[8] The inescapable conclusion is that in order to protect the ability of businesses to freely advertise, proponents of advertising freedom are willing to leave the majority of people to deal with marketing's effects as best they can, because, so the argument goes, respect for autonomy requires that the government not condescend to assume that people do not possess the ability to resist the blandishments of advertising. This expressed concern for others' autonomy allows supporters of freedom for commercial expression to both deny their own vulnerability and to defend marketing practices.

Defending Rationality

In much of the literature defending freedom of commercial expression, the consumer is portrayed as rationally pursuing his or her own ends and choosing goods that satisfy those ends, in a process with which defense of liberty requires that we not interfere. Preferences are exogenous and, unhelpfully for our purposes here, not discriminated among as long as they are legal. For some preferences, the state declares that however much the citizen might feel the good in question would assist in his or her self-definition or self-expression, it is not permitted. One is not free to choose to smoke marijuana or to consume LSD (or, rather, one is free to do so only if one is prepared to risk going to jail). Whether or not one ought to be free to do so is another question (and there is little in logic to recommend the choices in penalties and prohibitions when it comes to psychotropic substances in the U.S. drug enforcement scheme). But given these substantive constraints on expressive and consumption choices, it cannot be said that making distinctions between types of substances is theoretically improper or illegitimate, because the law already has such limits. So we cannot say, to paraphrase Milton Friedman, that the government ought not to interfere in economic choices as long as they are legal, since this statement sets up a tautology. That is precisely the question: what ought to be illegal?

Laws allocate risk and loss. A law that permits a consumer to recover for (or the government to sanction) false statements made in order to obtain the benefit of the sale represent the allocation of risk of falsity to the one making the statement. Conversely, caveat emptor allocates the risk of falsity on the consumer. Demanding procedural hurdles and high burdens of proof before obtaining a recovery allows for fine-tuning and allocates risks along a continuum of these two extremes, ranging from strict liability to intentional wrongdoing, depending on the circumstances that lawmakers wish to discourage versus those for which they seek to offer incentives. The proper functioning of the market and the public welfare suggest that false commercial speech should be discouraged. Consumers require truthful speech to make informed decisions, and sometimes they have expressed the preference to be free of advertising.

Antipaternalists suggest that claims of the universality of various cognitive limitations, limitations that could be exploited by marketers, are exaggerated.[9] They argue that because debiasing sometimes works or that experience can teach people to compensate for cognitive biases, this means that people should be exposed to, rather than shielded from, these bracing learning opportunities, lest we create moral hazards through offering the wrong incentives.[10]

In this view, even if we know that many consumers do not wish to be exposed to marketing messages (which we do), the freedom of the advertiser to reach these audiences should be supported, because it is better for the audience and, thus, ultimately for society as a whole to be offered this opportunity to learn to resist such blandishments rather than to be shielded from the benefits of trial and error. It is as if the proponents of advertising freedom are saying, "Yes, we know that you might rather avoid this advertising, but it is good for you to be exposed to it. You can build up resistance to it! You'll thank me for this later!" Now who is being paternalistic?

When we consider this argument, that learning to resist advertising will be better in the long run, we must also consider whether people might have long-run preferences other than learning to resist advertising or not to believe everything they hear, preferences that, if given the choice, they might put in front of this putative learning experience. For example, they might also prefer to resist impulses to eat a donut or smoke a cigarette or drink a high-calorie beverage, and they might prefer not to have advertising pushing these products in their faces every day. Short-term preferences to indulge often overwhelm these long-term preferences, with or without advertising. However, advertising acts as a thumb on the scale. It is intended to intensify the pull of the immediate, and there is evidence that it works, even on well-educated people who might fondly imagine they are immune.

Fatal Attraction

In 1976 Harvard law professor Vern Countryman was speaking at a conference on commercial speech at the University of Miami. In the context of making a point about the informational aspects of advertising, he made the following offhand remark: "I have recently been persuaded that I can safely keep on smoking if I change to a cigarette that is advertised to have less tar and nicotine than the brand I previously smoked."[11] This, he argued, was an example of the sort of useful, informational function performed by advertising that would be lost if commercial speech were subject to excessive regulation. Ironically, his example perfectly illustrates how misplaced his characterization was. The advertising that suggested that smoking light cigarettes was safer was not information, because it was not true. Smoking "light" cigarettes does not make smoking safe or even safer.

The tobacco companies encouraged beliefs like Professor Countryman's through commercial expression that took many forms: advertising, PR news placements, seemingly authoritative figures' denials of health detriments, and many other communications efforts. But all the while, the tobacco companies knew what the rest of the public did not: that there was no health benefit to smoking light cigarettes, because nicotine is addictive (and virtually all smokers are addicted), and smokers who smoked cigarettes with lower tar and nicotine would compensate for the lower nicotine by sucking harder on the cigarette.[12] They would smoke the cigarette further down to the butt and smoke more of them, so any virtue of the lower tar and nicotine content (assuming there was any at all) was completely lost.[13] This information was locked in the tobacco companies' proprietary archives. They actively attempted to prevent the negative information from becoming public and did everything in their power to discredit and suppress truthful information that was available about the health risks. In these efforts, the companies could take advantage of the psychological vulnerability of their customers, vulnerabilities they knew about through their research.

As an industry official noted in 1982, "[M]ost of those who have smoked for any significant time would like to stop."[14] Yet because nicotine is addictive, nicotine made it difficult to quit smoking. The companies knew that smokers would grasp at any justification, no matter how thin, to continue smoking. Consequently, a good deal of their marketing efforts involved giving smokers reasons for why they did not have to quit. They intended to provide what they described as a "psychological crutch and a self-rationale to continue smoking."[15] One such crutch was the oft-repeated claim that there was no clear link between smoking and cancer. Another was offering the irrelevant choice of "light" and "low tar" cigarettes. This language implied, without actually claiming, that these features made smoking safer, even though the industry wanted to claim that smoking was not unsafe in the first instance.

Bombarding smokers who want to quit with false information intended to suggest that they do not need to quit and to keep them from getting access to accurate information hardly seems calculated to further their autonomy interests. People who succumbed to the addictive properties of cigarettes and subsequently wanted to quit might experience the confrontation with cigarette ads, the placement of attractive rationalizations for not quitting, and the glamorization of smoking as ways in which the industry undermined their ability to actualize their desire to quit. If a Harvard law professor believed the pitch, perhaps there is not much hope for the rest of us.

Regulation for the People

Defenders of freedom for commercial expression respond to concerns about the manipulative aspects of advertising and marketing practices by charging that the concerns are based on exaggerated representations about the effectiveness of advertising. These exaggerations have created "the folk myth of managerial infallibility in divining the consumer's psyche."[16] But the evidence does not support the proposition that advertising mostly does not work. Even if these attempts to manipulate consumers' choices based on appeals to unconscious motivations were to work even *half* of the time it would be a big problem where dangerous products like cigarettes are concerned and a significant encroachment on consumer autonomy in every case. When the question is what is the best rule to enact for the public welfare — that is, what is best for most people, not what is best for most exceptionally intelligent people or what is best for capital—regulation of commercial speech seems appropriate and not at all paternalistic. It may seem overwhelmingly persuasive to some observers that there is some evidence that debiasing works, that it is more respectful to allow people to make their own mistakes and to learn from those mistakes, but where the costs of mistakes are sufficiently high, it is not good public policy to adopt a policy of unyielding caveat emptor.

Where the consequences for mistakes are particularly high and the likelihood of errors is also fairly high, it becomes harder to make the case for a laissez-faire approach to commercial speech. Most of us are eager for ways in which to make a priori assessments about the safety of products rather than learning the hard way. As Ezra Mishan observed (in a piece published from the same symposium at which Professor Countryman made the comment quoted earlier), relying on experience to decide which products are safe is less than ideal.

> On this interpretation, a parent who is anxious to know whether a pet boa constrictor is likely to make a meal of a human infant ought to be persuaded to buy one and find out for himself. Surely the demand by the consuming public for product information arises just from a desire to avoid incurring the costs, *sometimes very heavy costs,* involved in the actual experience of the products.[17]

Human beings are concerned with freedom in many respects, and freedoms of choice and action exist in time, such that a choice made may often foreclose other choices. There is little moral force to the argument that people are justly left to the outcomes of their choices when those choices have been shaped in material ways without their knowledge or consent and without some element of material information. Commercial speech practices offer substantial evidence that they employ means of persuasion that are nonobvious or subconscious and that enormous resources have been devoted to attempting to affect those choices without appealing to rational thought. Such evidence makes it more difficult to describe the choices made within that system as "free." It offers correspondingly weaker support for protecting the modes of speech that channel those choices, on the grounds that doing so is antipaternalistic.

There are, no doubt, moral reasons to approve of a policy that allows people to "pay for their mistakes," particularly when the alternative is to let other people pay for their mistakes. Allocation of risks also entails allocation of burdens. But why should this principle be limited to consumers? For example, the blame for the subprime mortgage crisis and the ripple shocks it caused across the spectrum of the whole economy falls on lenders and predatory lending practices as much as or more than on the borrowers who borrowed money that they ended up being unable to repay. The lenders are in the business of lending money to make a profit and have at their disposal tools for making sophisticated risk assessments that the individual buyer does not have.[18] Would it not create a moral hazard for lenders if they were allowed to avoid the consequences of their irresponsible lending practices? In the wake of "too big to fail," one could argue that the greater moral hazard is not one facing individual borrowers but the one facing the institutions.

Of course, because the failure of large institutions affects not only those connected to it directly but many others, there may be prudential reasons to insulate them from the consequences that (ultimately) will only be "felt" in any meaningful sense not by the entity but by the people. Although, as a general matter, self-discipline and restraint are admirable qualities that a nation might rationally attempt to cultivate, there is no question that deciding what is good for someone else, whether restricting or enlarging choices, is always a proposition fraught with the potential for (at best) well-meaning overreaching and (at the worst) self-serving despotism. However, that may apply as much to the aim of developing self-discipline and restraint in a populace as to attempting to protect them from themselves.

Risk allocations are a topic that a people can presumably democratically decide. On many questions, the electorate may be of two minds on marketing, because people have multiple roles in society. For example, many people want to avoid direct mail solicitations. When considering a ban on direct mail, if people are thinking and voting as owners of small businesses that rely heavily on direct mail, they might vote against a ban. But if they are thinking and voting as potential recipients of direct mail, they might vote for a ban. We rely on voting and representative democracy to sort out these preferences.

Corporations that send direct mail would obviously not be in favor of a ban, but (theoretically) they do not get to vote. If a majority of the electorate voted to ban commercial direct mail on the grounds that it was wasteful and annoying and that, in the main, they preferred not to receive commercial solicitations at home, why should it offend the First Amendment for them to do so? Why does this present a moral hazard? Does our interest in autonomy reflected in the First Amendment really require us to submit ourselves—our mailboxes, our eyes, our ears, our senses—to unremitting sales pitches?

Apparently, to the antipaternalists, the answer is yes. The antipaternalists appear to believe that restrictions on marketing communications should be rejected because people ought to be required to learn how to resist the hard sell. This learning is, they say, made possible by exposure. Through exposure, consumers can learn to resist these endless blandishments. We are better off, so the argument goes, with a rule that cautions the buyer to beware, caveat emptor, rather than one that interposes a governmental assessment of what is in our best interest. The doctrine of caveat emptor (and, for that matter, the puffing doctrine) justifies leaving buyers where they lie after a sales pitch has convinced them to buy a product that does not deliver what was promised, on the grounds that the buyers ought to have been more careful.

Experience with this rule has suggested that most of us do not actually want to transact business in this sort of Hobbesian war of all against all. So at least politically and probably economically as well, regulation has sprung up to mitigate the harshness of rigid caveat emptor. Such regulation may in some cases help avert costly market failures. These laws range from securities regulations, labeling regulation, prohibitions on false advertising, disclosure requirements, warning labels, disclaimers, and a host of other regulations of speech—regulations that the proponents of full protection for commercial speech would presumably prefer to see set aside as overly paternalistic. Even if voters have lobbied their representatives for a particular rule, the antipaternalistic argument appears to be an assertion that voters cannot be trusted to know what is best for them,[19] for if they did, they would surely choose a regime of caveat emptor. This assertion is both paternalistic and antidemocratic.

Putting aside the paternalism reflected in existing laws regulating commercial speech, it is not clear why antipaternalism justifies less regulation rather than more in the current marketing climate, where marketers have far more knowledge about purchasing behavior and persuasion techniques than buyers do. A refusal to intervene means leaving the overwhelming majority of people at the mercy of professional persuaders, on the grounds that it is better for people to learn from their mistakes. While this may be true as a moral hypothetical, what such a rule does in reality is permit predation.

The law already makes distinctions among types of transactions, so why not do so in other cases as well, like those where the stakes are very high for health and safety? In some cases, for some people, mistakes are fatal. Do we want people to run the risk of fatal mistakes, like overdosing on a medication, rather than require an effective warning? (The distinction of effectiveness is important, since not all warnings are effective.) One of the legitimate functions of government is to regulate for the public's health, safety, and welfare. Thus, from a public policy perspective, the government has a legitimate role in assuring that people have accurate information with which to make decisions with rather more serious consequences than the "mistake" of buying a refrigerator in avocado green. Consider the following examples:

- There is some evidence that credit cards encourage people to spend more than they ordinarily would, by bypassing the pain of paying cash. Should it be appropriate to market credit cards to college students?[20]
- Drug companies have, some argued, created disorders that they then developed medications to treat. Direct-to-consumer advertising for an illness like social anxiety disorder is intended to inspire people to ask their doctor for these medications,[21] ones that could potentially have serious side effects. Is that practice consistent with sound strategy for public health?

- Imagery, packaging, and promotional appeals are often designed to increase logo recognition among children and teens for products like tobacco or alcohol, which are not legal for them to use.[22] Are limitations on this marketing really "paternalistic"? If so, are children not appropriate targets for paternalism in the first place?
- Some banks engage in data mining to identify people who are experiencing financial difficulties. Should it be appropriate to send "convenience checks" for balance transfer or cash advance loans to these people where the loan terms, including interest rates and terms relating to what constitutes an instance of default, are not clearly disclosed and where the bank knows that the form of this solicitation is particularly likely to overcome resolutions to resist new loans?[23]
- Many sellers of grooming or diet products that may have negative health consequences to users deliberately employ marketing techniques that rely on stimulating anxieties about appearance.[24] Is this consistent with public health and safety?

It is one thing for a person who does not have any financial insecurity to be bombarded with blank checks for lines of credit. It is another thing altogether to direct such a blizzard at someone who may be dealing with health problems or a job loss. These circumstances make having to repeatedly throw these checks away a never-ending exercise in self-restraint. Many consumers will predictably lose such an exercise. Indeed, the blitz is predicated on the knowledge that while many people will throw these checks away, the industry will be kept afloat by those who will not. (The checks thrown away create another public hazard—the risk of identity theft.) How does permitting these and other sorts of bombardments enhance the targets' autonomy? Moreover, false speech is theoretically not entitled to protection under the First Amendment, and much commercial expression is false. It is difficult to follow why anyone's autonomy is enhanced by allowing marketers to inject false statements or noise into the stream of communications.

Truth, Freedom, and Autonomy

There are at least a couple of possible responses to this objection. The first is the familiar dicta from *New York Times v. Sullivan* to the effect that we may have to tolerate a certain amount of false speech in order to get the optimal amount of speech, that the cost to our civil liberties in attempting to suppress all false speech would be too great. This is the "optimal fraud" argument. Still, while it might be dangerous for the government to be in the truth-verifying business, is it any less dangerous to leave that function to those very powerful entities directly interested in the outcomes where the management has not been elected to its positions of power over the public? Which approach is less dangerous may be an open question. Which is less democratic does not seem open to question.

When we compare the relative strength of the three interested groups—big businesses, the government, and consumers—we might be tempted to conclude that the dangers of an unfettered, free-for-all of communication in the commercial arena are worse than the specter of governmental regulation of commerce, particularly when you consider that the government has at least some pretensions to legitimacy in regulating for the public welfare. Corporate social responsibility initiatives notwithstanding, there is little evidence that corporations are designed to or in fact do largely view themselves as institutions run for the benefit of the public. In contrast, government is supposed to be run for the benefit of the public. It may often not live up to its promise, but that is its legitimate object, and it can be called to account by the electorate when it fails in this task. It is much harder to counter efforts like those of the tobacco companies to inject false information in the public sphere.

Sometimes tobacco is cited as a special case. However, the incentives and the devices employed by the industry to defend itself from the truth and support its profitability are indistinguishable from many of those used by oil companies to deny global warming, by Nike to defend its labor practices, or by cereal makers to defend marketing sugary cereals to children. It does not advance consumers' autonomy to tell them that they can "make a difference" in global warming, breast cancer, labor exploitation, or animal cruelty by buying a particular product or service if it is not true. Requiring a connection between such claims and their truth would, however, enhance consumers' autonomy.

Of course, sometimes marketing claims are inherently unconnected to any empirical reality, so the inability to substantiate them is intrinsic to the claim. There is no way to verify a claim that a particular brand is "cool" or "hip." The same cannot be said of the claim "We comply with all minimum wage laws." That claim is susceptible to verification. It is the sort of claim that courts test the truth of every day. It hardly seems paternalistic to give people information relevant for their decisions, and to refuse them access to this information or to allow institutions that have devoted substantial resources to discovering how to manipulate consumer responses at a preconscious level to say whatever they please without any consequences does not seem to enhance truth or autonomy.

Similarly, when the Federal Communications Commission and the Center for Media and Democracy sought to require stations airing video news releases (VNRs) to disclose the sources of those releases rather than presenting them as straight news, several media outlets claimed that a limitation on VNRs (or even disclosure) would infringe on their First Amendment rights. They made this argument notwithstanding that one result of this practice may be the corruption of the reliability of news. When the news becomes sufficiently corrupted that the public no longer believes the news or cannot distinguish between it and advertising, the very thing that made it desirable to use this device in the first place, the apparent disinterestedness of the news source and its authority, will be destroyed as well. The practice suggests that both media and advertisers are heedlessly poisoning the well of the resource on which they both depend. Presumably, the same First Amendment claim would be made to any attempt to require disclosures of PR content in the print context. Can it be the case that the First Amendment also renders us powerless to protect the integrity of the press? If so, that would be deeply ironic.

The paternalism argument must presuppose some sort of rough equivalence of starting points that justifies leaving people where they lie. Otherwise, it hardly seems to make sense to accord the antipaternalistic stand as having moral weight, since there is no particular virtue associated with taking candy from a baby or, more to the point, getting a baby to take it. When it comes to commercial speech, even a cursory review of the existing landscape, pitting the individual consumer against the accumulated institutional knowledge and the forces in play, suggests that the analogy is not far off. When it comes to advertising to children, getting candy to a baby is not even a figure of speech. It is simply reality. Moreover, as we know, children are one of the most beloved targets of advertising messages. It is appropriate to be paternalistic with respect to children. Why should the First Amendment shield marketing to children?

Paternalism and Children

There is a great deal of evidence that children between the ages of two and eight cannot sort out the difference between advertising and editorial or informational content.[25] A task force of the American Psychological Association has observed that children below seven or eight years old are particularly susceptible to advertising, tending "to accept commercial claims as truthful and accurate because they fail to comprehend the advertiser's motive to exaggerate and embellish."[26] For these reasons, the task force identified advertising directed at children in this age range "inherently unfair."[27]

Litigation against the tobacco industry has revealed evidence supporting a connection between advertising strategies and tobacco use among teenagers.[28] It also revealed that, representations to the contrary notwithstanding, the industry had intentionally been attempting to appeal to what it referred to as "presmokers," out of recognition that the industry would have to continue to add to its customer base as its customers died or quit smoking in the face of the evidence of health risks of smoking. It is also clear that these marketing efforts have had some effect.[29] One study reported that Joe Camel scored a recognition rate of 91.3 percent among six-year-olds.[30]

It is not unusual for an industry to have the best information about the behavior of the consumers that make up its potential base, since those industries have a powerful incentive to investigate that behavior and, in many cases, the resources to pursue it. Thus, we should not be so quick to dismiss the claims of advertising professionals about what they can deliver. The question is, why should techniques that seem offensive to the dignity and autonomy of the individual be constitutionally protected? This question is particularly apt when considering promotional speech aimed at children.

No one argues that children have the same cognitive abilities as adults or that they are exercising their autonomy interests in the processing of commercial messages. We know that they do not understand the motives of advertisers and cannot distinguish between advertising and editorial content until they are about eight years old. We do sometimes encounter the claim that although children are not themselves capable of satisfactorily sorting out commercial messages, parents are ultimately responsible for the outcome, since they control all spending and (so the argument goes) can control children's access to media.

With respect to the last argument, control of access and the admonition to parents to control their children's TV watching, the claim that this is an adequate response to 24-7, 360-degree marketing efforts is unconvincing. Anyone who is a parent can attest that it is well nigh impossible to shield your child from commercial culture even if you allow them to watch no TV at all, because advertising and promotion saturates the environment. Unless they also never attend movies, do not have any friends whose parents allow their children to watch TV, and are homeschooled and thus safe from the endorsements channeled through the public schools, children will be exposed to products that they may well ask for but that parents would prefer their children not have. Even such a cloistered child will encounter billboards; point-of-purchase displays in stores; ads in magazines, newspapers, and other print media; or pop-ups and video on the Internet. Once you begin to think about how to actualize this mythical parental control, it becomes apparent how unworkable it is.

Some would say, however, that, no matter what children ask for, it is the parents who hold the purse strings and therefore can control spending and, thus, the effect of the advertised products on children. This argument is only slightly more plausible than the cloistering scenario. Although obviously true in theory, this argument also breaks down on closer inspection. In the first place, although adults make the large purchases, children often have access to their own incomes, whether through their parents in the form of allowances or payment for chores or directly through work. Access to cash, as well as opportunities to make unsupervised purchases, means parents have something less than perfect control. But more fundamentally, just as it is pleasant to imagine oneself as impervious to the blandishments of advertisers, it appears to be equally pleasant for some people to imagine that their own children are well supervised and that it is other people whose children experience difficulties, because their parents fail to toe a hard line on purchasing and instead "cave in" to children's requests that they should refuse.

Alternatively, some people appear to fall back on the notion that all this advertising is largely inconsequential, just a part of "the ways things are." They argue that people who worry about advertising's effect on their children are just worriers or, as they call Vance Packard, "paranoid." If so, what advertisers say about what they do fuels that paranoia.

A good part of the art of marketing is to unchain favorable purchase motives, or at least somehow to persuade the potential buyer that these desires are actually worthy and legitimate. So consumer marketing isn't so
much a job of instilling motives and desires as it is of opening up the ones
that are already there, of freeing up strong vital, but closely fettered urges
and impulses. (Of course, any similarity between this description and a
seduction is purely coincidental.)[31]

The argument that commercial speech contributes to autonomy seems in-
apposite for many reasons, and refusal to protect those who need or ask for
protection does not seem to entail respect for autonomy. The promotion of a
product like cigarettes, which so many users want to stop using but feel in-
capable of quitting, hardly seems to promote autonomy, particularly where it
is promoted to children. Addiction does not contribute to any reasonable notion of autonomy.

But some people might object that most people do not smoke and that
many people who used to smoke have managed to quit, so while addiction
may impinge on autonomy to some extent, it is simply a cost of that same autonomy by which the smoker first picked up a cigarette and began the process
of becoming addicted. That people quit proves freedom exists, according to
this argument, so we should not concern ourselves with the less rational or
those with weaker wills. Quite apart from the facts that this argument treats
the deaths and health care costs associated with smoking as simply an unavoidable cost of liberty, that the exercise of that liberty may come too late
to be meaningful for those who quit but nevertheless experience the negative
health costs, or even that the majority of smokers acquired the habit before
they were fully mature and thus, by definition, were perhaps not capable of
assessing the risks properly even had they been clearly presented, what is
more fundamental is that we are comparing the wrong liberties.

The correct assessment is not between a person's liberty to smoke and a
person's liberty not to smoke. The real question is whether the exercise of this
liberty requires unrestrained liberty for the seller to try to persuade the potential smoker by any means possible to exercise his or her own liberty to
smoke the cigarette that the producer has to sell. It is not immediately self-evident why, given a toxic product with such demonstrable social costs, liberty

requires that the public be assailed with promotional materials in favor of adopting this habit. This becomes a particularly pressing question when one considers the highly sophisticated mechanisms that have been developed to help these commercial communications along and that this and other similarly dangerous products are intentionally marketed to those too young to legally consume them.

Until now, I have been exploring the effect of commercial expression on the autonomy, expressive interests, and welfare of the consumer/listener, the person for whose benefit the commercial speech doctrine was developed. A close look reveals that very little commercial speech, except the truthful speech the doctrine identified for protection, contributes to any real autonomy for the listener. Any expressive interests seem rather insubstantial compared to the significant impairments it may impose on autonomy, freedom, and self-actualization. Compulsion is the antithesis of freedom.

There is, however, one more perspective. What are the interests of the speaker, particularly the corporate speaker, in commercial expression? In one sense, the answer to this question is easy—a commercial speaker's interest in commercial speech is identical to his or her interest in conducting a legal business. If the Commerce Clause has any meaning, there are legitimate limits that may be imposed on the conduct of a business. But recently there are suggestions that expressive rights arise from some notion of the commercial speaker as a separate entity with an interest different than the mere conduct of a business. Since much of the commercial expression this discussion is concerned about is conducted by corporations, I must ask, can a corporation have expressive interests? That question is the subject of the next chapter.

CHAPTER 8

The Corporate Person

> Did you ever expect a corporation to have a conscience, when it has no soul to be damned, and no body to be kicked?
>
> —attributed to Baron Edward Thurlow,
> seventeenth-century lord chancellor of Britain[1]

The idea of the "corporate speaker" is, for many people, inextricable from the legal and intellectual construction of the corporate person. There may be other grounds on which to extend First Amendment protection to commercial speakers, but this is the one that seems to most thoroughly capture popular and legal imagination. If the arguments that commercial speech contributes greatly to listener autonomy interests seem, at best, exaggerated and, at worst, to obscure the very real ways in which commercial speech impairs personal autonomy by limiting choices (even as consumers are made to feel their choices are expanded), the question remains, is there an autonomy interest for the speaker when the speaker is a corporation? This raises an interesting question: can a legal fiction have cognizable autonomy interests? Who *is* ExxonMobil? Does Nike have a personality? Do these questions even make sense? As noted twentieth-century legal realist and author Felix Cohen put it, "What right have we to believe in corporations if we don't believe in angels?"[2]

Yet, whether because of long judicial practice or just because of decades of advertising, we are accustomed to thinking this way, so that "What is the personality of McDonald's?" is a meaningful question. We are accustomed to thinking this way. Image advertising encourages it. It makes it seem like there can be such a thing as a "bad" corporation or, for that matter, a "good" corporation. Consistent with these tropes, some claim that the social artifact of corporate personhood, in combination with the legal fiction of corporate personhood, compels the conclusion that corporations should have First Amendment rights.[3] This contention is profoundly mistaken. Corporations are not organic creatures with a moral consciousness (or any consciousness at all for that matter) and so, as an entity, cannot be said to have personalities. Nor do they react to incentives as people do. Perhaps most significantly for this discussion, corporate persons do not have the needs human beings do: "[T]o dignify a profoundly non-human entity by awarding it rights [is] to confuse basic categories—like trying to control the behavior of animals by handing them pamphlets, or trying to make a machine operate more reliably by promising it a ticket to the movies."[4]

What's in a Name?

What does it mean for a corporation to be a person in the law? In the first place, legal personhood solves many prosaic, unglamorous problems. For example, can a corporation sue and be sued? Where is a corporation located for purposes of jurisdiction? Exploring these mundane questions reveals the almost metaphysical nature of the inquiry; it can lead to mistaking the legal fiction for the thing itself. Indeed, this was the thrust of Felix Cohen's famous article "Transcendental Nonsense." He argued that trying to answer questions such as "Where is a corporation?" by exploring the "nature" of the corporation resulted in absurd and futile jurisprudential inquiries and obscured that the correct response was to ask which answer would make the most sense as a matter of policy, given the task we want corporations to perform. He believed that facts and social and economic policy should inform how courts answered such questions, not treating metaphors as if they were real. But he lamented that lawyers were particularly prone to making this sort of error: "[L]awyers trained by long practice in believing what is impossible, will accept this reasoning as relevant, material, and competent."[5] As he put it, "When the vivid fictions and metaphors of traditional jurisprudence are thought of as *reasons for* decisions, rather than poetical or mnemonic devices for formulating decisions reached on other grounds, then the author, as well as the reader, of the opinion or argument, is apt to forget the social forces which mold the law and *the social ideals by which the law is to be judged.*"[6]

Despite Cohen's trenchant criticisms, the "thingification" of corporations continued throughout the twentieth century. It included the enactment of numerous criminal laws creating criminal liability not just for those who run corporations but for the corporations themselves. Yet those criminal laws are notoriously difficult to apply effectively.[7] Small fines simply become a cost of doing business; large ones are passed through the corporation and are borne mostly by consumers or innocent investors or, if the entity goes under, by innocent and guilty employees alike, as well as all the others—creditors and customers—with which it interacted.[8] There is no way to punish an entity that does not exist. Moreover, the entity cannot feel shame (even if shame or the threat of individual prosecution can operate as a modest deterrent to managers). Furthermore, a bad corporate reputation can be refurbished with a name change.

There are also a number of concepts critical to the law, particularly the criminal law, that would seem to have little or no operational effect with respect to a fictional entity. How can a nonhuman actor feel, think, or—crucially—be responsible? What does it mean to make an institution responsible? Can a corporation have malice or intent? Can it be "insincere"? There are no easy answers to these questions. However, calling a corporation a person makes the questions seem rational rather than nonsensical, obscures questions of policy, and diverts the fact finder to the sort of metaphysical questions Cohen criticized. It inspires the search for analogous substitutes or the development of new fictions rather than an admission that the fiction is only of limited usefulness to some inquires and of no use at all to others. In the introduction, I argued that all the expressive activity of a for-profit corporation is commercial speech because the organizational imperatives for a for-profit corporation limit its reason for being to engaging in commerce. Thus, anything the entity says is, by definition, "commercial." In this chapter, I explore this idea further and argue that the structure of a corporation, its absence of human interests, and its organizational dynamics offer pressing reasons for distinguishing between the corporate person and the natural (human) person for purpose of the First Amendment.

Corporate Misconduct and a "Few Bad Apples"[9]

If you opened a newspaper in the United States in the early part of the new century, it was difficult to escape news of the fallout from corporate excesses, involving such corporations as WorldCom, Enron, Arthur Andersen, Tyco, and American International Group (AIG).[10] Citigroup agreed to pay a $2 billion settlement in relation to its role in the Enron fiasco.[11] That settlement may have been a bargain, since, according to some observers, Citigroup's exposure in the Enron matter could have been far greater.[12] Many of the individuals associated with these failures went to prison, such as Bernard Ebbers (former CEO of WorldCom),[13] Dennis Kozlowski (CEO of Tyco),[14] and Ken Lay and Jeffrey Skilling of Enron.[15] Yet these failures were dwarfed by later failures of companies like Lehman Brothers and then by the potential failures of companies "too big to fail," like AIG and General Motors. Given the example of the early cases such as Enron, the subsequent failures in 2008 suggest that achieving the sort of fundamental change in corporate governance that would have prevented such failures has been an elusive goal.

Back in 2002, when it still seemed possible to say that "the rot," as represented by spectacular failures like Enron, could be contained, Congress passed the Sarbanes-Oxley Act to reform corporate governance to protect the public from similar meltdowns.[16] Sarbanes-Oxley was intended as a comprehensive reform of corporate governance. It was meant to prevent future failures like those of Enron, Tyco, and WorldCom.[17] It has obviously failed. It is probably impossible to identify all of the reasons for its failure and the persistence of problems in corporate governance. Deep structural failures in the system of public accounting, the commercialization of public accounting standards,[18] and regulatory failures are all undoubtedly a part of the explanation. But surely one reason can be found in the slipperiness of the corporate identity itself, the elusiveness of a figure to hold responsible for wrongdoing—the very feature Baron Thurlow claimed would permit corporations to "do as they like."[19]

Consider this: eleven years before Sarbanes-Oxley was passed, the United States Sentencing Commission had made a similar bid to discourage corporate wrongdoing by revising the federal sentencing guidelines to provide tougher penalties for criminal wrongdoing by corporations.[20] These changes were also intended to prevent corporate malfeasance. However, a study published in the *Journal of Law and Economics,* several years after these reforms were passed, found that those sentencing enhancements had had little effect on corporate behavior.[21] The experience with the efforts at reforming the sentencing guidelines offered a reason to be skeptical from the beginning that Sarbanes-Oxley would solve the problems it was meant to solve. Subsequent events seem to bear out that skepticism.

Surely, one of the reasons why such reform efforts fail is that the corporate person, by virtue of its incorporeal status, is, as noted, an elusive target for sanctions. In the first place, the corporation is indifferent to the most severe criminal penalty—the loss of liberty. For most purposes, the flesh-and-blood actors in the corporation—shareholders, officers and directors, executives—are shielded by law from personal liability for things that go wrong in the corporation. This law is found in legal doctrines such as the business judgment rule, in statutory exemptions from liability, in the contractual provisions for indemnification that most corporation statutes permit, in incorporation documents that limit liability, and in liability insurance policies for officers and directors.[22] All are various devices that shelter the human actors from responsibility.

Even in those circumstances where liability could theoretically attach to such persons, responsibility is often hard to locate in practice, because corporate officers, directors, and managers act within a collective.[23] The collective diffuses both knowledge and responsibility in such a way that no one person may really possess the sort of guilty knowledge that serves, in most cases, as a prerequisite for liability, certainly for criminal liability.[24] Consequently, criminal conviction of individuals for corporate wrongdoing is relatively rare. Undoubtedly, many of those executives who did find themselves convicted of a crime could say, along with former WorldCom accountant Betty Vinson, "I never expected to be here."[25]

The Amoral Person

In *The Corporation,*[26] author and legal scholar Joel Bakan engaged in a thought experiment; he took the notion that the corporation is a person and asked, "If it is a person, what *sort* of person is it?" Applying the criteria in the DSM-IV, the diagnostic manual for psychologists, he concluded that if a corporation is a person, that person is a psychopath. According to Bakan, the corporation is a psychopath because the focus on the economic welfare of the entity makes it relentlessly self-serving, something that is in many ways perfectly appropriate and desirable in a for-profit, nonhuman entity (as long as it is properly restrained by law) but that is less so in a human being. This is a brilliant exercise, because it illustrates the absurdity of taking the legal fiction of corporate personhood literally. Of course, corporations are not psychopaths (even if they often behave as if they were). The problem with corporations is not so much that they are "bad" persons. It is that they are not persons at all.

The Corporation has been subjected to withering criticism on the right for its purportedly one-sided and simplistic view of the corporation. But this mistakes the critique. Of course, corporations are not people; therefore, applying the DSM-IV to a corporation does not make sense. That is the point: it does not make sense. If it does not make sense to apply a tool intended to analyze human behavior to a nonhuman entity, perhaps it also does not make sense to push the legal fiction of corporate personhood too far and endow the corporation with expressive rights. This point seems largely to have eluded most critics. Bakan's genius was that in applying some of the problematic aspects of corporate conduct and calling them "personality" characteristics, he highlighted that these characteristics are stable enough to bear analogy to what we call "personality" in human beings and that they are arguably structural and endemic to corporations, not episodic or particular.

There is no doubt that The Corporation is polemical. However, Bakan is not alone in his criticism of the legal treatment of corporations as persons. The same criticism has been voiced by other commentators in the last decade or so, many of whom are themselves coming at the topic from careers in business or consulting,[27] a fact that ought to give pause to those who would dismiss Bakan's critique as wacky, left-wing, corporation bashing. The evidence that there might be something amiss with our corporate governance structures is all around us, not only in the numerous spectacular corporate failures of the twenty-first century, but also in the apparently routine amount of corporate misconduct.

The Structure of a Corporation

How the law ought to deal with corporations has always been a matter of some conceptual difficulty. Exactly what a corporation is or ought to be is a debate that has been pursued for most of the last century and that promises to continue into this one.[28] Is it a nexus of contracts and relationships, or is it a mere legal form? Is it an institution among many institutions in the modern economy (only partially distinguished by its pursuit of profit), or is it *defined* by pursuit of profit? In one sense, of course, the answer seems straightforward. If we were going to be descriptive, we would have to concede that for-profit corporations are one institution in a complex, interdependent web of institutions. Looked at from this perspective, it may not seem so irrational to consider, as indeed was reflected in the famous Berle-Means debate, that for-profit organizations ought to have and will sometimes behave as if they have social obligations. Moreover, they might be organized to enhance the likelihood that they will behave as if they have social obligations.[29]

This is the hope of the proponents of corporate social responsibility. Their view finds historical grounding in the original requirement that a corporate charter could only be granted for a public purpose.[30] Of course, corporate purpose has long since come unmoored from this limitation to public purpose, unless we conclude that conducting a business and accumulating capital is always a public purpose. That seems a step too far and is in conflict with other law that defines these institutions as "private."

Another approach has been to say that corporations are "institutions," with complex goals and social meaning that are not so different from many other institutions. Yet if we take this notion of "institution" seriously and treat the for-profit corporation as merely one of many institutions, so that the term *institution* encompasses not only for-profit companies but also not-for-profit corporations and government, then the term *institution* is so indefinite that it is not of much use analytically in deciding concrete cases.[31] If the word *institution* encompasses for-profit private companies and governmental organizations equally, it would seem to give corporations (again) a sort of quasi-public/quasi-governmental status. We are then no better off (if we are seeking a basis for finding a corporate speech right) in First Amendment terms, since, doctrinally, the First Amendment's injunction is against the government. If corporations become public actors in that sense, it seems that the First Amendment's strictures would apply to restrain corporate speech, not enlarge it. The government may have a right (or is it merely a power?) to speak, but it is not a right that stems from the First Amendment. If we adopt an institutional speech right, we are back in the business of drawing lines between covered and noncovered institutions.[32] Coverage may presumably be based on the very same sorts of distinctions between types of institutions (government or nongovernment, for-profit or not-for-profit) that some have argued is an analytically inappropriate basis on which to make distinctions among corporations in terms of the First Amendment.

Governments are the product of political and social forces. Law serves to legitimate and even limit power. You can have government without much law. But you cannot have law without government. Some institutions are creatures of law, and some are merely subject to it. Law may regulate churches, but it does not (at least in the United States) constitute it. Although people may band together to conduct a business, there is no necessity that they do so in the form of a corporation. They can choose many different forms. The corporation is one such form created by law. A corporation, unlike a church or a government or a political organization, is *purely a creation of law*. A corporation is what the law organizing its existence says it is. The defining characteristic of a for-profit corporation, under the law, is that it is *for-profit*. Exactly what the term *for-profit* means, to whom the duties to seek profit run, and what they must entail are less clear.

The Primacy of the Profit Motive

Pursuant to conventional interpretations of black letter corporate law, the corporation's officers and directors have primarily one duty—to maximize shareholder value.[33] Furthermore, as Professor Daniel Greenwood has observed, it turns out, both in theory and in practice, that this duty accrues not to real shareholders who can be expected to have a multiplicity of concerns but to the *idea* of a shareholder, the fictional shareholder who cares for nothing but short-term financial gain.[34]

> [H]uman shareholders who are also neighbors or employees or customers or friends may have other commitments beyond an extra nickel in the quarterly dividend. . . . A decrease in your phone bill is likely to be worth more to you than the commensurate drop in the price of the telephone company shares held by your pension fund. Only foreign shareholders with little connection to the American economy or politics beyond their

shareholdings approximate this conventional image of a shareholder always interested in higher stock returns.[35]

Officers and directors of corporations owe fiduciary duties to these fictional shareholders.[36] This construction of the shareholder has a lot in common with the economists' workhorse *homo economicus,* or the "rational actor." Like the economists' fictional rational actor, the fictional shareholder bears little resemblance to a real person. Yet the notion of the fictional shareholder offers analysts and managers an attractively simple and comparatively straightforward way to analyze a company's performance. Orienting management duties toward the interests of this fictional shareholder who cares for nothing but an economic return permits the administration of a corporation on behalf of a large group of shareholders, who might in fact have many disparate interests, by narrowing the focus of managers' duties to a relatively manageable set of goals. As it turns out, even this relatively narrow set of goals can be incredibly complex.[37]

There is a great deal of ambiguity about what exactly is best for shareholders—long-run stability, short-term gain, corporate image, and so on. The business judgment rule, together with management perceptions about what sorts of profit-sacrificing behavior is appropriate and necessary to conform to law and to social norms, allows corporations to engage in some behavior that is not straightforwardly profit-seeking. The personalities of (and choices made by) a corporation's executive officers can and do make a great deal of difference to the corporation's conduct of its affairs and the speech it issues, not solely in the negative ways of a Dennis Kozlowski or a Jeffrey Skilling, but also in positive ways through the values of a Warren Buffet or a Ray Anderson.[38] There undoubtedly is such a thing, from an anthropological point of view, as a "firm culture."[39]

All these things can be true and yet not add up to the conclusion that we must give the legal entity the status of a human being and protect its speech the same way that we would a human being's. This is because the legal structure of corporations also channels the behavior of the human beings within it in ways that may be distinctive *because* it takes place within the corporate entity. This may be true in other institutions as well. For example, soldiers may behave in ways inside the institution of the military that are distinct from the behavior they exhibit privately—say, to defer more to authority or to react with aggression. These behaviors are consistent with or at least related to the socially sanctioned behavior the institution valorizes and encourages. With respect to for-profit corporations, the behavior it valorizes is profit seeking (or sometimes just rent seeking). Arguably, it is this focus on the bottom line, combined with the degree to which the largest firms can shape and spin reality by virtue of their access to vast sums and the media platforms with a broad reach, that contributes to an atmosphere in which there may be large gaps between apparent commitments and actual practices. It leads to a situation where Enron could have, as many observers noted, a model code of ethics, an exemplary corporate governance structure, impeccable rhetoric related to ethical commitments, and yet a culture that exemplified the opposite of its stated goals.

The relentless forces of the market and the primacy of economic welfare as the legal imperative systematically channel even the most dedicated advocates of a different kind of corporate model into the same old pattern.[40] For example, sometimes a corporation's management will feel compelled by the consideration of profit to take actions that seem, on their face, to put the company in an unsympathetic light or to violate social norms (if not legal rules), in order to protect perceived value to shareholders. Managers justify such actions, as unpalatable as they may be, on the grounds that their duties to shareholders require it of them. We all know the phrase "Well, if it were up to me I would do (or not do) X. But I have a duty to my shareholders to do Y."

One of the more comical examples of this sort of move occurred when Johnson & Johnson sued the American Red Cross for trademark infringement. It had grounds. J&J *did* use the red cross mark first. When Clara Barton established the charitable organization the American Red Cross, she sought and received from J&J a license to use the mark, and she acknowledged J&J's priority. Presumably, the company granted the license believing that there was no danger that the charitable organization would ever be a competitor. Recently, however, the American Red Cross had been licensing the use of the mark to some of J&J's competitors, including the manufacturers of emergency first aid kits typically sold in drug stores. J&J was thus confronted with a dilemma. Pursuant to trademark law, if it did not sue to enforce the mark, it might be deemed to have surrendered its rights to the logo.

But as *Advertising Age* reported, J&J probably knew that "suing the American Red Cross for using—of all things, the Red Cross logo—wasn't a slick public-relations move."[41] That might be an understatement.

So why did J&J do it? One manager of a consulting firm contacted about the case claimed, "J&J did the right thing for both its reputation and its financial position. 'They absolutely had to [sue],' he said, regardless of the relatively small revenue impact and the reputation risk in taking on the Red Cross because 'estimates now are that 65%–70% of the total value of Fortune 500 companies are in their intangible assets.'"[42] Presumably he meant that even though the revenue risk today was small, the loss of a valuable intangible asset such as a logo, through acquiescence to infringing uses, would represent a greater financial loss in the long term than any harm to J&J's reputation from suing a humanitarian organization. The logo (asset) had to be protected, even if J&J had to sue the Red Cross (and eat up the charity's resources defending the litigation) to do it.

Needless to say, the CEO of the American Red Cross did not see it that way. When the suit was filed, he issued a press release saying, "For a multibillion-dollar drug company to claim that the Red Cross violated a criminal statute that was created to protect the humanitarian mission of the Red Cross—simply so that J&J can make more money—is obscene."[43] Since the Red Cross claimed to be engaging in this licensing practice in order to support hurricane awareness but was licensing products like humidifiers that do not qualify as hurricane relief supplies, we should not take this burst of outrage too seriously. Still, "obscene" or not, from the perspective of J&J's management, the shareholders made them do it.

The Responsible Company

This tendency of the profit imperative (however conceived) to generate what are antisocial, undesirable, or just plain unpopular activities is perhaps partly attributable to the laws governing for-profit corporations and partly a function of the difficulties in running large organizations, difficulties that make profit a seemingly straightforward and quantifiable goal compared to a morass of less-definable goals. It may also be partly attributable to social attitudes about what constitute legitimate goals in the context of business. But that the profit imperative eventually overwhelms alternative business models seems undeniable. One example of the force of this pull is the case of the Body Shop.

Anita Roddick founded the Body Shop, a cosmetics company, with the avowed goal of running a different sort of company, one that would be environmentally responsible and that would eschew ethically troubling animal testing. She was an outspoken advocate of corporate social responsibility. Nevertheless, Roddick eventually had to step down from her position as CEO, because her leadership was seen by those who mattered, the analysts, as not profitable.[44] As Roddick's successor at the Body Shop said, "We believe in social responsibility but we are very hard-nosed about profit. *We know that success is measured by the bottom line.*"[45] As noted by Joel Bakan, "Roddick's story illustrates how an executive's moral concerns and altruistic desires must ultimately succumb to her corporation's overriding goals."[46]

The history of the Ben & Jerry's ice cream company offers another familiar example. The founders of Ben & Jerry's, like the Body Shop's Roddick, made their business model a part of their marketing pitch. They wanted to appeal to consumers who wanted to support socially responsible businesses while also eating tasty ice cream. Yet despite the founders' commitment to social responsibility, the company was ultimately sold to Unilever, a large multinational Dutch/UK company. Unilever most assuredly does not have an image as a "different" sort of company. To some, the sale to Unilever undermined Ben & Jerry's credibility as a company committed to social justice.[47] Whether or not this is really the case or whether Ben & Jerry's was ever really "different" is almost beside the point. Either way, it seems that all roads lead back to the profit imperative.

These sorts of cases suggest that it is difficult to run a business in a way that is not business as usual—economic gain. Perhaps this is because, as Milton Friedman and so many others have argued, management, at the end of the day, has a duty to shareholders, not to the whole world. Moreover, managers have not been elected by anyone (except maybe the shareholders in some cases), and they have little or no training in what is good for the world. Their focus is on how to make the company profitable. The only limitations on how managers may carry out that duty to shareholders are those imposed by law, law written by legislators who are accountable to the electorate, a larger group than just shareholders.

Encouraging Bad Behavior

As we have seen, even law may represent a very weak deterrent to bad behavior, to the extent that managers may rationally (if not legally) decide to break the law and pay fines rather than comply with it. They may also calculate that the odds of being prosecuted are tiny. Or they may conclude that the odds of still being with the company when the day of reckoning comes for bad (but personally profitable) decisions are infinitesimal due to today's revolving door at the top spots. Worse still, the legal interpretation of managers' and directors' duties to shareholders as duties to a fictional shareholder who cares nothing for anything but economic returns actually creates structural incentives for these managers and directors to make trade-offs that would presumably be morally repugnant in other circumstances (e.g., choosing to market a drug that may carry with it an unacceptably high risk of injury without disclosing that risk for fear of losing sales), on the grounds that business ethics require it.

Daniel Greenwood, who teaches corporate law, writes, "[T]he fictional shareholder allows people to take actions they know are wrong while believing they are doing the right thing."[48] Putting aside the difficulty, in some contexts, with knowing something is wrong before the law has declared it to be wrong (a concern that presumably does not apply to exposing others to risk of death or serious injury), the problem is that this legal construction of the managers' duties does not just *allow* people to take actions that are wrong. It actually *encourages* them to do so wherever it would appear to maximize shareholder value.

Professor Greenwood offers a vivid example of this tendency with a hypothetical he regularly gives to his corporations students. In the hypothetical, students are asked to imagine that they are the manager of a business running a lunch counter in the South in 1963. The business is organized as a corporation. As was common in the South at the time, the lunch counter is racially segregated. Such segregation is legal. The manager nevertheless believes segregation is wrong. He would like to desegregate the lunch counter. But he has concrete evidence that the corporation would go out of business if he does so. "What should the manager do?" Greenwood asks his classes. Year after year, class after class, the students conclude that the manager's only options, pursuant to his duties to shareholders, are to resign his position or to continue to engage in behavior he believes is morally wrong. They determine that as long as the behavior he finds morally repugnant is legal and the market forces seem to endorse this morally repugnant practice, his duty to shareholders is to maximize their profits, not to engage in social reeducation.

> [The law] strongly hinders attempts to take actions that may not only be right, but in the best interest of all the real people concerned: Even most of the students who do not take refuge in the role morality of serving the fictional shareholder *are unable to articulate a principled basis for ignoring it.* The most they can do in good conscience is resign, leaving the administration of the firm to those who have less problem following institutional norms.[49]

In contrast, the external force of law offers a plausible and acceptable rationale for the manager to decline to engage in an otherwise profitable practice, like making false statements about your product's origin. Even if some managers would nevertheless flout the law and pay fines, a law prohibiting a practice gives management a plausible reason to eschew otherwise profitable actions—it is forbidden. Taking that force away just makes profit, already a strong motivator, more irresistible. When legal prohibitions against certain behaviors are absent and when other law requires concern for economic welfare of the corporation, the morally repugnant decision actually gains apparent moral force.

In addition, large, publicly traded corporations are bureaucracies with many of the same undesirable features of governmental bureaucracies. This may be particularly true where a handful of firms dominate the market. These large aggregations of people increase the potential to diffuse and dissipate whatever individual, human moral impulses its officers, directors, and employees may have and contribute uncertainty about the moral and legal responsibilities of individual employees.[50] Diffusion of responsibility and the fiduciary duty to attend to profit then become convenient instruments for suppressing guilt feelings about any particular actions.[51] They even make it difficult to locate responsibility when things do go wrong.[52] These are all very good structural reasons for concern that large, for-profit entities could easily be the source of much destructive speech as long as it was or seemed profitable and that their existence thus requires legal sanctions to act as speed bumps to slow or prevent that speech. Taking away the brakes hardly appears to be advisable.

Of course, the primacy of the profit motive is not, by any means, always a morally pernicious influence on corporate decision making and therefore hazardous to society. In the first place, the profit motive has been an engine contributing to one of the highest standards of living ever achieved in human history. We can also find many places where the desire for profit, combined with the identification of a previously underserved market, has resulted in greater acceptance of groups that were previously discriminated against.[53] For example, many companies have integrated the images in their advertising to include more people of color or more women (outside of advertising for cosmetics, clothing, and the like) and have discovered that it pays to recognize the Hispanic market or the African American market.[54]

Arguably, these trends all represent social advances for which we can thank corporate indifference to anything but the profit motive. (If you believe materialism is itself immoral, however, then you may regard the impulse to translate everything into market terms as immoral.) We do not need to resolve the question of whether the profit motive is or is not immoral in itself to decide whether corporations' single-mindedness on this issue may be one reason to treat the for-profit corporation differently than human beings or nonprofits in terms of the First Amendment. Moreover, focus on profit is simpler for the entities themselves than trying to embrace many other goals.

Corporate Social Responsibility

The singularity of corporate purpose offers managers some analytical clarity with respect to decision making, at least when compared to more nebulous social goals like "the general welfare" or "happiness." Despite multiple ways of calculating what constitutes the bottom line,[55] such options are models of clarity compared to attempts to assess nonmonetary contributions or impacts on social welfare. Thus, although the idea of corporate social responsibility (CSR), attempting to incorporate social responsibility into the legal duties of a corporation by taking account of the interests of constituencies beyond shareholders,[56] has gained popularity, that movement suffers from the absence of a legal structure (or indeed even a definition) that offers officers and directors clear guidance on what is a permissible departure from the profit maximization model.

On the one hand, the business judgment rule has generally proven capacious enough to protect judgments that trade off short-term profits for long-term benefits, including social ones. So shifting between long- and short-term payoffs could (theoretically) offer no obstacle to the implementation of CSR without any further amendment of existing corporate codes. On the other hand, when the magnitude of long-term gains is difficult to predict with any certainty or is intangible, managers could still expose themselves to shareholder liability if the alleged long-term benefits are intangible enough and the sacrificed short-term profits are very large.[57] In addition, there is no clear definition of what "corporate social responsibility" means:[58] "[C]ompanies fasten the label to a quite bewildering variety of supposedly enlightened, progressive or charitable corporate actions."[59] It is also often unclear whether actions undertaken in the name of CSR actually produce the aimed-for results. Moreover, since the corporation is not a democratic institution and its management is not elected by the public at large, it is reasonable to ask whether the acquisition of such public welfare responsibilities is appropriate.

Perhaps this is why the *Economist* suggested, in an editorial, that CSR as a theory is unnecessary.

> The goal of a well-run company may be to make profits for its shareholders, but merely in doing that—*provided it faces competition in its markets, behaves honestly and obeys the law*—the company, without even trying, is doing good works. . . . There is no need for selfless sacrifice when it comes to stakeholders. It goes with the territory.
>
> . . . All things considered, there is much to be said for leaving social and economic policy to governments. They, at least, are accountable to voters.[60]

While there is evidence that the rosy picture of an identity of interests between the corporation's pursuit of its profits and the general welfare is overstated in this quotation,[61] it is beyond dispute that private corporations are not accountable to voters as voters, except through the mechanism of governmental control. Whether what is in the best interest of business is necessarily always in the best interest of society as a whole has been an issue of fierce debate and fluctuating legislative trends from the inception of the United States. The argument that these interests converge and that many public welfare goals are best left to the market is an argument that has enjoyed a resurgence in the latter part of the twentieth century. It continues to be popular even into the present, despite the ample evidence of rather severe limits to that approach.[62] So it is worthwhile to reiterate what may seem to be obvious questions.

First, the *Economist* editorial observes, albeit in the manner of brushing aside an obvious and unproblematic constraint, that a company may only maximize profits within the limits of the law. Milton Friedman made a similar observation: "[T]here is one and only one social responsibility of business—to use its resources and engage in activities designed to increase its profits *so long as it stays within the rules of the game,* which is to say, engages in open and free competition without deception or fraud."[63] These statements offer no help at all in discerning what the limits of the law or the "rules of the game" ought to be.

When it comes to corporate speech, this is precisely the problem: what are the limits of the law? What *should* they be? It cannot be the case that the current laws represent a fixed state, from which no legal reform is legitimate. Presumably, it is possible to reform the treatment of corporate and commercial speech and thus what it means to "obey the law."[64] The question "What should the law be?" cannot be analyzed apart from the incentive structures within a for-profit corporation. Assuming that the law shields false statements, even those intentionally made, would a corporation (or, more accurately, its officers) not have a duty to make false statements whenever truthful statements might negatively affect profits?[65] Under the current understanding, it seems likely that many officers and directors would interpret their duty precisely that way, just as Professor Greenwood's students believe that the law required their fictional lunch counter manager to continue to engage in racial segregation.

Similarly, while it is true that people who make false statements might have many motivations to do so apart from financial ones, a financial motive is singled out as a singularly significant motive in a number of contexts. In some, a financial interest may constitute dispositive grounds to disqualify someone as a decision maker, if what we want is a detached decision maker. A financial interest is routinely considered a motivation of a different order and magnitude than other motives. Here are a few examples:

- Many state laws governing corporations define "conflict of interest" transactions as those where the members of boards of directors have a personal financial stake in a transaction.[66]
- Judges must automatically recuse themselves if they have a financial interest related to one of the parties before them.[67]
- For many crimes, a financial motive can be an aggravating factor in sentencing or even an element of the crime.[68]
- That unauthorized copying of copyrighted material is done for a commercial purpose (as opposed to a political or an educational purpose) may be a consideration in whether the copying qualifies as "fair use."[69]

In short, there are any numbers of areas where the law singles out financial benefit as a motivation that presents a heightened danger of the corruption of truth or impairment of the ability to render detached judgments. So why should it be so troubling to say that a for-profit corporation's status as a for-profit means that its speech should not be protected to the same degree as speech in other contexts? It seems reasonable to view the profit motive with the same cautiousness in the First Amendment arena as we do in others. This is particularly the case when we consider the problem of externalities.

Corporations as "Externalizing Machines"[70]

Economic activity can generate what economists call externalities, that is, costs to third parties. Something is "external" by virtue of its cost being absorbed by a party external to the transaction, that is, neither buyer nor seller. Environmental pollution is often cited as the paradigmatic example of an externality.[71] More subtle, corporate-created externalities may include the social costs to individuals caused by requiring that human capital, particularly top executives, be highly mobile;[72] by requiring working hours that some feel are incompatible with raising a family or caring for an elderly parent or other dependent person;[73] or by requiring workers to rapidly (or even instantly) acquire new skills in order to adapt to changing economic conditions.[74]

In some cases, corporate managers may conclude that a particular practice, characterized as a "cost," might actually represent an investment, because it will generate (or it is hoped it will generate) long-run benefits. For example, some companies adopt family leave policies more generous than those required by law because management believes it will help them recruit the best workers. But in many cases, companies have only internalized externalities because it was required by law (basic family leave policies, minimum wage laws, environmental laws). In other words, as long as the law does not require a particular practice, the logic of profit maximization suggests that the company should externalize the cost if possible. Social norms may result in internalizing a particular cost, but there is glaring evidence that this is not, by itself, a reliable source of internalizing social costs.[75]

"The corporation is an externalizing machine, in the same way that a shark is a killing machine,"[76] says Robert Monks, a business consultant and advocate for stronger shareholder rights, in an interview in *The Corporation*. "The corporation," he explains, "is deliberately programmed, indeed legally compelled, to externalize costs without regard for the harm it may cause to people, communities and the natural environment."[77] While his phrase "legally compelled" may be overstating the case, the preceding discussion suggests that the management of a corporation is certainly encouraged to externalize costs where possible. This does not make the corporation as a legal entity or any specific corporation "evil."[78] Rather, it illustrates that the corporation in general is inherently amoral. Its moral content is dependent on either the positive law or the vagaries of the personalities of the specific persons in charge at any given moment. If slave labor became legal, corporations might have a duty to engage in it under the current legal regime. If it became legal to kill rival executives, steal trade secrets, or kill people for lucrative body parts, presumably all or most corporations would do those things—not just the renegade few.[79] If the law makes it legal to lie (indeed, erects an almost impenetrable shield against liability), most corporations will disseminate falsehoods whenever it seems in their interests to do so.

Moreover, while neutrality may be desirable in a pluralistic society in which the content of such terms as "morally worthwhile" and "morally bankrupt" are fiercely contested, there are some public welfare goals that cannot be reduced to their economic terms or be allowed to be "neutrally" sorted on economic grounds. As Professor Greenwood observes,

[T]he . . . internal mechanisms of the corporation do not differentiate between making money by creating a good product or lobbying the law to
avoid the costs of a bad one. *A corporation driven by the profit motive is
morally indifferent* . . . [unless] those effects are not reflected in the returns to the shares.[80]

Law can be a force to set preferences outside of the profit motive as a disci-
plining force.

Legal Incentives

The law ostensibly sets the limits for corporate behavior, but because a corporation has no corporeal existence, the penalties for transgressing these
laws largely consist of monetary penalties.[81] Calibrating the amount of the
penalty to represent a real disincentive to future misconduct has always been
a difficult undertaking. Profits of many of those multinational corporations
that are most likely to have widespread impact on the public welfare are so
enormous that proportional penalties assume a size that, taken in a vacuum,
seem self-evidently excessive. It is politically difficult to assess fines that are
large enough. But taken in the context of the amount at stake, large penalties
may not seem so excessive.

For example, the majority of the penalty of $253.5 million set in a verdict
against Merck in one of the Vioxx cases included punitive damages. The
amount of those damages was "not picked at random."[82] Rather, it was
taken from "a 2001 Merck estimate of *additional profit* the company might
make if it could delay an F.D.A. warning on Vioxx's heart risk."[83] Note the
calculus that Merck engaged in when deciding whether or when to disclose
information: it estimated what a truthful communication of the risks of the
drug would cost the company. It should never be permissible to keep back a
critical piece of information, relevant to people's health, on the basis that
people's ignorance is more profitable. Nevertheless, companies do, and because defendants such as Merck have successfully managed to convince the
public and the legislatures to focus on the size of verdicts like this one in iso-
lation, they have succeeded in securing caps on damages that diminish the effectiveness of damages as penalties.

Even these restraints, such as they are, will be insufficient if a corporation's executives conclude that the penalties exacted by law will not diminish profits as much as the failure to engage in the prohibited activity. As author Joel Bakan notes, "Corporate illegalities are rife throughout the economy. Many major corporations engage in unlawful behavior, and some are habitual offenders with records that would be the envy of even the most prolific human criminals."[84] In support of this assertion, he lists the 42 violations or judgments (most relating to environmental infractions) issued against General Electric for the period between 1990 and 2001.[85] Moreover and perhaps more important, because a corporation is a conduit, any penalty assessed against it can potentially be passed on to the end user in the form of a higher price for the product or service.

Of course, not every company is in the position to raise its prices in order to pass on these costs. But if it cannot, any disability it incurs, whether diminution in revenues or, in the worst case, bankruptcy, ends up falling mainly on the heads of shareholders and employees, most of whom have had no role to play in making the decision to violate the law. This is not a very happy outcome. Civil sanctions in the form of regulation, permitting private rights of action for damages, injunctions, and the like, are thus only somewhat effective in deterring corporate misconduct. However, the availability of even these sanctions may be severely diminished if commercial speech receives full First Amendment protection.

All these aspects of the corporate person suggest that it does not have human need for self-expression. Moreover, they illustrate structural reasons for supposing that for-profit corporations cannot be expected to produce truthful or reliable information when it is not in their economic interest to do so. Because the world's largest corporations wield tremendous power, with the potential of imposing astronomical costs on millions of people (as with the blowout of the BP Deepwater Horizon oil rig), it is particularly important that some sort of mechanism can be used to counter the forces within the corporation that push it to suppress truthful information that is inconvenient or to engage in untruthful or harmful communications when it is in their economic interest to do so. That is an appropriate role for government, but it is one that it is made more difficult by the deep penetration of corporate participation and the marketing mentality into the political system.

PART III

DEMOCRACY AND STABILITY

CHAPTER 9

Commercial Democracy

Which way will capital vote?
—*Economist,* July 19, 2008

Individual interests in autonomy and self-expression and in the production of information are not the only interests the First Amendment is said to protect. They are, however, the ones particularly focused on the rights and interests of the individual—whether as speaker or listener. But many observers, like Thomas Emerson, believe that the First Amendment is also intended to promote collective interests. As Emerson put it, "Maintenance of a system of free expression is necessary . . . (3) as a method of securing participation by the members of the society in social, including political, decision-making, and (4) . . . as a means of maintaining the balance between stability and change in the society."[1] I propose that a closer study of the actual operation of commercial expression suggests that neither of these values is advanced by greater protection for commercial expression. In this chapter, I address the problem of the influence of commercial expression and commercial interests in the democratic process.

Commercial influence in politics is harmful in a number of ways. First, as noted earlier, the corporate form allows for the accumulation of wealth in a manner that means that corporations have amplified voices. This makes the claim that corporations' voices need to be heard or that they need equal time particularly galling, because the truth is that the largest

corporations already enjoy a virtual monopoly on access to the mainstream media. Moreover, corporations themselves are not democratic institutions. The decision-making process within corporations by which priorities are set and money is spent on speech efforts is not a democratic
one. Indeed, as pointed out in the preceding chapter, it is even questionable whether management is responsive to the constituents it is supposed
to serve—the shareholders. However, management is certainly not at all
accountable to the public at large unless the law requires it to be. In addition, to the extent that corporate decision making (e.g., to resist health
care reform) may have enormous social consequences that the public is
unable to remedy directly by voting, corporate influence seems antidemocratic and troubling.

Second, marketing mindsets and techniques have so thoroughly infiltrated the political sphere that many of the participants are no longer able to
tell the difference between what is real and what "works," and sometimes
display a rather shocking disregard for facts. Perhaps politicians and governors have, from time immemorial (certainly since Niccolo Machiavelli wrote
The Prince), been chiefly concerned with appearances and "manufacturing
consent."[2] Nevertheless, the infiltration into politics of extremely sophisticated manipulation techniques that were developed in connection with marketing and marketing research seems particularly troubling. This is the world
envisioned by Aldous Huxley in his novel *Brave New World*. Edward
Bernays argued that democracy was unworkable without propaganda. He
thought that commercial interests would and should play an important role
in the "invisible government" that made democracy work. The problem now
may be, can democracy survive its influence?

Equal Time

As objectionable, on many fronts, as advertising may often be, perhaps no
area of commercial expression, as I have broadly defined it, is as troubling as
speech that takes place in contexts that are clearly political. It is here that
misdirection in the argument about corporations as political participants is
most apparent. Many of commercial speech's defenders suggest that distinguishing between the levels of protection on the basis of the identity of the

speaker when that speaker is a nonhuman entity is a form of invidious discrimination and that there is nothing about the corporate status of the speaker that invalidates or undermines the legitimacy of its contribution. These claims echo the flights of rhetoric along the same lines in the Supreme Court's *Citizens United* decision. They make it sound as if commercial speakers have difficulty having their voices heard, when nothing could be farther from the truth.

Corporate influence in the legislative process through lobbying and other forms of political speech is so pervasive as to constitute an unfair distortion of the democratic process. Corporate money floods into the political process every day, arguably distorting the priorities of elected representatives. Perhaps more insidiously, marketing mentality dominates politics so thoroughly that politicians use the same polling firms, the same consultants, and the same techniques that many marketers feel comfortable using, including ones that are unambiguously deceptive.[3]

Corporate speakers attempt to manage impressions with massive expenditures for speech of all kinds, some of which is truthful and informational but often not. For example, *New York Times* media columnist Frank Rich claims that it was public relations propaganda that propped up Enron's "house of cards."[4] An intensive spin campaign may explain how the company managed to convince investors, the financial media, and the public at large that it was spectacularly successful, despite little in the way of factual support for its claims of profits and many good reasons for skepticism.[5] Spin—managing how a story "plays" in appropriately small, 30-second sound bites—dominates how we receive a great deal of information of all kinds: consumer, political,[6] and personal. A closer look at this influence suggests that unfettered corporate participation in the political arena results in corporations gaining a disparate influence in government in a manner that hardly seems to advance the democracy-enhancing concerns of Emerson.

Hanging Out with a Bad Crowd

If there was any doubt that PR techniques have infiltrated government communications, that doubt should have been removed by the events of October

23, 2007. On that day the Federal Emergency Management Agency (FEMA) called a press conference to report on measures it was taking in response to wildfires raging out of control in California. Reporters and news agencies were given 15 minutes' notice of the conference. Those who could not attend (which was everyone who did not happen to have a reporter within 15 minutes of FEMA's headquarters) were given a number to call so they could listen in on the conference. It would be "listen only," and reporters would not be able to ask questions. Reporters who listened and viewers who watched the conference on TV[7] saw or heard the FEMA representative field some remarkably softball questions from persons who were off camera. The scene *seemed* to be a news press conference. There was just one small problem: there was no press. FEMA employees posed as reporters.[8]

Later, David Paulison, the agency's administrator, sent out a memo to all FEMA employees in which he acknowledged that "there were no media representatives present"[9] at the press conference. He confirmed that employees from the agency's External Affairs Division posed the questions to the deputy administrator during the conference and that media were given short notice and listen-only telephone access.[10] He said that all of these actions were "inappropriate" and "inexcusable" and that the appropriate disciplinary actions would be forthcoming. However, he asserted that agency employees had acted in good faith and had made these "poor decisions" in "a rush to get information out" and to "rapidly respond to the media."[11]

It is difficult to know how such overt playacting—a performance that included a FEMA employee interjecting, "One more question," and employees asking their boss, "Are you happy with FEMA's response?"—could be done in good faith, if, as Paulison claimed, "under no circumstances is it appropriate for FEMA employees to pose questions during a FEMA press event."[12] What is the good-faith explanation for the listen-only call-in? Even apart from the implausibility of the proposition that Deputy Administrator Harvey Johnson, who was the one standing before the cameras,[13] did not know that it was FEMA employees and not reporters asking the questions (perhaps it is a big office), there does not seem to be any way to explain this as a mistake. There may be a simpler explanation: it was standard operating procedure. To test the plausibility of this explanation, we can first examine the stated rationale: haste.

Where's the Fire?

According to Paulison, the "real story" of the week of October 23, 2007, was "how extraordinarily well the response and recovery operation" being conducted by FEMA in California was going.[14] It may be, in light of the widespread condemnation of FEMA's performance after Hurricane Katrina, that FEMA's good performance would be news of a sort (although representative of a sad state of affairs), but it hardly seems to qualify as breaking news. To be fair, there were some nuggets of actual news about the fires in the statement offered that day.[15] Nevertheless, it is impossible to avoid the impression that the most immediate concern of the agency was its need for some positive press coverage and that the reason for the short notice and the absence of reporters was to allow for softball questions about the agency's performance that might not have been asked by real reporters. Real reporters might (or, sadly, might not) have asked questions that would have been more difficult to answer—such as whether the fact that the victims in the California fires appeared to be, on the whole, more affluent than those of Katrina was a factor in the agency's responsiveness.

Real reporters have a tendency to ask such embarrassing questions for which there is no good answer. As any lawyer knows, ask the right questions and even the truth sounds self-serving. Such questions can have a negative impact just by virtue of being asked. Given this fact, practitioners of PR are always seeking ways to massage press coverage. One way to do it is to stage-manage the press conference by casting your own people in the role of the press. This is not a technique unfamiliar to recent administrations, perhaps most notably the Bush administration.

Virtual Reality

The Bush administration engaged in several fairly high-profile attempts to manipulate media coverage, from a photo op of a "mission accomplished" landing on an aircraft carrier to managed "town hall meetings" that limited attendance to friendly audiences. It was associated with making payments to columnists to promote No Child Left Behind and granting press credentials to one Jeff Gannon of Talon News—both (the reporter and the news agency) of dubious journalistic credentials—apparently for no other purpose than to allow Mr. Gannon to ask the president softball questions during press conferences. Perhaps the most famous of all efforts at press management was the Bush administration's connection to "leaks" about the war in Iraq to reporter Judith Miller of the *New York Times* (who apparently could not tell the difference between a whistle-blower and a press release). Repeatedly representatives of the government demonstrated that they were operating from the PR industry playbook. In that world, perception is everything, memories are short, and selling a policy is simply a matter of framing it properly and suppressing or spinning bad facts.

Of course, we could say that spinning facts is the lawyer's stock-in-trade and hardly the exclusive province of marketing people. Nevertheless, it seems that there will be times when the rubber of spin hits the road of reality. Global warming, recession, and war cannot be spun entirely away. But perhaps spin is good enough for government work. As discussed earlier with respect to brands and meaning, it is true, in a sense, that perceptions have an independent reality, a reality that may change behaviors and thus events. Based on their conduct, it seems that many in the Bush administration really thought that marketing and packaging could overcome any defect in "the product" and that the reality was what they said it was. This was reflected in the infamous quote of an unidentified Bush administration official who said, "When we act, we create our own reality."[16]

What does it mean for democracy that those with the most access to the creating of this reality have so much influence on government. What does it mean that government, in turn, borrows so much of its own communication practices and strategies from an industry that, in the words of one insider, "would gladly sell colored sugar cubes to toddlers if it could get away with it"?[17] The government, of course, has a bully pulpit. Almost by definition, anything it does is news simply because it says it is. The question is whether, in a culture in which communication has been so thoroughly dominated by the ethos of marketing, the public has been inured to the revelation that news has been staged or that appearances are deceiving. Former U.S. secretary of labor Robert Reich has argued, "Democracy has become enfeebled largely because companies, in intensifying competition for global consumers and investors, have invested ever greater sums in lobbying, public relations, and even bribes and kickbacks, seeking laws that give them a competitive advantage over their rivals. The result is an arms race for political influence that is drowning out the voices of average citizens."[18] Columnist David Brooks said something similar when he wrote, "[T]he biggest threat to a healthy economy is not the socialists of campaign lore. It is chief executives. It's politically powerful crony capitalists who use their influence to create a stagnant corporate welfare state."[19]

Finding the Right Words?

Politicians use marketers' research methods to assess the reception of their messages and selling of their "brands." These methods involve reliance on polling, surveys, and focus groups. Perhaps no one has done more to popularize the techniques of marketing in politics in the last several years than Republican strategist Frank Luntz. He describes the techniques he uses to discover the "words that work"[20] as essentially democratic because he says he listens to America.[21] Luntz says he listens "[t]hrough national telephone surveys, focus groups, one-on-one interviews, content analysis, and simple day-to-day interaction with people," in order to give people what they want.[22] One of the most straightforward of these efforts is his infamous dial survey. In the dial survey, Luntz gathers a focus group, which he hopes is representative of the target audience, and then exposes it to a speech about the subject he is trying to test. Members of the group are given a response box with a dial (approximately the size of a kitchen timer) that registers a range of reactions, from very positive to very negative. They are asked to move the dial in accordance with how much they like or dislike what they are hearing. Luntz has used this method to tease out specific words that he asserts "work"—hence the title of his book, *Words That Work*.[23]

   Luntz's technology may appear to be sophisticated, but he is essentially simply employing the tried-and-true techniques of marketers who are trying to figure out how to get consumers to buy what they have to sell as much as they are trying to figure out what consumers really want. What consumers want and what marketers have to sell is not necessarily the same thing. Successful marketing often seeks to tie the sale to some intangible—like a sense of belonging. Marketers associate products with some intangible like love or self-esteem (something that clearly cannot be reliably provided by a product), in the hopes that this association will inspire consumers to buy the product.

Sometimes it involves associating the product with staving off some feared outcome—a dateless Saturday, an illness, a job loss, an accident, or any one of the numberless ways in which life's inherent uncertainty threatens that the future will fail to conform to our hopes or expectations.

Either way, the object is to persuade the audience, not necessarily to inform it. Indeed, if a party (or a politician) has a position it would like to take (as opposed to finding out what constituents would like), it will be interested in knowing the best way to frame the position for maximum appeal. It is appeal, not information, that is central. In fact, according to Luntz, there can be such a thing as too much information and an appeal that is pitched too high. He urges those who would be this century's invisible governors to use simple words and short sentences, because, he writes, although "[s]ophistication is certainly what Americans *say* they want in their politics, . . . it is certainly not what they buy."[24] Most Americans, he notes, have not gone to college and are suspicious of big words and long sentences. For these reasons, Luntz suggests that those who seek to communicate with the public do so in short sentences.

Vivid words and short sentences are undoubtedly features of good communication. Virtually every writer who has written about effective communication, from Strunk and White to Orwell to Annie Lamott, has said much the same thing. It may be that it is possible to communicate sophisticated ideas to the unsophisticated (and assumptions about who is and who is not unsophisticated seem fraught with their own perils). Presumably though, there are some limits to how simply you can express your idea before it becomes oversimplified. However, Luntz apparently thinks that there is no such thing as oversimplification. Instead, he observes, "At work, and at home, in business and in our personal lives, we're actually writing more than ever before—but what we're writing looks less like an old-fashioned letter and more like what you'd see on a vanity license plate."[25] This sounds like an exaggeration. It is not. Can this be a good thing?

Puppet Government

Perhaps Bernays was right that a democracy inevitably needs a cadre of "invisible wire-pullers,"[26] although it is depressing to think so. However, it is clear that democracy or, indeed, any institution needs to act through designees. Pure democracy with every decision made by a vote of the whole is not practical, nor is it always consistent with notions of civil liberties, since a majority of people could vote to oppress a minority, as indeed they have done from time to time in history. Submitting everything to a vote threatens to bog an organization down in minutiae.

At the same time, a democracy requires some accountability to the demos. Bernays's comment is depressing less for its reference to wire-pullers than for his use of the word *invisible*. Accountability depends on some transparency. (It is also worth observing that Bernays himself thought the government should regulate the public relations industry, presumably to keep standards high.)[27] Although the argument to exert more control over commercial expression invariably inspires charges of paternalism and elitism from proponents of more freedom for commercial expression, it should be observed that *any* form of government entails entrusting much decision making to an elite few. The differences between political theories involve differences in how those few are chosen and the terms under which they may remain in their positions of power. Bernays's invisible wire-pullers, like the management of today's global corporations, are mostly chosen from among their own group and often have little accountability outside of that group to the thousands, if not millions, of people whom their decisions may affect.

Down on Democracy

It appears that democracy as an institution is getting a rather bad rap recently. Economist Bryan Caplan writes that democracy is "widely over rated"[28] relative to markets. He argued that voters regularly vote for bad economic policies and thus cannot be trusted to vote for good laws. To remedy this problem, Caplan would offer more economics education. After the calamitous events of the last couple of years in the banking industry, however, that recommendation seems of dubious value, and economics seems aptly named the "dismal science."[29] Among Caplan's many other suggestions are proposals for an economics literacy test in order to vote or extra votes for the educated.[30] He appears to realize that these proposals have little chance of acceptance and offers them only halfheartedly.[31] That they are rather nakedly antidemocratic does not appear to him to be a defect. What is this argument if it is not some conception of the "good" that suggests that people do not know what is good for them?

Arguments that the electorate is not to be trusted with the facts lest they make bad decisions come from all sides of the political spectrum. A psychology professor, Drew Westen, urges the Democratic Party to appeal more to the emotions than to the brain, because, according to Westen, rationality is also widely overrated as a basis for political decision making.[32] While this is a slightly different argument, many of the consequences are the same: someone else, someone who knows better, needs to direct the public to what is good for them. As examined earlier, Richard Thaler and Cass Sunstein suggest that the public at large could do with a little nudging in the right direction, the "right" direction being the direction that someone else has determined is in their best interest.[33] Again, the specter of invisible wire-pullers is raised. On this topic, there seems to be consensus. There is no way to do without the wire-pullers. The question raised is whether such wire-pulling by business interests, in a fashion that is nontransparent and not accountable, is a good thing. Is it true that "what is good for GM is good for America?"[34] If it is not, we ought to be concerned, because if commercial expression is completely shielded by the First Amendment, that attitude is what we will get. Indeed, we might have it already.

One of the topics that appears throughout this book is the idealization of rationality and the ways in which this idealization works to the advantage of those who would profit from the degree to which we fall short from the ideal. Nevertheless, there is something profoundly unsettling about the prospect that, as a people, we are willing to explicitly abandon hope of governance by the people except through the manipulation of sound bites and slogans appropriate to an ad campaign. It may well be that it has been ever thus and that it does not do to romanticize some distant past in which the general electorate was supposedly more engaged, involved, or informed. But can it be a good thing to jettison not only reasoned debate but also facts, to shrug our shoulders at the prospect of a government divorced from the "reality-based community"? If voters cannot be counted on to make the right choices unless they are guided to it, who is in the position to guide them, and what prevents the guiders from giving the country a bum steer?

There is a group that stands ready to guide the great masses where they want them to go as well as to helpfully point out the path to legislators who may not be sufficiently enlightened. These are for-profit corporations and the various nonprofit groups that they create and support. The metaphor of corporate personhood and the use of various "hot-button" words, whether accessed intuitively by the speaker or road tested by Dr. Luntz in his dial groups, have resulted in a circumstance in which words and phrases like *freedom, individual responsibility, autonomy,* and *freedom of speech* are used to activate cherished political concepts in a way that obscures the actual role of commercial speech in the society by building word associations that make the corporate speaker just another "voice" rather than a dominant wire-puller.

Corporate Lobbying

A democracy is not really a democracy without the participation of its citizens, the demos. Citizens do require protection for their expression in order to fully participate. Corporations, however, are not citizens. They have no interest in democratic participation as such. For-profit corporations have an interest in supporting whatever legal or political regime guarantees the most congenial environment in which to generate profits. Often this is not a particularly democratic regime, as decades of commercial involvement in political regimes in South America,[35] the Middle East,[36] and Africa[37] have illustrated.

Moreover, no matter where a corporation is located or incorporated, its management often does not hesitate to reincorporate in Liberia or the Bahamas, or to move certain parts of their operations to other countries, whenever it is profitable to do so. The fact of initial incorporation in the United States is not an insurmountable obstacle to this practice and makes large multinational corporations indifferent "citizens" of any country and perhaps only nominally subject to any laws. As institutions, they have no allegiance to any particular nation, although the people who run them may. As noncitizens, corporations have (or, rather, ought theoretically to have) no role of participation in democracy.[38]

This is not to say that corporate representatives ought never to be able to offer opinions. It *is* to say that there is no clear reason to conclude that corporations must be entitled to a voice in matters of public concern as a matter of democratic participation. Yet they do have a voice—and a deafening one at that. The July 19, 2008 issue of the *Economist* put it bluntly: "Which way will capital vote?"[39] Of course, capital does not actually vote. It does not need to. It has lobbyists. It is difficult to think of any other institution in American life that has so thoroughly enlisted the cooperation of the government in the passage of laws. Although the *Economist* article put its question in terms of small business owners (as apologists for industry so often do, since it makes the argument far more attractive), it is the largest businesses that have the most lobbying voice.

Corporations cannot vote, yet it is apparent that corporations have a major, if not a dominant, role in our democracy. They play key roles in urging legislation on Congress and have a large measure of success, as the recent revisions to the bankruptcy code, urged by the credit card companies for their own benefit, illustrate.[40] Typically, industry has drafted the legislation in question as well as funded the research and engaged in public relations campaigns to get the issue before key members of the public and the legislatures.[41] In the past, corporations could offer legislators attractive trips to luxurious locales under the pretext of "education."[42] They can invest billions in nonprofit organizations that act as fronts, such as the now-defunct Council for Tobacco Research. They can also invest billions in putting together "astroturf" organizations to lobby legislators,[43] and form industry and trade groups like the Business Roundtable, an organization made up of the CEOs of the largest companies, like Archer Daniels Midland and American Express. The Business Roundtable was formed in 1972 with the express purpose of playing a more effective role in influencing government.

> Under the banner of "tort reform" and backed by huge political contributions at the national, state, and even local levels, BRT and its allies managed to paint Corporate America as the victim and those injured and otherwise damaged by corporate neglect as the assailants—a seismic shift that continues to this day. For the past 25 years, the group's task force on corporate governance has been shaping the nation's definition and understanding of that critical term, invariably in ways that entrench management and disempowered shareholders.[44]

If that was what the Business Roundtable did for shareholders, one can only imagine how much less assiduously it has represented the rest of the public.[45]

Ghostwriting the Law[46]

The granddaddy of all lobbying efforts is perhaps represented by ALEC, the American Legislative Exchange Council. The council is made up of legislators (the association proudly announces that over 100 legislators are members) and representatives from industry. One of the announced goals of the organization is to uphold "Jeffersonian principles."[47] It apparently does this by writing model legislation friendly to business interests—draft legislation that is not open to inspection to anyone except members of the organization. Membership fees for private-sector members range from $7,000 to $50,000. (Public-sector members (elected officials) get a break. Their memberships are only $100 to $200. Still, it is quite a trick that ALEC manages to collect any fees at all, when you consider that this amounts to elected officials paying for the privilege of being lobbied.)

The rest of us, nonmember citizens will just have to wait until the model legislation is proposed to Congress and subject to sunshine laws before we can get a peek at its contents. However, there is some evidence in the titles that this model legislation was influenced by efforts like those of Frank Luntz to find attractive names for what might be less-attractive policies. For example, there is the "Resolution to Establish an Office of Men's Health" (part of a section entitled "Men's Health") and the "Resolution Supporting Private Market Initiatives to Fund Children's Health Insurance."[48] No doubt, efforts such as these are why the recent bankruptcy legislation appears to have been written by the American Bankers Association.

Corporate influence is not limited, however, to the legislature. It is also felt in the well-known phenomenon of agency capture, a phenomenon that, by the way, illustrates that even regulation is no panacea for social ills. Agency capture describes the situation in which the regulated and the regulators are all part of the same small group, because the people with the necessary expertise must be drawn from industry and are likely to go back to industry at the conclusion of their public service. Agency capture can also occur when governmental employment is sufficiently politicized that it informs the judgments of governmental employees in the discharge of their duties. This kind of politicization is surely always a potential problem. It is a problem singled out with the word *corruption* when there is an explicit exchange of money for political favor. Such corruption was part of the reason that access to the corporate form was made freely available in the nineteenth century—to avoid valuable corporate charters being handed out as political favors. It is surely not much help for a particular regulatory effort if the head of that effort, be it an agency or a prosecutor, views his or her job as being in partnership with business[49] or decides that he or she is not in favor of a particular regulatory or disciplinary effort and wants to withdraw it.[50]

One particularly stark example of this occurred in the early 1980s when the head of the Federal Trade Commission publicly described his understanding of his job as one of urging Congress to narrow the scope of the agency's jurisdiction.[51] While it is certainly true that narrowing the scope of an agency's jurisdiction might sometimes be in the public interest, his understanding was in some conflict with the legislative direction that had been given by statute that established the FTC. How much of this understanding sprang from political pressure from the potential targets of regulation is probably impossible to say. But it is commonplace to suppose that politicians are rather more solicitous of industry interests than of those members of the public with less to offer in the way of campaign contributions. Thus, when the Department of Justice reduced the requested damages in the tobacco lawsuit brought by the United States against various tobacco companies, from the $130 billion it had originally sought to "only" $10 billion, some felt it might be connected to the tobacco lobby's influence.[52] Lawyers for the Justice Department denied that they had reduced the damages demand because of political pressure.[53] However, many observers were skeptical.

These incidents and others are suggestive of widespread corporate influence on government. Despite having no vote, large corporations have far more voice, more participation, in shaping the law and government policy than most flesh-and-blood citizens.[54] It is difficult to understand how requiring that corporate communications be truthful (where the truth can be ascertained) will injure democracy, especially where the communications are designed to affect policy.

In addition, corporate speech is not itself the result of a democratic process, so it has no claim to be respected as a contribution to the democratic process. Corporate positions on political or social issues are not produced via a democratic process. There is no shareholder democracy with respect to the

issuance of corporate speech, since shareholders' participation in a corporation is extremely circumscribed and largely relegated to issues of the delega-
tion of control. When managers craft corporate speech, including draft legislation, they do so with one overriding goal—maximizing shareholder value.
When a corporation lobbies it is not hobbled by conflicting goals. Its aim is
to maximize returns to the corporation by creating an environment most hospitable for its purposes. Moreover, unlike a citizen group, when it speaks, it
speaks with a single voice, unburdened by the need to compromise or muffle
its demands to suit its coalition partners.[55]

As Robert Monks, an investor activist and consultant recounts, even in
those circumstances explicitly dedicated to receiving shareholder views (e.g.,
shareholders' meetings), corporations such as ExxonMobil have demonstrated a positive hostility toward receiving dissenting opinions or shareholder resolutions.[56] Shareholders who wish to speak are subject to rigidly
controlled time limits and a system of green, amber, and red lights that parallels that of the courts—except apparently the management does not always
even feel the need to pay lip service to the idea that these are views of which
they should take notice. Monks records as illustrative the following exchange
from May 26, 2004, between Dale McCormick, representing the Maine State
Retirement System, and ExxonMobil chairman Lee Raymond. McCormick
had asked whether he could pose a question about Exxon's provisions in its
financial statements for damages relating to global warming.

RAYMOND: You may not.

MCCORMICK: Why, sir?

RAYMOND: Because that's not—the audit committee looks at the recommendations of management. That's properly the responsibility of the
controller of the corporation.

MCCORMICK: May I pose it to you?

RAYMOND: Oh sure. You can pose anything to me. (*laughter*)

MCCORMICK: Will you answer me?

RAYMOND: Oh, that's a different question? (*more laughter*)

MCCORMICK: Sir, I do not think it is a matter of laughter when an institutional investor representing over 3 million shares cannot get answers
to an important question like this.[57]

If an institutional investor the size of McCormick's cannot participate meaningfully in a corporation's decision making, what hope is there for non-shareholders? Yet the decisions of ExxonMobil and other corporations like it have major public consequences—both long-term (e.g., global warming) and short-term (e.g., the Exxon Valdez oil spill), both general (e.g., the price of fuels) and specific (e.g., refinery closings or other decisions that may affect jobs). Companies can support slavery, violate human rights, support genocide (or the regimes that engage in them), and generally affect foreign policy, yet the many people whose lives they influence in this quasi-governmental way do not elect their boards of directors. Moreover, their processes are not transparent. We have observed this in the area of international banking law; in the shrouding in secrecy of the action of the MPPA ratings board, which prevents filmmakers from knowing the identity of the raters who have such power over them or effectively appealing their judgments;[58] and in the work of groups like ALEC, where sponsored legislation is available only to members. When corporate decisions stand in for government action or are influencing the law in corporations' favor, it seems unconscionable, in a democracy, to shroud them in secrecy.

If, as many on the right are fond of saying, "Democracy is the worst form of government . . . except any other that has ever been tried," it would seem self-evident that what Robert Monks has called a "corpocracy"[59] is even worse. This picture of the corporation acting on behalf of a fictional shareholder leads to the conclusion that the law and the market define corporations in a way that makes them inappropriate participants in political debate. Far from there being a need to protect corporations so that they can offer their point of view, it would seem that it is the public that needs protection from corporations' ability to impose their point of view on the electorate without having to answer for it or explain it. Without restrictions on corporate speech, the democratic process and the legitimacy of government is likely to be overrun by these special interests.

Discredited Precedent for Control

Once upon a time, the Supreme Court thought a for-profit corporation's participation in the democratic process could be appropriately circumscribed. Although the Supreme Court held in *First National Bank of Boston v. Bellotti*[60] that a corporation had a right to participate in political debates in some fashion, it retreated some from this position in the now overruled *Austin v. Michigan Chamber of Commerce,*[61] with a reminder that corporations are, after all, creatures of the state and recipients of special benefits from the state that are not enjoyed by natural persons.

> State law grants corporations special advantages—such as limited liability, perpetual life, and favorable treatment of the accumulation and distribution of assets—that enhance their ability to attract capital and to deploy their resources in ways that maximize the return on their shareholders' investments. These state-created advantages not only allow corporations to play a dominant role in the Nation's economy, but also permit them to use resources amassed in the economic marketplace to obtain an unfair advantage in the political marketplace.[62]

The decision also asserted that

> the political advantage of corporations is unfair because "*[t]he resources in the treasury of a business corporation . . . are not an indication of popular support for the corporation's political ideas.* They reflect instead the economically motivated decisions of investors and customers. The availability of these resources may make a corporation a formidable political presence, even though the power of the corporation may be no reflection of the power of its ideas."[63]

Moreover, many observers have suggested that the techniques of advertising and promotion are corrosive of democracy to the extent that these techniques have bled into political communication.[64] Frank Luntz describes his techniques as relevant to both business and politics and consults for both.[65] The interpenetration into political speech of the strategies, ethics, and techniques of marketing that do not seek primarily to inform but to persuade may explain why President Bush's spokesperson Andrew Card compared the announcement regarding the invasion of Iraq to a "product launch." It may also explain the increased acceptability of paying pundits to promote government programs or to carry government messages, a PR technique that, in the hands of the government, appears to be prohibited propaganda.[66] It may explain why politics looks and sounds so much like marketing and why the Bush administration appeared to think, like the quoted marketing executive, that "truth is irrelevant" on the issues of weapons of mass destruction, whether there had actually been a terrorist plot that was foiled by the authorities, or whether anyone remembers who told what to whom about CIA agent Valerie Plame. These are simply problems of spin control, not reasons to fear troubling backlash from the electorate.[67]

It is undoubtedly the case that politicians have always been in the persuasion business. Politicians, like lawyers, do not enjoy the highest reputations for honesty. That does not mean that there is not something vaguely troubling about this unselfconscious adoption of marketing techniques and attitudes in politics. When we consider for-profit corporations' very powerful interest and influence in government, their antidemocratic structure, and their singular organizational imperatives, it hardly seems that democracy would be well served by offering them even more leeway in the form of a constitutional shield for their expressive activities. Protection for either democracy or the democratic process seems to offer little support for the proposition that for-profit corporations should enjoy the same rights to speech as human beings.

Even if you argue that the position of a corporation is somehow indicative of the accumulated preferences of its owners, you still need a theory for why that means a corporation should have independent speech rights, a theory that roots the corporation in both democratic process and commitment to something other than what *homo economicus* would choose. There does not appear to be one. To the contrary, an examination of the reality of the corporate accumulation of resources, access to media, and influence on government suggests that the corporation is properly restrained in support of the goal of the preservation of democracy. In part, this is because corporations spend money and time doing research not just trying to figure out what we want, but also trying to figure out how to circumvent what we want when what we want is to be free of advertising.

Professor Emerson suggested that protection for freedom of expression offered some play in the joints of democracy—some possibility for blowing off steam by those who might otherwise have incentives to foment unrest—and that such protection thereby contributed to social stability. Those persons he envisioned as needing a place to vent were undoubtedly the poor and dispossessed, those who the people in power must always fear lest they get excessively disgruntled. For-profit corporations may, as novelist Max Barry imagined in *Jennifer Government,* pose a real threat to government, but they do not pose that threat because of a lack of outlets for their expression. Rather, they pose a threat because they have too much. They are rivals for governmental power.

Moreover, as nonhuman entities, corporations do not have, in the first place, an emotional need to blow off steam. Given their privileged position in the American economy and in the political realm, it is difficult to characterize corporations as a despised and powerless minority having a grudge they need to vent lest they upset the government. Yet, despite corporations' privileged position, they argue they need First Amendment protection in order for there to be balance. But the environment in which discussion about many issues of public concern takes place is already severely imbalanced and compromised by the firm grip of consumerism and corporate structuring of our wants and needs—in the first world and elsewhere. Only the truly poor are largely free of the bombardment of commercial speech experienced by almost everyone else, since, because they do not have much money, poor people do not present a good market.[68] Nevertheless, even those not marketed to may suffer some of the social consequences of consumerism, albeit without any sponsor to voice their concerns more directly to government. Interest in balance hardly seems to support the argument for more protection for corporate speech.

Even putting aside economic imbalance, there is evidence that, on the merits, interest in balance goes in the other direction, because it is pro-corporate speech that appears neutral. It is the anticorporate argument that has difficulty getting aired, because of for-profit corporations' dominance of the media.[69] For example, in *Sultans of Sleaze,* author Joyce Nelson describes the efforts in 1988 of the British Columbia Council of Forest Industries to reposition their industries as "green."

> The council mounted a massive and expensive campaign to convince the public of its "sound forest and stewardship and reforestation programs." The campaign included educational displays in shopping malls, huge

posters at bus stops, ads inside buses, and colour supplements delivered to most households in the province. . . . But the biggest irritant, in the whole PR effort was the Council's "Forests Forever" ads: a $2 million pitch on billboards and TV and in the print media in which Council spokespeople say what a wonderful job they are doing in managing B.C. forests.[70] . . . The ads ran for over a year on CBC-TV despite protests by environmental groups; but when a counter-ad, "Mystical Forests," detailing the actual practices of the logging industry, was proposed by environmentalists and presented for CBC approval, it was turned down as "too controversial."[71]

Canadian journalist and social activist Kalle Lasn of AdBusters Media Foundation has encountered similar problems getting the broadcast media to air his organization's ads for "Buy Nothing Day" or its advertising parodies, leading the foundation to initiate legal action that has (so far) apparently been unsuccessful.[72]

Reflecting similar tendencies to reject controversy, Amtrak, a governmental corporation, attempted to refuse to carry artist Michael Lebron's ad that entailed a photo commentary on Coors Brewing Company's support for the Nicaraguan contras and other right-wing causes. The ad parodied a Coors ad campaign that proclaimed Coors to be the "Right Beer Now," with the line "Is It the Right's Beer Now?" Although Lebron paid for the ad, Amtrak refused it on the grounds that the corporation did not allow "political" advertising.[73] Of course, the characterization of Lebron's ad as "political" implies that the Coors ad is not political—and in a sense it is not: Coors just wants to sell beer. Lebron wanted to impeach the political choices the company had made by supporting the contras. So he sued, claiming that the First Amendment prohibited Amtrak from refusing to display his ad. He argued that because Amtrak was a government entity, it could not refuse to display his ad on the basis of its political content. In response, Amtrak claimed that its status as a corporation meant that Lebron could not raise a First Amendment claim. It argued that it was acting in its private capacity in refusing the ad and thus that there was no government action.[74]

The Supreme Court rejected Amtrak's argument, holding that where the government retains complete control over the corporation, the law may disregard the corporate form and view the corporation as an arm of the government. So it had to accept his ad. Nevertheless, this resolution of the case turns on Amtrak's status as a *governmental* corporation. An ordinary media company *would* be free to reject an ad like Lebron's, and they usually do, since one of the greatest concerns for advertisers, the lifeblood of all media, is that content in the media (or on the side of the bus, in the bathroom stall, etc.) presents the appropriate selling environment for their goods and services. It is easy to see why "[a] message in support of the status quo is typically considered to be 'neutral,' 'objective,' and 'non-controversial,' while a message that departs from the status quo position or criticizes it is considered to have a 'point of view' and 'bias.' "[75]

Distinctions between the political and the commercial such as those made in the *Lebron* case demonstrate that, contrary to the argument of many of commercial speech's supporters, making a distinction between commercial and political speech is not intellectually or practically impossible, even if commercial speech might be said to be political to the extent that it advances a materialist, consumerist point of view. It also reflects the mainstream orientation of the dominant powers of the society. The orientation of the media to the "noncontroversial" in many settings suggests that a balance of political points of view, particularly with regard to antimaterialism, anticorporatism, or anticonsumerism, is unlikely to emerge from the current environment.[76] That, in turn, suggests that drawing a line between commercial and political speech is not some kind of invidious discrimination, and it is difficult to discern how letting these powerful entities dominate so much of the political agenda contributes to a stronger democracy.

But perhaps it does contribute to stability in the sense that the frustration expressed on behalf of many in business about what they perceive as over-regulation and other impediments to an "unencumbered" environment could build to the degree that it becomes a threat to the government, particularly if these interests are successful through propaganda efforts to marshal the support of many ordinary people (Tea Party, anyone?). Giving them what they want, including protection for commercial speech, might lessen this threat. Yet this hardly seems like the sort of safety valve that Emerson had in mind. As will be discussed in the next two chapters, commercial speech demonstrably contributes to social instability in other ways.

CHAPTER 10

Commercial Expression and Economic Instability

[I]t pays to remember that the borrower is the amateur in this equation,
someone who might execute a mortgage twice in a lifetime.
A lender will do it a hundred times before lunch.

—Dean Starkman, "Boiler Room,"
Columbia Journalism Review, Sept./Oct. 2008

In the summer of 2008, the American economy appeared to be in free fall. Although it has rallied somewhat, it is not clear that more such economic shocks are not in our future. That summer appeared to bring a day of reckoning that some had long feared was coming and that was perhaps presaged by bubbles and "irrational exuberance" in more limited markets, like the dot-coms market, that also ultimately burst, causing significant losses. In those events, we might be able, although with perhaps too much hindsight, to discern warnings of the present problems—the susceptibility of securities markets to hype, overleveraging, and a boundless faith that values could not decline. Now we may be headed into a fundamental reordering of the economic system, a reordering that is likely to be harsh for many. How did we get here? At least one writer of a letter to the editor in *Advertising Age* thinks that advertising played a role. The letter said in part,

[O]verzealous marketing—"expansion for expansion's sake"—should take the lion's share of the responsibility for where we are, economically, politically, etc. Throw in short-term, quarter-by-quarter reporting of profits, and it is easy to see how we get in "crisis" mode from time to time. In short, the ever-increasing outrageous, unsupported claims made by marketing professionals has made it so our reality can never keep up with our expectations. . . . In the dot-com era, everyone wanted all these fantastic ROI numbers, so much so they threw all sensibilities out the door. Brick-and-mortar companies that had long and great profit histories at 7% to 8% were suddenly dinosaurs and being asked to come up with ways to attain percentages on par with what the dot-coms were saying they were producing. It all looked good over a couple quarters, but then reality hit. Same thing with the housing market. . . . If [China] ever stopped [buying U.S. Treasury bonds] or lost faith, then we would certainly have a very severe "correction," the likes of which no amount of consumer consumption could change. As marketers, we keep selling potential before things have been around long enough to gauge any real information on their real value.[1]

This letter was published in response to an article entitled "Marketing Must Take Its Share of Blame for the Economic Crisis."[2] Remember, you heard it there first, from the source—from someone in the industry.

Although it would be oversimplified to put the economic problems of the present down to the marketing practices of the last fifty years, it appears to have undeniably played a role. If so, freedom for commercial expression, far from contributing to the social stability that Thomas Emerson proposed was a reason to protect freedom of expression, appears to have contributed significantly to economic instability. In this chapter, I look at a few ways in which marketing helped to foster economic and thus social instability by contributing to the creation of a society comfortable with large amounts of debt, by focusing decision making on marketing inputs rather than investments in productive capacities, by encouraging a general focus by companies and investors on short-term returns on investment and arbitrage rather than in creating value, and by generally and gradually increasing people's comfort levels with assets and value located primarily in presentation rather than in creating a tangible fact. If it sounds like I am proposing that this was an orchestrated or conspiratorial effort, I am not. I do not think it was organized. It was, however, the logical outgrowth of a number of social attitudes about money, value, productivity, and what makes for a good society. It begins with economics.

The Value of Information

Since the late 1970s, a particularly strong view of the reliability of markets to solve economic and social problems has dominated American politics. Economists wielded great influence in politics (the collapse of communism) and law (efficiency). Economic explanations for virtually every sort of behavior (utility maximizing) were offered as the authoritative explanation for the operation of the economy and a guideline for solving virtually all social problems. At one point, it was even proposed (albeit controversially) that an open market might resolve the "baby shortage."[3] Economists exuded this confidence despite obvious shortcomings in basic economic models. The basic models often left out financial intermediaries and assumed perfect information. Such deficiencies were perhaps dictated by convenience, because accounting for financial intermediaries, for example, can make for complicated models.

Similarly, although economists understood that no market operated with perfect information and that market participants did not all behave "rationally" as commonly understood, the models (certainly as translated for mass consumption) often did not take this into account. It may have been as much for convenience as for anything, because attempting to account for these variables would make for an unwieldy model and diminish some of the virtues of modeling in the first place. However, as the *Economist* noted in the summer of 2009, "Convenience . . . is addictive. Economists can become seduced by their models, *fooling themselves that what the model leaves out does not matter.*"[4]

Perhaps no element that was "left out" or insufficiently modeled was as critical to the theory's validity as the role played by information, especially when that information is unreliable. This has particular significance for one model on which many legal arguments were based and that turned out to be, at least by some accounts, spectacularly wrong: the efficient capital market hypothesis. The efficient capital market hypothesis posits that the price of a security in the market accurately reflects all the information that is available about a firm, so that (theoretically) the market price of a security is an accurate reflection of its value. (This is an oversimplification, but one that nevertheless appears to have been widely accepted and to underlie some legislative and regulatory approaches.) Of course, if this theory were correct, it would be difficult to explain how bubbles would ever arise. However, arise they did. As a consequence, the notion that "the market price is the right price . . . has been badly dented."[5]

Part of what the efficient capital market hypothesis left out was what I have discussed in earlier chapters, the observation that people often behave in predictably irrational ways and that, in many cases, marketers have taken advantage of those cognitive tendencies to sell people things and services. Consumers may or may not have bought the product anyway, but the evidence suggests that the total volume of consumption is increased by advertising. The "noise," bubbles, and "irrational exuberance" in the financial sector suggest that similar limitations appear to apply to even sophisticated investors who perhaps had fallen prey to their own hype in building models relying on facially problematic assumptions, such as that housing values would never decline.

Even if you have a good model, however, you are likely to generate bad outcomes if the input is bad. When it came to the popular reliance on the variety of the efficient capital market hypothesis to support various "innovations" in the financial services market, many of the inputs were bad. As explained by Myron Scholes, Nobel Prize–winning economist and codeveloper of the popular Black-Scholes model for pricing options, "[T]he models used for structured products were pretty good, but the inputs were awful."[6] Sometimes they were more than just awful; sometimes they were intentionally false.

A key contributor to every significant corporate failure from Enron to AIG has been false information. In many instances, these organizations (or, rather, the people speaking on their behalf) did not disclose what needed to be disclosed or made statements intended to mislead investors (or others who might be expected to rely on these statements). Now, as regulators look to try to regulate the financial markets to prevent more spectacular failures like those we have seen in the last few years, it seems clear that reliable "information is crucial."[7]

Information, whether accurate or not, is what helps create market price. Where there are strong incentives to create false, favorable information and few checks or disincentives for doing so, it is fairly clear that you will get a great deal of false information. Furthermore, if the word *information* does not mean fact but, rather, propaganda and where (as in most cases) it is cheaper to manage the propaganda about your product or firm than it is to manage the facts *and* the information, there will be a competitive advantage to lying, and false information will proliferate. For example, if it is easier to simply say you pay your workers minimum wage than it is to actually do so, and there are few or no consequences for false claims, it is predictable that many will prefer to simply make claims rather than make good on claims.

False information will then contribute to an ever-widening gap between market prices and some external reality that will, one day, finally come to light and inspire a market correction. The term *market correction* is a euphemism for the decline in value when a bubble bursts, a phenomenon that usually means a great deal of economic hardship for a great many people, many of whom had no role in inflating the bubble in the first place. A strong constitutional defense to claims of falsity in commercial expression would exacerbate these tendencies. It is difficult to conclude that such a defense would do anything to prevent more such failures.

For example, the First Amendment is being raised as a defense to lawsuits against rating agencies like Standard & Poor's[8] for their role in the collapse of the housing market. Billions of dollars worth of debt that went bad was rated by credit rating agencies such as S&P, Moody's, or Fitch as high or investment grade. How could they have been so wrong? Perhaps it is a mystery. But perhaps it is not, when one considers that the entities that pay for the ratings are also the ones who are being rated. As *New York Times* reporter David Segal put it, having the rating agencies paid by the issuers of the bond that it rates sets up "what appears to be a rather spectacular conflict of interest—like a teacher appraising the work of the students who pay his salary."[9] It might explain, Segal writes, at least to critics, "why so many bonds that were later all but worthless were stamped triple-A."[10] Indeed it might. However, it seems difficult to know how we will prevent such events from happening in the future if S&P's lawyer, the famous First Amendment lawyer Floyd Abrams, wins his argument that these ratings are just "opinions" and, as such, are entitled to the same sort of constitutional deference given to opinions on the editorial page.[11]

There is irony in Abrams's comment, in that since, as described earlier, it is increasingly difficult to tell whether the editorial content in most newspapers or other sources of information is "sponsored content," we may well be wary of giving automatic protection to editorials as well. The problem of the penetration of marketing into news means that the distinctions between advertising and editorial content are not as great as one might hope. But hopefully this breakdown in journalistic integrity is not going to be further ammunition for the argument that the right "fix" is to protect the ratings agencies (and other commercial speech) rather than to call a halt to the practices of allowing PR news releases to pass as straight news or paying opinion columnists to produce favorable opinions. Whatever the case, many investors can say with some forcefulness that if you cannot rely on the major bond rating agencies, let alone the media, for information on investments, something is seriously wrong.

Of course, it is still possible to observe that commercial communications are, as the *Virginia Pharmacy* Court put it, "indispensible" to a market economy and that as long as we have such an economy, these communications must take place because, in the aggregate, they may contribute to economic stability. There seems to be no doubt, at least from reading the newspapers and business journals, that the American economy is more dependent than ever on high levels of consumption to fuel economic growth and to fuel confidence in the market, which, in turn, helps prop it up. If marketing stimulates consumption and if consumption is critical to welfare, then perhaps it is appropriate to consider the right to engage in commercial speech comfortably within the ambit of protected speech, for precisely the reasons Emerson identified.

However, Emerson located the stability claim as one that acted as a safety valve for the release of the pressures and discontents of dissenters and outsiders. He claimed that having protection for such dissident speech defused tensions that might otherwise erupt into rebellion and disruption of civil society. It is a stretch of this argument for it to encompass economic stability, so that Emerson's rationale for the protection of the *outsider* becomes a rationale for protection of *insiders*. This parallels the observation that although it is true that the Supreme Court sometimes plays the role of a countermajoritarian force to protect the civil rights of an oppressed minority, the analogy of corporations to civil rights protesters is misplaced. When insiders, the powerful majority, are engaging in speech that contributes to social instability, it does not seem that we can say that protecting it, rather than regulating it, contributes to social stability.

Even supposing, though, that economic welfare and stability is a good enough goal on its own without the outsider gloss, there is some reason to question whether unrestrained commercial expression and very high levels of consumption actually increase stability in the long term or whether they ultimately put the economy at risk by overheating it. The events of the subprime lending crisis and the resultant cascading crises at least suggest that if the high levels of consumption are built on high levels of debt not matched by sufficient and stable sources of income, this model is based on a shaky foundation, one inordinately susceptible to shocks and to sudden changes in levels of confidence. This did not happen by accident.

All Consuming

In 1947, the readers of *Life* magazine were treated to a story about the how the end of the war and the ramping up of production for peacetime involved a change from scrimping in consumption to help the war effort to consuming as a patriotic duty. The story, entitled "Family Status Must Improve: It Should Buy More for Itself to Better the Living of Others," explained how people would be contributing to a better way of life for everyone by upgrading their homes, modernizing their kitchens, purchasing new clothes, and redecorating, since these purchases supported industries that, in turn, employed workers whose salaries were dependent on a strong consumer demand.[12] The idea that well-being is dependent on consumption has continued relatively unabated until the present time, so that in the wake of the shock and resultant economic contraction after the terrorist attack on September 11, 2001, President Bush urged Americans to return to traveling and shopping to ensure that the terrorists did not "win." Unfortunately, a lot of that spending would have to be done on credit, something that might postpone the day of reckoning but would do little to address the fragility of the economy that the attack exposed. The problem was flat or declining incomes for too many.

The Role of Credit

In February 2008, two economists at the Federal Reserve Bank of Dallas published an op-ed in the *New York Times* suggesting that despite growing evidence of a large gap between the haves and the have-nots, things on the bottom end of the scale were not as bad as they appeared: "The bottom fifth [of American households] earned just $9,974, but spent nearly twice that—an average of $18,153 a year."[13] "How is that possible?" the authors ask. One obvious answer is credit. This was not, however, the answer the authors came up with. Instead, they argued that the disparity in spending was accounted for by "access to various sources of spending money"[14] that was not taxable as income. They described these sources as "portions of sales of property like homes and cars and securities that are not subject to capital gains taxes, insurance policies redeemed, or the drawing down of bank accounts."[15]

These kinds of resources do not strike me as good reasons not to be concerned about income inequality. It is unlikely that people making $10,000 a year have a great deal in the way of savings accounts, property, or other assets to convert to cash, although some may well have been retirees drawing on such reserves. But surely many of those in this category were simply poor. So what accounted for this consumption in excess of income? Again, the obvious answer seems to be access to credit—whether conventional credit cards or the ubiquitous and controversial payday loans that have proven so troublesome to so many low-income borrowers.

Moreover, if this op-ed was supposed to reassure those worried about income inequality by implying that the condition of the poor was not as bad as it seemed, it failed miserably. Even if a reader was convinced by the improbable suggestion that people earning less than $10,000 a year actually had access to things like savings accounts (an increasingly unfamiliar financial feature even to those in the $100,000 category) or property to sell, there was another disquieting element to identifying these sources of nonreported income. All of the potential sources of income the authors identified for this extra $8,000 in annual consumption were coming from nonrecurring sources. If you spend everything you earn *and* are withdrawing money from your savings account to finance your spending, it is axiomatic that your savings account is not being replenished. It is going to run out—unless you have a rich uncle who leaves you an inheritance. When it does run out, what will you do?

Americans have an unprecedented amount of consumer debt. Yet even with very high amounts of debt or after having declared bankruptcy, many are bombarded with offers for more credit, balance transfers, or moving purchases onto a revolving balance arrangement rather than a pay-balance-in-full arrangement.[16] The increased comfort with deficit spending that emerged in the late twentieth century was supported by the unceasing efforts of marketers who never stopped selling and, indeed, have not stopped to this day, flogging more and more credit.[17]

Generating a sense of urgency to acquire things that were previously thought to be luxuries was a part of the explicit post–World War II economic plan. It was truly an early example of a partnership between government and business. Now we have to ask if that plan has worked too well, whether the country is ill-equipped to reverse historic flat or negative savings rates and cut back on consumption in the face of higher commodity prices, particularly food, not because individuals necessarily lack the proper habits or moral fortitude (although they may), but because the economy as a whole may be dependent on a great deal of consumption.

Lots of people are living beyond their means,[18] although the new economy calls into question, to some degree, what that phrase means. If living within one's means involves having an adequate income stream to meet your needs and service any debts, many Americans meet that definition. If, instead, it means you have an adequate income stream to meet your needs and service your debts *and* adequate savings to survive unexpected reversals like the loss of a job or a major health setback, then many Americans do not meet that definition.[19] To meet this second definition, Americans would have to save much more money.

But if they save much more money, it will depress consumption, which will slow the economy. So they must continue to spend everything they have and then some. Given that the economy is dependent on their spending, where will this spending come from? One answer is debt. The usual source of deficit spending—the government—is already at fairly staggering levels and presumably cannot continue indefinitely. But a heavy burden seems to also rest on consumers. The economy appears to be dependent on people living beyond their means, if "beyond their means" equals not having adequate savings. If consumption fuels economic stability, then all those borrowers living beyond their means and all those who promptly went out and spent their 2009 incentive checks rather than saving them are patriots who have placed themselves in harm's way in service of the greater good. Yet few see them as such. Instead, they are reviled for their irresponsibility should they come to grief.

Harvard Law professor Elizabeth Warren and her coauthor (and daughter) Amelia Warren Tygai have called this the "myth of the immoral debtor"[20] and thoroughly debunked the idea of the "irresponsible borrowers." Instead, they convincingly demonstrate that what got most people into trouble was some large, unexpected financial hit—the loss of a job, a catastrophic medical expense, a divorce, a catastrophic property loss uncovered by insurance (e.g., as suffered by some residents of New Orleans following Katrina or in cases of similar natural disasters). Warren and Tygai have harsh criticism for the revisions to the bankruptcy code that made bankruptcy more difficult to obtain for people thus pressed by circumstances. These bankruptcy reforms were pushed by the banks and the credit card industry. They sold them to Congress as necessary protections against the "irresponsible borrowers."

But even if the banking industry's story about the need for these reforms—that too many people were in over their heads—was true, what responsibility did the banks themselves have? They relentlessly promoted their products to people to the brink of disaster and beyond. They specifically targeted people with riskier credit profiles for the most aggressive products, "free offers" and "convenience checks." They mined large databases of information to cull out the names of those with financial problems, knowing that they would be more susceptible to the pitch. If the bank tells you that you are worth $30,000 in credit, should you be deemed irresponsible for accepting that proposition?

Creating Comfort with Debt

A generation or more ago, no one would have argued that the equity in your home was unused money lying around that you should take advantage of, the way banks, brokers, financial advisors, and others did throughout the 1990s. That was precisely the pitch made to home owners as property values inflated, seemingly never to return to earth. In an earlier day, no one would have considered borrowing against their homes to fund a vacation. But that was precisely the sort of pitch banks made to potential borrowers. Indeed, such advertising was even directed toward people who were not in such good positions: "[T]he lending industry used marketing deception—including boiler room tactics—on a mass scale against a class of financially vulnerable borrowers (which subprime borrowers are, by definition) and other middle-class financial amateurs already laboring with stagnating incomes and rising costs for health care, education, and, of course, housing."[21]

If you had any equity at all in your home and sometimes even when you did not but there was simply an opportunity to book a loan commission and then sell the thing to someone else before it went bad, a home equity loan could be had. These loans had adjustable rates, balloons, and onerous terms that put borrowers back on their heels if they missed a payment on any bill. Even as the real estate market was tottering in 2008 and, in particular, the subprime market was crashing, the National Association of Realtors[22] and mortgage lenders like Ditech[23] were touting mortgages and refinance. Perhaps they were simply responding to desperate times with desperate measures. But as 2008 wore on, it became increasingly clear that the only thing that would get the country out of the terrible fix it was in was more lending, as the government stepped up with proposals of ever larger bailout packages for various players in the banking and financial industries and as the major automakers also teetered on bankruptcy.[24]

Throughout it all, the relentless pace of promotion continued. Some pitches bordered on fraudulent, as when the REAA claimed that an investment in a home was still solid and one of the most important that anyone could make or when Ditech tried to make a virtue of adversity by telling consumers that they could take their loan problems to Ditech. At best, these appeals seemed irresponsible. At worst, they constituted knowing misrepresentations. Yet many people blamed borrowers. Editorial pages carried solemn admonishments about "irresponsible borrowers" getting their comeuppance and cited borrower fraud as an important contributor to the crisis, even though the issuers themselves had relentlessly marketed credit cards and done their best to encourage their use.[25]

The Professionals

The increased comfort with deficit spending was supported by the unceasing efforts of marketers who never stopped selling (and indeed have not stopped to this day) more and more credit. It is not immediately apparent why the so-called irresponsible borrowers are more or even equally to blame for their plight as the irresponsible lenders. A lender is in the business of loaning money. In contrast, the borrower is the amateur in the transaction. Responsible lending entails risk management and lending ratios that are based on the ability to repay. Also, lenders can (and do) employ professional marketers who know how to pitch a product that is profitable for the bank, even if it is not particularly desirable for the consumer or is even, in some cases, inconsistent with a borrower's stated preferences.

It is the marketers' business to figure out ways of getting around stated preferences that are antagonistic to a sale, in order to persuade the customer that they really do need something that they think they can do without. Perhaps no one has been better at that than American marketers have in the latter part of the twentieth century and up to the present. Their job is to get around our resistance. Lenders could also assemble databases, commission marketing research to test how a particular message is working, hire accountants to track loan and borrower performance and run algorithms to predict problems, hire psychologists and language professionals to couch pitches in terms that would convey the impression of one thing while perhaps delivering a different reality, and hire lawyers to lobby for beneficial laws and to draft contracts with advantageous phrasing written in fine print that few borrowers would read and almost none would understand if they did read it. If, with all those advantages, lenders made many loans that were untenable—who is really, "irresponsible"?

The marketing environment in which we now live is a consequence of the responses generated by the need to create a market for the excess productive capacity freed up at the end of World War II. At that time, consumers were urged, as a patriotic matter, to buy houses and cars, to go into debt, and to do so on a scale that had been previously unheard of.[26] They responded. As people became accustomed to large debt burdens as a matter of course, the limits to those burdens began to be tested. This shift occurred not only in personal finance but also in the corporate world.

Don't Call It Debt

The corporate world does not speak about "debt"; it speaks about "leverage." *Debt* is a word freighted with negative and shameful connotations. *Leverage,* by contrast, is an action word; it implies skillfully manipulating circumstances to turn them to your advantage. In the latter part of the twentieth century, leverage came to be seen as a way to ensure that a company operated efficiently, that it was "lean and mean." Corporate raiders would make tender offers, at above-market prices, to shareholders of target companies, on the theory that the target was underperforming because of excess "fat" in management.

Buyers could make these takeover bids with other people's money by convincing investment banks to lend them the vast sums of money necessary. This phenomenon, known as a "leveraged buyout," took the country by storm. Takeover mania struck Wall Street, and incredibly large sums were routinely lent to finance takeover bids. Some of them worked out well for almost everyone—the buyers, the stockholders, and the lenders (maybe not so much for old management). Others did not do so well, and sometimes it was unclear whether anyone other than the investment banks themselves was better off. However, despite this strategy's popularity on Wall Street, many people saw it as wasteful of corporate resources and destructive of going concerns that employed many people. Executives of targeted companies were obviously alarmed.

The political response was a wave of anticorporate takeover devices meant to hinder attempts by "outsiders" to takeover a company without the blessing of management. These devices, whether statutory or dreamed up by lawyers, went by various colorful names in the popular culture of Wall Street—"poison pills," "shark repellent," and so forth. The drafters preferred to use rather more attractive names like "shareholders' rights agreements." But whatever they were called, the purposes of such devices was to make takeovers more expensive and unpopular. Some of these efforts did not fare so well in the courts, but others were upheld.

Over the course of the next couple of decades, there were several generations of such shareholders' rights agreements, until an uneasy equilibrium was achieved. Orchestrating takeovers was complex and costly, and battling through the legally sustainable antitakeover barriers was forbidding enough that the enthusiasm for leveraged buyouts appeared to diminish somewhat. The threat did not go away, but it no longer dominated the front pages. However, the takeover battles and leveraged buyouts left changes in their wake. One of those changes was an increased tolerance for debt. High levels of debt could make a company more profitable—as long as it could manage not to collapse. Another effect was a hypersensitivity on the part of management to variations in stock prices. A decline in the value of the price of a stock was never good news to a CEO. But the threat of a takeover bid made a decline particularly unnerving. They did have some countermeasures, though, to serve as insulation.

"We're in the Money!"

One group that appeared to benefit immensely (if somewhat belatedly) from these battles was the top executives. Executives fearing ouster through takeovers began to insist that their employment contracts contain buyout provisions, what became known as "golden parachutes." In the overheated environment of takeover bids, sums that once seemed exorbitant became routine, and executive compensation generally shot into the stratosphere, to levels previously not only unheard of but undreamed of.

In part, this was because stock options became a routine part of executive compensation packages. Stock options offered a way, or so many thought, to solve a problem that arguably had led to the takeover battles in the first place: a lack of commitment to the welfare of the company on the part of managers and directors who were simply employees and might be putting their own interests in front of those of the company. One way to try to align management and the company's interest was to give management a stake in the company through giving them options. It sounded like a good idea at the time. However, rather than generating enhanced attention to their fiduciary duties, it seemed such offers simply turned executives into speculators and manipulators of their own companies' stock, and enormous compensation packages became commonplace.[27] Over and over again, in the tales of wretched excess from the 1990s and well into the present, we have encountered corporate scandals like Enron's that were fueled at least in part by the desire to inflate stock value, a desire that can be traced back to options.

The enormous sums earned by top executives of major corporations can be seen as indicators of the general growth of income inequality more generally. Tolerance for compensation in the hundreds of millions[28] went side by side with tolerance for debt. Consumption, conspicuous and otherwise, assumed a starring role in the economy as a whole, making up, by some accounts, 70 percent of the gross national product.

All these developments were accompanied by the democratization of luxury, or at least the appearance of luxury. Many small "luxuries," in the form of designer goods and brand-name coffees for example, became routine parts of many people's lives, even if the people were not part of the executive elite—and most were not. Although luxury was democratized, making small luxuries more accessible, there was also during this period a slowing down of increases in real incomes. Income inequality increased, but the shortfalls in income, sometimes caused by unexpected drags on income through increased expenses for health care as employers cut back or reduced health care coverage for employees, may have been postponed because of widely available credit. Credit shored up both business and personal expenditures. Households and businesses appeared to be able to keep pulling rabbits out of hats—until they were not.

Who Is Minding the Store?

There is no doubt that many people borrowed more money than was prudent. Some of that money was, undoubtedly, spent unwisely. Borrowers are not professional borrowers. If someone is a professional borrower, there is a good chance that person is defrauding the bank or representing a hedge fund. Most people borrow as a means to an end, whether to own a home, to start and run a business, or simply to consume whatever it is that they are consuming. Lenders, however, are professionals in the borrowing business. They aim to make a profit, and they address lending issues—like the likelihood a particular borrower will pay back a loan—out of self-interest. Banks are in the business of attempting to calculate this risk. No bank is going to call loans right in every case. That is the role reserves and differential interest rates are meant to play. So how could things have gone so wrong? Does America *really* have that many deadbeats?

Actually, it does not.[29] The vast majority of people want to pay their debts, notwithstanding the credit card industry's representation of borrowers as increasingly willing to run up large debts that they are not willing to pay and will file bankruptcy to avoid. The industry got the bankruptcy legislation it wanted using this sort of imagery. But it did so knowing that the poorest people may be the best credit risks, long-sufferingly paying ruinous interest rates and staggering amounts of debt to demonstrate that they will meet their obligations. Indeed, credit cards, or something that looks like credit cards, have become a measure of status as a respectable citizen.[30]

Lenders know that those at the lowest end of the income scale are just as likely (if not more likely) to try to pay their debts as those at the upper end. They also know that these borrowers may be more inclined to test the affordability of a loan by the amount of the monthly payment rather than by the total cost of the loan. Most credit cards therefore set up as a monthly minimum payment an amount that, if adhered to, would not retire the debt for decades, thereby disguising the real interest rates. All borrowers are treated to loan terms that are essentially nonnegotiable and contained in the fine print, while they are bombarded with ever more urgent cries of "Take our money, please!" "Just think," so the marketing circulars urge, "of all that you can do with this extra cash!" They send consumers blank "convenience checks" that, if signed, end up committing the borrower to loan terms that they may not fully understand. Lenders inserted something called a universal default in the loan agreements, a provision that meant that even if the borrower did not make a late payment to the lender, a late payment to any other creditor or possibly even on a utility bill would constitute a breach of the agreement. These and other practices emerged at the same time as the federal government seemed to loosen restrictions on predatory lending practices.[31] If the trend has reversed or slowed somewhat in recent years with the passage of credit card reform, it has done so only slightly. Many claim that the reform is inadequate.

In sum, commercial actors were responsible for a great deal of the bad information in the market that undoubtedly contributed to the economic collapses in 2008–9. Relentless promotion of home equity loans and credit cards fueled the consumption that, when combined with negative or flat savings rates, made the economy precariously susceptible to any market correction in home prices, major institutional failure, sudden unemployment, or unexpected massive health care expenses. In the last century, we became inured to grotesque executive compensation packages and ever-widening inequality that seem to fuel political and economic instability, not the stability Emerson envisioned. The country has seen the collapse of housing prices and the bankruptcy of several major financial institutions and automakers. Many individuals have experienced a job loss or catastrophic illness (or both). These events exposed the weakness of our economy, an economy fueled by high levels of consumption that present a threat to the stability of the whole world through threats to the environment.

CHAPTER 11

Commercial Expression and Environmental Instability

Green is the new black.[1]
—Tamsin Blanchard, *Green Is the New Black:*
How to Change the World with Style

The final concern that Emerson identified as a reason to protect freedom of expression was that such protection acted as a safety value to promote social stability. As with the interest in promoting truth or democratic participation, social stability is a goal that reflects the interests of society as a whole, not the individual speaker. Emerson believed protection for freedom of expression permitted dissent to be expressed, which in turn allowed political change to occur through dialogue rather than through coercion or suppression. Suppression, he argued, could cause opposition both to be concealed and to harden. Protection for freedom of expression, in contrast, might allow for cathartic expression. It would allow dissenters to blow off steam and thereby lessen the urgency with which they sought to press their positions. In this way, the First Amendment could act as a more benign tool of social control than coercion.

It is not at all clear that protection for commercial expression would function this way. In the first place, since corporations are not human, they do not have any "frustrations" to express or cathartic benefits to be gained from blowing off steam. More fundamentally, as previously discussed, for-profit corporations have a very effective and powerful voice in government. Even if industry lobbyists are not invariably successful, they probably succeed in seeing their goals realized more often than any other single group in America. It *is* clear, however, that commercial expression contributes significantly to consumption practices that are destructive of the very physical basis on which all life depends—the integrity of the planet. While that may not be the sort of stability Emerson had in mind, global climate change and the political struggles surrounding the issue may ultimately endanger social and political stability.

Recycling

It has happened now more times than I can count. One of the grocery stores where I regularly shop has stopped using plastic bags and has begun selling reusable bags for loading groceries. Despite the fact that I have any number of saved shopping bags from shopping trips past that might have served as well (although I feel there is a curious etiquette about going into a store with a bag with someone else's logo, even if it is not a competing business), I bought two of these bags and put them in the trunk of my car. There they remain. So far, every time I have gone shopping since I bought those bags, I have gone into the store without them and discovered halfway through my shopping (or later) that I forgot to bring them in. On four or five occasions, I have made a trip back to the car to retrieve the bags. More often, I have just thought to myself, "Forget about it! I'll try to remember next time," and—yes, you guessed it—I forget again the next time. I suspect it will take several more trips back to the car before I reliably remember to bring my reusable bags into the store with me.

Of course, if everyone were bringing their bags, I would probably have an easier time remembering. This is one of the things that make environmental problems so frustratingly difficult to address—habits are very difficult to change. Until a lot of people change, it is hard to initiate change. But until some people initiate changes, widespread change will not occur. Stability of *bad* social practices is not necessarily desirable. Nevertheless, it is possible to change. The decline in smoking in the United States illustrates that, given the right incentives and information, people can change even very deeply ingrained habits like smoking, with its additional built-in mechanism of self-reinforcement and physical habituation. So why would we not be able to change consumption practices?

Initiating and reinforcing change is difficult when one of the principal targets for change—consumption practices—fuels the economic welfare of the world's largest enterprises and, by extension, perhaps the country as well. Many (if not all) of those enterprises see their very existence as dependent on the continuation (not to say acceleration) of those practices. In service of that continuation, they engage in a virtually nonstop barrage of speech. Some of this speech is useful and informative. Most of it is probably not. Some of it is entertaining. A lot of it is just annoying. Some of it is patently and demonstrably false or misleading. But *all* of it is intended to inspire the very thing that contributes to our current environmental dilemma—consumption.

Consumption lies at the heart of the motivation for the wave of enthusiasm for green marketing—seemingly an oxymoron. It is doubtful that green marketing can even meaningfully address, let alone solve, the world's environmental problems. If this is the case, commercial expression, far from contributing to social stability, may actually be contributing to the ultimate in instability: rendering the planet unfit for human existence. We are presumably very far away from such a doomsday outcome, and many things may intervene. However, if some critics of consumption are right, it is difficult to know how the problem will be brought under control without, at a minimum, setting and enforcing standards for what can qualify as "green" in environmental labeling and marketing efforts.

Green ($$) from "Green"

According to the *Economist*, there are several reasons why businesses might be concerned about their environmental practices and thus be positioning their companies to appear environmentally responsible. Some of it is driven by recruitment needs: "Oil companies need talented graduates, many of whom want to make the world a better place."[2] Some is about saving money, as (contrary to the usual assumption) sometimes saving money and saving the environment are not at odds—for example, with respect to energy efficiency. Sometimes government, in the form of regulation, drives a business interest in environmental efforts (more about that later). Lastly, many companies are driven by consumer demand, or at least perceived consumer demand, to address their environmental practices. There have been conflicting industry reports about whether interest in environmental concerns is declining,[3] static,[4] or increasing.[5] Nevertheless, it appears that at least advertisers think that many customers care about the environment, so they market accordingly. As Jeffrey Immelt, chairman of General Electric, said, "We see green is green."[6]

Green marketing is big business. There is a rush of enthusiasm for businesses to display their credentials as "green."[7] Marketers of every product and service imaginable—some incongruous and unlikely bearers of the green mantle, like oil companies[8]—have jumped on the green bandwagon. As Commissioner J. Thomas Rosch of the Federal Trade Commission observed in 2008, green marketing efforts have become "ubiquitous," "running the gamut" from luxury vodka and hotels to the Super Bowl and the Academy Awards.[9] In 2007 former vice president Al Gore was invited by the advertising industry to address marketers at the Cannes Lions International Advertising Festival.[10] Far from rejecting the Nobel Prize winner's message about climate change in *An Inconvenient Truth,* the industry has been eager to find ways to embrace it.[11] There is seemingly no end to the number of ways in which the public concern about environmental responsibility can be used to sell apparently unrelated products. For example, several "green" credit cards have been offered to let consumers choose carbon offset credits instead of reward points.[12] There was even the launch of a "green" TV channel expected to reach 50 million homes and provide what was called "eco-tainment."[13] (What that might be is unclear.)

Investors are also concerned about the environment. Multiple investment funds have sprung up to serve those investors who would like to align their investment decisions with their commitments to the environment.[14] Investors may represent a smaller slice of the public than consumers, but they are nevertheless significant because of the large numbers of people with small holdings through their retirement plans like TIAA-CREF and CalPERS.[15] Even the takeover sector has gone green, with leading acquisition firm Kohlberg Kravis Roberts brokering an agreement to take the Texas energy company TXU private and including in the negotiations two prominent environmental groups—the National Resources Defense Council and Environmental Defense Fund—in the largest takeover deal to that time.[16]

Some kinds of commercial expression are directed widely at both consumer and investor audiences (although these audiences obviously overlap, since all investors are also consumers, even if not all consumers are investors). Corporate *image advertising,* directed at improving the corporate image as a whole, and *issue adverting,* ads by companies about particular issues (e.g., Darfur or breast cancer), have multiple targets: investors, potential regulators, *and* consumers. Green marketing not only involves marketing products as "green" but marketing the companies as green as well, by advertising and public statements intended to position them as friends of the environment. With respect to corporate identity, however, these communications highlight some of the problematic (albeit perhaps not insoluble) identity questions corporations' structure presents. For example, is Burt's Bees a "green" company if it is owned by Clorox, the maker of, among other things, chlorine bleach, which is a pollutant?[17] Is General Electric, a major polluter, a "green" company because of its "Ecomagination" division?[18] Many would say not; but it is obviously a complicated determination.

Whether in consumption or investment decisions, "going green" holds out the possibility that people can, by their consumption decisions, contribute to resolution of a collective problem. It offers "individuals . . . an outlet for expressing public values," a way to influence "the policies and conditions of a deregulated, privatized, and globalized world."[19] As one investor puts it, [I was drawn to] "a green-oriented investment approach" in order to influence corporate behavior.[20] However, in order for these efforts to be even marginally effective, consumers and investors need reliable information about what makes a purchase or an investment "green." In a world of unrestrained commercial expression, this reliable information may be hard to come by. If calling a product or service "green" boosts revenues, it is unclear when companies would not want to do it. Where making such a claim falsely has few or no consequences, the temptation to engage in "greenwashing" may be irresistible.

Greenwashing

"[I]t is often difficult to distinguish between goods that offer a real environmental benefit from those that are simply making exaggerated claims."[21] For example, changing the color of a logo to green, as BP did as part of its green makeover, hardly seems to constitute concrete change.[22] Nevertheless, the logo change, along with some unknowable combination of other moves—some substantive, some not—has had an impact on the public perception of how "green" BP oil is.[23] Making irrelevant changes, like the color of a logo, that are intended to change the impression consumers have of the company but that are not followed by any change in actual practices is known as *greenwashing.*

Some of the following examples illustrate the problem. In Australia the *Sydney Morning Herald* accused Woolworth's of putting a "Sustainable Forest Fibre" logo on its premium house brand of facial tissues that was apparently just a marketing phrase and not actually linked to any environmental accreditation program.[24] Clorox signed a deal with the Sierra Club to share profits on a "Green Works" product line[25] and acquired Burt's Bees, a green company, but presumably it still makes Clorox bleach. General Electric touts its "Ecomagination" program while spending decades litigating an environmental action by the Environmental Protection Agency.[26] Despite BP's much-touted "Beyond Petroleum" campaign and the green logo, BP has engaged in several actions that are arguably in tension with its green image, such as its request for a permit to discharge 54 percent more ammonia and 35 percent more suspended solids into Lake Michigan.[27] BP and Shell Oil have paid fines of $1.5 million to settle fuel violations regarding emissions standards.[28]

Although many companies have loudly proclaimed their commitments to "sustainability," many of them have not followed through by establishing departments or officers dedicated to monitoring sustainability or environmental practices generally.[29] An industry insider noted that sustainability officers often "have very little budget, direct reports or organization authority."[30] Another observer, who has pegged "most companies' claims to green credentials as 'crass,'"[31] wrote, "Firms' assurances that they have properly assessed their social and environmental impacts are 'at best useless and at worst highly misleading.'"[32]

One of the consequences of all this empty marketing is that there is more public skepticism, which can fuel consumer/investor indifference or frustration. This frustration can lead to lack of follow-through or searching when it comes to green products because it is so difficult to tell what is true and false, what represents a genuine difference and what is window dressing. "What we've been seeing in focus groups is a real green backlash,"[33] says the president of one advertising and market research firm. Greenwashing, combined with legitimate ambiguity about which purchases further environmental goals, may have led to what some observers are reporting as an increased skepticism about environmental claims in general. "The sheer volume of these ads—and the flimsiness of their claims—seems to have shot the messenger. At best, it has led consumers to feel apathetic toward green claims, or at worst, even hostile, and suspicious of them."[34] When there is a lot of talk about being green but no clear way to sort the true from the false, the result is *green noise.*

Green Noise

Green noise is the "static caused by urgent, sometimes vexing or even contradictory information played at too high a volume for too long."[35] Noise (misinformation, inaccurate information, useless or unhelpful information), which is what greenwashing is, makes it difficult for businesses to profit from "going green," because if in decision making, consumers are unable to tell the difference between a true green claim and a false one, they will be more likely to default to price or other criteria that are more salient or readily confirmed. Manufacturers will be reluctant to adopt more environmentally sound methods of manufacture or sale if they are more costly, particularly if they impose costs that cannot be recouped because whatever green claims they make can be replicated by competitors who make the same claims without making the same investments. This is known as free riding, and it is easier to do where there is a lot of noise in the market. There are, of course, some additional problems. One of them is that it is not clear what makes something "green."

It's Not Easy Being Green

Even assuming perfect good faith and sincerity on the part of those at the helms of these companies (an assumption that, while not facially absurd, seems at least imprudent in light of experience), it is not easy to identify what makes a product "green." On many issues, there is little agreement (although consensus may be building) on how to measure environmental impact, which goods should be traded off, and whose interests must take priority—or even, with intergenerational equity, whether certain people's interests should be taken into account.[36] As Professor Doug Kysar of Yale has pointed out,

"[T]he sustainable development paradigm requires at a minimum some collective response to the question 'Sustainability of what?'"[37] Is it enough to put some solar panels on your factory roof? Is it possible that flying bottled water in from Fiji can be done in an environmentally sound, let alone "neutral," way?[38] What counts as green? Does recycling at the office count? Does reducing energy consumption at your stores make a company "green"?[39] Do instituting recycling or changing to energy efficient light bulbs? Most would probably say no—that these gestures are insufficient in themselves. Recent reports that those energy efficient bulbs contain mercury, another contaminant,[40] left at least some consumers uncertain about which consumption choices would vindicate their principles or support the cause with which they are concerned.

Moreover, the idea of a collective response conflicts with market liberalism, the dominant economic and political model of the developed world. If the developed and developing countries do not come to the same conclusions about what the appropriate collective response should be to the environment, how is the consumer in the developed world to choose between these visions and how can she actualize them in her purchasing decisions, when the very idea of more purchasing may be an imbedded artifact of the developed world? It is the developed world that largely dominates production and marketing and thus drives the idea that consumption and environmental responsibility are compatible. What if they are not?

"Is Earth Day the New Christmas?"[41]

While it surely makes sense to consider the ecological impact of our purchasing decisions, it seems equally clear that global climate change is not something we can buy our way out of. But you would not know it from listening to advertisers. An article in *Advertising Age* opened with the announcement "It's nearly Earth Day: Time to consume more to save the planet."[42] The incongruity of this statement appears to have been intentional, because the author was asking if consumerism had not overshadowed the meaning of the day. Still, that is what marketers do: market. So the comment cannot have been entirely tongue in cheek. Yet "[g]reen consumerism is an oxymoronic phrase," said environmentalist and author Paul Hawkin in the *New York*

Times.[43] "The assumption that by buying anything, whether green or not, we're solving the problem is a misperception,"[44] said another source, adding, "Consuming is a significant part of the problem to begin with."[45]

All that consumption has multiple impacts at every stage—the production stage, the packaging stage, the transportation to market stage, the purchasing stage, and the discard stage. On just the packaging and discarding issue, it appears that "[t]rash is clogging the arteries of the planet."[46] From that perspective, the most environmentally sound purchase is no purchase at all.[47] But on the trash front, some purchases are worse than others, and some marketing techniques themselves entail clear environmental detriments.

For example, Unilever and Proctor & Gamble sell antiperspirants. Their marketing research revealed that "clinical strength" antiperspirants can be sold at twice or three times the price as regular antiperspirants.[48] They can command this price in part on the perception that "clinical strength" is something different. Apparently, much of that impression is conveyed by an irrelevant fact—an extra box. "It would appear that the outer carton signals the idea of clinical, high-performance products,"[49] said Kevin Havelock, president of Unilever USA. Similarly, a P&G spokesman said, "[The outer box] serves as the extra real estate to get [consumers] *the information* we think they need."[50] This box obviously does not affect the contents. It only affects consumers' perception of the contents. Using this packaging is a marketing strategy pursued despite the questionable environmental practice of putting something in a superfluous box.[51] It remains unclear whether these antiperspirants are actually more effective or whether the "information," in the form of the box, is not information at all but merely an attempt to manipulate consumer perceptions. This example highlights that the "green" of economic viability will often trump the "green" of environmental responsibility—even where the company is eager to promote its green bona fides.

For this reason, some observers say that real change requires people to not only buy green but buy less—way less. Movements such as Voluntary Simplicity[52] and events such as "Buy Nothing Day"[53] have been started by those who believe that consumption practices need to be radically scaled back in order to achieve environmental stability.[54] Author Judith Levine is one of these people and, animated by the desire to explore the possibility of living on less, she decided to see if she could buy nothing in the course of one year. She kept a diary during this year and then published it as a book.[55] The year yielded some disturbing revelations. According to Levine, "because purchased experiences are so much a part of contemporary consciousness," she found excluding them to be "the hardest part of the experience":[56] "I felt stupid, boring, out of it, dulled,—boring to myself even."[57] It turns out that even if you are motivated to do so, changing your consumption habits is a very difficult thing to do. Since there is no economic benefit to less consumption, industry has understandably concentrated its messages on consuming differently, on emphasizing that being green need not entail sacrifice and that every little bit helps.

Green Lite

The marketing industry does not want you to feel, as Levine did, "out of it." It does not want you to have to try that hard. It would like to reassure you that you may, with just a few painless changes, basically continue consuming as you have been used to doing. As one advertising executive put it,

> O.K., so we like to consume. . . . [We aren't] here to tell you to start hugging trees and become an eco-warrior—although it's fine, if that's what you're into. Nah, all we are here to do is ask you to make little changes to the way you consume. *So small are these changes that you won't even notice them.*[58]

"Behavior change is a journey," says another executive about corporate responsibility,[59] adding, "People are more willing to change their light bulbs than their lifestyles."[60] Whether or not this "light green" activity constitutes meaningful action with respect to environmental concerns, it is popular with marketing professionals, since "easy" and "effortless" sell better than "difficult" or "sacrifice." That popularity is not surprising, since a move to consume less overall would probably mean fewer sales for most[61] and possibly no sales for some. Is there such a thing as a "green" Hummer?

This "light green" message dovetails nicely with the green noise problem. A situation where the truth is difficult to verify and much information is complicated or contradictory discourages inquiry. "People don't want to spend their lives wrapped up in ambiguities over one consumption decision," says Reid Lifeset of Yale's *Journal of Industrial Ecology,* commenting in the *New*

York Times[62]—and there is some evidence that they do not. Not only may consumers be inclined to accept marketers' suggestion that buying green is a reason to feel good about yourself, but they may also have fairly robust psychological defenses for continuing on with whatever practices they are currently engaged in, practices that reinforce the inertia of habit and avoidance of discomfort associated with change. One study published in the *Journal of Business Ethics* suggested that a psychological mechanism dubbed "neutralization" (which is really several techniques, including denial of responsibility and condemning the condemners) serves to interfere with the reliable translation of consumers' ethical commitments into purchasing decisions.[63] This echoes findings recently published in *Advertising Age* that consumers are not necessarily motivated by green marketing attempts, because while their aspirations may be lofty, their actions often undercut them.[64]

Moreover, consistent with the findings in the *Journal of Business Ethics* survey, there is evidence of some consumer defensiveness, so that while consumers may be "tepid about rewarding virtuous companies," they "could well be energetic about punishing the unvirtuous."[65] This makes the stampede to green claims and greenwashing even more explicable, since even if a company does not reap any benefit, it may want to avoid the tag of the environmentally unregenerate. Thus, "sincerity" and "authenticity" are buzzwords that marketing experts frequently invoke.[66] These are somewhat euphemistic ways of saying that such marketing efforts should be truthful in order to be effective. However, much of this marketing is not truthful.

Greenwashing is reflective of an attitude that is, as discussed in previous chapters, endemic to the public relations industry, an industry that is fundamentally involved in the business of marketing. That attitude is that ultimately everything can be spun and that facts are just the province of those quaint creatures still attached to the "reality-based community."[67] Although at least one PR executive has taken the position, with respect to the problem of global warming, that you can't spin Mother Nature and that the public relations industry itself has a PR problem when it comes to the environment,[68] this does not appear to be the norm. His remarks are in some sense indicative of the larger culture of PR in which the reverse is true—*anything* can be spun. In this view, the solution to the problem of acid rain is to change the perceptions about acid rain. The troubling thing is that this strategy often does work. It does not work all the time, and when it backfires, it can backfire spectacularly. But, for example, it has mostly worked for BP. That makes such greenwashing irresistible to businesses driven by a profit imperative.

Green image making is also the point of some charitable activities, like donations to universities that then become the basis for corporate image advertising. ExxonMobil, often singled out as particularly reprehensible on the environmental front, was apparently engaging in damage control in 2007 when it pledged $100 million to Stanford University to fund climate and energy research and then ran an ad campaign announcing the donation. The ad used engaging images of kids playing golf inexpertly, with the voiceover "Kids, they'll tackle anything. An approach we can learn from."[69] The ad suggested that while climate change was an enormous problem, it was one that the company had begun to address in its own small way with this donation.[70] Exxon's ad drew objections from some Stanford alums, who sought reassurance that Stanford's "research, faculty and good name are not for sale."[71]

While it seems undeniable that Exxon's contribution ought to advance climate and energy research, it seems unlikely, given the company's business, that it would want to support research that would point the way toward diminished reliance on oil. Instead, this donation was eerily reminiscent of the tobacco companies' efforts at research funding, efforts that clearly proceeded from an agenda that ultimately involved undermining the credence paid to the research on the health consequences of smoking and contributing to the appearance of scientific uncertainty where it did not exist. The point of such efforts is to reframe the product, to tell the company's "story"[72] and to offer the "other side."

The Corporate Story

An appeal to permit the airing of the "other side" acts as a siren song to conventional First Amendment thinking. But saying that there is a "side" to something about which there is little objective, scientific, empirical, or historical dispute is profoundly misleading. It suggests that everything in the material world is just framing. But there are not two "sides" to, for example, the laws of gravity. Some things are demonstrably true. That smoking increases the risk of cancer is a fact. However, that did not stop the tobacco companies from funding research to produce think pieces, op-eds, and other material suggesting that there were "two sides" to the issue of the health consequences of smoking. Of course, the tobacco companies did not really have a "side" in the sense of a difference of opinion on the facts; they had an economic interest to protect, regardless of the facts. A claim for freedom to promote the companies' "side" in this context is not an attempt to air a point of view but is, rather, an attempt to influence people to reject the facts in order for the company to benefit from the persistence of smoking.

Similarly, oil companies have funded think tank pundits and research to provide " 'logistical and moral support' to climate change dissenters" in order to undercut " 'the prevailing scientific wisdom.' "[73] At one point, the American Enterprise Institute (AEI), a think tank receiving some funding from major oil companies, including ExxonMobil, was offering $10,000 for papers critical of the conclusions of the most recent report on global climate change by the UN Intergovernmental Panel on Climate Change (IPCC).[74] Presumably such incentives had been offered in the past, and when the AEI or other groups offer such position papers, it creates the appearance of a dispute where there is little academic or scientific dispute even if there is a great deal of political dispute. But a political dispute is not the same thing as factual dispute. And unless the corporations are citizens whose political voice counts (which *Citizens United* appears to say they are), it is not clear why corporations are entitled to a voice in this political dispute, an entitlement that includes a virtual shield from liability for knowingly false statements.

If one side in the midst of a political dispute can muster apparently scientific support, it reinforces the impression of a dispute on the facts and triggers the journalistic tendency to demonstrate neutrality by reporting both "sides." As PR professional Hoggan noted,

> Reporters who are too busy to gain expertise in a contentious issue often try to achieve impartiality by quoting "experts" on both sides. But the public should be able to expect that reporters weigh carefully the relative merits of their opposing spokespeople—an expectation that falls down in this instance [i.e., climate change]. . . . [T]he mainstream media are presenting a controversy that doesn't appear in science—usually without mentioning when skeptical experts were unqualified or were associated with energy industry lobbying firms or Exxon-funded think tanks.[75]

Of course, one response to these efforts is to require transparency. This is what Hoggan calls for. However, in the absence of compulsion, this is a non-starter. As discussed earlier, it is PR's nontransparency that makes it effective. The American Enterprise Institute is far more credible on climate change than Exxon is, because Exxon obviously has an economic stake in things continuing largely as they have. It is putting your company's "story" into a credible third-party's mouth that makes the message credible.

In any event, it is primarily in the industry and in the journalism schools that there are calls for greater transparency for such marketing, as a matter of professionalism and professional integrity. Not everyone buys it. As one person in the industry put it, "PR practitioners shouldn't be expected to be totally transparent. It's not what our clients pay us for."[76] Thus, it seems unlikely that disclosure will be widely adopted as a professional norm. Disclosure could, however, be mandated by governmental regulations, and some have argued that this is what is called for in order to standardize environmental claims and to provide a stable basis for business response to public concerns about the environment.[77]

The Green Police

It is not clear what institution is positioned, willing, or able to act as green police to challenge greenwashing and reduce green noise. Nongovernmental organizations like the National Resources Defense Council, the Environmental Defense Fund, and the Sierra Club, as well as smaller groups like the Center for Science in the Public Interest and the Center for Media and Democracy, and even individual bloggers can all contribute to green policing by exposing inconsistencies and false claims when they encounter them. However, none of these entities can expect to make a profit in doing so, nor do they have the resources to match those of the commercial interests they are up against.

One possibility may be to establish voluntary industry guidelines, although there are serious concerns about whether voluntary guidelines will have real bite or, instead, just offer an opportunity for more corporate window dressing. Moreover, some have claimed that incremental and uncoordinated responses in this area are likely to fail, if not to be worse than no response at all.[78] Competitors may also act as police by raising objections to the dubious green claims of others under the Lanham Act. But where all companies are guilty of the same practices—tobacco companies, oil companies, Unilever, and Proctor & Gamble, for example—fear of retaliation against their own dubious marketing claims may inhibit many companies from bringing a claim.

So, the government is a natural place to look for an institution to police greenwashing and green noise, and some governments have taken up this role. For example, Royal Dutch Shell ran an advertising campaign in the UK that (1) claimed that Shell had discovered "creative ways to recycle" that allowed flowers to grow from its waste and (2) asserted that it used its waste sulfur to make superstrong concrete. The British Advertising Standards Authority found that the ad violated laws regarding "truthfulness" and "environmental claims."[79] Although the ad showed the outline of a factory with flowers spewing from its smokestack, it was not the imagery that violated the truthfulness standards but, rather, the slogan that implied that Shell had diverted all or a substantial amount of its waste products to these uses when, in fact, the amount diverted was trivial.[80]

But there has not been much enthusiasm for this sort of role for government in the United States. As Commissioner J. Thomas Rosch of the Federal Trade Commission noted, "the Commission has not brought any environmental marketing cases that relate to conduct described in the Guides since 2000."[81] Nevertheless, he opined that should "objectionable claims increase[] or the alternatives dissipate, the FTC cop can and should get on the beat vigorously—because these are very important claims in today's world (and they will be increasingly important, I think in our grandchildren's world)."[82] At present, however, the FTC "Green Guides" with respect to green marketing claims are only advisory and do not provide for any direct enforcement authority.[83] Rather, enforcement actions need to proceed under the general authority of the FTC to police false and misleading commercial claims. Given the proliferation of such claims, it would seem that the FTC "cop" is on a coffee break.[84]

For the last several years, lawmakers have shown little enthusiasm for this police officer role. The Bush administration, for example, was at best indifferent and, according to many, actually hostile to environmental concerns. In fact, the Bush administration's Council on Environmental Quality seemed to be pulling many of its programs from the PR playbook when it proceeded to name various initiatives that seemed to be an exercise in Orwellian dou-blespeak: "Lowering air quality became the 'Clear Skies Initiative,' while al-lowing timber companies to step up their clear cutting was dubbed the 'Healthy Forests Initiative.' "[85] For several years, the government's state-ments have read as if they were shaped by the oil industry. Even worse, it ap-peared that the White House engaged in tactics such as requiring the dele-tions of some facts from federal science reports on climate.[86] The authors of the reports were told by the director of the Environmental Protection Agency to take the position that greenhouse gasses could not be controlled under the Clean Air Act, and the White House refused to open an e-mail setting forth a contrary position.[87]

There is an additional obstacle to regulation. Many believe that it is in-appropriate for the government to police the truthfulness of such claims, and they would certainly argue that ads such as Royal Dutch Shell's were sufficiently directed at issues of public concern that they ought to be pro-tected by the First Amendment. If the proponents of freedom for commercial expression have their way, the First Amendment defense may deprive the FTC and other governmental agencies of even their marginal authority to po-lice truthfulness. In the absence of recognition that a corporate speaker is not the same as a human speaker, the First Amendment would seem to even more clearly represent an obstacle to regulating the use of the third-party technique to put out position papers and the like, because these communications seem, on their face, to be more like political speech than commercial speech.

The Problem of PR and the Third-Party Technique

In 2006, Senators Rockefeller and Snowe sent a letter to ExxonMobil urging it to cease funding for groups denying global warming and asking the com-pany to "publicly acknowledge both the reality of climate change and the role of humans in causing or exacerbating it"; to disassociate itself from skeptics of global warming; and to cease its funding of pseudoresearch in-tended not to "prevail in the scientific debate, but to obscure it."[88] On De-cember 7, 2006, the Ayn Rand Institute, a conservative think tank, issued a press release calling the plea of Senators Rockefeller and Snowe to Exxon-Mobil "an outrageous violation of ExxonMobil's right to free speech."[89] Without knowing whether the Ayn Rand Institute is funded by ExxonMobil or whether, like Working Families for Wal-Mart, it was not only funded but created by the company, one does not know how to assess the political import of such statements. As long as we consider statements like this protected speech, in an environment where companies may create front groups at will and then put their messages in those groups' mouths, the prospects seem dim for a diminishment of greenwashing or green noise.

While it is surely an exaggeration that people believe everything they read or hear in the media, it may be that people are particularly reliant on third-party sources about such complicated problems as global climate change or the environmental impact of the production of certain goods. As Professor Zygmunt Plater has noted, this operates at both the macro level of general policy formation and the micro level of trial strategy in enforcement actions and suits for damages:[90] "Media coverage is almost always an affirmative element—and is sometimes an indispensable determinant—for public interest environmental attorneys in litigation, as well as for those doing legislative, administrative, and political work."[91] Plater uses *Escamilla v. ASARCO*[92] as a case study for the importance of framing. In *Escamilla,* a low-income neighborhood at the fringes of Denver had been the site of many polluting industries, of which defendant ASARCO was the most notorious.[93] A group of plaintiffs sued ASARCO alleging harm from the pollution. Plater describes the plaintiffs' attorneys' efforts to bring the case to the media's attention and to offer an appealing frame, a sort of marketing approach, as key to the positive outcome for the plaintiffs. He makes a compelling case for why attorneys acting as advocates for environmental causes must adopt such marketing strategies.

This approach is echoed by two environmentalists who have been labeled the "'bad boys of American environmentalism,'"[94] Michael Shellenberger and Ted Nordhaus, who wrote a provocatively titled essay called "The Death of Environmentalism."[95] In the essay, they take environmentalists to task for working with what they consider outmoded paradigms—too much that sounds like bad news, too much defensiveness, and too much adherence to the "literal truth"—instead of launching a PR assault with the good news like "the millions of jobs that will be created by accelerating our transition to a clean energy economy."[96] As Yale law professor Doug Kysar observed in reviewing Shellenberger and Nordhaus's latest opus, *Break Through,* it seems the authors believe that "the future of environmentalism . . . lies not in stronger evidence, better science, or more reasoned appeals to the public, *but instead in sheer marketing acumen,* in forming and framing policy goals in a manner that activates the deeply embedded values and cognitive metaphors of the public."[97]

Since Shellenberger and Nordhaus are consultants, it is perhaps not surprising that they see the issue through a PR lens. Of course, there are a few small problems with this observation. Not all the news is good, and some of it simply defies being spun as good. Moreover, as Plater noted with respect to the *Escamilla* case, the polluter defendant objected to the plaintiffs' attempts to garner and shape publicity in the case as violative of the attorneys' professional responsibilities. They sought and obtained a gag order prohibiting the mention of the issues of race, poverty, and environmental justice raised by the case and filed a grievance with the state bar against one of the plaintiff's attorneys for his characterization of the action in a statement to the press that plaintiffs were trying to "potty-train a Fortune 500 company."[98] Defendants implied that plaintiffs were welcome to hire a PR firm to manage the publicity, as the defendant did, but that such comments by the attorney were inappropriate.[99]

Of course, since corporate defendants are far more likely to have the funds to launch PR campaigns, either directly or through third-party industry or trade groups like Energy Tomorrow, it is a rather uneven battle that reprises the difficulties raised for plaintiffs in cases in which expert testimony is required. As with expert witnesses, the services of which corporate defendants will have more access to than public interest groups, the access to press agents is another instance of inequality. Environmental groups seem similarly unlikely to be able to muster the sort of resources to launch PR campaigns of the sort Nordhaus and Shellenberger appear to contemplate. Moreover, few entities stand to make a profit from urging consumers to consume less. As noted previously, it is the profit motive tied up in the opportunities for marketing and positioning as "green" that have been driving some of the attention to green issues.

Still, there does seem to be some new impetus for change. Despite long resistance, it appears that there is general buy-in to the sense that there is a real emergency with respect to the environment. Perhaps it was Hurricane Katrina, Al Gore's *An Inconvenient Truth,* the IPCC's report, or all of the above, but the actions of wealthy individuals like Steve Bing and the apparently ever more serious rhetoric from traditionally conservative commentators like the *Economist* suggest the tide has turned, making it safe to be an environmentalist. As *Advertising Age* put it, "That elite shops [advertising and public relations firms] aren't scared off from crafting environmental messaging that could be tacitly critical of big business's sometimes unsustainable ways is yet another sign of the mainstreaming of green thinking within the corporate world at large."[100]

It remains to be seen whether this trend can be reconciled with the fundamental structural tensions between, on the one hand, businesses predicated on stimulating consumption where a decrease seems to be called for or comments to practices for which there is no immediate sustainable alternative and, on the other, what is needed for real amelioration of current harmful practices. But where there is no meaningful check on what can be said in aid of *appearing* green and where the profit-making imperative remains, the temptation to greenwash seems likely to be overwhelming for many and arguably just good business sense as long as it is legal to do so.

Commercial expression contributes to environmental problems in a number of ways. It serves as a stimulus to the hyperconsumption visited in the last chapter. Furthermore, much of this marketing is directed at a particular consumption style which may not be sustainable. It is probably impossible to catalog all of the myriad ways in which the consumption style is ecologically unsound.[101] The rough outlines are all too familiar now: a society heavily dependent on cars, a penchant for fuel-inefficient vehicles, excessive and extraneous packaging and corresponding mountains of garbage, inefficient appliances, planned obsolescence, a heavy reliance on disposable products, and so forth. Because many of these practices and products so deeply ingrained into the daily life of Americans were originally sold to us by those who wanted to sell us something,[102] it is difficult to know where the momentum to preach the gospel of conservation will come from unless someone can think of a way in which a profit can be turned by convincing us to consume less. Even supposing someone had such a motive, could the speech of such a gospel match or exceed the volume at which consumption is being pitched?

Even if it is possible (and some think it is not) to undo destructive habits through targeted purchasing, the proliferation of green claims contributes to green noise. Greenwashing and noise are a form of static that impedes attempts to harness the power of consumption to affect changes, because the market depends on accurate information. First Amendment protection for commercial expression would ensure more noise of this type. One might well ask whether the First Amendment ought to protect that kind of disinformation.

Commercial expression goes far beyond the direct attempts to further economic interests by stimulating consumption. It also includes speech aimed at legislators, investors, and the public at large that is often misleading. Some of this speech, such as the creation and use of front groups, the manipulation of media and other third parties to disguise the source of the communication, the funding of pseudoscience, and direct lobbying for such industry-friendly bills as the lifting of the ban on offshore drilling, has engendered significant setbacks or obstacles to meaningful change. Extending broader First Amendment protection to all of these practices, instead of instituting limits on them, would make it more difficult than ever either to curb persuasion activities that stand to have such potentially devastating consequences on our environmental future or even, at minimum, to reduce the static that obscures the need for meaningful change.

It seems unlikely that any effort to reverse or slow global climate change will be effective without the means to limit what can be said to spur consumption of some products or to prohibit false green claims or lobbying by giant global corporations, like oil companies, with a stake in the status quo. It is devilishly difficult to change consumption practices, but change they must, if only, as the best case scenario would have it, in small ways. Change seems needed with respect to not only things purchased but ways of living: for example, the residential development of towns and cities in a culture that takes automobiles as a given, the consumption of electricity and natural gas, the use of disposable items in place of reusable ones. The list could go on.

Virtually no part of daily life in the United States—showers, toothpaste, paper plates, disposable cleaning wipes, bottled water, transportation—remains untouched by the attitudes and preferences about how to live shaped by those in the marketing business. With climate change looming, however, what if it is no longer the case that "the increase of consumer spending on the things that consumers want and need" will provide a "basic and lasting solution to our economic future"?[103] Relying solely on individuals and nongovernmental organizations to ferret out the truth of environmental claims and to act as environmental watchdogs for consumers with respect to greenwashing is inadequate.

As the *Economist* noted in its special report on business and climate change, "Climate change is a collective problem, which can be dealt with only collectively. Voters can encourage that by electing governments committed to changing the rules to encourage companies to behave differently."[104] Indeed, it is government's function to deal with collective problems. How to inspire changes in consumption practices is a collective problem. Moderating and controlling the flow of commercial speech, which acts as a counterforce to efforts to change those practices by, at the very least, discouraging fraudulent green claims, seems not only a legitimate governmental task in this context but a critical one.

It might be necessary to go farther by prohibiting for-profit companies from making anonymous contributions to or establishing front groups that promote climate change denial and to require full disclosure of corporate funding sources for all scholarly articles. These actions are arguably constitutional as appropriate responses to a collective problem that is beyond the scope of individual solutions. The details of the governmental response may be less important than reestablishing the legitimacy of government action in general in this arena. Global climate change presents a real, looming social cost of a laissez-faire attitude with respect to marketing speech. As one Nobel Prize winner for work on climate change, Rajendra Pachauri, put it, "Awareness has to be raised in both the East and the West to deglamorize unsurvivable consumerism."[105] The parameters of the cost are still indistinct, but they are virtually certain to be large. This makes one of the most compelling cases for what Judge Richard Posner has called, in other circumstances, First Amendment "pragmatism." "[W]hile the risk of judges' overweighing the costs of free speech is a real one," wrote Posner, ". . . I don't know on what basis this risk can be pronounced greater than the risk of stifling beneficial government regulation."[106] In light of the dangers of climate change, curbing greenwashing and reducing green noise are legitimate areas for the exercise of governmental experimentation and for court engagement in a bit of First Amendment pragmatism.

Conclusion

[A] nation built for shopping cannot possibly endure as a democracy.
—Mark Crispin Miller, introduction to 2007 reissue of
Vance Packard's *The Hidden Persuaders*

In the wake of the Supreme Court's dismissal of the *Nike v. Kasky* case, it was still possible to imagine, even if it was not likely, that the Court might draw back from the path it was on to extend more protection for commercial speech. After *Citizens United* and *Sorrell v. IMS Health*,[1] that prospect seems less likely than ever. To the contrary, the rhetoric in these cases suggests that increased protection for commercial speech is almost inevitable. If that happens, it will seriously impair Congress's ability to regulate commerce. And if ever there was a time when it appeared that regulation of commerce was absolutely essential, that time is now. There are undoubtedly many lessons to be learned from the massive business failures and scandals of recent years, but surely one of them is that unfettered commercial speech can be extremely destabilizing to the economy. It may go some way toward explaining the degree to which the American economy is dependent on high levels of consumption, debt, and a low savings rate, factors that may make the country more vulnerable to phenomena like financial bubbles and uneven, dramatic market corrections.

As set out in the preceding chapters, the problems of unrestrained commercial expression go far beyond the dangers of financial instability. They are present in all, or virtually all, of the most pressing issues facing not just the United States but the world today—how to reconcile concern for the environment with economic development and stability, how to protect human health and well-being, how to defend democratic government from the en-croachments of powerful and essentially stateless nondemocratic institutions. If government lacks the ability to impose legitimate checks on how businesses promote their products and services, it would seem to pose grave dangers to the general welfare on many levels, particularly public health.[2]

Protection for freedom of speech under the First Amendment does not mean now, nor has it ever meant, absolute protection from consequences for all utterances. If that were the case, fraud, bribery, defamation, libel, con-spiracy, and many other speech acts would not be a basis for prosecution; the enforcement of contracts might be impossible. So, some restrictions on speech are permissible; the question is, which ones? Given the evidence, con-stitutional protection for truthful commercial speech is the outer limit for what ought to be protected under the First Amendment with respect to com-mercial expression.

This is consistent with the justifications under which protection was granted in the first place by the *Virginia Pharmacy* Court—the informational value of truthful commercial speech and the respect for autonomy of the in-dividual consumer, which entails not shielding consumers from the truth. However, that does not mean accepting a loose definition of what constitutes "information," nor does it mean that the government ought to be powerless to control the style of presentation or.manipulative techniques. Aspects of advertising that are designed to manipulate more than inform ought to be subject to regulation. The large, for-profit corporation has historically been a demonstrably unreliable source of information even with appropriate gov-ernmental controls (and often despite them).

Moreover, the definition of "commercial speech" should include any speech by a for-profit corporation. Full protection for commercial speech is not mandated by the Constitution, and corporations are not speakers just like any other speaker. Neither logic nor historical practice dictates that a corporation must be treated like a human being. A "corporation" is a legal entity that takes its character and purpose from the law that creates it. Just as it has "no body to kick or soul to be damned," it has no "self" to be ex-pressed. Such entities do not have "intentions" or "purposes" beyond the profit-centered ones provided for under the laws governing their creation. This renders all speech by for-profit corporations inherently "commercial" by definition.

It is not illegitimate to distinguish between for-profit and not-for-profit entities. The latter are often formed precisely to amplify the voices of their membership on a particular topic. Likewise, unions are representative organizations. But for-profit corporations are not representative organizations. They represent capital, not people. Not all human interests are reducible to an economic interest, but for-profit corporations' charters drive their employees to act as if they were. The peculiar tunnel vision of the for-profit corporate entity, which is so useful when appropriately limited to its proper sphere, is, as we have seen, dysfunctional if allowed to run amok with respect to interests in the public welfare like health, product safety, the environment, and other public goods.

Saying that there should be more regulation of commercial speech, however, does not mean that regulation is itself unproblematic or that a regulatory state represents some sort of democratic nirvana. It is undoubtedly a mistake to place too much confidence in regulation alone. Nevertheless, we have ample evidence that, in many cases, the market does not do much better in imposing appropriate limits and, in some key ways, is worse. The government is or can be somewhat responsive to the electorate. Elected representatives must pay at least lip service (and hopefully more) to the public interest, whether they serve it in fact or not. In contrast, the boards of directors and management of the world's largest companies, companies that have such profound effects on our lives, are not even nominally answerable to the public. The public has no say, even formally, over choices with dramatic impacts on it.

Social responsibility trends do not offer a meaningful solution to this problem. The corporate social responsibility initiatives adopted in the last few decades remain largely perfunctory, unenforceable, and opaque.[3] When practices are not mandatory and when reliable information is scarce, corporations are free to make whatever representations they like about corporate social responsibility, with few repercussions for false statements and little danger of discovery for many abuses. Competition similarly offers little solace if all participants in the industry engage in the same practices. Managers do not see themselves as having an incentive to depart from a practice by foregoing advertising (a sort of prisoner's dilemma) or by adopting costly labor or environmental practices and then advertising those practices so long as a competitor might make similar claims without similar investments. Too often, consumers' ability to withhold their business offers even less in the way of informational feedback to those companies than the power to withhold a vote does to politicians. So we cannot hope for consumer demand to push corporations to social responsibility. Consumers are at a grave informational disadvantage. It cannot be the case that we are "warranted in justifying manipulation on the ground that anything that increases the gross national product is 'good' for America?" Surely not *anything* is justified.

Balancing Competing Values

Commercial speech presents a question of balancing interests—public and private. The question that must be answered before commercial speech is offered expansive protection is whether the purported benefits of such protection outweigh the harms of fewer restrictions. The evidence suggests that they do not. Commercial speech's defenders claim that it supplies important information to consumers, enhances consumers' autonomy, and contributes to their opportunity for self-expression. Support for broad commercial speech protection also generally entails support for corporate political and issue advertising, on the grounds that corporations are "citizens" who have a right to contribute to issues of public concern and that it would "chill" or create "imbalance" in that sphere to subject corporate or commercial speakers to different restrictions than individuals.

Those claims do not appear to be well founded. Undoubtedly some autonomy and expressive interests for consumers are advanced through commercial expression, but given the degree of manipulation in which advertisers engage and the disparity in consumers' knowledge about manipulation techniques and the time and resources necessary to devote to defend against them, it is unlikely that the net effect of commercial expression is often more autonomy. To the contrary, the autonomy advertisers are most concerned with is their own—the preservation of an "unencumbered" marketing environment.

In addition, the concern about paternalism or moral hazards is misplaced. Advertisers and marketers have often overstated and inflated their degree of control over audiences, and many ads are ineffective, but it does not follow from these observations that ads are never effective or that the techniques employed to generate a response from consumers are of no consequence. Even if advertisers can only do half of what they claim, that half seems to involve encroachments into citizens' autonomy interests and to raise nontrivial concerns about the public health and safety consequences of allowing it to take place unmediated. Claiming, in the face of that evidence, that regulation is paternalistic seems to overlook the ways in which leaving the public undefended against false claims and manipulation by these institutions on the grounds that debiasing efforts sometimes work or that people sometimes learn from their mistakes seems to merely substitute one sort of paternalism for another.

Steven Shiffrin, a prominent, contemporary First Amendment scholar, has written that First Amendment jurisprudence is filled with "romantic generalizations"[4] that hinder our ability to deal with commercial speech because they oversimplify complex social, political and economic realities. "To formulate an organizing vision for the first amendment is to risk detachment from social reality."[5] According to Shiffrin, the reality is that "the commercial speech problem is in fact many problems,"[6] problems that raise "questions that will not go away."[7] These complex social realities often present the question of what is the proper balance in resolving tensions between competing values. Ronald Collins and David Skover have called this the "Huxleyan Dilemma,"[8] referring to the tension between the fear of a governmental orthodoxy and repression as represented in George Orwell's *1984*[9] and the dystopian vision of Aldous Huxley's *Brave New World,* in which a totalitarian government relied on consumption, eugenics, drugs, and entertainment to keep the masses happy and under control. It would certainly be premature[10] to say that there is no reason to fear George Orwell's nightmare. However, it is equally clear, given the dominant role corporations play in society, that we may not be far from the Huxleyan nightmare either—except that the totalitarian "government" is not government at all but the operation of multinational behemoths larger than most countries, against which we might expect the government to offer some shelter.

There is a legitimate role for governmental "paternalism" if paternalism means doing for citizens something that they are not able to do for themselves but that they indicate through their votes they want government to do. Government is the only force large enough to counter the power of the largest corporate actors. Whether any specific intervention is excessively paternalistic cannot be assessed in the abstract. Some ideas that seem appropriate today, under the present circumstances, may seem less appropriate to a later time. As Justice Holmes noted, "[C]ertainty generally is an illusion and repose is not the destiny of man."[11] In an area so central to the functioning of the economy and democracy as the First Amendment and the regulation of commerce, the boundary lines of appropriate regulation will always be contested, and "the means do not exist for determinations that shall be good for all time."[12] Much of the law will undoubtedly be "open to reconsideration upon a slight change in the habit of the public mind."[13] That does not mean that government should not act to try to prevent harm.

There may be unintended consequences of regulation and dangers on both sides. However, looking at the evidence, we must conclude that commercial expression contributes to, even if it is not solely responsible for, a number of social ills—the public health costs related to tobacco and alcohol, prescription and over-the-counter drugs, unhealthy foods, dangerous or simply ineffective dietary supplements, contaminated or adulterated foods, defective products, and environmental contamination. It also undermines public safety and welfare related to environmental degradation and global climate change and threatens global economic security. It does not do all of that by itself, of course. But I hope this book demonstrates that it plays a significant role.

Commercial expression also plays a role in boosting demand for products produced in a manner some find objectionable, whether because of animal testing, labor practices, or support for groups or causes offensive to some or many people. Although I have not discussed this here, it also reinforces gender and racial stereotypes that undermine other societal attempts to remove barriers to full equality for women and disadvantaged minority groups.[14] The dominance of commercial interests in the world of communication generally may not bode well for democracy.

As I hope the preceding chapters have made clear, few of these problems are likely to go away with more freedom for commercial expression. Our current problems have arisen under the present legal regime, where much commercial speech *is* (at least theoretically) highly regulated. Doing away with those limitations would not seem to ameliorate any of these problems.

It is not clear how to solve this dilemma or resolve these tensions, since it appears that there is no reasonable prospect that a developed economy can do without a great deal of promotional activity. Moreover, the genii may be out of the bottle when it comes to the application of marketing techniques to politics. Although Huxley deplored the notion that politicians might be "sold" with the same techniques used to sell soap, not everyone considered this a pernicious development. Edward Bernays thought it was the only way in which a democracy could be made manageable: "The conscious and intelligent manipulation of the organized habits and opinions of the masses is an important element in democratic society."[15] He wrote that, "*Those who manipulate this unseen mechanism of society constitute an invisible government that is the true ruling power of our country.* We are governed, our minds molded, our tastes formed, our ideas suggested, largely by men we have never heard of. This is a logical result of the way in which our democracy is organized."[16] Bernays saw nothing sinister or undemocratic in the prospect that a good many of the members of that "invisible government"[17] would include "the presidents of the chambers of commerce in our hundred largest cities, [and] the chairman of the boards of directors of our hundred or more largest industrial corporations."[18] Perhaps he saw it this way because he included academics, local political leaders, and labor as well and thought of business actors as but one group among many. But that is not as much the case today. Today those "hundred or more largest industrial corporations" have the dominant voice in our society.

Master political strategist Frank Luntz, the man who gave Newt Gingrich the "Contract with America" and who turned the estate tax into the "death tax," is clearly an heir of Bernays and represents the triumph of his vision. "Sophistication is certainly what Americans say they want in their politics, but it is certainly not what they buy," he writes. However, the largest corporations are no longer, if they ever were, just one voice among many. They often control the conversation on public issues so thoroughly, so seamlessly, that their influence is difficult to see because it is so ubiquitous.

Moral Questions

Many might say that we have arrived at the worst of both worlds. We have experienced, in some cases, tyrannical overstepping by government and a degraded level of discourse in the political arena, as envisioned by Orwell,[19] as well as a veritable landslide of cultural "junk" in the form of nonstop advertising and an abundance of entertainment that hardly bothers to disguise its real function as marketing and distraction, as envisioned by Huxley. Commercial speech stokes the desires for escapism, consumption, and endless entertainment, desires that serve to further undermine whatever enthusiasm or aptitude for political engagement the public may have.

Nonstop commercial expression seamlessly interwoven with informational communication from other sources contributes to a general increase in materialism, a tendency to apply economic criteria to noneconomic goods or to commodify even that which some would say ought not to be commodified.[20] Commodification can, in some circumstances, exacerbate disabilities arising from income inequalities. It may also be bad for the spirit. As legal scholar James Boyd White writes,

> [F]ar too much of our world of public speech consists of forms of expression that are designed simply to promote the sale of commodities or to advance a political position, and do so with very little respect for the audience or regard for the truth. Speech of this character works not by appealing to the thought and experience of the person it addresses . . . but through the manipulation of instincts, instincts that it in fact does a lot to form. *To put it in plain terms, I think our public world is dominated by the twin evils of advertising and propaganda; that these constitute in their own way an empire of might;* and that what to think or do about this fact is a serious problem for us both as individual people and as lawyers.[21]

Many of the moral questions Vance Packard raised half a century ago remain unanswered. What is the morality of advertising campaigns "designed to thrive" on the "weaknesses that [marketers] have diagnosed" through massive amounts of marketing research; of "manipulating small children even before they are legally responsible for their actions"; of "developing in the public an attitude of wastefulness toward natural resources by encouraging the 'psychological obsolescence' of products already in use"; of "treating voters like customers, and child customers seeking father images at that"?[22] Why should there not be limits on what corporations may say to peddle their wares? If there are to be rules, why should false statements, manipulation of fears and self-esteem, manipulation of cognitive biases and other means of exploitation not be considered means that are foul rather than fair?

These are important questions. There is little indication that they are being addressed with the sense of urgency that they warrant. There is yet a chance that the Supreme Court, when presented with an invitation to expand protection for commercial speech, will reconsider its expansive notions of the value of commercial and corporate participation in the polity. It should do so while there is still a chance for "we the people" to rein in those institutions whose power is already so great that they do not need the protection of the First Amendment. To the contrary, it is we who need protection from them.

Notes

Introduction

1. Nat Ives & Rich Thomaselli, "Marketing Takes a Beating in Beltway," *Advertising Age*, July 27, 2009, 19.

2. *Id.* (quoting Bob Liodice, president and CEO of the Association of National Advertisers).

3. Nicholas Quinn Rosenkranz has recently argued that the key instrument of constitutional analysis is focus on the subject to be restrained. Nicholas Quinn Rosenkranz, "The Subjects of the Constitution," 62 *Stan. L. Rev.* 1209 (2010). Rosenkranz argues that the First Amendment and the Commerce Clause are framed as diametrical opposites; the former is written in the active voice as a prohibition, ("Congress shall make no law . . ."); while the latter, also in the active voice, is written in terms of an affirmative grant of power ("Congress shall have . . ."). *Id.* at 1275. This is undoubtedly correct as a grammatical matter. It is unclear that it illuminates when something should be considered speech and when it should be considered commerce.

4. *Advertising Age*, Editorial, "Time for Industry Workers to Make Case to Congress," July 27, 2009, 9.

5. *Marbury v. Madison,* 5 U.S. (1 Cranch) 137 (1803).

6. John J. Walsh, "The Supreme Court Should Expand Commercial Speech Protection," *Legal Backgrounder* (online publication of Carter Ledyard & Milburn LLP), Sept. 8, 2000, available at http://www.clm.com/publication.cfm/ID/90 (last accessed May 24, 2010). It is interesting that in this article that is more than 10 years old, the author identifies Justices Kennedy, Stevens, Souter, Ginsburg, and Thomas as favoring strict scrutiny for commercial speech. Of course, Justice Souter has been replaced by Justice Alito, and Justice Stevens has retired. But

given the dissent of Stevens in *Citizens United,* in which Ginsburg joined, it is no longer clear that Ginsburg could be counted as among those who would favor strict scrutiny for commercial speech. However, *Citizens United* suggests there might still be five votes—from Roberts, Alito, Scalia, Thomas, and Kennedy—for strict scrutiny.

7. *Citizens United v. Federal Election Comm'n,* 130 S.Ct. 876 (2010).

8. *Id.*

9. *See generally* David D. Kirkpatrick, "Lobbyists Get Potent Weapon in Campaign Ruling," *N.Y. Times,* Jan. 21, 2010.

10. *See, e.g.,* Lawrence Lessig, "Institutional Integrity: *Citizens United* and the Path to a Better Democracy," *Huffington Post,* Jan. 22, 2010, http://www.huffing tonpost.com/lawrence-lessig/institutional-integrity-c_b_433394.html (last accessed May 24, 2010).

11. Tamara R. Piety, "*Citizens United* and the Threat to the Regulatory State," 109 *Mich. L. Rev* First Impressions 16 (2010), http://www.michiganlawreview .org/assets/fi/log/piety.pdf.

12. Bob Herbert, "Brutality in Vietnam," *N.Y. Times,* March 28, 1997, A29. *See also* Bob Herbert, "In America: Nike Blinks," *N.Y. Times,* May 21, 1998, A33; and Bob Herbert, "Let Nike Stay in the Game," *N.Y. Times,* May 6, 2002, A21. For one of the best summaries of the facts surrounding this case, *see* Ronald K. L. Collins & David Skover, "The Landmark Free-Speech Case That Wasn't: The *Nike v. Kasky* Story," 54 *Case W. Res. L. Rev.* 965 (2004).

13. *Id.*

14. *See, e.g.,* Deborah J. La Fetra, "Kick It Up a Notch: First Amendment Protection for Commercial Speech," 54 *Case W. Res. L. Rev.* 1205, 1210 (2004).

15. *N.Y. Times Co. v. Sullivan,* 376 U.S. 254 (1964). *See also* Walsh, "Supreme Court."

16. *See* Brief for Petitioners, at 43, *Nike, Inc. v. Kasky,* 539 U.S. 654 (2003) (No. 02-575) 2003 WL 898993. There is more to the *New York Times v. Sullivan* test than the malice element. A plaintiff must also show that he or she is not a public figure. That portion of the opinion is not relevant to the discussion here.

17. *Id.* at 44–45 (contending that some erroneous statement in speech is inevitable and that protection must be given to that error).

18. *See* Tamara R. Piety, "Grounding Nike: Exposing Nike's Quest for a Constitutional Right to Lie," 74 *Temp. L. Rev.* 151 (2004).

19. It is difficult to attribute any "state of mind" to a legal fiction, let alone a disordered state of mind. But a corporation might have a better basis for a claim to something like multiple personality disorder than a human being, given that there are several people "in there" in the corporate mind. Canadian author Joel Bakan claims that if you apply the diagnostic criteria in the DSM-IV to a corporation, the corporation is a psychopath. Joel Bakan, *The Corporation* (Toronto: Penguin, 2004), 56–59.

20. Piety, "Grounding Nike," at 166.

21. Thomas C. Goldstein, "*Nike v. Kasky* and the Definition of 'Commercial Speech,'" 2002–3 *Cato Sup. Ct. Rev.* 63, 79 (2003).

22. For a somewhat different angle on this case, *see* David C. Vladeck, "Lessons from a Story Untold: *Nike v. Kasky* Reconsidered," 54 *Case W. Res. L. Rev.* 1049 (2004). Those interested in the *Nike* case should read all of the articles in the *Case Western Reserve Law Review* symposium issue on the case, "Symposium: *Nike v. Kasky* and the Modern Commercial Speech Doctrine," 54 *Case W. Res. L. Rev.* 965 (2004).

23. For example, in the Nike suit, Kasky, the plaintiff, alleged that Nike spent "almost $1 billion" in 1997 on advertising and promotion. *Kasky v. Nike Inc.*, 45 P. 3d 243, 247 (Cal. 2002).

24. See *Katzenbach v. McClung*, 379 U.S. 294 (1964); *United States v. Lopez*, 514 U.S. 549 (1995); *Gonzales v. Raich*, 545 U.S. 1 (2005).

25. *Ohralik v. Ohio State Bar Ass'n*, 436 U.S. 447, 456 (1978).

26. *Id.*

27. *See, e.g.*, Brief of the Center for the Advancement of Capitalism (arguing that the Court should do away with the commercial speech doctrine), *Nike v. Kasky*, 539 U.S. 654 (2003) (No. 02-575) 2003 WL 834937. *See also* Bruce E. H. Johnson & Ambika K. Doran, "Amendment XXVIII? Defending Corporate Speech Rights," 58 *S.C. L. Rev.* 855 (2007); Vicki McIntyre, "*Nike v. Kasky*: Leaving Corporate America Speechless," 30 *Wm. Mitchell L. Rev.* 1531 (2004); Daniel E. Troy, "Advertising: Not 'Low Value' Speech, 16 *Yale J. Reg.* 85 (1999); Martin H. Redish & Howard M. Wasserman, "What's Good for General Motors: Corporate Speech and the Theory of Free Expression," 66 *Geo. Wash. L. Rev.* 235 (1998).

28. Roger Shiner, *Freedom of Commercial Expression* (Oxford: Oxford University Press, 2003), 70–93, 94–110 (describing similar moves to greater protections for commercial expression in Canada and Europe, respectively).

29. *See, e.g.*, 2003 O.J. (C 289): 57 (notice by Kreuzer Medien GmbH against the European Parliament and the Council for the European Union challenging the regulation of tobacco products as "infring[ing]" on "the freedom of expression safeguarded by Article 11 of the Charter of Fundamental Rights of the European Union and Article 1091 of the ECHR"). Attempts to limit the governmental regulation of products causing health risks have met with mixed success. *See, e.g.*, Opinion of Advocate General Fennelly (June 15, 2000), Case C-376/98, *Fed. Republic of Germany v. European Parliament and Council of Europe*, and Case C-74/99, *The Queen v. Sec'y of State for Health and Other, ex parte Imperial Tobacco Ltd. and Others*, 2000 E.C.R. I-8419, I-8494–95 ("I conclude, therefore, that the Advertising Directive does not constitute a disproportionate restriction of freedom of expression in so far as it imposes a comprehensive prohibition on the advertising of tobacco products."). *See also* European Court of Justice, Press Re-

lease, "Advocate General Fennelly Proposes That the Court of Justice Annul Directive on the Advertising and Sponsorship of Tobacco Products" (June 15, 2000), available at http://curia.europa.eu/en/actu/communiques/cp00/aff/cp0045en.htm (last accessed Mar. 16, 2010). The overall effect of decisions such as this one is ambiguous; *see* Benjamin Apt, "On the Right to Freedom of Expression in the European Union," 4 *Colum. J. Eur. L.* 69, 86–87 (1998). But such decisions are instructive because they help to shape public perceptions. For an overview of the approach to commercial speech in Canada and Europe, *see also* Shiner, *Freedom,* at 70–116.

30. For example, Sweden prohibits ads targeting children under the age of 12. Lennart Lindström & Mårten Stenström, "Sweden," in *The European Handbook on Advertising Law,* ed. Lord Campbell of Alloway & Zahd Yaqub (London: Cavendish, 1999), 775, 789 (citing Ch. 1(b) § Radio-och TV-lagen (SFS 1996:844) ("advertising must not be targeted at children below the age of 12 . . ."). In another example, in 2005, British regulators "introduced new rules barring depictions of links between sex and drinking in alcohol advertisements." Eric Pfanner, "No Hunks in the Alcohol Advertisements, Please; We're British," *N.Y. Times,* Aug. 1, 2005, C4. Such bans might be difficult to implement in practice. As the former deputy director of the Federal Trade Commission observed in commenting on the FTC's attempt to regulate advertising directed at children: "[W]e had trouble tailoring a regulation that would prohibit ads only in programs watched by young children because, it turns out there aren't any programs just watched by very young children; audiences are all intermixed together." *See* Tracy Westen, "Government Regulation of Food Marketing to Children: The Federal Trade Commission and the Kid-Vid Controversy," 39 *Loy. L.A. L. Rev.* 79, 85 (2006).

31. There are several philosophical roots for this position, but one of the most pertinent for purposes of constitutional analysis is John Locke and his observations in the *Second Treatise on Government* that human beings have equal rights to "life, liberty, health and property," an observation that was clearly influential on the Framers of the constitution. John Locke, *Second Treatise on Government: Political Writings of John Locke,* ed. David Wootton (Indianapolis: Hackett, 2003, 1993) (1689).

32. *See, e.g.,* Christine Chambers Goodman, "(M)Ad Men: Using Persuasion Factors in Media Advertisements to Prevent a 'Tyranny of the Majority' on Ballot Propositions," 32 *Hastings Comm. & Ent. L. J.* 247 (Winter 2010).

33. Stewart Brand, *Whole Earth Discipline* (New York: Penguin Group, 2009), 21.

Chapter 1

1. David Rabban, *Free Speech in Its Forgotten Years, 1870–1920* (Cambridge: Cambridge University Press, 1997).

2. Troy, "Advertising."

3. *See* C. Edwin Baker, "Paternalism, Politics, and Citizen Freedom: The Commercial Speech Quandary in *Nike*," 54 *Case W. Res. L. Rev.* 1161, 1162 (2003). For more of Professor Baker's magisterial work on this area see his book, *Human Liberty and Freedom of Speech* (New York: Oxford University Press, 1989) and *Media Concentration and Democracy: Why Ownership Matters* (Oxford: Oxford University Press, 2007).

4. *Valentine v. Chrestensen,* 316 U.S. 52, 54 (1942). For an excellent discussion of the definition problem, *see* Erwin Chemerinsky & Catherine Fisk, "What Is Commercial Speech? The Issue Not Decided in *Nike v. Kasky,*" 54 *Case W. Res. L. Rev.* 1143 (2004).

5. *Va. State Bd. of Pharmacy v. Va. Citizens Consumer Council,* 425 U.S. 748 (1976). The *Virginia Pharmacy* decision in 1976 is generally credited with establishing the commercial speech doctrine. However, another candidate is the earlier decision of *Bigelow v. Virginia,* 421 U.S. 809, 829 (1975), in which the Court held that a newspaper publisher could not be prohibited by the criminal law from running an ad noting the availability of abortions in New York that were illegal in Virginia. Because the Court's holding was identified as "limited" it was not really clear what the parameters of protection for commercial speech were, or on what theory it was grounded, until *Virginia Pharmacy.*

6. *Va. Pharmacy,* 425 U.S. at 749–53.

7. *Id.* at 766–70.

8. *Id.* at 770.

9. *Id.* at 756–70.

10. *Id.* at 765.

11. *Id.*

12. *Id.*

13. Alan B. Morrison, "How We Got the Commercial Speech Doctrine: An Originalist's Recollections," 54 *Case W. Res. L. Rev.* 1189 (2004).

14. Martin Redish, "The First Amendment in the Marketplace," 39 *Geo. Wash. L. Rev.* 429 (1971).

15. *Id.* at 432–48.

16. Actually, it is not entirely clear that only truthful information performs this function. Much false information may also stimulate economic activity, and if that were the sole reason for protecting speech there is no reason for limiting protection to truthful information.

17. Redish, "First Amendment in the Marketplace" (profit motive may be some insurance against the chilling effect of regulation of false advertising). *Cf. Va. Pharmacy,* 425 U.S. 748, 771 n. 24. Reading Professor Redish's article in tandem with the *Virginia Pharmacy* decision should be cheering to academics who despair of having any influence on the courts. One cannot read these two without concluding that Redish persuaded the Court to adopt his theory.

18. *Cent. Hudson Gas & Elect. Corp. v. Pub. Serv. Comm'n of N.Y.*, 447 U.S. 557 (1980).

19. *Id.* at 566 (describing test).

20. *Id.* at 563.

21. Redish, "First Amendment in the Marketplace," at 432.

22. *Va. Pharmacy*, 425 U.S. 769, 773 (using *advertising* and *commercial speech* interchangeably as if it was self-evident that advertising was equal to commercial speech). *See also* Redish, "First Amendment in the Marketplace," at 432 ("The subject of inquiry . . . is the value to society of traditional commercial advertising of products and services the public purchases and uses regularly.").

23. *Va. Pharmacy*, at 762 (quoting *Pittsburgh Press Co. v. Human Relations Comm'n*, 413 U.S. 376, 385 (1973)).

24. *44 Liquormart v. Rhode Island*, 517 U.S. 484 (1996).

25. *Bolger v. Youngs Drug Prods. Corp.*, 463 U.S. 60 (1983).

26. *Consol. Edison Co. of N.Y. v. Pub. Serv. Comm'n of N.Y.*, 447 U.S. 530 (1980).

27. *Posadas de Puerto Rico Assocs. v. Tourism Co. of Puerto Rico*, 478 U.S. 328 (1986).

28. *Zauderer v. Office of Disciplinary Counsel*, 471 U.S. 626 (1985); *Bates v. State Bar of Ariz.*, 433 U.S. 350 (1977).

29. *Id.* at 66, 67.

30. *Kasky v. Nike, Inc.*, 27 Cal. 4th 939, 966–67 (2002).

31. *First Nat'l Bank of Boston v. Bellotti*, 435 U.S. 765 (1978) (national banks challenged constitutionality of a state statute that criminalized contributions or expenditures by corporations to influence the outcome of a vote on any question submitted to voters that did not "materially affect the property, business or assets of the corporation").

32. *Bellotti*, 435 U.S. at 772. This limitation was arguably redundant since corporate law already precludes expenditures that are not in the corporation's economic interest. Although the Court suggested that the First Amendment did not permit the government to tell a corporation to "stick to its business" (*Bellotti*, 435 U.S. at 784–85), it did not comment on state statutes delineating the scope of corporate power and the duties to shareholders, which do exactly that insofar as they typically define the duty of the board and management as protecting shareholder financial interests. Presumably, a claim could still be made in a shareholders' derivative action that corporate spending for an apparently nonbusiness purpose in a particular case was a misuse of corporate funds. However, the practical realities of the capaciousness of the business judgment rule, combined with the procedural hurdles for shareholders to bring these suits, suggest that shareholders would have a difficult time maintaining such an action.

33. *Bellotti*, 435 U.S. at 775–76.

34. *Id.* at 776.

35. *Id.* at 777.

36. *Id.*

37. Charles L. Black Jr., "The Lawfulness of the Segregation Decisions," 69 *Yale L.J.* 421, 424 (1960).

38. This holding was reaffirmed in *Consol. Edison Co. of N.Y. v. Public Service Comm'n,* 447 U.S. 530, 533–34 n.1 (1980).

39. *Bellotti,* 435 U.S. at 825 (Rehnquist, C. J., dissenting) (internal citations omitted) (emphasis added). This is important because many supporters of strong protection for commercial speech, most significantly Martin Redish, seem to assume that opposition to protection for the speech of corporations or for commercial speech is predicated on hostility to commerce or to capitalism itself. *See* Martin H. Redish, "Commercial Speech, First Amendment Intuitionism, and the Twilight Zone of Viewpoint Discrimination," 41 *Loy. L.A. L. Rev.* 67, 69 (2007).

40. *Austin v. Michigan Chamber of Comm.,* 494 U.S. 652 (1990).

41. *Id.* at 659 (quoting *FEC v. Massachusetts Citizens for Life,* 479 U.S. 238, 258 (1986)).

42. The limitations on corporations that were upheld in *Massachusetts Citizens for Life* and *Austin* were put into question before being overruled outright when the Supreme Court declined to extend its reasoning in these two cases to a challenge in 2007 to limits on certain types of political advertising expenditures by corporations. *Fed. Election Comm'n v. Wisconsin Right to Life, Inc.,* 551 U.S 449 (2009). For more discussion of this issue, *see* Thomas W. Joo, "The Modern Corporation and Campaign Finance: Incorporating Corporate Governance Analysis into First Amendment Jurisprudence," 79 *Wash. U. L.Q.* 1 (2001).

43. *Buckley v. Valeo,* 424 U.S. 1 (1976).

44. For example, many of the amici in the *Nike v. Kasky* case cited *Bellotti* for the proposition that the status of the speaker as a commercial entity was irrelevant for First Amendment purposes, but they did not cite *Austin* or other cases, suggesting that this was not an unlimited principle. *Nike, Inc. v. Kasky,* 539 U.S. 654 (2003). Brief of Amici Curiae the Association of National Advertising, Inc., the American Advertising Federation and the American Association of Advertising Agencies in Support of Petitioners, 2003 WL 835112 at 8 (Feb. 28, 2003); Brief of ExxonMobil, Microsoft, Morgan Stanley and GlaxoSmithKline as Amici Curiae in Support of Petitioners, 2003 WL 835523 at 9–13 (Feb. 28, 2003); Brief for the National Association of Manufacturers as Amicus Curiae in Support of Petitioners, 2003 WL 835884 at 12–13 (Feb. 28, 2003).

45. *See, e.g.,* Brief of Amicus Curiae Center for Individual Freedom in Support of Petitioners at 23, *Nike, Inc. v. Kasky,* 539 U.S. 654 (2003) (No. 02-575) 2003 WL 835292.

46. *Citizens United v. Fed Election Comm'n,* 130 S.Ct. 876, 913 (2010) (*"Austin,* . . . should be and now is overruled.") (internal citation omitted).

47. 2 U.S.C. § 441b. An electioneering communication is defined in § 434(f)(3)(A) and in 11 C.F.R. § 100.29(a)(2) and § 100.29(b)(3)(ii).

48. The notice, coming on June 29, 2009, was succinct and heavily foreshadowed the decision: "This case is restored to the calendar for reargument. The parties are directed to file supplemental briefs addressing the following question: For the proper disposition of this case, should the Court overrule either or both Austin v. Michigan Chamber of Commerce, 494 U.S. 652 (1990), and the part of McConnell v. Federal Election Comm'n, 540 U.S. 93 (2003), which addresses the facial validity of Section 203 of the Bipartisan Campaign Reform Act of 2002, 2 U.S.C. § 441b?" Order of Sept. 9, 2009, *Citizens United v. Fed. Election Comm'n*, 130 S.Ct. at 888 (No. 08-205).

49. *Citizens United*, 130 S.Ct. at 899 (emphasis added).

50. *Id.*

51. *Id.* at 913.

52. *Id.* at 908 (characterizing corporations as "disfavored citizens").

53. *Id.* at 907 (quoting Justice Scalia claiming that the McCain-Feingold Act "muffle[d]" the voices that best represent the most significant segments of the economy").

54. *Id.* at 908.

55. *Lochner v. New York*, 198 U.S. 45 (1905).

56. There is something of a cottage industry around the interpretation of the *Lochner* decision, with a great deal seen to be rising on the issue of whether the decision was or was not an example of illegitimate "judicial activism" or depended on a notion that existing distributions of wealth were somehow "natural." *See, e.g.,* Jack M. Balkin, "Wrong the Day It Was Decided: *Lochner* and Constitutional Historicism," 85 *B.U. L. Rev.* 677 (2005); David E. Bernstein, "*Lochner's* Legacy's Legacy," 82 *Tex. L. Rev.* 1 (2003); Cass R. Sunstein, "*Lochner's* Legacy," 87 *Colum. L. Rev.* 873 (1987).While it cannot be said that these debates are irrelevant to my present purpose, they are not central. I do not claim *Lochner* was either rightly or wrongly decided as a matter of doctrine or of constitutional interpretation. Instead, I observe that the defeat of *Lochner* appeared to usher in an age of general acceptance for a broad mandate for governmental intervention in economic affairs but that this apparent victory for the government was quickly challenged using other theories.

57. *See, e.g.,* J. M. Balkin, "Some Realism about Pluralism: Legal Realist Approaches to the First Amendment," 1990 *Duke L.J.* 375, 379–80 (1990).

58. *See, e.g,* J. M. Balkin, "Wrong the Day It Was Decided: *Lochner* and Constitutional Historicism," 85 *B.U. L. Rev.* 677 (2005). For more discussion of the political implications of the commercial speech doctrine as it relates to these struggles between competing ideologies, see Reza R. Dibadj, "The Political Economy of Commercial Speech," 58 *S.C. L. Rev.* 913 (2007).

Chapter 2

1. Terence A. Shimp, *Advertising, Promotion, and Supplemental Aspects of Integrated Marketing Communications,* 6th ed. (Mason, Ohio: Thomson / South-Western, 2003), 6 (emphasis added).

2. For the contrary view, *see* Bruce E. H. Johnson & Jeffery L. Fisher, "Why Format, Not Content, Is the Key to Identifying Commercial Speech," 54 *Case W. Res. L. Rev.* 1243 (2004).

3. Shimp, *Advertising,* at 621 (glossary) (emphasis added).

4. *Va. Pharmacy,* at 765.

5. Shimp, *Advertising,* at 31.

6. Nick Southgate, "Coolhunting with Aristotle," *Int'l J. Market Res.,* Summer 2003, at 167.

7. Shimp, *Advertising,* at 33.

8. *See, e.g.,* Graeme W. Austin, "Trademarks and the Burdened Imagination," 69 *Brook. L. Rev.* 827, 843–44 (2004); Jean Wegman Burns, "Confused Jurisprudence: False Advertising Under the Lanham Act," 79 *B.U. Law. Rev.* 807, 823–25 (1999). For a review of the economic arguments at the point that the tide was turning against the position of advertising as "waste" to the position of advertising (trade symbols included) as information, *see* Ralph S. Brown Jr., "Advertising and the Public Interest: Legal Protection of Trade Symbols," 57 *Yale L.J.* 1165 (1948).

9. Shimp, *Advertising,* at 5.

10. *Id.* at 36 (emphasis in original).

11. Kevin Roberts, the CEO of the advertising agency Saatchi & Saatchi Worldwide, wrote a book about brands that inspire loyalty "beyond reason" entitled *Lovemarks: The Future beyond Brands* (Brooklyn: PowerHouse Books, 2005).

12. Shimp, *Advertising,* at 56–75.

13. *Id.* at 285.

14. Rich Thomaselli, "Will Harry and Louise Succeed for the Other Side?" *Advertising Age,* July 27, 2009, 6.

15. Rich Thomaselli, "Big Pharma's Deal with White House Threatened Despite $100 Mil Ad Outlay," *Advertising Age,* Mar. 15, 2010, 2, 27.

16. Tamara R. Piety, "Free Advertising: The Case for Public Relations as Commercial Speech," 10 *Lewis & Clark L. Rev.* 367 (2006).

17. Edward L. Bernays, *Propaganda* (New York: H. Liveright, 1928; reprinted with introduction by Mark Crispin Miller, Brooklyn: Ig, 2005), 64 (page references are to the 2005 edition).

18. Michael Schudson, *Advertising, the Uneasy Persuasion: The Dubious Impact on American Society* (New York: Basic Books, 1984), 100.

19. Fraser P. Seitel, *The Practice of Public Relations,* 8th ed. (Upper Saddle River, N.J.: Prentice Hall, 2001), 8.

20. Øyvind Ihlen, Betteke van Ruler, & Magnus Fredriksson, eds. *Public Relations and Social Theory: Key Figures and Concepts* (New York & London: Routledge, 2009), 27.

21. *Id.* at 9 (from a longer definition developed by the Foundation of Public Relations Research).

22. Shimp, *Advertising,* at 569.

23. *Id.*

24. *Id.*

25. Stuart Ewen, *PR! A Social History of Spin* (New York: Basic Books, 1996): 399, 400.

26. Shimp, *Advertising,* at 14.

27. This is probably not surprising, since he was Freud's nephew. *See* Larry Tye, *The Father of Spin: Edward L. Bernays and the Birth of Public Relations* (New York: Henry Holt, 1998), 8–9.

28. Bernays, *Propaganda,* at 75.

29. Al Ries & Laura Ries, *The Fall of Advertising and the Rise of PR* (New York: Harper Business, 2002), xx.

30. VNRs are preproduced tapes that are sent to television stations and can be run as news. David Barstow, "Report Faults Video Reports Shown as News," *N.Y. Times,* Apr. 6, 2006, A19.

31. Neil Henry, "Truth Be Told: Saving the Soul of Journalism," *Chron. Higher Educ.,* May 25, 2007, B11.

32. Seitel, *Practice of Public Relations,* at 38 (emphasis added).

33. Henry, "Truth Be Told."

34. John Stauber & Sheldon Rampton, *Toxic Sludge Is Good for You: Lies, Damn Lies, and the Public Relations Industry* (Monroe, Maine: Common Courage, 1995), 183–84. *See also* Jeff Blyskal & Marie Blyskal, *PR: How The Public Relations Industry Writes the News* (New York: William Morrow, 1985); Patrick Weever, "All the Spin Doctors' News That's Fit to Leak," *Observer,* Nov. 9, 2003, 7.

35. Trudy Lieberman, "The Epidemic," *Colum. Journalism Rev.,* Mar./Apr. 2007, 38–43.

36. The Radio-Television News Directors Association and a group of broadcasters filed a protest with the Federal Communications Commission objecting to four Notices of Apparent Liability for forfeitures that total $20,000 against Comcast for violation of the sponsorship disclosure rules for stations available through its service for using video news releases without disclosing their source. *See* Letter of Kathleen Kirby of October 31, 2007, to the FCC on Behalf of RTNDA and Various Network Broadcasters, available at http://www.odwyerpr.com/editorial/1101vnr_letter_rtnda.pdf (last accessed Mar. 3, 2010). *See also* Liz Cox Bar-

rett, "Wrist? Slap! FCC Fines Comcast Four Figures for Fake News," *Colum. Journalism Rev.*, Sept. 26, 2007.

37. Sara Ivry, "Marketers Say They Pay for Play in News Media," *N.Y. Times*, June 26, 2006.

38. *E.T.: The Extra-Terrestrial,* directed by Steven Spielberg (Universal Studios, 1982). For the story of how Reese's Pieces got product placement instead of M&Ms in *E.T., see* the link on IMDb, http://www.imdb.com/title/tt0083866/ trivia (last accessed Mar. 3, 2010).

39. *See* Steve Miller, "Coalition Urges FCC to Adopt Product Placement Rules," *Brandweek.com,* June 20, 2008, bw/content_display/news-and-features/ automotive-travel/e3i50d4ccb4056bd834ba90cdf3639ae183.

40. Jean Halliday, "Nissan's Rogue Joins Cast of 'Heroes,'" *AdAge.com,* Aug. 29, 2007, http://adage.com/mediaworks/article?article_id=120143 (last accessed May 18, 2010).

41. *Id.*

42. *Id.*

43. *See* Claire Atkinson, "Absolut Hunk: Story of Wildly Successful Product Placement," *AdAge.com,* Aug. 4, 2003, http://adage.com/article/news/absolute-hunk-story-a-wildly-successful-product-placement/38094/ (last accessed March 2, 2011).

44. Andrew Hampp & Emily Bryson York, "How Miracle Whip, Plenty of Fish Tapped Lady Gaga's 'Telephone,'" *AdAge.com,* Mar. 13, 2010, http://adage .com/madisonandvine/article?article_id=142794 (last accessed Mar. 27, 2010). Interestingly, music videos were originally produced by record companies as a form of advertising to pitch a particular album or artist. They have since developed into freestanding artistic projects.

45. *Up in the Air,* directed by Jason Reitman (Paramount Pictures, 2009).

46. Andrew Hampp, "How American Airlines Got a Free Ride in 'Up in the Air,'" *AdAge.com,* Dec. 14, 2009, http://adage.com/print?article_id=141059 (last accessed Mar. 27, 2010). You can go too far, however, as the negative reaction to the second film in the *Sex and the City* franchise illustrated, since a good deal of the criticism seemed to be of how product placement had taken over the movie. Manhola Dargis, "Un-Innocents Abroad: The Drubbing," *N.Y. Times,* June 6, 2010, AR8.

47. Motoko Rich, "Product Placement Deals Make the Leap from Films to Books," *N.Y. Times,* June 12, 2006, C1.

48. Ellen Goodman, "Stealth Marketing and Editorial Integrity," 85 *Tex. L. Rev* 83 (2006).

49. Warren Strugatch, "L.I. @ Work: When Advertising Mixes Fact and Fiction," *N.Y. Times,* Sept. 8, 2002.

50. Rick Lyman & Stuart Elliot, "Sony Admits It Used Employees as Bogus Fans," *N.Y. Times,* June 16, 2001, B11.

51. Shimp, *Advertising,* at 169–71.

52. *See, e.g.,* Alissa Quart, *Branded: The Buying and Selling of Teenagers* (New York: Basic Books, 2003), 37–45 (describing peer-to-peer marketing and cool hunting); Juliet B. Schor, *Born to Buy: The Commercialized Child and the New Consumer Culture* (New York: Scribner, 2004), 74–81 (describing buzz or viral marketing); Lucas Conley, *OBD: Obsessive Branding Disorder; The Illusion of Business and the Business of Illusion* (New York: Public Affairs, 2008), 111–29.

53. *See* Malcolm Gladwell, "The Coolhunt," *New Yorker,* Mar. 17, 1997; Quart, *Branded;* Schor, *Born to Buy;* Douglas Rushkoff, "Merchants of Cool," *Frontline* (PBS television broadcast, Feb. 1, 2001), http://www.pbs.org/wgbh/pages/frontline/shows/cool/etc/hunting.html (last accessed Mar. 3, 2010). There are also websites for cool hunting. *See* http://www.coolhunting.com/ (last accessed Mar. 3, 2010).

54. Stuart Elliott, "Any Way It's Sliced, Appeal of Social Media Grows," *N.Y. Times,* Feb. 22, 2010.

55. *See* Center for Media and Democracy, "Latest Version of Pay for Play: Bucks for Blogs," *Los Angeles Times,* Mar. 9, 2007, http://www.prwatch.org/node/5846 (last accessed May 18, 2010) (describing PayPerPost, ReviewMe, Loud Launch, and SponsoredReviews).

56. *See* Rob Walker, "The Brand-ness of Strangers," *N.Y. Times,* Nov. 16, 2008.

57. *See* Shelly Jofre, "Doctoring the Evidence: GlaxoSmithKline Pushes Depression Drug," *CorpWatch,* July 30, 2007, http://corpwatch.org/article.php?id=14606 (last accessed Mar. 3, 2010); *Economist,* "Devil in the Details: The Art of Pushing Pills," June 18, 2005, 11–13; Gardiner Harris, Benedict Carey, & Janet Roberts, "Psychiatrists, Troubled Children, and Drug Industry's Role," *N.Y. Times,* May 10, 2007, A1; Julie Bosman, "Reporters Find Science Journals Harder to Trust, but Not Easy to Verify," *N.Y. Times,* Feb. 13, 2006, C1; Susan Haack, "Scientific Secrecy and 'Spin': The Sad, Sleazy Saga of the Trials of Remune," 69 *Law & Contemp. Probs.* 47 (2006). For a book length treatment of the perversion of science by commercial interests *see* David Michaels, *Doubt Is Their Product: How Industry's Assault on Science Threatens Your Health* (New York: Oxford University Press, 2008).

58. Jofre, "Doctoring the Evidence."

59. *Id.*

60. Hill & Knowlton resigned the account in 1969, reportedly because of ethical concerns about the tobacco industry's application of the strategy the firm developed for it. Karen S. Miller, *The Voice of Business: Hill & Knowlton and Postwar Public Relations* (Chapel Hill: University of North Carolina Press, 1999), 141, 45. The basic strategy of "creating doubt about the health charge without actually denying it," characterizing smoking as a "right," and claiming that objective scientific research would be the "only way to resolve the question of health hazard" continued for several more decades. *Id.* at 143.

61. *U.S. v. Philip Morris USA, Inc.*, 449 F. Supp.2d 1, 15–212 (D.D.C. 2006), *aff'd* 566 F.3d 1095 (D.C. Cir. 2009), *cert. denied* 130 S.Ct. 3501 (2010).

62. Extensive documentation of these efforts is available in Allan M. Brandt, *The Cigarette Century* (New York: Basic Books, 2007). *See also U.S. v. Philip Morris USA, Inc.*, 449 F. Supp.2d 1 (D.D.C. 2006).

63. Sharon Begley, "The Truth about Denial," *Newsweek*, Aug. 13, 2007, 20. Begley reports that the American Enterprise Institute, an organization that has received funding from ExxonMobil, was offering $10,000 for articles to dispute the latest report from the Intergovernmental Panel on Climate Change that reflected a consensus that the 1990s "were likely the warmest on record" and that the warming was at least partially attributable to human activities. For a response to an earlier report on the charge that AEI was offering $10,000 for articles critical of the IPCC report, *see* Kenneth P. Green & Steven Hayward, "Scenes from the Climate Inquisition," American Enterprise Institute for Public Policy Research, Feb. 19, 2007, http://www.aei.org/docLib/20070222_OTI.pdf (last accessed March 3, 2011). *See also* Paul Krugman, "Enemy of the Planet," *N.Y. Times*, Apr. 17, 2006, A21.

64. *See, e.g.*, Sheldon Rampton & John Stauber, *Trust Us, We're Experts! How Industry Manipulates Science and Gambles with Your Future* (New York: Jeremy P. Tarcher/Putnam, 2001), 79. For a definition of the term *front group*, *see* SourceWatch, http://www.sourcewatch.org/index.php?title=Front_groups (last accessed Mar. 3, 2010). SourceWatch is a project of the Center for Media and Democracy, an organization in which both Rampton and Stauber are involved.

65. Regardless of the circumstances in its creation, it may well have played that role, since the creation of the forum may have inspired members of the public to join the organization. The website had a link entitled "Share Your Story," and it appeared from the link that many people did just that. But because no last names were provided, it might be difficult to verify whether these were genuine posts or fictional characters. The degree to which the organization was independent of Wal-Mart (if at all) is unclear.

66. *See* http://www.prwatch.org/node/5316 (last accessed Mar. 3, 2010).

67. *Id.*

68. *Id.*

69. For more information on the group, *see* http://www.sourcewatch.org/index.php?title=Working_Families_for_Wal-Mart (last accessed Mar. 3, 2010), sponsored by the Center for Media and Democracy.

70. http://www.sourcewatch.org/index.php?title=SourceWatch.

71. *See* http://www.sourcewatch.org/index.php?title=Freedom_Works (last accessed March 2, 2011).

72. Julian Zelizer, "Commentary: When Interest Groups Go Too Far," *CNNPolitics.com*, Aug. 11, 2009, http://edition2.cnn.com/2009/POLITICS/08/10/zelizer.town.halls.index.html (last accessed March 2, 2011).

73. *See* SourceWatch, http://www.sourcewatch.org/index .php?title=60_Plus _Association (last accessed Mar. 3, 2010), with links to other media about 60 Plus.

74. This material was formerly available here. *AARP Newsletter,* Editorial, "Pulling Strings From Afar," http://bulletin.aarp.org/yourworld/politics/arti cles/pulling_strings_from.html (last accessed Mar. 3, 2010). The AARP has apparently since taken this article down. For multiple links to these and other sources, *see* the website for the Rachel Maddow Show, http://www.msnbc.msn.com/id/ 26315908/ns/msnbc_tv-rachel_maddow_show/#32372457 (last accessed Mar. 3, 2010).

75. For a discussion of some of these practices and their role in the present subprime lending crisis, see Kathleen C. Engel & Patricia A. McCoy, "Turning a Blind Eye: Wall Street Finance of Predatory Lending," 75 *Fordham L. Rev.* 2039 (2007). For a critique of the banking industry's incorrect or misleading representations about irresponsible borrowers in lobbying for bankruptcy reform, *see* Elizabeth Warren, Op-Ed, "Show Me the Money," *N.Y. Times,* Oct. 24, 2005 (describing banks' role in lobbying for the bankruptcy law revisions).

76. Douglas Rushkoff, Introduction to "The Persuaders," *Frontline* (PBS television broadcast, Nov. 9, 2002), http://www.pbs.org/wgbh/pages/frontline/ shows/persuaders/etc/synopsis.html (last accessed Mar. 3, 2010).

77. Bradley Johnson, "Spending Fell (Only) 2.7% in '08; The Real Issue: '09," *Advertising Age,* June 22, 2009.

78. *APA Online,* Press Release, "Television Advertising Leads to Unhealthy Habits in Children, Says APA Task Force" (Feb. 23, 2004, 1), available at http://www.apa.org/news/press/releases/2004/02/children-ads.aspx (last accessed Feb. 17, 2011).

79. Bradley Johnson, "Leading National Advertisers Report: Spending Up 3.1% to $105 Billion," *Advertising Age* (June 25, 2007). Another source pegs total U.S. advertising spending for all traditional media categories to be $152.3 billion. TNS Media Intelligence, "TNS Media Intelligence Forecasts 1.7 Percent Increase in U.S. Advertising Spending for 2007," June 12, 2007, http://www.tnsglobal .com/news/news-41B1D08CEF094A98AAD79C2FABF263EB.aspx (last accessed Feb. 17, 2011).

80. *Economist,* "Back on Top: A Revival in Advertising Spending," Jan. 1, 2005, 48.

81. *N.Y. Times,* "Tune in; No, Log on," May 23, 2005 (graphic breaking out ad expenditures for 2004 into various categories).

82. TNS Media Intelligence, "Increase in U.S. Advertising Spending."

83. Nat Ives, "Ad Spending Barely Budged in 2007," *AdAge.com,* Mar. 25, 2008, http://adage.com/mediaworks/article?article_id=125921 (last accessed May 18, 2010).

84. Ries & Ries, *Fall of Advertising,* at 9.

85. *Id.* at 84.

86. One relatively new place is on the back of tray tables on airplanes. Eric Pfanner, "At 30,000 Feet, Finding a Captive Audience for Advertising," *N.Y. Times,* Aug. 27, 2007.

87. The resources available to large multinational commercial enterprises often outstrip those of all but the richest nations. *See* Institute for Policy Studies, "Research Institute Releases Study on Corporate Power on 1st Anniversary of Seattle Protests," http://www.ips-dc.org/reports/top200.htm (last accessed Aug. 15, 2007) (top 200 companies are larger than the combined economies minus the top 10 countries).

88. For a book-length discussion of the government's attempt to use advertising techniques to "sell" U.S. foreign policy in Iraq and, more generally, the War on Terrorism, through what the State Department called its "Shared Values Initiative," *see* Jami Fullerton & Alice Kendrick, *Advertising's War on Terrorism* (Spokane, Wash.: Marquette Books, 2006).

89. *See, e.g.,* Kim Severson, "Seduced by Snack? No, Not You," *N.Y. Times,* Oct. 11, 2006; Gale Group, "MarketResearch C'mon, Mom! Kids Nag Parents to Chuck E. Cheese's," Selling to Kids, May 12, 1999, http://findarticles.com/p/articles/mi_m0FVE/is_9_4/ai_54631243/?tab=content;col1 (last accessed Feb. 17, 2001); Clotaire Rapaille, *The Culture Code* 2007 (New York: Broadway Books, 2006) (cultural anthropologist uses insights from psychology and focus group research to purport to identify cultural "codes" that tap into the "reptilian brain" and bypass rational thought processes to sell products). For more on Dr. Rapaille, *see* PBS, "The Persuaders," *Frontline* (PBS television broadcast, Nov. 9, 2003), http://www.pbs.org/wgbh/pages/frontline/shows/persuaders/ (last accessed Mar. 3, 2010). *See also* Patrick Renvoisé & Christophe Morin, *Neuromarketing: Is There a "Buy Button" in the Brain? Selling to the Old Brain for Instant Success* (San Francisco: SalesBrain Publishing, 2005) (purporting to use research in neurology to find the "buy button" in the brain and obtain "instant success"); *Economist,* "The Triumph of Unreason: Why You Are Not Always Rational with Your Credit Card," Jan. 13, 2007 (reporting on similar research in economics identified as neuroeconomics, a field that perhaps overlaps with what is described as "behavioral economics").

90. *See, e.g.,* Douglas A. Kysar, "Kids & Cul-de-sacs: *Census 2000* and the Reproduction of Consumer Culture," 87 *Cornell L. Rev.* 853 (2002) (census data used for marketing purposes).

91. *See* Washburn, *University, Inc.: The Corporate Corruption of Higher Education* (New York: Basic Books, 2005), 125–36.

92. For a comprehensive look at the regulation of research on human subjects in all public and some private contexts, *see* Carl H. Coleman, Jerry A. Menikoff, Jesse A. Goldner, & Nancy Neveloff Dubler, *The Ethics and Regulation of Research with Human Subjects* (Eagan, Minn.: West, 2005). *See also* Christopher Shea, "Don't Talk to the Humans: The Crackdown on Social Science Research," *Lingua Franca,* Sept. 2000, 26–34.

93. *See, e.g.,* Jon Gertner, "Hey, Mom, Is It O.K. If These Guys Market Stuff to Us?" *N.Y. Times,* Nov. 28, 2004. *See also* Schor, *Born to Buy;* Quart, *Branded.*

Chapter 3

1. Steven Shiffrin, "The First Amendment and Economic Regulation: Away from a General Theory of the First Amendment," 78 *Nw. U. L. Rev.* 1212 (1983).

2. Thomas I. Emerson, *Toward a General Theory of the First Amendment* (New York: Vintage Books, 1966).

3. Stanley Fish has made this point fairly forcefully. Stanley Fish, *There's No Such Thing as Free Speech—and It's a Good Thing, Too* (New York: Oxford University Press, 1994).

4. *See, e.g.,* Anthony Lewis, *Freedom for the Thought We Hate: A Biography of the First Amendment* (New York: Basic Books, 2007).

5. Thomas I. Emerson, "Toward a General Theory of the First Amendment," 72 *Yale L.J.* 877, 879 (1963). Emerson later republished this article as the book cited in note 2 to this chapter. The remaining references are to the law review article unless otherwise indicated.

6. For works criticizing the degree of employer control over issues of grooming and dress, *see* Deborah L. Rhode, *The Beauty Bias: The Injustice of Appearance in Life and Law* (New York: Oxford University Press, 2010); Bruce Barry, *Speechless: The Erosion of Free Expression in the American Workplace* (San Francisco: Berrett-Koehler, 2007).

7. European Convention on Human Rights, available at http://www.hri.org/docs/ECHR50.html (last accessed May 25, 2010).

8. *Id.*

9. One scholar has recently challenged the conventional reading of the First Amendment's prohibition as applicable to the judicial and executive branches, despite the amendment's clear subject (Congress), as difficult to defend. Rosenkranz, "Subjects of the Constitution."

10. Emerson, "Toward a General Theory," at 880.

11. It is not possible to probe all the definitional difficulties in distinguishing between speech, action, and "speech acts." *See, e.g., O'Brien v. U.S.,* 391 U.S. 367, 376–84 (1968) (burning a draft card). For an illustration of the difficulties in drawing speech/act distinctions, see Frederick Schauer, "Categories and the First Amendment: A Play in Three Acts," 34 *Vand. L. Rev.* 265, 272, 276 (1981). For more vivid examples, *see* Catharine A. MacKinnon, *Only Words* (Cambridge, Mass.: Harvard University Press, 1993), 28 ("Is a rape a representation of a rape if someone is watching it?").

12. *See, e.g., Barnes v. Glenn Theatre, Inc.,* 501 U.S. 560, 565 (1991) (nude dancing as "expressive conduct").

13. Leonard W. Levy, *Emergence of a Free Press* (Chicago: Ivan R. Dee, 1985),

266–74. For a critical interpretation of Levy's reading, *see* David A. Anderson, "The Origins of the Press Clause," 30 *UCLA L. Rev.* 455 (1983).

14. Alexander Meiklejohn, *Free Speech and Its Relation to Self-Government* (New York: Harper Brothers, 1948).

15. Milton's *Areopagitica,* with its argument against prior restraints, is often cited as one of the intellectual inspirations for the Framers in drafting the First Amendment. *See* Vincent Blasi, "The Elliot Lecture: Milton's *Areopagitica* and the Modern First Amendment," in *Ideas of the First Amendment* (St. Paul, Minn.: Thomson West, 2006), 52–56, 102–7. For a full discussion of Milton's influence as well as excerpts from many others on this topic, *see id.* at 34–145.

16. Leonard Levy wrote, "Apathy, ambiguity, and brevity characterize the comments of the few Congressmen who spoke on the First Amendment. The House did not likely understand the debate, care deeply about its outcome, or even share a common understanding of the finished amendment." Levy, *Emergence of a Free Press,* 267.

17. Emerson, "Toward a General Theory," at 948–49 n. 93.

18. *See* John H. Garvey & Frederick Schauer, *First Amendment: A Reader,* 2nd ed. (St. Paul, Minn.: West, 1996) (chapter II, "Philosophical Foundations of Freedom of Speech," discusses primarily Emerson's structure and introduces variations and other arguments in "Additional Perspectives," 126–67).

19. Emerson, *Toward a General Theory* (book). *See also* Stanley A. Ingber, "Rediscovering the Communal Worth of Individual Rights: The First Amendment in Institutional Contexts," 69 *Texas L. Rev.* 1 (1990).

20. Emerson, "Toward a General Theory," at 878.

21. *Id.* This argument was repeated by Nike and by most of the amici supporting Nike. *See, e.g.,* Brief for the Center for the Advancement of Capitalism, *Nike v. Kasky,* 539 U.S. 654 (2003) (No. 02-575), 2003 WL 834937. *See also* Richard A. Posner, "Bad News," *N.Y. Times Book Review,* July 31, 2005.

22. *See Va. Pharmacy,* 425 U.S. at 763–65.

23. Emerson, "Toward a General Theory," at 878. *See also* Alexander Meiklejohn, "The First Amendment Is an Absolute," 1961 *Sup. Ct. Rev.* 245 (1961).

24. Emerson, "Toward a General Theory," at 878–79. To make things even more complicated, Schauer argues that it may be a mistake to look for a single core value rather than a multiplicity of values underlying protection for speech. Schauer, "Categories and the First Amendment," at 276–77. *See also* Shiffrin, "First Amendment and Economic Regulation."

25. Burt Neuborne, "The First Amendment and Governmental Regulation of Capital Markets," 55 *Brook. L. Rev.* 5 (1989).

26. Professor James Weinstein offered one of the latest rebuttals of the first two arguments. According to Weinstein, neither the self-actualization nor truth theories are supported by the case law. *See* James Weinstein, "Speech Categorization

and the Limits of First Amendment Formalism: Lessons from *Nike v. Kasky,*" 54 *Case W. Res. L. Rev.* 1091, 1100–1101 (2004).

27. *See* Blasi, *Ideas of the First Amendment,* at 832.

28. There are a number of sources for this position, of which the "natural rights" theory of John Locke was one. Locke proposed that human beings belonged to God and, as such, should not interfere with one another's life, health, liberty, or property, because human beings, "being furnished with like faculties, . . . cannot be supposed any such subordination" as between each other "as if we were made for one another's uses, as inferior ranks of creatures are for ours." John Locke, *Second Treatise on Government* (ca. 1681), 6, reprinted in *Political Writings of John Locke,* ed. David Wootton (Indianapolis: Hackett, 2003, 1993) (1689). In his introduction to his volume of Locke's writings, Wootton describes the American Constitution as "founded on Lockean principles" (8). *See also* David L. Wardle, "Reason to Ratify: The Influence of John Locke's Religious Beliefs on the Creation and Adoption of the United States Constitution," 26 *Seattle U. L. Rev.* (2002): 291. As Eduardo Peñalver has persuasively argued, a natural rights approach can be consistent both with "a robust sphere of individual autonomy and with active state regulation." Eduardo M. Peñalver, "Restoring the Right Constitution?" 116 *Yale L.J.* 732 (2007).

29. *Whitney v. California,* 274 U.S. 357 (1927) (Brandeis, J. concurring).

30. *Id.* at 375.

31. Susan H. Williams, *Truth, Autonomy, and Speech* (New York: New York University Press, 2004), 33.

32. *Wilson v. U.S.,* 221 U.S. 361 (1911).

33. *California Bankers Ass'n v. Schultz,* 416 U.S. 21 (1974).

34. *First Nat'l Bank of Boston v. Bellotti,* 435 U.S. 765, 778 n. 14 (1978).

35. Emerson, "Toward a General Theory," at 879.

36. For a wonderful discussion of this issue, noting the absence of an author, see Randall Bezanson, "Institutional Speech," 80 *Iowa L. Rev.* 735 (1995).

37. The business judgment rule gives management substantial scope to determine what constitutes the best strategy for achieving that goal. *See Kahn v. Sullivan,* 594 A.2d 48 (Del. 1991) (shareholder dispute over Occidental Petroleum's use of corporate funds to establish an art museum in Los Angeles to house the art collection of former chairman Dr. Armand Hammer; the court upheld a lower court finding that although corporate justifications for expenditure merited some skepticism and although settlement of lawsuits offered meager benefits to shareholders, it fell within the definition of reasonableness, since the court should not substitute its judgment for that of the parties.

38. Daniel J. H. Greenwood, "Essential Speech: Why Corporate Speech Is Not Free," 83 *Iowa L. Rev.* 995, 1002 (1998) (emphasis added). *See also* Daniel J. H. Greenwood, "First Amendment Imperialism," 1999 *Utah L. Rev.* 659 (1999);

Daniel J. H. Greenwood, "Fictional Shareholders, for Whom Are Corporate Managers Trustees, Revisited," 69 *S. Cal. L. Rev.* 1021 (1996).

39. Despite its obvious creativity, advertising, for the most part, does not have "authors." For an interesting discussion of this aspect of advertising and the intersection with copyright and First Amendment law, *see* Catherine L. Fisk, "The Modern Author at Work on Madison Avenue," in *Modernism and Copyright*, ed. Paul Saint-Amour (New York: Oxford University Press, 2010).

40. Greenwood, "Essential Speech," at 1057.

41. As Professor David Vladeck notes, the Supreme Court appears to have incorporated some notion of speaker's rights into the commercial speech doctrine, despite the absence of this element in the earlier law, in two recent cases. *See* David Vladeck, "Lessons from a Story Untold," 1072–73 (citing *Lorillard Tobacco Co. v. Reilly,* 533 U.S. 525 (2001); *Thompson v. W. States Med. Ctr,* 535 U.S. 357 (2002)).

42. Martin H. Redish, "Self-Realization, Democracy, and Freedom of Expression: A Reply to Professor Baker," 130 *U. Pa. L. Rev.* 678, 682 (1982).

43. For arguments in this vein, *see* James B. Twitchell, *Adcult USA* (New York: Columbia University Press, 1996).

44. David Brooks, "The Culture of Debt," *N.Y. Times,* July 22, 2008, A19. For a scholarly expression of the same idea, *see* Xi Zou, Kim-Pong Tam, Michael W. Morris, Sau-lai Lee, Ivy Yee-Man Lau, & Chi-yue Chiu, "Culture as Common Sense: Perceived Consensus vs. Personal Beliefs as Mechanisms of Cultural Influence," 97(4) *J. Personality & Soc. Psychol* 579 (2009).

45. Redish & Wasserman, "What's Good for General Motors."

46. There is some evidence that, as with much self-reporting that involves potentially moral claims, there may be some divergence between what people say will influence their decision-making process and what actually does. *See* Andreas Chatzidakis, Sally Hibbert, & Andrew P. Smith, "Why People Don't Take Their Concerns about Fair Trade to the Supermarket: The Role of Neutralisation," 74 *J. Bus. Ethics* 89 (2007).

47. Emerson, "Toward a General Theory," at 882.

48. John Stuart Mill, *On Liberty,* chapter 2, http://ebooks.adelaide.edu.au/m/mill/john_stuart/m6450/chapter2.html (last accessed Mar. 16, 2010).

49. *See, e.g.,* Thomas I. Emerson, *The System of Freedom of Expression* (New York: Random House, 1970), 6–8. Robert Post, "Reconciling Theory and Doctrine in First Amendment Jurisprudence," 88 *Cal. L. Rev.* 2353, 2365–66 (2000). *Truth* is a highly charged word with many complexities, and distinguishing between fact and opinion is often difficult. Nevertheless, making this distinction is a common legal task. *See, e.g.,* Federal Rules of Evidence 102 ("These rules shall be construed to secure fairness in administration, elimination of unjustifiable expense and delay, and the promotion of growth and development of the law of evidence *to the end that the truth may be ascertained* and proceedings justly deter-

mined.") (emphasis added). For purposes of this chapter, I use the word *truth* in the same way it is used generally in the law, to refer to a fact capable of proof or falsification. I am inclined to think that a "global denial of objective truth is unwarranted." Alvin I. Goldman & James C. Cox, "Speech, Truth, and the Free Market for Ideas," 2 *Legal Theory* 1, 8 (1996).

50. *N.Y. Times Co. v. Sullivan*, 376 U.S. 254, 271–72 (1964) (citing *N.A.A.C.P. v. Button*, 371 U.S. 415, 433 (1963)).

51. *Id.* at 376 U.S. at 279, n. 19 (quoting J. S. Mill, *On Liberty* [Oxford: Blackwell, 1947], at 15).

52. *Abrams v. U.S.*, 250 U.S. 616, 630 (1919) (Holmes, J., dissenting). Robert Post has argued that the use of this metaphor, rather than an invitation to actually apply economic theory, is an "expression of American pragmatic epistemology." Post, "Reconciling Theory," at 2360 (citing Thomas C. Grey, "Holmes and Legal Pragmatism," 41 *Stan. L. Rev.* 787, 788 (1989)). For more on Holmes's connection to the American pragmatists, *see* Louis Menand, *The Metaphysical Club: A Story of Ideas in America* (New York: Farrar, Strauss & Giroux, 2001). For more on pragmatism in America generally, *see* Cornel West, *The American Evasion of Philosophy: A Genealogy of Pragmatism* (Madison: University of Wisconsin Press, 1989).

53. Barry Meier, "Narcotic Maker Guilty of Deceit over Marketing," *N.Y. Times*, May 11, 2007, A1. *See also U.S. v. Purdue Frederick Co.*, 495 F. Supp.2d 569 (2007).

54. Tobacco Industry Research Committee, Press Release, "New Evidence Shows Complexities of Lung Cancer, Scientists Say" (Sept. 27, 1960), available at http://legacy.library.ucsf.edu/tid/nqh79d00 (last accessed Mar. 20, 2010) (quoted in Brandt, *Cigarette Century*, at 202).

55. Rampton & Stauber, *Trust Us*, at 86 (quoting material distributed in 1962 from Gulf Oil Company to its workers, attributed to Jim Morris, "Worked to Death," *Houston Chronicle*, Oct. 9, 1994, A1).

56. Eminent economist Ronald Coase was perhaps one of the first to take this metaphor somewhat literally, although he also acknowledged that it was not a perfect one. *See* R. H. Coase, "The Market for Good and the Market for Ideas," 64 *Am. Econ. Rev.* 384 (1974).

57. The trend to commercialize everything is beyond the scope of this book. However, it has been noted by several writers as applied to many areas of social life thought to be untouched or superior to assessment in market terms. *See, e.g.,* Vincent J. Miller, *Consuming Religion: Christian Faith and Practice in a Consumer Culture* (New York: Continuum International, 2005).

58. Fred Schauer has described the doctrine of chill as part of the substantive ordering of values under the First Amendment, as it implies the inevitability of error and a preference that those errors run in favor of protecting more speech.

Frederick Schauer, "Fear, Risk, and the First Amendment: Unraveling the 'Chilling Effect,'" 58 *B.U. L. Rev.* 685 (1978).

59. *N.Y. Times Co. v. Sullivan*, 376 U.S. at 270.

60. Amended Complaint, *Sharper Image Corp. v. Consumers Union of U.S. Inc.* (N.D. Cal. 2003) (No. 03-4094 MMC), 2003 WL 23796370.

61. Order Granting Consumers Union's Special Motion to Strike at 13–14, *Sharper Image*, (N.D. Cal., 2004) (No. 03-4094 MMC), 2004 WL 2554451.

62. A feature-length documentary was made about the case, *McLibel: The Postman and the Gardner Who Took on McDonald's*, http://www.spannerfilms .net/?lid=161 (last accessed Mar. 18, 2010).

63. The organization London Greenpeace was not affiliated in any way with the more well-known organization Greenpeace.

64. *See Steel and Morris v. United Kingdom*, 2005-II Eur.Ct.H.R. 13 (describing McDonald's infiltration of group meetings).

65. McDonald's had earlier extracted apologies and retractions from some media organizations that had reproduced the leaflet or discussed the claims. *Id.* at 14.

66. *Id.* at 14–15.

67. *Id. See also BBC News–UK*, Editorial, "'McLibel' Pair Win Legal Aid Case," Feb. 15, 2005, http://news.bbc.co.uk/2/hi/uk_news/4266209.stm (last accessed May 19, 2010).

68. Darren Rovell, "Investors Fret about Nike's Star Endorsements," *CNBC on MSN Money*, Sept. 22, 2006, http://articles.moneycentral.msn.com/Invest ing/CNBC/TVReports/NikeStarEndorsements.aspx (last accessed Mar. 18, 2010).

69. Ben Casselman, "Three Stories a Day? How Young Reporters Learn to Skim," *Colum. Journalism Rev.*, May/June 2004, 65.

70. *Id. See also* Eric Alterman, *What Liberal Media? The Truth about Bias and the News* (New York: Basic Books, 2003).

71. *See* Meiklejohn, *Free Speech*.

72. Another famous advocate for this position, albeit from a different ideological perspective, is Judge Robert Bork. Robert H. Bork, "Neutral Principles and Some First Amendment Problems," 47 *Ind. L.J.* 1 (1971).

73. Emerson, *Toward a General Theory*, at 9.

74. *See, e.g.*, Cynthia L. Estlund, "Free Speech and Due Process in the Workplace," 71 *Ind. L.J.* 101 (1995); Richard Michael Fischl, "Labor, Management, and the First Amendment: Whose Rights Are These, Anyway?" 10 *Cardozo L. Rev.* 729 (1989); Lawrence Soley, *Censorship, Inc.: The Corporate Threat to Free Speech in the United States* (New York: Monthly Review Press, 2002). *See also* Cindy Boren, "Packers Necktie Gets Chicago Car Salesman Fired," *The Early Lead* (blog), Jan. 25, 2011, *Washington Post*, http://voices.washingtonpost.com/ early_lead/2011/01/packers_necktie_gets_chicago_c.html.

75. Bruce Barry, *Speechless: The Erosion of Free Expression in the American Workplace* (San Francisco: Berrett-Koehler, 2007), 5.

76. *Id.* at 8.

77. Andrew Pollack & Duff Wilson, "Former Pfizer Scientist Wins Whistle-blower Suit," *N.Y. Times,* Apr. 3, 2010, B3.

78. This does not even include the suppression of expression mandated by the prohibition on discrimination, which can affect such issues as sexual harassment and hate speech. *See* Barry, *Speechless,* at 156–65.

79. For example, there is some evidence that the whistle-blower protection provisions of Sarbanes-Oxley have not proven particularly effective. *See* Jayne O'Donnell, "Blowing the Whistle Can Lead to Harsh Aftermath, Despite Law," *USA Today,* Aug. 1, 2005, 1B.

80. Nasrin Shahinpoor & Bernard F. Matt, "The Power of One: Dissent and Organizational Life," 74 *J. of Bus. Ethics* 37 (2007).

81. *See* Jad Mouawak, "Shell to Pay $15.5 Million to Settle Nigerian Case," *N.Y. Times,* June 9, 2009.

82. Steven Ratner, "Corporations and Human Rights: A Theory of Legal Responsibilities," 111 *Yale L.J.* 443 (2001).

83. Adriadne K. Sacharoff, "Multinationals in Host Countries: Can They Be Held Liable under the Alien Tort Claims Act for Human Rights Violations?" 23 *Brook. J. Int'l L.* 927 (1998).

84. Victoria Shannon, "French Court Affirms Auction Site Ruling: Yahoo Faces Deadlines to Block Nazi Items," *Int'l Herald Tribune,* Nov. 21, 2000), 1.

85. Surya Deva, "Corporate Complicity in Internet Censorship in China: Who Cares for the Global Compact or the Global Online Freedom Act?" 39 *Geo. Wash. Int'l L. Rev.* 255 (2007).

86. Emerson, *Toward a General Theory* (book), at 11.

87. *Id.* at 13.

88. *See, e.g.,* Owen Fiss, "Why the State?" 100 *Harv. L. Rev.* 781 (1987); Cass Sunstein, "Free Speech Now," 59 *U. Chi. L. Rev.* 255 (1992). *See generally* C. Edwin Baker, *Human Liberty and Freedom of Speech* (New York: Oxford University Press, 1989).

89. *See* Brief for the Petitioners at 50, *Nike, Inc. v. Kasky,* 539 U.S. 654 (2003) (No. 02-575), 2003 WL 898993 (2003) and Brief for the U.S. at 39, *Nike, Inc.,* 539 U.S. 654 (No. 02-575) WL 899100. (Nike had not released its corporate responsibility report because of fears of liability in light of California Supreme Court opinion.) Not everyone agrees that the decision hurts corporate social responsibility reporting. *See* Adam M. Kanzer & Cynthia A. Williams, "The Future of Social Reporting Is on the Line," *Bus. Ethics Q.,* Summer 2003, available at http://www.dominiadvisor.com/advisor/About-Domini/News/Press-Release-Archive/Nike_Kasky_Oped_6-03_cut.htm. Ironically, the 2004 corporate responsibility report's disclosures suggest that Kasky's allegations may have been true.

90. *See, e.g.,* Thomas H. Clarke Jr., "Will *Nike v. Kasky* Ignite Corporate Social Responsibility Trade Wars between the U.S. and European Union?" *SRI Me-*

dia, Corporate Governance News, June 28, 2003 (no longer available online; on file with author) ("Those companies that do not publish CSR reports, or generally obfuscate their positions on matter diverse as global warming to supply chain economics, will be much less inclined to publicize their progress for fear of California litigation.").

Chapter 4

1. Emerson, *Toward a General Theory* (book), at 3.
2. *Id.* at 4.
3. *Id.* at 5.
4. Christina E. Wells, "Reinvigorating Autonomy: Freedom and Responsibility in the Supreme Court's First Amendment Jurisprudence," 32 *Harv. C.R.-C.L. L. Rev.* 159, 165 (1997).
5. Martin H. Redish, "The Value of Free Speech," 130 *U. Pa. L. Rev.* 591 (1982). *See also* Redish, "First Amendment in the Marketplace"; Redish & Wasserman, "What's Good for General Motors"; Redish, "First Amendment Intuitionism."
6. *See* Ronald K. L. Collins & David Skover, *The Death of Discourse,* 2nd ed. (Durham, NC: Carolina Academic Press, 2005); James B. Twitchell, *AdcultUSA* (New York: Columbia University Press, 1996); Tyler Cowen, *In Praise of Commercial Culture* (Cambridge, Mass.: Harvard University Press, 1998).
7. *See, e.g.,* Jean Kilbourne, *Deadly Persuasion: Why Women and Girls Must Fight the Addictive Power of Advertising* (New York: Free Press, 1999).
8. Richard H. Fallon Jr., "Two Senses of Autonomy," 46 *Stan. L. Rev.* 875, 876 (1994).
9. *Id.*
10. Emerson, *Toward a General Theory,* at 4–5.
11. *Id.* at 5.
12. *See, e.g.,* Daniel M. Wegner, *The Illusion of Conscious Will* (Cambridge, Mass.: Bradford Books / MIT Press, 2002).
13. Daniel Kahneman, Paul Slovic, & Amos Tversky, *Judgment under Uncertainty: Heuristics and Biases* (Cambridge: Cambridge University Press, 1982).
14. Cordelia Fine, *A Mind of Its Own: How Your Brain Distorts and Deceives* (New York: W. W. Norton, 2006).
15. *See, e.g.,* Antonio Damasio, *Descartes' Error: Emotion, Reason, and the Human Brain* (New York: Avon Books, 1994).
16. Robert A. Burton, *On Being Certain: Believing You Are Right Even When You Are Not* (New York: St Martin's Press, 2008).
17. Antonio Damasio, *The Feeling of What Happens: Body and Emotion in the Making of Consciousness* (Orlando, Fla.: Harcourt, 1999); Burton, *On Being Certain.*
18. Philosopher Gerald Dworkin suggests that some restraints on liberty are

consistent with autonomy. Gerald Dworkin, *The Theory and Practice of Autonomy* (Cambridge: Cambridge University Press, 1998), 12–28.

19. *See, e.g.,* Manuel A. Utset, "Time-Inconsistent Management and the Sarbanes-Oxley Act," 31 *Ohio N.U. L. Rev.* 417 (2005).

20. *See, e.g.,* Daniel Gilbert, *Stumbling on Happiness* (New York: Alfred A. Knopf, 2006).

21. *See, e.g.,* Jonathan Klick & Gregory Mitchell, "Government Regulation of Irrationality: Moral and Cognitive Hazards," 90 *Minn. L. Rev.* 1620 (2006).

22. *See* Wendy's Soviet fashion show ad at http://www.youtube.com/watch?v=DWAKtYGJZSM (last accessed Mar. 18, 2010). Burger King advertised its own customization options with a similar injunction to "have it your way."

23. Sheena Iyengar, *The Art of Choosing* (New York: Hachette Book Group, 2010).

24. Although our culture generally celebrates choice as an unquestioned good, philosophers and psychologists have noted that choice can sometimes create distress. *See, e.g.,* Dworkin, *Theory and Practice of Autonomy*, at 62–81.

25. Barry Schwartz, *The Paradox of Choice* (New York: Harper Collins, 2004).

Chapter 5

1. *See* James B. Twitchell, *Branded Nation: The Marketing of Megachurch, College Inc., and Museumworld* (New York: Simon & Schuster, 2004); Naomi Klein, *No Logo* (New York: Random House, 2000).

2. Vincent J. Miller, *Consuming Religion: Christian Faith and Practice in a Consumer Culture* (New York: Continuum International, 2005).

3. *See* Robert A. Weisbuch, "Branding Isn't a Dirty Word," *Chron. Higher Educ.,* Jan. 26, 2007, C3; Thomas Bartlett, "Your (Lame) Slogan Here," *Chron. Higher Educ.,* Nov. 23, 2007, A1 (universities' efforts to develop slogans through focus group testing and other marketing research devices).

4. Adam Nagourney & Carl Hulse, "Republican Election Losses Stir Fall Fears," *N.Y. Times,* May 15, 2008 (quoting Rep. Devin Nunes of California saying, "The Republican brand is down," and Rep. Tom Cole of Oklahoma saying, "When you lose three of these in a row you have to get beyond campaign tactics and take a hard look and ask if there is something wrong with your product") (internal quotes omitted).

5. Jeff Leeds, "The New Deal: Band as Brand," *N.Y. Times,* Nov. 11, 2007, Arts & Leisure, 1 (describing what are termed "360° deals" for developing new musical groups that entail not only recording but merchandising rights).

6. Tom Peters, "The Brand Called You," *FastCompany,* Aug. 31, 1997, http://www.fastcompany.com/magazine/10/brandyou.html (last accessed Mar. 24, 2010).

7. Rob Walker, "The Brand Underground," *N.Y. Times Magazine,* July 30, 2006, SM 28; Mya Frazier, "When a Brand Buster Becomes a Brand," *Advertising Age,* Nov. 26, 2007.

8. Klein, *No Logo,* at 3–5. *See also* Susan Strasser, *Satisfaction Guaranteed: The Making of the American Mass Market* (Washington, D.C.: Smithsonian Books, 1989).

9. Kathryn A. Braun & Elizabeth F. Loftus, "Advertising's Misinformation Effect," 12 *Applied Cognitive Psychol.* 569 (1998).

10. Conley, *OBD,* at 7.

11. *Id.* at 11 ("Branding distracts companies and executives from doing what they ought to be doing.").

12. *Id.* at 5.

13. Rob Walker, *Buying In: The Secret Dialog between What We Buy and Who We Are* (New York: Random House, 2008), 8.

14. *See* http://www.starbucks.com/aboutus/Company_Factsheet.pdf (last accessed Mar. 20, 2010).

15. *See* http://www.kraftfoodscompany.com/Brands/index.aspx (last accessed Apr., 4, 2010).

16. *See* http://www.unilever.com/ourbrands/ (last accessed Mar. 20, 2010).

17. *See* http://www.kelloggcompany.com/ (last accessed Mar. 20, 2010).

18. Gabriel J. Biehel & Daniel A. Sheinin, "Managing the Brand in a Corporate Advertising Environment: A Decision-Making Framework for Brand Managers," *J. Advertising,* Summer 1998, 99–111.

19. *See* Burns, "Confused Jurisprudence," 822–23. For a seminal article discussing the social utility of brands and advertising, *see* Brown, "Advertising and the Public Interest." For an update on Brown's article, *see* Mark Lemly, "The Modern Lanham Act and the Death of Common Sense," 108 *Yale L.J.* 1687 (1999).

20. Jules Backman, *Advertising and Competition* (New York: New York University Press, 1967), 28–39 (citing studies identifying advertising as waste or as anticompetitive).

21. *Economist,* "The Case for Brands," Sept. 8, 2001, 11.

22. Ralph Cassady Jr. & E. T. Grether, "The Proper Interpretation of 'Like Grade and Quality' within the Meaning of the Section 2(a) of the Robinson-Patman Act," 30 *S. Cal. L. Rev.* 241, 278 (1957).

23. Emily Bryson York, "McNuggets Are Good, but Branded McNuggets Are Even Better," *AdAge.com,* Aug. 8, 2007, http://adage.com/article?article_id= 119753. *See also Advertising Age,* Editorial, "McD's Likely to Get Fried by Passive Response to Study," Aug. 11, 2007, 10.

24. "Brainy Brand Research," 19 *Marketing Res.* 5 (Summer 2007).

25. Conley, *OBD,* at 5.

26. As Felix Cohen observed in 1935, the brand is not protected because it has value; it is valuable because it is protected. If it were not protected, it would be less valuable. Felix S. Cohen, "Transcendental Nonsense and the Functional Approach," 35 *Colum. L. Rev.* 809, 815 (1935).

27. Robert B. Settle & Pamela L. Alreck, *Why They Buy: American Consumers Inside and Out* (New York: John Wiley & Sons, 1986), 95.

28. Settle & Alreck, *Why They Buy,* at 16.

29. Shimp, *Advertising,* at 301. David Finkle, "Television Q-ratings: The Popularity Contest of the Stars," *N.Y. Times,* June 7, 1992. For more information, go to the website of the company that pioneered the concept in 1963, Marketing Evaluations: http://www.qscores.com/ (last accessed Feb. 17, 2011).

30. Vicki R. Lane, "The Impact of Ad Repetition and Ad Content on Consumer Perceptions of Incongruent Extensions," 64 *J. Marketing* 80 (2000).

31. *CMO Magazine,* "The Strategic Significance of Brands," Sept. 24, 2005 (interview with Virgin America's Spence Kramer).

32. Naomi Klein, *No Logo.*

33. Shimp, *Advertising,* at 31.

34. Susan Fournier, "Consumers and Their Brands: Developing Relationship Theory in Consumer Research," 24 *J. Consumer Res.* 343 (1998).

35. *Id.* at 345.

36. *CMO Magazine,* "Strategic Significance of Brands" (discussing Virgin America's brand image).

37. Ira Teinowitz, "GM Breaks Up with Big Oil," *Advertising Age,* June 10, 2008.

38. Claudia H. Deutsch, "Mum's the Word: We've Found a Greener Gas," *N.Y. Times,* Nov. 7, 2007, explaining the PR problem presented by switching to CO_2, paradoxically a more environmentally friendly choice than hydrofluorocarbons, for refrigeration.

39. Rob Walker, "Organic Growth: Name Brand? Store Brand? Safeway's Virtue-Food Products Aim to Blur the Line," *N.Y. Times Magazine,* July 13, 2008, SM 22.

40. *Id.*

41. Jack Neff, "Recall Sheds Light on Pet-Food Industry's Little Secret: Consumers See That Premium, Private-Label Products Can Come from the Same Place," *Advertising Age,* Mar. 20, 2007.

42. Walker, "Organic Growth."

43. *Id.* (emphasis added).

44. Walker, *Buying In,* at 8.

45. *Advertising Age,* "Time for Industry Workers to Make Case," 9 (emphasis added).

46. B. R. Hergenhahn & Matthew H. Olson, *An Introduction to Theories of Learning* (Upper Saddle River, N.J.: Prentice Hall, 2001), 157–95.

47. *See* Renvoisé & Morin, *Neuromarketing.*

48. *See, e.g.,* Emily Bryson York, "Shopping Aisles at Cutting Edge of Consumer Research and Tech: They Learned It from You; Marketers Working to Better Understand Supermarket Psychology," *Advertising Age,* Mar. 15, 2010, 1, 29.

49. *Economist,* "Who's Wearing the Trousers?" Sept. 8, 2001, 27 (special report on brands).

50. *Id.* at 28.

51. http://www.lovemarks.com/index.php?pageID=20020 (last accessed Mar. 20, 2010).

52. Guido Palazzo & Kunal Basu, "The Ethical Backlash of Corporate Branding," 73 *J. Bus. Ethics* 333, 337 (2007).

53. Walker, "Brand Underground," at 30.

54. Douglas Atkin, *The Culting of Brands: When Customers Become True Believers* (New York: Penguin, 2004), xiii.

55. Strasser, *Satisfaction Guaranteed.*

56. *Id.* at 123.

57. *See, e.g.,* Stuart Elliot, "Switch to Daylight Time Joins the List of Special Occasions Made for Merchandising," *N.Y. Times,* Mar. 31, 2005.

58. *Business Week,* Editorial, "A Trojan Horse for Advertisers," Apr. 3, 2000, 10.

59. For more information about advertising directed at children, *see* the website for the Center for a New American Dream, http://www.newdream .org/kids/problem.php (last accessed Mar. 20, 2010). The center also publishes a 32-page guide titled *Tips for Parenting in a Commercial Culture.*

60. Deborah Roedder John, "Consumer Socialization of Children: A Retrospective Look at Twenty-Five Years of Research," 26 *J. Consumer Research* 183, 207 (1999).

61. *See, e.g.,* Jean McDougall & David Chantry, "The Making of Tomorrow's Consumer," 5(4) *Young Consumers* 8 (2004).

62. Vance Packard, *The Hidden Persuaders* (New York: Simon & Schuster), 154 (quoting Clyde Miller from *The Process of Persuasion* [New York: Crown, 1946]).

63. Packard, *Hidden Persuaders,* at 154 (quoting an ad Packard identified as appearing "several years ago" in *Printer's Ink,* a trade publication for the advertising industry).

64. *Id.*

65. *Id.*

66. Paul M. Fischer, Meyer P. Schwartz, John W. Richards Jr., Adam O. Goldstein, & Tina Rojas, "Brand Logo Recognition by Children Aged 3 to 6 Years: Mickey Mouse and Old Joe the Camel," 266 *JAMA* 3145 (1991).

67. *Id.*

68. Elizabeth S. Moore & Richard J. Lutz, "Children, Advertising, and Product Experiences: A Multimethod Inquiry," 27 *J. Consumer Research* 31 (2000).

69. Brooks Barnes, "Toys for Toddlers From PG-13 Movie," *N.Y. Times,* July 2, 2007 ("Warning: 'Transformers' is steering toward your toddlers.").

70. Rick Lyman & Julian E. Barnes, "The Toy War for Holiday Movies Is a

Battle among 3 Heavyweights," *N.Y. Times,* Nov. 12, 2001, C1; Manohla Dargis, "Car Wars With Shape-Shifter 'R' Us," *N.Y. Times,* July 2, 2007, E1.

71. *See, e.g.,* Deron Boyles, *American Education and Corporations: The Free Market Goes to School* (New York: Falmer, 2000).

72. George Will, "The New Adulthood," *Tulsa World,* Nov. 15, 2001, A16.

73. PBS, "Persuaders." *See also* Douglas Rushkoff, *Coercion: Why We Listen to What "They" Say* (New York: Riverhead Books, 1999).

74. Gale Group, "MarketResearch C'mon, Mom! Kids Nag Parents to Chuck E. Cheeses," Selling to Kids, May 12, 1999, http://findarticles.com/p/articles/mi _m0FVE/is_9_4/ai_54631243/?tag=content;col1 (last accessed Feb. 17, 2011).

75. Schor, *Born to Buy,* at 11.

76. Brian Steinberg, "Need a Slogan? Ask Your Harshest Critic," *AdAge.com,* July 23, 2008, http://adage.com/print?article_id=129837.

77. *Id.*

78. *Id.*

79. Kevin W. Saunders, *Saving Our Children from the First Amendment* (New York: New York University Press, 2003).

80. Rupal Parekh & Natalie Zmuda, "JC Penney Upset at Racy Cannes-Winning Ad," *Advertising Age,* June 24, 2008.

81. *See, e.g.,* Lois Biener & Michael Siegel, "Tobacco Marketing and Adolescent Smoking: More Support for a Causal Inference," 90 *Amer. J. Pub. Health* 407 (2000); Elizabeth A. Gilpin et al., "Receptivity to Tobacco Advertising Promotions among Young Adolescents as a Predictor of Established Smoking in Young Adulthood," 97 *Amer. J. Pub. Health* 1489 (2007).

82. *U.S. v. Philip Morris USA, Inc.,* 449 F. Supp.2d 1 at 234 (D.D.C. 2006), *aff'd* 566 F.3d 1095 (D.C. Cir. 2009), *cert. denied,* 130 S.Ct. 3501 (2010).

83. Report of Marketing Innovations, Inc. to Brown & Williamson Tobacco Corporation in conjunction with Youth Cigarette—New Concepts project (Sept. 1972), http://legacy.library.ussf.edu/tid/ons 56600. *See also* Jennifer M. Kreslake et al., "Tobacco Industry Control of Menthol in Cigarettes and Targeting of Adolescents and Young Adults," 98 *Am. J. Pub. Health* 1685 (2008).

84. In January 1990, a public relations manager for R. J. Reynolds Tobacco Company wrote a letter to the principal and a student of a grade school claiming that "scientists do not know the cause or causes of the chronic diseases reported to be associated with smoking." *United States v. Philip Morris USA, Inc.,* 449 F. Supp.2d at ¶ 784. Some 1,000 pamphlets about smoking were sent to schoolchildren in 1971 and 500 more in 1973. *Id.* at 714.

85. James Bates & Greg Miller, "Selling 'R' Movies to Teens," *San Jose Mercury News,* Sept. 30, 2000, 9A; Deborah Lohse, "Violence Knowingly Marketed to Kids," *San Jose Mercury News,* Sept. 10, 2000, 1A, 10A.

86. Gina Keating, "LA Sues over 'Grand Theft' Game," *Reuters,* Jan. 27, 2006.

87. Join Together, *CAMY: Kids Still See More Alcohol Ads than Adults,*

http://www.jointogether.org/news/research/summaries/2005/camy-kids-still-see-more-ads.html.

88. Jennifer L. Harris, Jennifer L. Pomeranz, Tim Lobstein, & Kelly D. Brownell, "A Crisis in the Marketplace: How Food Marketing Contributes to Childhood Obesity and What Can Be Done," 30 *Annu. Rev. Public Health* 211 (2009). *See also* Adam Benforado, Jon Hanson, & David Yosifon, "Broken Scales: Obesity and Justice in America," 53 *Emory L.J.* 1645 (2004).

89. *See* Kelly D. Brownell & Kenneth E. Warner, "The Perils of Ignoring History: Big Tobacco Played Dirty and Millions Died; How Similar Is Big Food?" 87 *Milbank Q.* 259 (2009).

90. Elizabeth Jensen, "'Sesame' Upgrading Its Address on the Web," *N.Y. Times*, July 15, 2008 (noting difficulties *Sesame Street* has in competing with commercial programs).

91. *Business Week*, "Trojan Horse" (reporting on commercial tie-in arrangement between *Teletubbies* and McDonald's in Happy Meals).

92. *See* Federal Trade Commission, "FTC Staff Report on TV Advertising to Children" (Feb. 1978), http://www.eric.ed.gov/ERICWebPortal/detail?accno=ED178083. *See also* Newton N. Minow & Craig LaMay, *Abandoned in the Wasteland: Children, Television, and the First Amendment* (New York: Hill & Wang, 1995), 166 (on children's difficulty in distinguishing between programs and commercials).

93. Bill Carter, "MTV Plans to Increase Its Lending of Ads and Shows," *N.Y. Times*, May 8, 2008.

94. Abbey Klaassen, "Social Networking Reaches Near Full Penetration among Teens and 'Tweens," *AdAge.com*, June 25, 2007, http://adage.com/digital/article?article_id=118763.

95. *See, e.g.*, Andrew Martin, "Kellogg to Phase Out Some Food Ads to Children," *N.Y. Times*, June 14, 2007; Ira Teinowitz, "Big Food Cuts $1B in Kids Ads; Pols' Hunger Still Not Sated," *Advertising Age*, July 23, 2007; Ira Teinowitz, "More Major Food Marketers Establish Kid-Advertising Limits," *Advertising Age*, July 18, 2007. There are industry groups set up that purport to monitor standards of advertising to children. They include the Children's Food and Beverage Initiative (CFBAI) and the Children's Advertising Review Unit (CARU).

96. Ira Teinowitz, "FTC Subpoenas Food Advertisers," *Advertising Age*, Aug. 13, 2007; Ira Teinowitz, "Marketers, Media Get Chewed Out about Childhood Obesity: FCC Officials and Senator Want More Health-Oriented Advertising," *Advertising Age*, Mar. 21, 2007. *See also* Center for Science in the Public Interest, *Pestering Parents: How Food Companies Market Obesity to Children* (Washington, D.C.: CSPI, 2003); Brownell & Warner, "Perils of Ignoring History."

97. Sarah Ellison & Janet Adamy, "Activists Plan to Sue Viacom and Kellogg over Ads to Children," *Wall Street Journal*, Jan. 19, 2006, A1, A12.

98. Brian Wilcox, Dale Kunkel, Joanne Cantor, Peter Dorwick, Susan Linn, &

Edward Palmer, *Report of the APA Task Force on Advertising and Children* (Feb. 20, 2004), http://www.apa.org/pi/families/resources/advertising-children.pdf (last accessed May 18, 2010). *See also* Judith Gaines, "Mind Games: Psychologists Debate Ethics of Helping Sell to Children," *Boston Globe,* Mar. 26, 2000, A1, B4.

99. *St. Louis Post Dispatch,* Editorial, "Credit Cards: Teach Your Children Well," July 15, 2001, B2.

100. Larry Magid, "Kids Need to Think Critically to Weed Out Unsavory Marketing," *San Jose Mercury News,* Sept 25, 2000, 4F.

101. Wilcox et al., *Advertising and Children,* at 9.

Chapter 6

1. Richard H. Thaler & Cass R. Sunstein, *Nudge: Improving Decisions about Health, Wealth, and Happiness* (New Haven, Conn.: Yale University Press, 2008).

2. Kahneman, Slovic, & Tversky, *Judgment under Uncertainty.*

3. Dan Ariely, *Predictably Irrational* (New York: Harper Collins, 2008).

4. Haipeng (Allan) Chen & Akshay R. Rao, "When Two Plus Two Is Not Equal to Four: Errors in Processing Multiple Percentage Changes," 34 *J. Consumer Res.* 327 (2007) (internal citations omitted).

5. This seems to be the consensus, at least to the *New York Times* reviewer of work by researchers Christopher Chabris and Daniel Simons on what is called "inattentional blindness," the phenomenon of not seeing what you are not looking for. Paul Bloom, "What We Miss," *N.Y. Times,* June 6, 2010, BR 30 (reviewing Christopher Chabris & Daniel Simons, *The Invisible Gorilla* (New York: Crown, 2010)). *See also* Daniel J. Simons & Christopher F. Chabris. "Gorillas in Our Midst: Sustained Inattentional Blindness for Dynamic Events," 28 *Perception* 1059 (1999).

6. Chen, "When Two Plus Two Is Not Equal to Four," at 328.

7. Leonard Mlodinow, *The Drunkard's Walk: How Randomness Rules Our Lives* (New York: Vintage Books, 2008), 45.

8. Malcolm Gladwell makes a similar point in his analysis of some of this literature. Malcolm Gladwell, *Blink: The Power of Thinking without Thinking* (New York: Little, Brown, 2005).

9. *See, e.g.,* Fine, *Mind of Its Own;* Gilbert, *Stumbling on Happiness.*

10. Fine, *Mind of Its Own,* at 137.

11. Elizabeth Loftus, "Creating False Memories," *Scientific American,* Sept. 1997, 70–75.

12. *See* Damasio, *Descartes' Error.*

13. Damasio, *Feeling of What Happens;* Burton, *On Being Certain.*

14. Neale Martin, *Habit: The 95% of Behavior Marketers Ignore* (Upper Saddle River, NJ: FT Press, 2008), 147.

15. *Id.*

16. Robert B. Cialdini, *Influence: The Psychology of Persuasion,* rev. ed. (New York: HarperCollins, 2007).

17. *Id.*

18. Settle & Alreck, *Why They Buy*, at 38.

19. Farhad Manjoo, "Branded," *N.Y. Times*, July 27, 2008 (book review of Rob Walker's *Buying In: The Secret Dialog between What We Buy and Who We Are* [New York: Random House, 2008]).

20. There is a lot of dispute in the industry about what makes an ad effective. Al and Laura Ries (*Fall of Advertising*) have observed that effective ads are often not particularly good from an artistic point of view. *See also* Mya Frazier, "This Ad Will Give You a Headache, but It Sells," *Advertising Age*, Sept. 24, 2007 (recounting the success of obnoxious HeadOn ads).

21. Jack Neff, "P&G Rewrites Its Definition of 'Ad Spend,'" *Advertising Age*, Sept. 3, 2007, available at http://adage.com/article/news/p-grewrites-it-definition -ofad-spend/120213.

22. Bradley Johnson, "More Ad Spend, Better Economy," *Advertising Age*, Oct. 8, 2007. *See also* Maximilien Nayaradou, Doctoral Thesis in Economics submitted to University of Paris, "Advertising and Economic Growth" (Ph.D. diss., University of Paris, 2006), available at http://www.wfanet.org/documents/3/WFA -UDA_Advertising&Economic_Growth.pdf.

23. Walker, *Buying In*, at 36.

24. These are referred to as market "niches." *See, e.g.*, Emily Bryson York, "Social Media Allows Giants to Exploit Niche Markets," *Advertising Age*, July 13, 2009, 3; Natalie Zmuda, "Facebook Turns Focus Group with Splenda Product-Sampling App," *Advertising Age*, July 13, 2009, 18; Michael Learmouth, "Tracking Makes Life Easier for Consumers," *Advertising Age*, July 13, 2009, 3, 25.

25. On August 3, 2008, the Sunday edition of the *New York Times* included a special section on the upcoming Olympic Games, which was chock-full of Nielsen ads announcing that Nielsen was "always surfing the net" for information and collecting it, including 70 percent of all U.S. book purchases. *See also* Douglas Kysar, "Kids and Cul-de-sacs"; Shimp, *Advertising* (targeting customers and prospects), at 56–75 (describing data gathering and data mining).

26. Timothy D. Wilson, *Strangers to Ourselves: Discovering the Adaptive Unconscious* (Cambridge, Mass.: Belknap, 2002), 187.

27. Walker, *Buying In*, at 111.

28. York, "Shopping Aisles at Cutting Edge."

29. Gregory Mitchell, "Tendencies versus Boundaries: Levels of Generality in Behavioral Law and Economics," 56 *Vand. L. Rev.* 1781, 1811–12 (2003).

Chapter 7

1. Thaler & Sunstein, *Nudge* (labeling their recommendations as "libertarian paternalism"). Some have argued that "libertarian paternalism" is an oxymoron.

2. Abbey Klaassen & Ira Teinowitz, "Privacy Groups Propose Do-Not-Track

List: Demands Would Hinder Marketers' Behavioral-Targeting Practices On-Line," *Advertising Age,* Oct. 30, 2007. *See also* Kevin J. O'Brien, "Privacy Laws Trip Up Google's Expansion in Parts of Europe," *N.Y. Times,* Nov. 18, 2008, B8.

3. *See, e.g.,* N. Gregory Mankiw, "Can A Soda Tax Save Us from Ourselves?" *N.Y. Times,* June 6, 2010, BU 4.

4. *See, e.g.,* Brownell & Warner, "Perils of Ignoring History."

5. *Id.*

6. Some would say that writing is what distinguishes human beings. Natalie Goldberg, *Writing Down the Bones: Freeing the Writer Within* (Boston, Mass.: Shambhala, 2005).

7. Settle & Alreck, *Why They Buy,* at 38.

8. *See, e.g., In re Gen. Motors Corp., Anti-Lock Brakes Prods. Liab. Litig.,* 966 F. Supp. 1525 (E.D. Mo. 1997), *aff'd* 172 F.3d 623 (8th Cir. 1999); David A. Hoffman, "The Best Puffery Article Ever," 91 *Iowa L. Rev.* 1395 (2006); Richard J. Leighton, "Materiality and Puffing in Lanham Act False Advertising Cases: The Proofs, Presumptions, and Pretexts," 94 *Trademark Rep.* 585 (2004).

9. Klick & Mitchell, "Government Regulation of Irrationality."

10. *Id.*

11. Vern Countryman, "Advertising Is Speech" (speech given at a conference on the First Amendment and commercial speech, University of Miami, April 1976), in *Advertising and Free Speech,* ed. Allen Hyman & M. Bruce Johnson (Lexington, Mass.: Lexington Books, 1977), 40.

12. *See* Richard Craswell, "Taking Information Seriously: Misrepresentation and Nondisclosure in Contract Law and Elsewhere," 92 *Va. L. Rev.* 565 (2006) ("[T]he effect of the prohibition was to remove a source of relative information about differences in risks across brands, thereby reducing firms' incentives to make marginal improvements in their tar and nicotine levels."); Paul Robbennolt, "Not Just Smoke and Mirrors: Free Expression and EC Restrictions on Tobacco and Alcohol Advertising," 1992 *U. Chi. Legal F.* 419, 438–39 (1992) (restrictions deprived consumers of information about lower tar and nicotine); John E. Calfee, "The Ghost of Cigarette Advertising Past," *Regulation,* Summer 1997, available at http://www.cato.org/pubs/regulation/regv10/v10n6-5.pdf (last accessed Mar. 21, 2010) ("But the fact remains that successive restrictions on advertising have tended to undermine improvements in cigarettes while doing nothing to reduce smoking.").

13. *U.S. v. Philip Morris,* 566 F.3d 1095, 1107 (D.C. Cir. 2009) (describing evidence presented at trial). *See also* Brandt, *Cigarette Century.*

14. Statement by Robert DiMarco, vice president of research and development for R. J. Reynolds, reprinted in Final Opinion Findings of Fact and Conclusions of Law, *U.S. v. Philip Morris USA, Inc.,* 449 F. Supp.2d 362, 380 (D.D.C. 2006) *aff'd* 566 F.3d 1095 (D.C. Cir 2009), *cert. denied,* 130 S.Ct. 3501 (2010). *See also id.*

comments at 369 ("I realize that research tells us that the majority of smokers wished they did not smoke.").

15. *U.S. v. Philip Morris,* at ¶ 636 (statement of George Weissman, executive vice president of R. J. Reynolds, responding to the 1964 surgeon general's report).

16. John A. Howard & James Hulbert, Report to the U.S. Federal Trade Commission, *Advertising and the Public Interest* (Washington, D.C.: Crain Communications, 1973), III-35. The authors cite Vance Packard's *The Hidden Persuaders* as partially responsible for this "myth." *Id.* It is fairly common to dismiss Packard's book as alarmist, paranoid, and exaggerated. However, many of those making these claims are in the ad industry themselves and offer no reasons for the conclusion announced ipse dixit. *See, e.g.,* Mya Frazier, "Hidden Persuaders or Junk Science?" *Advertising Age,* Sept. 10, 2007, 36.

17. Ezra Mishan, "Commercial Advertising: A Skeptical View," in *Advertising and Free Speech,* ed. Allen Hyman & M. Bruce Johnson (Lexington, Mass.: Lexington Books, 1977), 16 (emphasis added).

18. *See, e.g.,* Dean Starkman, "Boiler Room," *Colum. Journalism Rev.,* Sept./Oct. 2008, 49–53, at 53.

19. Economist Bryan Caplan has made precisely this argument in *The Myth of the Rational Voter: Why Democracies Choose Bad Policies* (Princeton, N.J.: Princeton University Press, 2007), asserting that voters do not know what is good for them, a position somewhat difficult to square with antipaternalism.

20. Priya Raghubir & Joydeep Srivastava, "Monopoly Money: The Effect of Payment Coupling and Form on Spending Behavior," 14 *J. Experimental Psychol.: Applied* 213 (2008).

21. David C. Vladeck, "The Difficult Case of Direct-to-Consumer Drug Advertising," 41 *Loy. L.A. L. Rev.* 259, 269 (2007).

22. There is a wealth of information on this topic concerning tobacco alone. *See* Brandt's *Cigarette Century* and Judge Kessler's decision in the conspiracy case brought by the Clinton administration against the tobacco companies (*U.S. v. Philip Morris USA, Inc.; see* n.14). For more recent examples, *see* Kreslake et al., "Tobacco Industry Control"; Biener & Siegel, "Tobacco Marketing." On alcohol, *see* Stuart Elliott, "Youth Exposure to Alcohol Marketing Still Too High, Study Says," *N.Y. Times Media Decoder* (blog), June 24, 2008, http://mediade coder.blogs.nytimes.com/2008/06/24/youth-exposure-to-alcohol-marketing-still -too-high-study-says/.

23. Brad Stone, "Banks Mine Data and Pitch to Troubled Borrowers," *N.Y. Times,* Oct. 22, 2008, B1.

24. This technique is ubiquitous and has been particularly used against women, as is evidenced by Dove's "Onslaught" campaign. However, both genders' desire to be attractive to potential sexual partners (of either gender) is manipulated to sell products.

25. Jennifer L. Pomeranz, "Television Marketing to Children Revisited: The Federal Trade Commission Has the Constitutional and Statutory Authority to Regulate," 38 *J.L. Med. & Ethics* 98, 99 (2010).

26. Wilcox et al., *Advertising and Children,* at 35.

27. *Id.* at 7.

28. *U.S. v. Philip Morris USA, Inc.,* 449 F. Supp.2d 1, 561–691 (D.D.C. 2006), *aff'd* 566 F.3d 1095 (D.C. Cir. 2009).

29. Fischer et al., "Brand Logo Recognition."

30. *Id.* at 3147.

31. Settle & Alreck, *Why They Buy,* at 46–47.

Chapter 8

1. The source of this famous quote, often used in corporate law, is unclear and has been variously attributed. *See, e.g.,* John C. Coffee Jr., "No Soul to Damn, No Body to Kick: An Unscandalized Inquiry into the Problem of Corporate Punishment," 79 *Mich. L. Rev.* 386 (1981) (quoting M. King, *Public Policy and the Corporation* (New York: Chapman and Hall, 1977), 1; Ted Nace, *Gangs of America: The Rise of Corporate Power and the Disability of Democracy* (San Francisco: Berrett-Koehler, 2003), 5 (attributing the quote to Baron Edward Thurlow, lord chancellor of Great Britain during the seventeenth century).

2. Cohen, "Transcendental Nonsense," at 811. Cohen was assuming that sensible people did not believe in angels. He might have been mistaken about that.

3. Professor Adam Winkler argues, I think mistakenly, that critics who tie corporate personhood to freedom for commercial expression are making a doctrinal claim that the case law reflects judicial reliance on this notion of corporate personhood as an explicit justification for their decisions. Adam Winkler, "Corporate Personhood and the Rights of Corporate Speech," 30 *Seattle U. L. Rev.* 863, 866–67 (2007). *See also* Linda L. Berger, "What Is the Sound of a Corporation Speaking? How the Cognitive Theory of Metaphor Can Help Lawyers Shape the Law," 2 *Ass'n Legal Writing Directors* 169 (2004). However, the metaphor only goes so far, as the Supreme Court decided that corporations do not enjoy "personal privacy." *FCC v. AT&T.* No. 09-1279 (Mar. 1, 2011) (slip op.).

4. Nace, *Gangs of America,* at 172.

5. *See* Cohen, "Transcendental Nonsense," at 811 (footnote omitted).

6. *Id.* at 812 (emphasis added).

7. *See, e.g.,* William S. Laufer, *Corporate Bodies and Guilty Minds: The Failure of Corporate Criminal Liability* (Chicago: University of Chicago Press, 2006).

8. For an excellent early discussion of all these shortcomings and many more, as well as an attempt to offer a solution that (as far as I know) has never been adopted, *see* Coffee, "No Soul to Damn."

9. In the film *The Corporation,* inspired by the book of the same name by Joel Bakan, the filmmakers collect news and commentary clips repeating the "few bad

apples" trope. *See The Corporation,* directed by Mark Achbar & Jennifer Abbott (Big Picture Media Corporation, 2003). *See also* http://www.thecorporation.com/ (last accessed Apr. 12, 2010); Bakan, *Corporation.*

10. The June 4, 2005, Saturday issue of the *New York Times* carried at least five stories related to corporate misconduct, including Julie Creswell, "Citigroup Agrees to Pay $2 Billion in Enron Scandal," B13; Business Briefs, "Jurors in Trial of Two Tyco Executives End the Week without Completing a Verdict," C2; Associated Press, "A Second Guilty Plea in A.I.G.-Related Case," B13; Ken Belson, "Ebbers Pleads for Leniency in Sentencing," C13.

11. Creswell, "Citigroup Agrees to Pay."

12. *Id.* "The potential exposure to the banks in this case could have been really large," said Joseph A. Grundfest, a law professor at Stanford University and a former commissioner at the Securities and Exchange Commission. *Id.*

13. Krysten Crawford, "Ex-WorldCom CEO Ebbers Guilty," *CNNMoney .com,* Mar. 15, 2005, http://money.cnn.com/2005/03/15/news/newsmakers/ ebbers/ (last accessed Mar. 24, 2010).

14. Grace Wong, "Kozlowski Gets up to 25 Years," *CCNMoney.com,* Sept. 19, 2005, http://money.cnn.com/2005/09/19/news/newsmakers/kozlowski_sentence/ (last accessed Mar. 24, 2007).

15. Mary Flood, Mark Babineck, & John Roper, "Guilty! Guilty! Verdict Will Mean Prison for Ex-Enron Chiefs," *Houston Chronicle,* May 25, 2006.

16. Sarbanes-Oxley Act of 2002, Pub. L. No. 107-204, 2002 U.S.C.C.A.N. 116 Stat. 745 (codified in scattered sections of 15 and 18 U.S.C.).

17. *See, e.g.,* Roberta Romano, "The Sarbanes-Oxley Act and the Making of Quack Corporate Governance," 114 *Yale L.J.* 1521 (2005). For a somewhat more optimistic analysis of the potential of Sarbanes-Oxley to spur positive change, *see* Lawrence E. Mitchell, "The Sarbanes-Oxley Act and the Reinvention of Corporate Governance?" 48 *Vill. L. Rev.* 1189 (2003).

18. *See* PBS, "Bigger than Enron," *Frontline* (PBS television broadcast, June 20, 2002), http://www.pbs.org/wgbh/pages/frontline/shows/regulation/ (last accessed Mar. 24, 2010).

19. John Poynder, *Literary Extracts from English and Other Works; Collected during Half a Century: Together with Some Original Matter,* vol. I (London: John Hatchard & Son, 1844), 268 (attributed to "Lord Chancellor Thurlow" from Miscellaneous).

20. U.S. Sentencing Guidelines Manual § 8 (Nov. 2005).

21. Jeffrey S. Parker & Raymond A. Atkins, "Did the Corporate Criminal Sentencing Guidelines Matter? Some Preliminary Empirical Observations," 42 *J.L. & Econ.* 423, 424 (1999) ("generally finding no significant effect"). Indeed, the authors speculated that if "the 1991 guidelines were never intended to do anything other than meet a demand for political rhetoric rather than law enforcement," their lack of impact may have been "the best of all possible worlds." *Id.* at 449.

See also William S. Laufer, *Corporate Bodies and Guilty Minds: The Failure of Corporate Criminal Liability* (Chicago: University of Chicago Press, 2006) (identifying much of the reform in corporate criminal law to have taken place in the sentencing guidelines).

22. *See, e.g.,* Jeffrey D. Bauman, Alan R. Palmiter, & Frank Partnoy, *Corporations Law and Policy,* 6th ed. (St. Paul, Minn.: Thomson West, 2007). Under exceptional circumstances, officers, directors, and/or shareholders can be held liable for the debts or obligations of the firm where there are grounds for piercing the corporate veil. *Id.* at 268–300.

23. For a description of the collective nature of the firm, *see* Greenwood, "Essential Speech," at 995, & 1021–34.

24. In general, it is difficult to hold a firm liable for violations where intent or state of mind is relevant. *See, e.g.,* Stacey Neumann Vu, "Corporate Criminal Liability: Patchwork Verdicts and the Problem of Locating a Guilty Agent," 104 *Colum. L. Rev.* 459 (2004). *See also Arthur Andersen L.L.P. v. U.S.,* 544 U.S. 696 (2005) (overturning conviction because jury instruction failed to adequately convey to jury the requirement of intent).

25. Erin McClam, "WorldCom Figures Sentenced," *Tulsa World,* Aug. 6, 2005, E6 (quoting Betty Vinson at her sentencing). It is not clear whether Ms. Vinson meant that she was sorry and surprised because she had not started out to do wrong or simply that she had not expected to get caught.

26. Bakan, *Corporation.*

27. *See, e.g.,* Charles Derber, *Corporation Nation: How Corporations Are Taking Over Our Lives and What We Can Do About It* (New York: St. Martin's Press, 1998); Nace, *Gangs of America;* Ralph Estes, *The Tyranny of the Bottom Line: Why Corporations Make Good People Do Bad Things* (San Francisco: Berrett-Koehler, 1996); Richard Sennett, *The Corrosion of Character: The Personal Consequences of Work in the New Capitalism* (New York: W. W. Norton, 2006); Russell Mokhiber & Robert Weissman, *Corporate Predators: The Hunt for Mega-Profits and the Attack on Democracy* (Monroe, Maine: Common Courage, 1999); Harry Glasbeck, *Wealth by Stealth: Corporate Crime, Corporate Law, and the Perversion of Democracy* (Toronto: Between the Lines, 2002); Thom Hartmann, *Unequal Protection: The Rise of Corporate Dominance and the Theft of Human Rights* (Emmaus, Pa.: Rodale Books, 2002).

28. C. A. Harwell Wells, "The Cycles of Corporate Social Responsibility: An Historical Retrospective for the Twenty-First Century," 51 *Kan. L. Rev.* 77 (2002).

29. Kent Greenfield, "Proposition: Saving the World with Corporate Law," 57 *Emory L.J.* 948 (2008).

30. For the proposition that early corporations were chartered for public purposes see Morton J. Horwitz, *The Transformation of American Law 1870–1960* (New York: Oxford University Press, 1992), 72–73; Samuel Williston, "History of the Law of Business Corporations before 1800," 2 *Harv. L. Rev.* 105, 110–15

(1888). For a discussion of the corporate social responsibility issue and the ways in which it represents only the latest iteration of the struggle to build some public accountability into business corporations *see* Wells, "The Cycles of Corporate Social Responsibility."

31. Some interesting work done in this area suggests that the way out of the difficulties of commercial speech are through a more subtle and nuanced assessment of the interactions of institutions. *See, e.g.,* Randall Bezanson, "Institutional Speech," 80 *Iowa L. Rev.* 735 (1995); Joseph Blocher, "Institutions in the Marketplace of Ideas," 57 *Duke L.J.* 821 (2008); Frederick Schauer, "Towards an Institutional First Amendment," 89 *Minn. L. Rev.* 1256 (2005); Michael R. Siebecker, "Building a 'New Institutional' Approach to Corporate Speech," 59 *Ala. L. Rev.* 247 (2008); Douglass C. North, "Institutions," 5 *J. Econ. Persp.* 97 (1991).

32. *See, e.g.,* Blocher, "Institutions."

33. This black letter law has always been significantly modified by the business judgment rule. *See* Einer Elhauge, "Sacrificing Corporate Profits," 80 *NYU L. Rev.* 733, 740–44 (2005). However, even Professor Elhauge agrees that profit maximization is the management's "primary obligation" to shareholders. *Id.* at 745. The business judgment rule represents an implicit understanding that transferring the decision to the courts of what specific action would be "profit maximizing" in any particular situation would result in significant increases in transaction costs and that the resultant inefficiency would virtually guarantee further reductions in profits. Nevertheless, the existence of such discretion represents no assurance that the discretion will be exercised in a manner consistent with the public interest. *See Economist,* "The Good Company," Jan. 22, 2005, S3. It is not clear that adopting a nexus of contracts theory makes a meaningful difference with respect to this issue. *See* Stephen Bainbridge, "In Defense of the Shareholder Wealth Maximization Norm: A Reply to Professor Green," 50 *Wash. & Lee L. Rev.* 1423, 1427, 1446–47 (1993) (arguing that despite the replacement of the "outdated [shareholders as owners] model of the firm" with a nexus of contract model, the shareholder wealth maximization norm is nevertheless still dominant and appropriately so). *See also* Daniel J. H. Greenwood, "The Dividend Problem: Are Shareholders Entitled to the Residual, or Faith Based Investing: Why Economics Can't Explain Shareholder Returns." 32 *J. Corp. L.* 103 (2006).

34. *See* Greenwood, "Fictional Shareholders."

35. Greenwood, "Essential Speech," at 1036.

36. *See, e.g., Dodge v. Ford Motor Co.,* 170 N.W. 668, 684 (Mich. 1919).

37. Within this economic interest is, of course, an enormous range of movement. Saying that the fiduciary is to take into account the shareholders' economic interests does not self-evidently further dictate whether those interests are long- or short-term, must take the form of dividends paid out or value of the stock, or many other permutations of how the fiduciaries may act out their responsibilities. For a report on some of the current debate about short-term versus long-term

business planning, *see Economist,* "Jam Today: Worries about Short-Termism Grip America's Business Elite—Wrongly, Perhaps," July 14, 2007, 67. Moreover, with the advent of socially responsible investing (SRI), some investors are attempting to bring their investments in line with their overall moral convictions through shareholder resolutions, divestitures of stocks of companies that do not fit investors' agenda, and similar actions. *See, e.g.,* Daska Slater, "Public Corporations Shall Take Us Seriously," *N.Y. Times Magazine,* Aug. 12, 2007, 22.

38. Ray Anderson is the "founder and chairman of Interface, Inc., the world's largest commercial carpet manufacturer," and an outspoken proponent of a switch to manufacturing processes that contribute to sustainability. Bakan, *Corporation,* at 71.

39. Milton C. Regan Jr., "Moral Intuitions and Organizational Culture," 51 *St. Louis U. L.J.* 941 (2007).

40. *See, e.g.,* Lawrence E. Mitchell, "Cooperation and Constraint in the Modern Corporation: An Inquiry into the Causes of Corporate Immorality," 73 *Tex. L. Rev.* 477 (1995).

41. Jack Neff, "J&J Targets Red Cross, Blunders into PR Firestorm," *Advertising Age,* Aug. 13, 2007.

42. *Id.*

43. *Id.*

44. Bakan, *Corporation,* at 51–53.

45. *Id.* at 53 (emphasis added).

46. *Id.* It is worth noting that Roddick's sincerity in her commitment to these goals has been questioned, with some claiming that her much-vaunted values had been more cosmetic than substantive. *See, e.g.,* Stauber & Rampton, *Toxic Sludge,* at 73–76; Jon Entine, "The Stranger-Than-Truth Story of the Body Shop," in *Killed: Great Journalism Too Hot to Print,* ed. David Wallis (New York: Nation Books, 2004), 179–212.

47. David Goodman, "Culture Change," *Mother Jones,* Jan./Feb. 2003, 52. It is difficult to know whether this loss of credibility is more apparent than real. At least some commentators have attributed the founders' willingness to sell to Unilever to information about Unilever's "funding programs for hospitals in Vietnam and schools in Ghana." Laura P. Hartman, Robert S. Rubin, & K. Kathy Dhanda, "The Communication of Corporate Social Responsibility: United States and European Union Multinational Corporations," 74 *J. Bus. Ethics* 373 (2007).

48. Greenwood, "Fictional Shareholders," at 1092.

49. *Id.* (emphasis added).

50. *See, e.g.,* O'Donnell, "Blowing the Whistle."

51. *See, e.g.,* Geraldine Szott Moohr, "An Enron Lesson: The Modest Role of the Criminal Law in Preventing Corporate Crime," in *Enron: Corporate Fiascos and Their Implications,* ed. Nancy B. Rapoport & Bala G. Dharan (New York: Foundation Press, 2004), 431, 448–50.

52. *Id.* at 450–52.

53. *See, e.g.,* David M. Skover & Kellye Y. Testy, "Lesbigay Identity as Commodity," 90 *Cal. L. Rev.* 223 (2002). Many advertisers are now making one ad with alternate endings or elements depending on what market the ad is aimed at. Andrew Hampp, "An Ad in Which Boy Gets Girl . . . or Boy," *AdAge.com,* Aug. 6, 2007, http://adage.com/article?article_id=119705 (last accessed Mar. 25, 2010).

54. A recent article in *Advertising Age* identified the Hispanic and Spanish language market as an area of expected growth in an otherwise somewhat flat trajectory for advertising expenditures. Nat Ives, "Media Spending Declines as Marketers Tap the Brakes," *AdAge.com,* June 5, 2007, http://adage.com/mediaworks/article?article_id=117103 (last accessed Mar. 24, 2010).

55. *See, e.g.,* Estes, *Tyranny of the Bottom Line.*

56. *See, e.g.,* Bauman et al., *Corporations Law,* at 116–17; Cynthia A. Williams, "Corporate Social Responsibility in an Era of Economic Globalization," 35 *U.C. Davis L. Rev.* 705 (2002); Paul N. Cox, "The Public, the Private, and the Corporation," 80 *Marq. L. Rev.* 391 (1997).

57. Economist Milton Friedman suggested there is only "one instance when corporate social responsibility can be tolerated—when it is insincere." Bakan, *Corporation,* at 28.

58. *Economist,* "The Union of Concerned Executives: CSR as Practiced Means Many Different Things," Jan. 22, 2005. This article forms part of a special report entitled *A Survey of Corporate Social Responsibility. PRWeek* reports that the editorial staff of the *Economist* remains skeptical about CSR's value to shareholders. *See* Steve Hemsley, "Who's Responsible?" *PRWeek,* Aug. 12, 2005, 22.

59. *Economist,* "Union of Concerned Executives."

60. *Economist,* "Good Company."

61. For more discussion of the tendency of the marginal utility of efficient bargaining to enhance disparities in wealth, *see* Daniel J. H. Greenwood, "Torts in Corporate Law: Do Corporations Have a Fiduciary Obligation to Commit Torts?" in *Tortious Liability: Emerging Trends,* ed. M. N. Bhavani (Hyderabad: Icfai University Press, 2008).

62. *See, e.g.,* Henry Hansmann & Reinier Kraakman, "The End of History for Corporate Law," 89 *Geo. L.J.* 439 (2000–2001).

63. Milton Friedman, "The Social Responsibility of Business Is to Increase Its Profits," *N.Y. Times Magazine,* Sept. 13, 1970, available at http://www.colorado.edu/studentgroups/libertarians/issues/friedman-soc-resp-business.html (last accessed Mar. 25, 2010) (emphasis added).

64. Some observers think that CSR should entail more than what the law requires in order to really count as "social responsibility." "Many businesses think that merely complying with environmental regulations is CSR, when they are only doing what they must by law." Hemsley, "Who's Responsible?" 1 (internal quotes omitted).

65. "The corporate law that corporations have chosen directs corporate decision-makers to cause 'accidents' *deliberately* (even if statistically) in the name of profit." Greenwood, "Torts in Corporate Law," at 5 (emphasis in original).

66. *See, e.g., Model Bus. Corp Act* § 8.31(a)(2)(iii) & (v) (describing circumstances that might constitute a conflict of interest). This is not an automatic basis for finding a breach of loyalty. *See* § 8.31(b)(1)(i)–(ii) (placing the burden of showing harm on the party challenging the conduct). Many states have adopted these provisions of the Model Business Corporation Act.

67. *See, e.g.,* 28 U.S.C. §§ 455(b)(4) & (c) (mandating recusal where a judge has a financial conflict of interest).

68. *See, e.g.,* Fl. Stat. § 921.141 (providing enhancement for a homicide committed for financial gain). *See also Gore v. Sec. for Dept. of Corrections,* 493 F.3d 1273 (11th Cir. 2007).

69. *See, e.g., Sun Trust Bank v. Houghton Mifflin Co.,* 268 F.3d 1257, 1267–71 (11th Cir. 2001) (owners of copyright for *Gone with the Wind* sued for alleged infringement by publication of parody *Wind Done Gone;* court held plaintiff unlikely to overcome fair use defense for parody even though parody was produced for a commercial purpose, because commercial purpose is only one consideration and not dispositive). For a discussion of how fair use limits First Amendment protection, *see* Rebecca Tushnet, "Copy This Essay: How Fair Use Doctrine Harms Free Speech and How Copying Serves It," 114 *Yale L.J.* 535 (2004).

70. *See* Bakan, *Corporation,* at 60.

71. As Professor Douglas Kysar has pointed out, casting pollution as an externality may be an unduly limited lens through which to view the problem of environmental pollution, because it casts it in the role of side effect rather than fundamental. *See* Douglas A. Kysar, "The Consultants' Republic," 121 *Harv. L. Rev.* 2041, 2056–57 (2008).

72. *See* Peter T. Kilborn, "The Five-Bedroom, Six-Figure Rootless Life," *N.Y. Times,* June 1, 2005, A1.

73. *See* Marleen O'Connor-Felman, "American Corporate Governance and Children: Investing in Our Future Human Capital during Turbulent Times," 77 *S. Cal. L. Rev.* 1258 (2004).

74. Sennett, *Corrosion of Character,* at 96–97.

75. For example, as Gail Collins observed, many argued that this would be why most companies would begin offering day care to working women. But it did not happen. "[B]y 1987 the Bureau of Labor Statistics said only 2 percent of the 1.1 million American workplaces it studied offered child-care services to their employees, and only about 3 percent helped pay for it elsewhere." Gail Collins, *When Everything Changed: The Amazing Journey of American Women from 1960 to the Present* (New York: Little, Brown, 2009), 304–5.

76. Bakan, *Coporation,* at 70 (quoting Robert Monks).

77. *Id.* at 72–73.

78. In one article, Douglas Litowitz asks the question "Are Corporations Evil?" and concludes that it is actually size, not the corporate form, that generates social problems. Douglas Litowitz, "Are Corporations Evil?" 58 *U. Miami L. Rev.* 811, 814–15 (2004).

79. In the satirical novel *Jennifer Government* (New York: Vintage Books, 2003), author Max Barry creates just such a world. In it, everyone takes on as a surname the name of the company they work for, and the government is available for hire on a private contract basis and has a fairly minor role as referee in the corporate violence competition generates. The novel begins with a marketing plan by a fictional Nike to kill 10 customers in order to generate buzz about a new model of sneakers.

80. Greenwood, "Essential Speech," at 1053 (emphasis added).

81. Monetary penalties can include both civil and criminal fines as well as laws exposing the company to civil liability. Typically, multiple enforcement mechanisms coexist and overlap. In addition, regulatory agencies can have specific enforcement powers to order things like recalls, cleanups, corrective statements, and other affirmative steps. Some feel that the ability to fine is more likely to inspire compliance than the recall power alone. Eric Lipton & Louise Story, "Bid to Root Out Lead Trinkets Falters in U.S.," *N.Y. Times,* Aug. 6, 2007. *See also* Environment News Service, "Oil Companies Settle Fuel Violations for 1.5 Million," Oct. 6, 2006, http://corpwatch.org/article.php?id=14165 (last accessed Mar. 25, 2010) (violations of Clean Air Act).

82. Alex Berenson, "For Merck, the Vioxx Paper Trail Won't Go Away," *N.Y. Times,* Aug. 21, 2005, A1, 17.

83. *Id.* at 17 (emphasis added).

84. Bakan, *Corporation,* at 75.

85. *Id.* at 75–79.

Chapter 9

1. Emerson, *Toward a General Theory,* at 3.

2. *See* Edward S. Herman & Noam Chomsky, *Manufacturing Consent: The Political Economy of Mass Media* (New York: Pantheon, 2002).

3. Lisa Lerer, "Lobbyists Sent 13 Fake Letters to Hill," *Politico* (blog), Aug. 18, 2009, http://www.politico.com/news/stories/0809/26229.html (last accessed Apr. 24, 2010) (Bonner & Associates, a lobbying group, sent letters to congressmen using phony letterhead from the NAACP and other groups, urging congressional representatives to oppose climate change legislation). *See also* Andrea Seabrook, "House Scrutinizes Fake Letters Sent to Congress," NPR, Oct. 30, 2009, http://www.npr.org/templates/story/story.php?storyId=114303819 (last accessed Apr. 24, 2010).

4. Frank Rich, "Enron: Patron Saint of Bush's Fake News," *N.Y. Times,* Mar. 20, 2005. One example of such PR efforts was the infamous tour that Enron ex-

ecutives gave to financial analysts of Enron's newly launched EES division in 1998. *See* Bethany McLean & Peter Elkind, *The Smartest Guys in the Room: The Amazing Rise and the Scandalous Fall of Enron* (New York: Penguin, 2004), 179–80.

5. Enron's continuing to post profits despite being unable to show how it generated them and despite a refusal to offer balance sheets and cash flow statements led some observers to refer to it as a "black box." McLean & Elkind, *Smartest Guys*, at 320–21. At least one commentator makes a similar criticism of the Tyco collapse. *See* Jeff Matthews, "This Just In: 'Spin' Becomes 'Lying,'" *Jeff Matthews Is Not Making This Up* (blog), June 19, 2005, http://jeffmatthewsisnot makingthisup.blogspot.com/2005/06/this-just-in-spin-becomes-lying.html (last visited Mar. 24, 2010).

6. How would one explain widespread apathy with respect to the failure to find weapons of mass destruction in Iraq? One of the most blatant examples of the language of marketing infiltrating the political sphere is the explanation President Bush's chief of staff Andrew Card gave for the timing of the Iraq War invasion—"You don't introduce new products in August." George Packer, "Comment: Name Calling," *New Yorker,* Aug. 8, 2005, 33.

7. One report in the *Washington Post* attributed the live feed to Fox News, but the link in the article on MSNBC had been taken down. Al Kamen, "FEMA Meets the Press, Which Happens to Be—FEMA," *Washington Post,* Oct. 26, 2007. Many of the other sources for this story did not identify the video as coming from Fox News. One wonders whether this is because of Fox News's reputation for responding to criticism with such a furious defense that reporters are to delete reference to the organization when possible. *See* David Carr, "When Fox News is the Story," *N.Y. Times,* July 7, 2008.

8. Kamen, "FEMA Meets the Press."

9. Eric Lipton, "FEMA Aide Loses New Job Over Fake News Conference," *N.Y. Times,* Oct. 30, 2007, A19. R. David Paulison, memo to FEMA employees, Oct. 29, 2007, http://graphic8.nytimes.com/packages/pdf/national/2007/030 _FEMA _Paulison_memo.pdf.

10. Paulison memo.

11. *Id.*

12. *Id.*

13. It is unclear where the cameras came from. There was a suggestion that Fox News supplied them. It may be that it was run on the Virtual News Network. The VNN is a PR vehicle offering video news releases to the press but not created by the press.

14. Paulison memo.

15. The conference gave the public a phone number for people separated from their families by the fire to call, to help them find each other. It reassured people

that the emergency shelters would have enough supplies and that they should obey evacuation orders.

16. Ron Suskind, "Without a Doubt: Faith, Certainty, and the Presidency of George W. Bush," *N.Y. Times Magazine*, Oct. 17, 2004 (quoting an anonymous senior advisor to President Bush).

17. Ken Wheaton, "Agencies Have a Funny Way of Showing 'Commitment' to Diversity," *AdAge.com*, July 8, 2008, http://adage.com/bigtent/post?article_id =128219 (criticizing the ad industry's poor showing on commitment to diversity in hiring).

18. Robert B. Reich, "How Capitalism Is Killing Democracy," *Foreign Policy*, Sept./Oct. 2007, 38, 41.

19. David Brooks, "Bailout to Nowhere," *N.Y. Times*, Nov. 14, 2008, A33.

20. Frank L. Luntz, *Words That Work: It's Not What You Say, It's What People Hear* (New York: Hyperion Books, 2007).

21. *Id.* at 4.

22. *Id.*

23. *Id.*

24. *Id.* at 5 (emphasis added).

25. *Id.* at 6.

26. Bernays, *Propaganda*, at 60.

27. Tye, *Father of Spin*, at 236.

28. Caplan, *Myth of the Rational Voter*.

29. Scottish writer Thomas Carlyle first referred to economics as "dismal science." That he did so in the text of a racist screed in support of slavery is deeply ironic. *See* "The Carlyle-Mill 'Negro Question' Debate," http://cepa.newschool .edu/het/ texts/carlyle/negroquest.htm (last accessed Mar. 24, 2010). Carlyle's opponent on this question, John Stuart Mill, had the better of the argument on both slavery and economics.

30. Caplan, *Myth of the Rational Voter*, at 197–98.

31. Caplan's most comical suggestion is for economists to abandon their "misguided humility." *Id.* at 204. I leave it to the reader to judge whether humility is a characteristic often exhibited by the economists.

32. Drew Westen, *The Political Brain: The Role of Emotion in Deciding the Fate of the Nation* (New York: Public Affairs, 2007).

33. Thaler & Sunstein, *Nudge*. *See also* Dan M. Kahan, "The Cognitively Illiberal State," 60 *Stan .L. Rev.* 115 (2007). Kahan's theory is far too sophisticated and complex to summarize adequately here. Of all the theories, I find myself most in sympathy with this one. Although it does beg the question of who will be in the position to see that these norms are adopted and to implement them, it is not unreasonable to suppose that such norms may spontaneously emerge as groups, including business, see the long-term benefit in this approach. It is unclear whether

asymmetrical adoption of such norms might not disadvantage one side. But like Dr. Martin Luther King and Gandhi's strategy of nonviolence, it may give the side that adopts it the appearance of a moral advantage that could in time cause capitulation. This is pure speculation on my part, and more on it is beyond the scope of this book.

34. *See* Redish & Wasserman, "What's Good for General Motors." Redish was paraphrasing something said by Charles Erwin Wilson, a former CEO of GM, in his confirmation hearings for secretary of defense to President Eisenhower before the Senate Armed Services Committee. When asked whether he could ever imagine making a decision as secretary of defense that might be adverse to the interests of GM, Wilson answered that he could but that "for years I thought what was good for the country was good for General Motors and vice versa." *See Time* magazine, http://www.time.com/time/magazine/article /0,9171,827790,00.html (last accessed Mar. 24, 2010).

35. *See, e.g.,* John Gerassi, *The Great Fear in Latin America,* paperback ed. (New York: Collier Books, 1971); Dan Koeppel, Op-Ed, "Yes, We Will Have No Bananas," *N.Y. Times,* June 18, 2008, A21 (tracing the rise of popularity of bananas in the United States to marketing campaigns, then efforts to keep the costs low once the market was established, "by exercising iron-fisted control over the Latin American countries where the fruit was grown," including supporting antidemocratic regimes that protected business rather than workers).

36. James Glanz & Richard A. Oppel Jr., "Panel Questions State Dept. Role in Iraq Oil Deal," *N.Y. Times,* July 3, 2008, A1 (reporting on Hunt Oil signing an oil exploration deal with the Kurdistan Regional Government with the assistance and encouragement of the State Department, despite an official State Department stance that such deals were to be discouraged; given that the Iraqi government has passed no comprehensive oil policy, a policy that once passed might impact such deals negatively).

37. *BBC News–UK,* Editorial, "Nigeria's Removal of Shell Hailed," June 5, 2008, http://news.bbc.co.uk/2/hi/africa/7437247.stm (last accessed Mar. 25, 2010); *BBC News–UK,* Editorial, "Shell Admits Fueling Corruption," June 11, 2008, http://news.bbc.co.uk/2/hi/business/3796375.stm) (last accessed Mar. 25, 2010).

38. *See, e.g.,* Baker, "Paternalism," at 1178–83 (part III, "A Corporation Is Not a Citizen").

39. *Economist,* "Which Way Will Capital Vote?" July 19, 2008. Ironically, this issue contained multiple articles about the emerging bank and market crisis in the United States, attributing some of the problems in the mortgage crisis to both too much regulation and too little. *See Economist,* "Toxic Fudge," July 19, 2008, 80 (faulting Fannie Mae and Freddie Mac for being entities given a public subsidy for "private profit").

40. *See, e.g.,* Teresa Sullivan, Elizabeth Warren, & Jay Lawrence Westbrook, "Less Stigma or More Financial Distress: An Empirical Analysis of the Extraor-

dinary Increase in Bankruptcy Filings," 59 *Stan. L. Rev.* 213, 253–54 (2006) (industry lobbying efforts on the bill by one account exceed $100 million, but there was no organization with comparable assets lobbying on behalf of debtors). In 2007, Congress passed a bill with extensive limits on certain types of lobbying; but, based on newspaper accounts, it appears to be primarily directed at the practice of wining and dining legislators, not at prohibiting the practice of drawing up proposed legislation. David D. Kirkpatrick, "Tougher Rules Change Game for Lobbyists," *N.Y. Times,* Aug. 7, 2007.

41. *See* Sullivan, Warren, & Westbrook, "Less Stigma." *See also* Rafael Efrat, "Attribution Theory Bias and the Perception of Abuse in Consumer Bankruptcy," 10 *Geo. J. on Poverty L. & Pol'y* 205, 220 (2003) ("The subtle mass media message of consumer bankruptcy abuse has been recently steered, to some extent, by an aggressive public relations campaign by the credit card industry."); Elizabeth Warren, "The Market for Data: The Changing Role of Social Sciences in Shaping the Law," 2002 *Wis. L. Rev.* 1, 22 (2002) (describing the credit industry's role in generating research); Robert Cwiklik, "Ivory Tower Inc: When Research and Lobbying Mesh," *Wall Street Journal,* June 9, 1998, B1.

42. The recent rule changes make that practice suspect and apparently largely out of bounds. *See* Kirkpatrick, "Tougher Rules." On the issue of corporate lobbying generally, *see* Stauber & Rampton, *Toxic Sludge;* Rampton & Stauber, *Trust Us;* Joyce Nelson, *Sultans of Sleaze* (Toronto: Between the Lines, 1989).

43. The term *astroturf organizations* refers to organizations created by paid PR firms or other corporate sponsorship organizations that resemble grassroots organizations put together by citizens but that are really made up of persons paid by the industry in question to pose as "concerned citizens." *See* Stauber & Rampton, *Toxic Sludge,* at 79 (describing "astroturf lobbying" efforts).

44. Robert A. G. Monks, *Corpocracy: How CEOs and the Business Roundtable Hijacked the World's Greatest Wealth Machine—and How to Get it Back* (Hoboken, N.J.: John Wiley & Sons, 2007), 61.

45. The Business Roundtable, joined by the Chamber of Commerce of the United States of America, sued the Securities and Exchange Commission (SEC) to prevent the adoption of a new rule for publicly traded corporations that would, in some circumstances, require companies to include shareholder nominees for director in the corporation's proxy statement. Among other things, the Business Roundtable claimed that this rule violates corporations' First Amendment rights. *See* Brief for Petitioner at 55–59, *Business Roundtable, et al. v. SEC,* No. 10-1305 (D.C. Circuit appeal from SEC filed Nov. 30, 2010. The Court of Appeals struck down the SEC rule on other grounds. See *Business Roundtable, et al. v. SEC,* 647 F.3d 1144 (D.C. Cir., 2011)

46. *See* Karen Olsson, "Ghostwriting the Law," *Mother Jones,* Sept./Oct. 2002, 17.

47. ALEC website, http://www.alec.org/am/template.cfm?section=home (last accessed Mar. 24, 2010).

48. *Id.*

49. "The notion that business and government are and should be partners is ubiquitous, unremarkable, and repeated like a mantra by leaders in both domains." Bakan, *Corporation,* at 108.

50. There is often something of a revolving door between the firms in the industry to be regulated and the employees of the governmental agencies doing the regulating. *N.Y. Times,* Editorial, "Lobbying from Within," June 17, 2005. There are perfectly understandable reasons for this movement that are not in any way sinister. Nevertheless, the degree of movement is often troubling and raises concerns about agency capture.

51. *See, e.g.,* Peter Grier, "FTC Chief Changes Role of 'Nation's Nanny,'" *Christian Sci. Monitor,* Dec. 6, 1983, 5 (describing the chief of the Federal Trade Commission as pushing Congress for narrower tailoring of his agency's authority). As recently as 2003, an FTC commissioner described the agency's mission as allied to that of advertisers. Commissioner Thomas B. Leary, FTC, "Allies in a Common Cause" (speech at a conference at the Food and Drug Law Institute, Jan. 16, 2003), transcript available at http://www.ftc.gov/speeches/leary/fdli.pdf (last accessed Mar. 25, 2010).

52. *See* Eric Lichtblau, "Lawyers Fought U.S. Move to Curb Tobacco Penalty," *NY Times,* June 16, 2005, A1.

53. *Id.*

54. This observation constitutes at least a rebuttal to the recent claim by George Mason University economist Bryan Caplan (*Myth of the Rational Voter*) that it is irrational voters, unschooled in the verities of economics, who are responsible for bad laws and bad policies, because they keep voting for politicians pursuing bad economic policies. There is some question whether the voters are actually getting what they are voting for in the first place. *See* Thomas Frank, *What's the Matter with Kansas? How Conservatives Won the Heart of America* (New York: Henry Holt, 2005). But based on the amount of money spent by corporations on lobbying, including drafting legislation, it might seem fair to say that the actual content of the laws owes far more to the more economically sophisticated corporate lawyers, executives, and lobbyists.

55. Greenwood, "Essential Speech," at 1054.

56. Monks, *Corpocracy,* at 3–15 (describing an ExxonMobil shareholders' meeting).

57. *Id.* at 13–14.

58. *This Film Is Not Yet Rated,* directed by Kirby Dick (IFC Films, 2006).

59. Monks, *Corpocracy.* Monks believes the answer to the dilemma created by corporate dominance of government is to grant shareholders greater power or corporate actions. I am not sure I agree that this alone is the right approach. But Monks's position, given that he is an avowedly enthusiastic booster of business

and capitalism, surely demonstrates that my own observations are neither outlandish nor evidence that I am antibusiness.

60. *First Nat'l Bank of Boston v. Bellotti,* 435 U.S. 765 (1978).

61. *Austin v. Michigan Chamber of Commerce,* 494 U.S. 652 (1990).

62. *Id.* at 658–59 (internal quotations and citations omitted).

63. *Id.* at 659 (quoting *FEC v. Massachusetts Citizens for Life,* 479 U.S. 238, 258 (1986)) (emphasis added).

64. PBS, "Persuaders" (interview with Bob Garfield, describing his views of the negative effects of what he deems blatantly false political ads with content influenced by advertising trends); Bruce Ledewitz, "Corporate Advertising's Democracy," 12 *B.U. Pub. Int. L.J.* 389 (2003) (advertising as antidemocratic).

65. "Language, politics, and commerce have always been intertwined, both for better and for worse." Luntz, *Words That Work,* at xii. *See also id.* at 127–78 (corporate and political case studies).

66. *See* Gia Lee, "Persuasion, Transparency, and Government Speech," 56 *Hastings L.J.* 983, 984 n. 5 (2005) (accompanying text).

67. Frank Rich, *The Greatest Story Ever Sold: The Decline and Fall of Truth From 9/11 to Katrina* (New York: Penguin, 2006) (exhaustive review of the Bush administration's use of PR techniques).

68. Poor people may find themselves disproportionately the target of advertising of products like tobacco, alcohol, and lottery tickets. One recent contributor to *Advertising Age* urges marketers to realize that even people earning only $2,000 a year can represent an untapped market that will be responsive to the right approach. Michelle Kristula-Green, "How to Market to Asia's Masses," *AdAge.com,* Aug. 6, 2007, http://adage.com/print?article_id=119637 (last accessed Mar. 25, 2010). Given, however, that the author was touting marketers' success in converting many Vietnamese from riding bicycles to riding motorcycles and scooters (a somewhat troubling shift in light of the problem of global climate change, although someone driving a car in North America is not in the best position to point fingers) and the successful promotion of powdered milk (a product of dubious utility if there is no reliable source of clean water), it is not clear that these efforts represent an overall net *gain* to either the consumers or the society at large.

69. *See, e.g.,* Alterman, *What Liberal Media?*

70. Nelson, *Sultans of Sleaze,* at 133.

71. *Id.*

72. *See* Kalle Lasn, *Culture Jam: The Uncooling of American* (New York: Eagle Brook, 1999), 196–97.

73. *Lebron v. Nat'l R.R. Passenger Corp.,* 513 U.S. 374, 376–77 (1995). The adoption of the Coors' company slogan to more effectively convey the message is an example of the "culture jamming" described by Lasn (*Culture Jam*).

74. *Lebron,* 513 U.S. at 377–78.

75. Nelson, *Sultans of Sleaze,* at 133.

76. Another example of this phenomenon of defining for-profit commercial speech as normatively neutral in contrast to noncommercial interests is the charge, in the now-defunct publication *Brill's Content,* that Consumers Union compromised its "neutrality" by accepting "grant money from foundations with specific agendas—such as limiting the use of pesticides—and the magazine [*Consumer Reports*] has then run stories supporting those foundations' goals." Jennifer Greenstein, "Testing *Consumer Reports,*" *Brill's Content,* 72 (Sept. 1999).

Chapter 10

1. Michael J. Brown, Letter to the Editor, "Marketing Helped Make This Mess," *Advertising Age,* July 13, 2009, 14 (Brown is identified as associated with the Other Awareness Project in Long Beach, California).

2. Rance Crain, "Marketing Must Take Its Share of Blame for the Economic Crisis," *Advertising Age,* June 29, 2009, 11.

3. Elisabeth M. Landes & Richard A. Posner, "The Economics of the Baby Shortage," 7 *J. Leg. Studies* 323 (1978). For an interesting discussion of commodification generally, which includes excerpts from this article, see, Martha M. Ertman & Joan C. William, *Rethinking Commodification: Cases and Readings in Law and Culture* (New York: New York University Press, 2005).

4. *Economist,* "The Other-Worldly Philosophers," July 16, 2009, 66 (emphasis added).

5. *Economist,* "Efficiency and Beyond," July 16, 2009, 69.

6. *Id.*

7. *Id.*

8. David Segal, "A Matter of Opinion?" *N.Y. Times,* July 18, 2009, BU 1, 6.

9. *Id.* at 6.

10. *Id.*

11. The tide may, however, be turning on receptiveness to this defense. *See* David Segal, "Suddenly the Ratings Agencies Don't Seem Untouchable," *N.Y. Times,* May 21, 2010.

12. Lizabeth Cohen, *A Consumers' Republic: The Politics of Mass Consumption in Postwar America* (New York: Vintage Books, 2003), 112–13.

13. W. Michael Cox & Richard Alm, "You Are What You Spend," *N.Y. Times,* Feb. 10, 2008. The online version of this article is accompanied with a response by Nobel-winning economist and *Times* columnist Paul Krugman disputing the sources on which the authors rely.

14. *Id.*

15. *Id.*

16. For example, through the Sign and Travel program, American Express of-

fered to move ever-lower dollar purchases—first purchases over \$500, then those over \$300, and finally those over \$100—to long-term payment plans.

17. Oren Bar-Gill, "Seduction by Plastic," 98 *Nw. U. L. Rev.* 1373 (2004).

18. There is some dispute about whether there is any "overconsumption" problem at all. *Cf.* Elizabeth Warren & Amelia Warren Tyagi, *The Two-Income Trap: Why Middle-Class Mothers and Fathers Are Going Broke* (New York: Perseus Books, 2003).

19. Of course, the latter definition begs the question about what constitutes "unexpected." Some sort of health or other crisis could be viewed as prudent to expect, since it seems inevitable that everyone will experience a reversal of some sort. Yet good mental health seems to require a suspension of belief or unreasonable optimism about future events. Good financial planning, in contrast, seems to call for a pessimistic turn of mind. However, the truly unexpected—something like, say, worldwide market crash—might be what author Nassim Nicholas Taleb calls a "black swan," that is, something that is so unusual it makes a hash of probabilities. Nassim Nicholas Taleb, *The Black Swan: The Impact of the Highly Improbable* (New York: Random House, 2007). The irony of this example is that many observers thought the current crisis was completely predictable. Eric Jansen, "The Next Bubble: Priming the Markets for Tomorrow's Big Crash," *Harper's Magazine*, Feb. 2008, 39–45.

20. Warren & Tyagi, *Two-Income Trap*. *See also* Tamara Draut, *Strapped: Why America's 20- and 30-Somethings Can't Get Ahead* (New York: Anchor Books, 2005).

21. Jansen, "Next Bubble."

22. Bob Garfield, "Pay Heed to What Realtors Don't Say in Their Latest Pitch," *Advertising Age*, Jan. 28, 2008 (critiquing the National Association of Realtors ad in 2008 claiming that "buyer opportunities had never been better" even as many Americans were "upside down on their mortgages or worse").

23. Rance Crain, "Ad Industry Has Another Chance to Respond to Financial Fraud," *Advertising Age*, Aug. 20, 2007 (describing Ditech "People Are Smart" ad and noting, "Ditech knows full well that people aren't smart when it comes to financial matters, but the slogan makes everyone involved feel better"); Timothy Sexton, "People Are Smart? It is Time to Sue Ditech for Blatant False Advertising," Associated Content, Sept. 28, 2007, http://www.associatedcontent.com/arti cle/392848/people_are_smart_its_time_to_sue_ditechcom.html?cat=35 (last accessed Apr. 10, 2010).

24. *See, e.g.,* Gretchen Morgenson, "Your Money at Work, Fixing Others' Mistakes," *N.Y. Times*, Sept. 21, 2008, B1, 6. *See also* Brooks, "Bailout to Nowhere."

25. Robert D. Manning, *Credit Card Nation: The Consequences of America's Addiction to Credit* (New York: Basic Books, 2000).

26. *See, e.g.,* Lizabeth Cohen, *A Consumer's Republic: The Politics of Mass Consumption in Postwar America* (New York: Alfred A. Knopf, 2003); Gary Cross, *An All-Consuming Century* (New York: Columbia University Press, 2000).

27. Gretchen Morgenson, "The Quick Buck Just Got Quicker," *N.Y. Times,* Apr. 15, 2009.

28. Steve Lohr, "In Bailout Furor, Wall Street Pay Becomes a Target," *N.Y. Times,* Sept. 24, 2008, A1 (tolerance waned after the crash of 2008).

29. Oren Bar-Gill & Elizabeth Warren, *Making Credit Safer,* New York University School of Law, Working Paper No. 137 (2008).

30. Rob Walker, "Social Currency," *N.Y. Times Magazine,* Nov. 11, 2008, 26.

31. For discussions of predatory lending practices such as these, *see* Lauren E. Willis, "Decision-making and the Limits of Disclosure: The Problem of Predatory Lending; Price," 65 *Md. L. Rev.* 707 (2006).

Chapter 11

1. This slogan has been touted around a fair amount, appearing in different forms. *See* Emily Tan, "Survey: 'Good Is the New Black,'" *Advertising Age,* July 12, 2007.

2. *Economist,* "A Coat of Green: Business Is Becoming More Environment-Minded, but Only Because Government Is Pushing," Sept. 9, 2006, 19 (special report—a survey of climate change).

3. Alex Williams, "That Buzz in Your Ear May Be Green Noise," *N.Y. Times,* June 15, 2008, ST8 (a study by the Shelton Group suggested that consumers were "less likely to buy a wide range of green products" than in the prior year).

4. Mark Dolliver, "Deflating a Myth: Consumers Aren't as Devoted to the Planet as You Wish They Were," *Adweek,* May 12, 2008 ("[T]he percentage of adults saying they personally worry a great deal about global warming hasn't changed much during the past two decades of Gallup's polling on the subject.").

5. Sheila Bonini & Jeremy Oppenheim, "Cultivating the Green Consumer," *Stan. Social Innovation Rev.* 56, 56 (Fall 2008).

6. Miguel Bustillo, "A Shift to Green," *Los Angeles Times,* June 12, 2005, C1.

7. *Id.*

8. BP is an oft-cited example of a "green" oil company. *See also* Clive Thompson, "A Green Oil Baron?" *N.Y. Times Magazine,* June 22, 2008, 26–31. This is ironic in light of the incredibly toxic Deepwater Horizon blowout. *See* Julia Whitty, "BP's Deep Secrets," *Mother Jones,* Sept./Oct. 2010, 29.

9. J. Thomas Rosch, *Responsible Green Marketing,* FTC, 2008 W.L. 2557919 (2008) (remarks at the American Conference Institute's Regulatory Summit for Advertisers and Marketers, Washington, D.C., June 18, 2008).

10. Eric Pfanner, "Gore to Bring Talk of Green to Ad Festival," *N.Y. Times,* June 18, 2007.

11. Despite all the reporting of this in the trade publications as if it were a new

trend, there is some evidence that marketing professionals were predicting a move to environmental marketing as early as the late 1980s. *See, e.g.,* Ann Lallande, "Environmental Marketing: The Next Wave," 23 *Marketing & Media Decisions* (Vol. 12) 174 (Dec. 1988).

12. Claudia H. Deutsch, "G.E. Unveils Credit Card Aimed at Relieving Carbon Footprints," *N.Y. Times,* July 25, 2007, C9.

13. Brian Stelter, "A Network to Make an Environmental Point," *N.Y. Times,* June 2, 2008 (Discovery launching Planet Green channel to replace Discovery Home channel).

14. *See, e.g.,* Green Century Funds, http://www.greencentury.com/?utm_source=SIF&utm_medium=supp_banner&utm_content=logo&utm_campaign=feb10.

15. As one industry group noted, approximately 55 million households in the United States have an interest in a mutual fund. "Do you own an oil company?" recited an ad sponsored by a group called Energy Tomorrow in the *Economist* on May 17, 2008. According to their website, Energy Tomorrow is "the only trade organization that represents all aspects of America's oil and natural gas industry." http://www.energytomorrow.org/ (last accessed Apr. 10, 2010).

16. *N.Y. Times,* Editorial, "Talking about Green (the Other Kind)," Feb. 27, 2008 (DealBook blog); *N.Y. Times,* Editorial, "In TXU's $45 Billion Deal, Many Shades of Green," Feb. 26, 2008.

17. Jack Neff, "Clorox: Bleach, Charcoal, and . . . Burt's Bees; Company Pays $ 950 Million for Leading Natural Personal-Care Brand," *Advertising Age,* Oct. 31, 2007.

18. Claudia H. Deutsch, "Saving the Environment, One Quarterly Earnings Report at a Time," *N.Y. Times,* Nov. 22, 2005.

19. Douglas A. Kysar, "Sustainable Development and Private Global Governance," 83 *Tex. L. Rev.* 2109, 2166 (2008).

20. Kate Fitzgerald, "Financial Services: Portfolio 21," *Advertising Age,* June 9, 2008. Note that many of these articles in *Advertising Age* read like PR news releases touting particular companies. *See also* Deutsch, "Saving the Environment."

21. David Hoch & Robert Franz, "Eco-Porn versus the Constitution: Commercial Speech and the Regulation of Environmental Advertising," 58 *Alb. L. Rev.* 441 (1994) (quoting Hubert Humphrey III, then Minnesota attorney general).

22. Samar Farah, "The Thin Green Line," *CMO Magazine,* Dec. 2005, available at http://www.greenmarketing.com/files/news/cmomag_dec05.pdf. ("British Petroleum had its own idea of a green makeover: The oil giant changed its logo to a helios and began billing itself 'Beyond Petroleum.' ").

23. Jean Halliday, "BP Touts Greenness, Then Asks to Dump Ammonia," *Advertising Age,* Aug. 20, 2007. Halliday notes that despite public exposure of various actions in conflict with BP's green marketing campaign, "BP's green positioning has resonated with U.K. consumers who ranked BP ninth among their top 20

'green' brands in an online survey by Landor Associates." These survey outcomes may be the result of putting BP on a "green" list; Halliday's article does not say. Other surveys suggest that BP is only in the "middle of the pack" on this issue. Dolliver, "Deflating a Myth." Whether even being in the "middle of the pack" represents a triumph of marketing for an oil company is another question.

24. *Sydney Morning Herald,* Editorial, "Woolworths Blows Away Dodgy Tissues," Aug. 27, 2007.

25. Center for Media and Democracy, "Making Green Off of Green While Dividing Greens," June 17, 2008, http://www.prwatch.org/node/7453 (last accessed Mar. 27, 2010).

26. *See* Farah, "Thin Green Line" (GE involved in cleanup of PCBs in the Hudson River "for more than two decades"); National Resource Defense Council, "Historic Hudson River Cleanup to Begin after Years of Delay, but Will General Electric Finish the Job?" news release, March 23, 2007, http://www.nrdc.org/water/pollution/hhudson.asp. It is sobering to consider what the lawyers' fees for litigation lasting that long would be and whether that money might not have been more beneficially spent.

27. Halliday, "BP Touts Greenness."

28. Environmental News Service, "Companies Settle Fuel Violations."

29. Mya Frazier, "Who's in Charge of Green?" *Advertising Age,* June 9, 2008.

30. *Id.* (quoting Adam Werbach, former environmental activist now with Saatchi & Saatchi).

31. Rob Edwards, "Study Slams 'Trivial' Social Responsibility Reports," *Sunday Herald,* June 25, 2006 (reporting on a study published by a professor at St. Andrews University).

32. *Id.*

33. Williams, "Buzz in Your Ear," at 8.

34. Eric Pfanner, "Cooling Off on Dubious Eco-friendly Claims," *N.Y. Times,* July 18, 2008.

35. Williams, "Buzz in Your Ear," at 8.

36. *See, e.g., Economist,* "Not on the Label: Why Adding 'Carbon Footprint' Labels to Foods and Other Products Is Tricky," May 19, 2008, 84; *Economist,* "Voting with Your Trolley: Can You Really Change the World Just by Buying Certain Foods?" Dec. 9, 2006, 73–75.

37. Kysar, "Sustainable Development."

38. Rob Walker, "Water Proof," *N.Y. Times Magazine,* June 1, 2008, 22 (describing Fiji Water's efforts to communicate a "green" image and the obstacles presented to that effort, which start with the observation that the company's water must be flown into everywhere it is distributed *but* Fiji). *See also* Anna Lenzer, "Fiji Water: Spin the Bottle," *Mother Jones,* Sept./Oct. 2009.

39. Jeffrey Goldberg, "Selling Wal-Mart," *New Yorker,* Apr. 2, 2007, 32, 38 (de-

scribing PR firm Edelman's efforts to improve Wal-Mart's image, which include energy conservation measures); Michael Barbaro & Felicity Barringer, "Wal-Mart to Seek Savings in Energy," *N.Y. Times,* Oct. 25, 2005; Claire Hoffman, "Wal-Mart Warms to a Green Outlook: The Retailer Works Hard to Polish Its Image; Environmental Groups Have Mixed Reviews," *Los Angeles Times,* July 13, 2006.

40. Elizabeth Shogren, "CFL Bulbs Have One Hitch: Toxic Mercury," *All Things Considered,* NPR, Feb. 15, 2007, http://www.npr.org/templates/story/story.php?storyId=7431198 (last accessed Mar. 27, 2010).

41. Natalie Zmuda, "Is Earth Day the New Christmas? As More Marketers Pile On, Consumerism May Eclipse the Spirit of the Event," *Advertising Age,* Apr. 14, 2008.

42. *Id.*

43. Alex Williams, "Buying into the Green Movement," *N.Y. Times,* July 1, 2007, ST1, 8.

44. *Id.* at 1.

45. *Id.*

46. Donovan Hohn, "Sea of Trash," *N.Y. Times,* June 22, 2008, 41–45 (quoting Sylvia Earle, former chief scientist at the National Oceanic and Atmospheric Association) (internal quotations marks omitted); Elizabeth Royte, *Garbage Land: The Secret Trail of Trash* (New York: Little Brown, 2005).

47. Royte, *Garbage Land,* at 242 ("Persuading Americans to consume less stuff, probably the single best thing we could do to save the planet (besides promoting energy conservation and zero population growth), isn't a big part of the environmental agenda. Instead we are exhorted to buy green.").

48. Jack Neff, "Unilever, P&G War over Which Is Most Ethical," *Advertising Age,* Mar. 3, 2008 ("Wanting less but buying more").

49. *Id.*

50. *Id.* (emphasis added).

51. *Id.*

52. *See, e.g.,* Duane Elgin, ed., *Voluntary Simplicity: Responding to Consumer Culture* (Lanham, Mass.: Rowman & Littlefield, 1993). There are multiple websites devoted to simple living or voluntary simplicity. *See, e.g.,* http://www.choosingvoluntarysimplicity.com/ (last accessed Mar. 27, 2010).

53. "Buy Nothing Day" is organized by Adbusters and urges people not to go to the stores the day after Thanksgiving, a day now often referred to as "Black Friday."

54. For more critiques of consumption, critiques that include but go beyond its environmental impacts, *see* Benjamin R. Barber, *Consumed: How Markets Corrupt Children, Infantilize Adults and Swallow Citizens Whole* (New York: W. W. Norton, 2007) (focus on consumption is infantilizing and destructive of democ-

racy); John DeGraaf, David Wann, & Thomas H. Naylor, *Affluenza: The All-Consuming Epidemic* (San Francisco: Berrett-Koehler, 2001) (analogizing excessive consumption to an illness).

55. *See, e.g.,* Rachel Fudge, "Shop in the Name of Love: Judith Levine Explains Why She Is Not Buying It," *Bitch,* Summer 2006, 36–39, 994–95 (interview with author Judith Levine about her book *Not Buying It: My Year Without Shopping* (New York: Simon & Schuster, 2006)).

56. *Id.* at 38.

57. *Id.*

58. Pfanner, "Gore to Bring Talk of Green" (emphasis added).

59. Dolliver, "Deflating a Myth."

60. *Id.*

61. *Economist,* "Stimulus and Shopping," May 31, 2008, 34.

62. Walker, "Water Proof."

63. Andreas Chatzidakis, Sally Hibbert, & Andrew P. Smith, "Why People Don't Take Their Concerns about Fair Trade to the Supermarket: The Role of Neutralisation," 74 *J. Bus. Ethics* 89 (2007). Although the sample size was small and the fair trade example may be distinguishable from environmental concerns, it seems plausible that there are enough similarities to hypothesize that some of the same attitudes may be at work with respect to environmentally oriented consumption).

64. Dolliver, "Deflating a Myth."

65. *Id.*

66. Farah, "Thin Green Line" ("The burden is on marketers to be as transparent as possible about environmental claims—no easy task given the scientific and political nature of this information."); Brooke Capps, "Green Is Good, Environmentally-Friendly Marketers Say; But to Make It Work, Policies Have to Be Integrated into Corporate Practices," *Advertising Age,* June 12, 2007.

67. Suskind, "Without a Doubt."

68. Jim Hoggan, "Slamming the Climate Skeptic Scam," June 15, 2009 (DeSmog Blog), http://www.desmogblog.com/slamming-the-climate-skeptic-scam.

69. Julie Sevrens Lyons, "Donor to Stanford: No Big Oil; University Donation Rescinded over Ad," *San Jose Mercury News,* Mar. 11, 2007 (recounting Stanford alum and donor Steve Bing's decision to rescind his own donation upon learning of the ExxonMobil donation through the ads; Bing's representative accused Exxon of attempting to use Stanford as the "brush" to greenwash Exxon).

70. *Id.*

71. *Id.*

72. *See, e.g.,* Peter Gruber, "The Four Truths of the Storyteller," *Harv. Bus. Rev.,* Dec. 2007, 53–59. For a book-length treatment of this effort, *see* Roland Marchand, *Creating the Corporate Soul: The Rise of Public Relations and Cor-*

porate Imagery in American Big Business (Berkeley: University of California Press, 1998), 10. Marchand argues that corporations need to establish their social and moral legitimacy in the face of moral concerns about size, operational norms, and social impact; that "one corporation after another recognized the need to devote resources to the systematic construction of a corporate image"; and that these images, in the aggregate, form a sort of " 'creation story' of corporate imagery."

73. Krugman, "Enemy of the Planet."

74. AEI fellows Kenneth Green and Steven Hayward published an article in which they did not deny that ExxonMobil had donated $1.6 million to AEI, but they argued that it represented "over the last seven years" "less than 1 percent of AEI's total revenue during that period." Kenneth P. Green & Steven F. Hayward, "Scenes from the Climate Inquisition," American Enterprise Institute for Public Policy Research, Feb. 19, 2007, http://www.aei.org/docLib/2007022_OTI.pdf. They also did not deny the offer of $10,000, but they claimed that it was an "honorarium . . . entirely in line with honoraria the AEI and similar organizations pay to distinguished economists and legal scholars for commissioned work." Law professors on an environmental law professors' electronic mailing list disputed whether such payments were routine for reanalysis, not additional empirical research, particularly of questions that do not appear to be open ones (e-mails on file with author). For more reaction from some environmental law professors on ExxonMobil's funding of global-warming "deniers," *see* http://lawprofessors .typepad.com/environmental_law/2008/02/exxonmobil-de-1.html (last accessed Mar. 27, 2010). For more about the PR efforts to engage scientific support for skepticism *see* Naomi Oreskes & Eric M. Conway, *Merchants of Doubt* (New York: Bloomsbury Press, 2010), 169–215.

75. *See* Krugman, "Enemy of the Planet" (the practice of issuing position papers from industry-funded think tanks "plays into the he-said-she-said convention of 'balanced' journalism").

76. Eric Webber, "Transparency Schmansparency: It's Not the Business of PR," *Advertising Age*, Apr. 10, 2007.

77. Eric W. Orts, "Reflexive Environmental Law," 89 *Nw. U. L. Rev.* 1227 (1995). *See also Economist*, Editorial, "Cleaning Up: How Business Is Starting to Tackle Climate Change, and How Governments Need to Help," June 2, 2007, 13.

78. *See* Cary Coglianese & Jocelyn D'Ambrosio, "Policymaking under Pressure: The Perils of Incremental Responses to Climate Change," 40 *Conn. L. Rev.* 1411 (July 2008). The authors are speaking primarily of state and local rule making rather than that of industry, but the objections to incremental change may remain the same.

79. *See* Center for Media and Democracy, "Shell Oil's Flower Claims Wilt upon Examination," Nov. 8, 2007, http://www.prwatch.org/node/6692 (last accessed Mar. 27, 2010).

80. *See* Associated Press, "UK Bans Shell Ad of Refinery Sprouting Flowers,"

Nov. 6, 2007, http://www.msnbc.msn.com/id/21659526/ (last accessed Mar. 27, 2010).

81. Rosch, *Responsible Green Marketing,* at 5.

82. *Id.*

83. 16 C.F.R. § 260 (2008). *See also* Rosch, *Responsible Green Marketing* (explaining that the industry guides are administrative interpretations and "do not have the force and effect of law and are not independently enforceable.")

84. It is of some interest that a marketing employee of Toyota claimed that it was the "legal department" that did not allow Toyota to use the word *green* with respect to the popular Prius. Farah, "Thin Green Line." Presumably, this was a cautious response to the possibility that such a claim could be deemed fraudulent or misleading rather than because it would clearly be illegal.

85. Tim Dickinson, "The Secret Campaign of President Bush's Administration to Deny Global Warming," *Rolling Stone,* June 28, 2007.

86. Sharon Begley, "The Truth about Denial," *Newsweek,* Aug. 13, 2007.

87. Felicity Barringer, "White House Refused to Open Pollutants E-Mail," *N.Y. Times,* June 25, 2008, A15.

88. *See* Senator Snowe's website for a copy of the press release and letter, http://snowe.senate.gov/public/index.cfm?FuseAction=PressRoom.PressRe leases&ContentRecord_id=9acba744-802a-23ad-47be2683985c724e&Region _id=&Issue_id=d6938819-e35b-b44f-421f-729717308f35 (last accessed Mar. 27, 2010). For more on these efforts, *see* http://lawprofessors.typepad.com/envi ronmental_law/2008/02/exxonmobil-de-1.html (last accessed Mar. 27, 2010).

89. Ayn Rand Institute, Press Release, "Senators' Letter Is a Violation of ExxonMobil's Freedom of Speech" (Dec. 7, 2006).

90. Zygmunt J. B. Plater, "Law, Media, and Environmental Policy: A Fundamental Link in Sustainable Democratic Governance," 33 *Environmental Affairs* 511 (2006).

91. *Id.* at 517–18.

92. *Escamilla v. ASARCO, Inc.,* No. 91 CV 5716 (D.Colo.1993).

93. Plater, "Law, Media, and Environmental Policy," at 513–17.

94. Douglas A. Kysar, "The Consultants' Republic," 121 *Harv. L. Rev.* 2041, 2043 (2008) (reviewing Ted Nordhaus & Michael Shellenberger, *Break Through: From the Death of Environmentalism to the Politics of Possiblity* [New York: Houghton Mifflin, 2007]).

95. Michael Shellenberger & Ted Nordhaus, "The Death of Environmentalism: Global Warming Politics in a Post-Environmental World," http://www.the breakthrough.org/PDF/Death_of_Environmentalism.pdf (2004), 29–30.

96. *Id.*

97. Kysar, "Sustainable Development," at 2043 (emphasis added).

98. Plater, "Law, Media, and Environmental Policy," at 517.

99. *Id.*

100. Matthew Creamer, "Madison Ave. Warms to Climate Change," *Advertising Age,* Aug 27, 2008.

101. For a good attempt, *see* Royte, *Garbage Land.*

102. For some insight into the way commercial propaganda campaigns created the notions of the bacon-and-egg breakfast or the mall as the nexus for shopping, entertainment, and leisure, *see* Tye, *Father of Spin,* 51–52 (bacon and eggs); Cohen, *Consumers' Republic,* 257–89 (malls). There are too many of such incidents to count. For a description of the efforts of Western marketers to change Japanese breakfast habits to include cereal, *see* Kysar, "Sustainable Development," at 2139 n. 136.

103. Cohen, *Consumers' Republic,* at 116 (quoting Chester Bowles, former chief of the Office of Price Administration, formed to administer price controls during World War II).

104. *Economist,* "The Final Cut: Business Can Do It, with Governments' Help," May 2, 2007, 30.

105. Julia Whitty, "The Last Taboo," *Mother Jones,* May/June 2010.

106. Richard Posner, "Pragmatism versus Purposivism in First Amendment Analysis," 54 *Stan. L. Rev.* 737 (2002).

Conclusion

1. *Sorrell v. IMS Health,* 131 S.Ct. 2653 (2011).

2. Lawrence O. Gostin, *Public Health Law: Power, Duty, Restraint,* 2nd ed. (Berkeley: University of California Press, 2008), 347 ("Indeed, modern commercial speech doctrine is so uncertain, but still potentially so forceful, that it chills public health regulation.").

3. *See, e.g.,* Aneel Karnani, "Doing Well by Doing Good—Case Study: 'Fair & Lovely' Whitening Cream," 28 *Strategic Mgmt. J.* 1351, 1355–56 (2007).

4. Shiffrin, "First Amendment and Economic Regulation," at 1212.

5. Steven Shiffrin, *The First Amendment, Democracy, and Romance* (Cambridge, Mass.: Harvard University Press, 1990), 3.

6. Shiffrin, "First Amendment and Economic Regulation," at 1216.

7. *Id.*

8. *See* Collins & Skover, *Death of Discourse,* at xx–xxv.

9. George Orwell, *1984* (London: Harcourt, 1949).

10. *See Economist,* "Justice Is Not Blind," July 7, 2007, 13–14.

11. Oliver Wendell Holmes, "The Path of Law," 10 *Harv. L. Rev.* 457 (1897).

12. *Id.*

13. *Id.*

14. *See* Tamara R. Piety, "Onslaught: Commercial Speech and Gender Inequality," 60 *Case W. Res. L. Rev.* 47 (2009). *See also* Rhode, *Beauty Bias* (identifying advertising as a major contributor to the importance of appearance for women and to resulting burdens on gender equality).

15. Bernays, *Propaganda,* at 37.

16. *Id.* (emphasis added).

17. Bernays also called them "invisible wire-pullers." *Id.* at 60. Luntz argues that simplicity is necessary for good communication. Luntz, *Words That Work,* at 5. He is undoubtedly right. What is less clear is whether what the public "buys" ought to be the touchstone of truth and whether there is a duty to convey complicated truths to the public without oversimplifying and running the risk that you are simply, as Bernays put it, attempting to get "approval of the masses" by manipulating their emotional reactions and encouraging them to use mental "rubber stamps." Bernays, *Propaganda,* at 48–55.

18. Bernays, *Propaganda,* at 59–60. He also included the presidents of labor unions, professional and fraternal organizations, authors, educators, and what might today be called "interest groups." *Id.* at 60.

19. *See, e.g.,* Rich, *Greatest Story Ever Sold.*

20. *See, e.g.,* Michael J. Sandel, "What Money Can't Buy: The Moral Limits of Markets," in *Rethinking Commodification: Cases and Readings in Law and Culture,* ed. Martha M. Ertman & Joan C. Williams (New York: New York University Press, 2005).

21. James Boyd White, "Free Speech and Valuable Speech: Silence, Dante, and the 'Marketplace of Ideas,'" 51 *UCLA L. Rev.* 799, 809 (2004) (emphasis added).

22. Packard, *Hidden Persuaders,* 258.

Bibliography

AARP Newsletter. Editorial. "Pulling Strings from Afar." http://www.indiadi
vine.org/audarya/ayurveda-health-wellbeing/940512-pulling-strings-afar-
page-1-a.html.

Abrams v. U.S. 250 U.S. 616 (1919).

Advertising Age. Editorial. "McD's Likely to Get Fried by Passive Response to
Study." Aug. 11, 2007, 10.

Advertising Age. Editorial. "Time for Industry Workers to Make Case to Congress." July 27, 2009, 9.

Alterman, Eric. *What Liberal Media? The Truth about Bias and the News*. New
York: Basic Books, 2003.

Anderson, David A. "The Origins of the Press Clause." 30 *UCLA L. Rev.* 455
(1983).

APA Online. Press Release. "Television Advertising Leads to Unhealthy Habits in
Children, Says APA Task Force." Feb. 23, 2004. Available at http://www.apa
.org/news/press/releases/2004/02/children_ads.aspx.

Ariely, Dan. *Predictably Irrational*. New York: HarperCollins, 2008.

Arthur Andersen L.L.P. v. U.S. 544 U.S. 696 (2005).

Associated Press. "A Second Guilty Plea in A.I.G.-Related Case." *N.Y. Times*,
June 4, 2005.

Associated Press. "UK Bans Shell Ad of Refinery Sprouting Flowers." Nov. 6,
2007. http://www.msnbc.msn.com/id/21659526/.

Atkin, Douglas. *The Culting of Brands: When Customers Become True Believers*.
New York: Penguin, 2004.

Atkinson, Claire. "Absolut Hunk: Story of a Wildly Successful Product Placement." *AdAge.com*, Aug. 4, 2003. http://adage.com/article/news/absolut
-hunk-story-a-wildly-successful-product-placement/38094/.

Austin v. Michigan Chamber of Commerce. 494 U.S. 652 (1990).

Ayn Rand Institute. Press Release. "Senators' Letter Is a Violation of ExxonMobil's Freedom of Speech." Dec. 7, 2006.

Backman, James. *Advertising and Competition.* New York: New York University Press, 1967.

Bainbridge, Stephen. "In Defense of the Shareholder Wealth Maximization Norm: A Reply to Professor Green." 50 *Wash. & Lee L. Rev.* 1423 (1993).

Bakan, Joel. *The Corporation.* Toronto: Penguin, 2004.

Baker, C. Edwin. *Advertising and a Democratic Press.* Princeton, N.J.: Princeton University Press, 1994.

Baker, C. Edwin. *Human Liberty and Freedom of Speech.* New York: Oxford University Press, 1989.

Baker, C. Edwin. *Media Concentration and Democracy: Why Ownership Matters.* Oxford: Oxford University Press, 2007.

Baker, C. Edwin. "Paternalism, Politics, and Citizen Freedom: The Commercial Speech Quandary in *Nike.*" 54 *Case W. Res. L. Rev.* 1161 (2003).

Balkin, J. M. "Some Realism about Pluralism: Legal Realist Approaches to the First Amendment." 1990 *Duke L.J.* 375 (1990).

Balkin, J. M. "Wrong the Day It Was Decided: *Lochner* and Constitutional Historicism." 85 *B.U. L. Rev.* 677 (2005).

Barbaro, Michael, & Felicity Barringer. "Wal-Mart to Seek Savings in Energy." *N.Y. Times,* Oct. 25, 2005.

Barber, Benjamin R. *Consumed: How Markets Corrupt Children, Infantilize Adults, and Swallow Citizens Whole.* New York: W. W. Norton, 2007.

Bar-Gill, Oren. "Seduction by Plastic." 98 *Nw. U. L. Rev.* 1373 (2004).

Bar-Gill, Oren, & Elizabeth Warren. *Making Credit Safer.* New York University School of Law, Working Paper No. 137, 2008.

Barnes, Brooks. "Toys for Toddlers from PG-13 Movie." *N.Y. Times,* July 2, 2007.

Barnes v. Glenn Theatre, Inc. 501 U.S. 560 (1991).

Barrett, Liz Cox. "Wrist? Slap! FCC Fines Comcast Four Figures for Fake News." *Colum. J. Rev.,* Sept. 26, 2007.

Barringer, Felicity. "White House Refused to Open Pollutants E-Mail." *N.Y. Times,* June 25, 2008, A15.

Barry, Bruce. *Speechless: The Erosion of Free Expression in the American Workplace.* San Francisco: Berrett-Koehler, 2007.

Barry, Max. *Jennifer Government.* New York: Vintage Books, 2003.

Barstow, David. "Report Faults Video Reports Shown as News." *N.Y. Times,* Apr. 6, 2006, A19.

Bartlett, Thomas. "Your (Lame) Slogan Here." *Chron. Higher Educ.,* Nov. 23, 2007, A1.

Bates v. State Bar of Arizona. 433 U.S. 350 (1977).

Bauman, Jeffrey D., Alan R. Palmiter, & Frank Partnoy. *Corporations Law and Policy.* 6th ed. St. Paul, Minn.: Thomson West, 2007.

BBC News–UK. Editorial. "'McLibel' Pair Win Legal Aid Case." Feb. 15, 2005. http://news.bbc.co.uk/2/hi/uk_news/4266209.stm.

BBC News–UK. Editorial. "Nigeria's Removal of Shell Hailed." June 5, 2008. http://news.bbc.co.uk/2/hi/africa/7437247.stm.

BBC News–UK. Editorial. "Shell Admits Fueling Corruption." June 11, 2008. http://news.bbc.co.uk/2/hi/business/3796375.stm.

Begley, Sharon. "The Truth about Denial." *Newsweek,* Aug. 13, 2007, 20.

Belson, Ken. "Ebbers Pleads for Leniency in Sentencing." *N.Y. Times,* June 4, 2005, C13.

Benforado, Adam, Jon Hanson, & David Yosifon. "Broken Scales: Obesity and Justice in America." 53 *Emory L.J.* 1645 (2004).

Ben-Ze'ev, Aaron. *The Subtlety of Emotions.* Cambridge, Mass.: MIT Press, 2000.

Berenson, Alex. "For Merck, the Vioxx Paper Trail Won't Go Away." *N.Y. Times,* Aug. 21, 2005, A1.

Berger, Linda L. "What Is the Sound of a Corporation Speaking? How the Cognitive Theory of Metaphor Can Help Lawyers Shape the Law." 2 *J. Ass'n Legal Writing Directors* 169 (2004).

Bernays, Edward L. *Propaganda.* New York: H. Liveright, 1928. Reprinted with introduction by Mark Crispin Miller. Brooklyn: Ig, 2005.

Bernstein, David E. "*Lochner*'s Legacy's Legacy." 82 *Tex. L. Rev.* 1 (2003).

Bezanson, Randall. "Institutional Speech." 80 *Iowa L. Rev.* 735 (1995).

Biehel, Gabriel J., & Daniel A. Sheinen. "Managing the Brand in a Corporate Advertising Environment: A Decision-Making Framework for Brand Managers." *J. Advertising,* Summer 1998, 99–110.

Biener, Lois, & Michael Siegel. "Tobacco Marketing and Adolescent Smoking: More Support for a Causal Inference." 90 *Am. J. Pub. Health* 407 (2000).

Black, Charles L., Jr. "The Lawfulness of the Segregation Decisions." 69 *Yale L.J.* 421 (1960).

Blanchard, Tamsin. *Green Is the New Black: How to Change the World with Style.* New York: HarperCollins, 2008.

Blasi, Vincent. *Ideas of the First Amendment.* St. Paul, Minn.: Thomson West, 2006.

Blocher, Joseph. "Institutions in the Marketplace of Ideas." 57 *Duke L.J.* 821 (2008).

Bloom, Paul. "What We Miss." *N.Y. Times,* June 6, 2010, BR 30.

Blyskal, Jeff, & Marie Blyskal. *PR: How the Public Relations Industry Writes the News.* New York: William Morrow, 1985.

Bolger v. Youngs Drug Products Corp. 463 U.S. 60 (1983).

Bonini, Sheila, and Jeremy Oppenheim. "Cultivating the Green Consumer." *Stan. Social Innovation Rev.* (Fall 2008), 56.

Boren, Cindy. "Packers Necktie Gets Chicago Car Salesman Fired." The Early Lead, *Washington Post.* http://washingtonpost.com/early-lead/2011/01/pack ers_necktie_gets_chicago_chtml.

Bork, Robert H. "Neutral Principles and Some First Amendment Problems." 47 *Ind. L.J.* 1 (1971).

Boyles, Deron. *American Education and Corporations: The Free Market Goes to School.* New York: Falmer, 2000.

Brand, Stewart. *Whole Earth Discipline.* New York: Penguin Group, 2009.

Brandt, Allan M. *The Cigarette Century.* New York: Basic Books, 2007.

Braun, Kathryn, & Elizabeth F. Loftus. "Advertising's Misinformation Effect." 12 *Applied Cognitive Psychol.* 569 (1998).

Brooks, David. "Bailout to Nowhere." *N.Y. Times,* Nov. 14, 2008, A33.

Brown, Michael J. Letter to the Editor. "Marketing Helped Make This Mess." *Advertising Age,* July 13, 2009, 14.

Brown, Ralph S., Jr. "Advertising and the Public Interest: Legal Protection of Trade Symbols." 57 *Yale L.J.* 1165 (1948).

Brownell, Kelly D., & Kenneth E. Warner. "The Perils of Ignoring History: Big Tobacco Played Dirty and Millions Died; How Similar Is Big Food?" 87 *Milbank Q.* 259 (2009).

Buckley v. Valeo. 424 U.S. 1 (1976).

Burns, Jean Wegman. "Confused Jurisprudence: False Advertising under the Lanham Act." 79 *B.U. L. Rev.* 807 (1999).

Burton, Robert A. *On Being Certain: Believing You Are Right Even When You Are Not.* New York: St. Martin's Press, 2008.

Business Roundtable, et al. v. SEC. 647 F.3d 1144 (D.C. Cir., 2011).

Business Week. Editorial. "A Trojan Horse for Advertisers." Apr. 3, 2000, 10.

Bustillo, Miguel. "A Shift to Green." *Los Angeles Times,* June 12, 2005, C1.

Calfee, John E. "The Ghost of Cigarette Advertising Past." *Regulation,* Summer 1997. Available at http://www.cato.org/pubs/regulation/regv10n6/v10n6-5.pdf.

California Bankers Association v. Schultz. 416 U.S. 21 (1974).

Caplan, Bryan. *The Myth of the Rational Voter: Why Democracies Choose Bad Policies.* Princeton, N.J.: Princeton University Press, 2007.

Capps, Brooke. "Green Is Good, Environmentally-Friendly Marketers Say; But to Make It Work, Policies Have to Be Integrated into Corporate Practices." *Advertising Age,* June 12, 2007.

Carter, Bill. "MTV Plans to Increase Its Lending of Ads and Shows." *N.Y. Times,* May 8, 2008, C5.

Carr, David. "When Fox News Is the Story." *N.Y. Times,* July 7, 2008.

Cassady, Ralph, Jr., & E. T. Grether. "The Proper Interpretation of 'Like Grade and Quality' within the Meaning of Section 2(a) of the Robinson-Patman Act." 30 *S. Cal. L. Rev.* 241 (1957).

Casselman, Ben. "Three Stories a Day? How Young Reporters Learn to Skim." *Colum. Journalism Rev.,* May/June 2004, 65–66.

Center for Media and Democracy. "Latest Version of Play for Pay: Bucks for Blogs." Mar. 9, 2009. http://www.prwatch.org/node/5846.

Center for Media and Democracy. "Shell Oil's Flower Claims Wilt upon Examination." Nov. 8, 2007. http://www.prwatch.org/node/6692.

Central Hudson Gas & Electric Corp. v. Public Service Comm'n of N.Y. 447 U.S. 557 (1980).

Chabris, Christopher, & Daniel Simons. *The Invisible Gorilla.* New York: Crown, 2010.

Chambers Goodman, Christine. "(M)Ad Men: Using Persuasion Factors in Media Advertisements to Prevent a 'Tyranny of the Majority' on Ballot Propositions." 32 *Hastings Comm. & Ent. L.J.* 247 (Winter 2010).

Chatzidakis, Andreas, Sally Hibbert, & Andrew P. Smith. "Why People Don't Take Their Concerns about Fair Trade to the Supermarket: The Role of Neutralisation." 74 *J. Bus. Ethics* 89 (2007).

Chemerinsky, Erwin, & Catherine Fisk. "What Is Commercial Speech? The Issue Not Decided in *Nike v. Kasky.*" 54 *Case W. Res. L. Rev.* 1143 (2004).

Chen, Haipeng (Allan), & Akshay R. Rao. "When Two Plus Two Is Not Equal to Four: Errors in Processing Multiple Percentage Changes." 34 *J. Consumer Res.* 327 (2007).

Cialdini, Robert B. *Influence: The Psychology of Persuasion.* Rev. ed. New York: HarperCollins, 2007.

Citizens United v. Federal Election Comm'n. 130 S.Ct. 876 (Jan. 21, 2010).

Clarke, Thomas H., Jr. "Will *Nike v. Kasky* Ignite Corporate Social Responsibility Trade Wars between the U.S. and European Union?" *SRI Media, Corporate Governance News,* June 28, 2003. No longer available online. On file with author.

CMO Magazine. "The Strategic Significance of Brands." Sept. 24, 2005.

Coase, R. H. "The Market for Goods and the Market for Ideas." 64 *Am. Econ. Rev.* 384 (1974).

Coffee, John C., Jr. "No Soul to Damn, No Body to Kick: An Unscandalized Inquiry into the Problem of Corporate Punishment." 79 *Mich. L. Rev.* 386 (1981).

Coglianese, Cary, & Jocelyn D'Ambrosio. "Policymaking under Pressure: The Perils of Incremental Responses to Climate Change." 40 *Conn. L. Rev.* 1411 (July 2008).

Cohen, Felix S. "Transcendental Nonsense and the Functional Approach." 35 *Colum. L. Rev.* 809 (1935).

Cohen, Lizabeth. *A Consumers' Republic: The Politics of Mass Consumption in Postwar America.* New York: Alfred A. Knopf, 2003.

Coleman, Carl H., Jerry A. Menikoff, Jesse A. Goldner, & Nancy Neveloff Dubler. *The Ethics and Regulation of Research with Human Subjects*. Eagan, Minn.: West, 2005.

Collins, Gail. *When Everything Changed: The Amazing Journey of American Women from 1960 to the Present*. New York: Little, Brown, 2009.

Collins, Ronald K. L., & David Skover. *The Death of Discourse*. 2nd ed. Durham, NC: Carolina Academic Press, 2005.

Collins, Ronald K. L., & David Skover. "The Landmark Free-Speech Case That Wasn't: The *Nike v. Kasky* Story." 54 *Case W. Res. L. Rev.* 965 (2004).

Conley, Lucas. *OBD: Obsessive Branding Disorder; The Illusion of Business and the Business of Illusion*. New York: Public Affairs, 2008.

Consol. Edison Co. of N.Y. v. Pub. Serv. Comm'n of N.Y. 447 U.S. 530 (1980).

The Corporation. Directed by Mark Archbar & Jennifer Abbott. Big Picture Media Corporation, 2003.

Countryman, Vern. "Advertising Is Speech." In *Advertising and Free Speech*, ed. Allen Hyman & M. Bruce Johnson. Lexington, Mass.: Lexington Books, 1977.

Cowen, Tyler. *In Praise of Commercial Culture*. Cambridge, Mass.: Harvard University Press, 1998.

Cox, Paul N. "The Public, the Private, and the Corporation." 80 *Marq. L. Rev.* 391 (1997).

Cox, W. Michael, & Richard Alm. "You Are What You Spend." *N.Y. Times*, Feb. 10, 2008.

Crain, Rance. "Ad Industry Has Another Chance to Respond to Financial Fraud." *Advertising Age*, Aug. 20, 2007, 11.

Crain, Rance. "Marketing Must Take Its Share of Blame for the Economic Crisis." *Advertising Age*, June 29, 2009, 11.

Craswell, Richard. "Taking Information Seriously: Misrepresentation and Nondisclosure in Contract Law and Elsewhere." 92 *Va. L. Rev.* 565 (2006).

Crawford, Krysten. "Ex-WorldCom CEO Ebbers Guilty." *CNNMoney.com*, Mar. 15, 2005. http://money.cnn.com/2005/03/15/news/newsmakers/ebbers/.

Creamer, Michael. "Madison Ave. Warms to Climate Change." *Advertising Age*, Aug. 27, 2008, 1, 24.

Creswell, Julie. "Citigroup Agrees to Pay $2 Billion in Enron Scandal." *N.Y. Times*, June 4, 2005, B13.

Cross, Gary. *An All-Consuming Century*. New York: Columbia University Press, 2000.

Cwiklik, Robert. "Ivory Tower Inc.: When Research and Lobbying Mesh." *Wall Street Journal*, June 9, 1998, B1.

Damasio, Antonio. *Descartes' Error: Emotion, Reason, and the Human Brain*. New York: Avon Books, 1994.

Damasio, Antonio. *The Feeling of What Happens: Body and Emotion in the Making of Consciousness*. Orlando, Fla.: Harcourt, 1999.

Dargis, Manohla. "Car Wars with Shape-Shifter 'R' Us." *N.Y. Times,* July 2, 2007, E1.

Dargis, Manohla. "Un-Innocents Abroad: The Drubbing." *N.Y. Times,* June 2, 2010.

DeGraaf, John, David Wann, & Thomas H. Naylor. *Affluenza: The All-Consuming Epidemic.* San Francisco: Berrett-Koehler, 2001.

Derber, Charles. *Corporation Nation: How Corporations Are Taking Over Our Lives and What We Can Do about It.* New York: St. Martin's Press, 1998.

Deutsch, Claudia H. "G.E. Unveils Credit Card Aimed at Relieving Carbon Footprints." *N.Y. Times,* July 25, 2007, C9.

Deutsch, Claudia H. "Mum's the Word: We've Found a Greener Gas." *N.Y. Times,* Nov. 7, 2007.

Deutsch, Claudia H. "Saving the Environment, One Quarterly Earnings Report at a Time." *N.Y. Times,* Nov. 22, 2005.

Dibadj, Reza R. "The Political Economy of Commercial Speech." 58 *S.C. L. Rev.* 913 (2007).

Dickinson, Tim. "The Secret Campaign of President Bush's Administration to Deny Global Warming." *Rolling Stone,* June 28, 2007.

Director, Aaron. "The Parity of the Economic Marketplace." 7 *J.L. & Econ.* 1 (1964).

Dodge v. Ford Motor Co. 170 N.W. 668 (Mich.1919).

Dolliver, Mark. "Deflating a Myth: Consumers Aren't as Devoted to the Planet as You Wish They Were." *Adweek,* May 12, 2008.

Draut, Tamara. *Strapped: Why America's 20- and 30-Somethings Can't Get Ahead.* New York: Anchor Books, 2005.

Dworkin, Gerald. *The Theory and Practice of Autonomy.* Cambridge: Cambridge University Press, 1998.

Economist. "The Case for Brands." Sept. 8, 2001, 11.

Economist. "Cleaning Up: How Business Is Starting to Tackle Climate Change, and How Governments Need to Help." June 2, 2007, 13.

Economist. "A Coat of Green: Business Is Becoming More Environment-Minded, but Only Because Government Is Pushing." Sept. 9, 2006, 19.

Economist. "Devil in the Details: The Art of Pushing Pills." June 18, 2005, 11–13.

Economist. "Efficiency and Beyond." July 16, 2009, 68–69.

Economist. "The Final Cut: Business Can Do It, with Governments' Help." May 2, 2007, 30.

Economist. "The Good Company: A Skeptical Look at Corporate Social Responsibility." Jan. 22, 2005, S3.

Economist. "Jam Today: Worries about Short-Termism Grip America's Business Elite—Wrongly, Perhaps." July 14, 2007, 67.

Economist. "Justice Is Not Blind." July 7, 2007, 13–14.

Economist. "Not on the Label: Why Adding 'Carbon Footprint' Labels to Foods and Other Products Is Tricky." May 19, 2008, 84.

Economist. "The Other-Worldly Philosophers." July 16, 2009, 65–67.

Economist. "Stimulus and Shopping." May 31, 2008, 34.

Economist. "Toxic Fudge." July 19, 2008, 80.

Economist. "The Triumph of Unreason: Why You Are Not Always Rational with Your Credit Card." Jan. 13, 2007, 73.

Economist. "The Union of Concerned Executives: CSR as Practiced Means Many Different Things." Jan. 22, 2005.

Economist. "Voting with Your Trolley: Can You Really Change the World Just by Buying Certain Foods?" Dec. 9, 2006,73–75.

Economist. "Which Way Will Capital Vote?" July 19, 2008, 40–41.

Economist. "Who's Wearing the Trousers?" Sept. 8, 2001, 26–28.

Edwards, Rob. "Study Slams 'Trivial' Social Responsibility Reports." *Sunday Herald,* June 25, 2006, News, 12.

Efrat, Rafael. "Attribution Theory Bias and the Perception of Abuse in Consumer Bankruptcy." 10 *Geo. J. on Poverty L. & Pol'y* 205 (2003).

Elgin, Duane, ed. *Voluntary Simplicity: Responding to Consumer Culture.* Lanham, Mass.: Rowman & Littlefield, 1993.

Elhauge, Einer. "Sacrificing Corporate Profits." 80 *NYU L. Rev.* 733 (2005).

Elliott, Stuart. "Any Way It's Sliced, Appeal of Social Media Grows." *N.Y. Times,* Feb. 22, 2010.

Elliott, Stuart. "Switch to Daylight Time Joins the List of Special Occasions Made for Merchandising." *N.Y. Times,* Mar. 31, 2005, C4.

Elliott, Stuart. "Youth Exposure to Alcohol Marketing Still Too High, Study Says." *N.Y. Times Media Decoder* (blog), June 24, 2008. http://mediadecoder.blogs.nytimes.com/2008/06/24/youth-exposure-to-alcohol-marketing-still-too-high-study-says/.

Ellison, Sarah, & Janet Adamy. "Activists Plan to Sue Viacom and Kellogg over Ads to Children." *Wall Street Journal,* Jan. 19, 2006, A1, A12.

Emerson, Thomas I. *The System of Freedom of Expression.* New York: Random House, 1970.

Emerson, Thomas I. "Toward a General Theory of the First Amendment." 72 *Yale L.J.* 877 (1963).

Emerson, Thomas I. *Toward a General Theory of the First Amendment.* New York: Vintage Books, 1966.

Engel, Kathleen C., & Patricia A. McCoy. "Turning a Blind Eye: Wall Street Finance of Predatory Lending." 75 *Fordham L. Rev.* 2039 (2007).

Entine, Jon. "The Stranger-than-Truth Story of the Body Shop." In *Killed: Great Journalism Too Hot to Print,* ed. David Wallis. New York: Nation Books, 2004.

Environment News Service. "Oil Companies Settle Fuel Violations for 1.5 Million." Oct. 6, 2006. http://corpwatch.org/article.php?id=14165.

Ertman, Martha M., & Joan C. Williams. *Rethinking Commodification: Cases and Readings in Law and Culture.* New York: New York University Press, 2005.

Escamilla v. ASARCO, Inc. No. 91 CV 5716 (D.Colo. 1993).

Estes, Ralph. *The Tyranny of the Bottom Line: Why Corporations Make Good People Do Bad Things.* San Francisco: Berrett-Koehler, 1996.

Estlund, Cynthia L. "Free Speech and Due Process in the Workplace." 71 *Ind. L.J.* 101 (1995).

E.T.: The Extra-Terrestrial. Directed by Steven Spielberg. Universal Studios, 1982.

Ewen, Stuart. *PR! A Social History of Spin.* New York: Basic Books, 1996.

Fallon, Richard H., Jr. "Two Senses of Autonomy." 46 *Stan. L. Rev.* 875 (1994).

Farah, Samar. "The Thin Green Line." *CMO Magazine,* Dec. 2005. Available at http://www.greenmarketing.com/files/news/cmomag_dec05.pdf.

FCC v. AT&T, No. 09-1279 (March 1, 2011) (slip op.).

FEC v. Massachusetts Citizens for Life. 479 U.S. 238, 258 (1986).

FEC v. Wisconsin Right to Life, Inc. 551 U.S 449 (2009).

Fine, Cordellia. *A Mind of Its Own: How Your Brain Distorts and Deceives.* New York: W. W. Norton, 2006.

Finkle, David. "Television Q-ratings: The Popularity Contest of the Stars." *N.Y. Times,* June 7, 1992.

First National Bank of Boston v. Bellotti. 435 U.S. 765 (1978).

Fischer, Paul, Meyer P. Schwartz, John W. Richards Jr., Adam O. Goldstein, & Tina Rojas. "Brand Logo Recognition by Children Aged 3 to 6 Years: Mickey Mouse and Old Joe the Camel." 266 *JAMA* 3145 (1991).

Fischl, Richard Michael. "Labor, Management, and the First Amendment: Whose Rights Are These, Anyway?" 10 *Cardozo L. Rev.* 729 (1989).

Fish, Stanley. *There's No Such Thing as Free Speech—and It's a Good Thing, Too.* New York: Oxford University Press, 1994.

Fisk, Catherine L. "The Modern Author at Work on Madison Avenue." In *Modernism and Copyright,* ed. Paul Saint-Amour. New York: Oxford University Press, 2010.

Fiss, Owen. "Why the State?" 100 *Harv. L. Rev.* 781 (1987).

Fitzgerald, Kate. "Financial Services: Portfolio 21." *Advertising Age,* June 9, 2008.

Fletcher, Michael A. "Tobacco's Ties to Minority Groups Put Their Leaders in a Bind." *Washington Post,* May 17, 1998.

Flood, Mary, Mark Babineck, & John Roper. "Guilty! Guilty! Verdict Will Mean Prison for Ex-Enron Chiefs." *Houston Chronicle,* May 25, 2006.

44 Liquormart v. Rhode Island. 517 U.S. 484 (1996).

Fournier, Susan. "Consumers and Their Brands: Developing Relationship Theory in Consumer Research." 24 *J. Consumer Res.* 343 (1998).

Frank, Thomas. *What's the Matter with Kansas? How Conservatives Won the Heart of America.* New York: Henry Holt, 2005.

Frazier, Mya. "Hidden Persuaders or Junk Science?" *Advertising Age,* Sept. 10, 2007, 36.

Frazier, Mya. "This Ad Will Give You a Headache, but It Sells." *Advertising Age,* Sept. 24, 2007, 3, 34.

Frazier, Mya. "Who's in Charge of Green?" *Advertising Age,* June 9, 2008.

Friedman, Josh. "Blogging for Dollars Raises Questions of Online Ethics." *Los Angeles Times,* Mar. 9, 2007.

Friedman, Milton. "The Social Responsibility of Business Is to Increase Its Profits." *N.Y. Times Magazine,* Sept. 13, 1970, SM 17.

Fudge, Rachel. "Shop in the Name of Love: Judith Levine Explains Why She Is Not Buying It." *Bitch,* Summer 2006, 36.

Fullerton, Jami, & Alice Kendrick. *Advertising's War on Terrorism.* Spokane, Wash.: Marquette Books, 2006.

Gaines, Judith. "Mind Games: Psychologists Debate Ethics of Helping Sell to Children." *Boston Globe,* Mar. 26, 2000, A1, B4.

Gale Group. "Market Research C'mon, Mom! Kids Nag Parents to Chuck E. Cheese's." Selling to Kids, May 12, 1999. http://findarticles.com/p/articles/mi_M0FVE/is_9_4/ai_54631243/?tab=content;col1.

Garfield, Bob. "Pay Heed to What Realtors Don't Say in Their Latest Pitch." *Advertising Age,* Jan. 28, 2008, 41.

Garvey, John H., & Fredrick Schauer. *First Amendment: A Reader.* 2nd ed. St. Paul, Minn.: West, 1986.

Gerassi, John. *The Great Fear in Latin America.* Paperback ed. New York: Collier Books, 1971.

Gertner, Jon. "Hey, Mom, Is It Okay If These Guys Market Stuff to Us?" *N.Y. Times,* Nov. 28, 2004.

Gilbert, Daniel. *Stumbling on Happiness.* New York: Alfred A. Knopf, 2006.

Gilpin, Elizabeth A., Martha M. White, Karen Messer, & John P. Pierce. "Receptivity to Tobacco Advertising Promotions among Young Adolescents as a Predictor of Established Smoking in Young Adulthood." 97 *Am. J. Pub. Health* 1489 (2007).

Gladwell, Malcolm. *Blink: The Power of Thinking without Thinking.* New York: Little, Brown, 2005.

Glanz, James, & Richard A. Oppel Jr. "Panel Questions State Dept. Role in Iraq Oil Deal." *N.Y. Times,* July 3, 2008, A1.

Glasbeck, Harry. *Wealth by Stealth: Corporate Crime, Corporate Law, and the Perversion of Democracy.* Toronto: Between the Lines, 2002.

Goldberg, Jeffry. "Selling Wal-Mart." *New Yorker,* Apr. 2, 2007, 32, 38.

Goldberg, Natalie. *Writing Down the Bones: Freeing the Writer Within.* Boston, Mass.: Shambhala, 2005.

Goldman, Alvin I., & James C. Cox. "Speech, Truth, and the Free Market for Ideas." 2 *Legal Theory* 1 (1996).

Goldstein, Thomas C. "*Nike v. Kasky* and the Definition of 'Commercial Speech.'" 2002–3 *Cato Sup. Ct. Rev.* 63 (2003).

Gonzalez v. Raich. 545 U.S.1 (2005).

Goodman, David. "Culture Change." *Mother Jones* 52 (Jan./Feb. 2003).

Goodman, Ellen. "Stealth Marketing and Editorial Integrity." 85 *Tex. L. Rev.* (2006).

Gore v. Sec. for Dept. of Corrections. 493 F.3d 1273 (11th Cir. 2007).

Gostin, Lawrence O. *Public Health Law: Power, Duty, Restraint.* 2nd ed. Berkeley: University of California Press, 2008.

Green, Kenneth P., & Steven F. Hayward. "Scenes from the Climate Inquisition." American Enterprise Institute for Public Policy Research, Feb. 19, 2007. http://www.aei.org/docLib/20070222_OTI.pdf.

Green Century Funds. http://www.greencentury.com/?utm_source=SIF&utm_medium=supp_banner&utm_content=logo&utm_campaign=feb10.

Greenfield, Kent. "Proposition: Saving the World with Corporate Law." 57 *Emory L.J.* 948 (2008).

Greenstein, Jennifer. "Testing Consumer Reports." *Brill's Content*, Sept. 1999, 72.

Greenwood, Daniel J. H. "The Dividend Problem: Are Shareholders Entitled to the Residual, or Faith Based Investing: Why Economics Can't Explain Shareholder Returns." 32 *J. Corp. L.* 103 (2006).

Greenwood, Daniel J. H. "Enronitis: Why Good Corporations Go Bad." 2004 *Colum. Bus. L. Rev.* 773 (2004).

Greenwood, Daniel J. H. "Essential Speech: Why Corporate Speech Is Not Free." 83 *Iowa L. Rev.* 995 (1998).

Greenwood, Daniel J. H. "Fictional Shareholders, for Whom Are Corporate Managers Trustees, Revisited." 69 *S. Cal. L. Rev.* 1021 (1996).

Greenwood, Daniel J. H. "Markets and Democracy: The Illegitimacy of Corporate Law." 74 *UMKC L. Rev.* 41 (2005).

Greenwood, Daniel J. H. "Torts in Corporate Law: Do Corporations Have a Fiduciary Obligation to Commit Torts?" In *Tortious Liability: Emerging Trends,* ed. M. N. Bhavani. Hyderabad: Icfai University Press, 2008.

Grey, Thomas C. "Holmes and Legal Pragmatism." 41 *Stan. L. Rev.* 787 (1989).

Gruber, Peter. "The Four Truths of the Storyteller." *Harv. Bus. Rev.,* Dec. 2007, 53–59.

Haack, Susan. "Scientific Secrecy and 'Spin': The Sad, Sleazy Saga of the Trials of Remune." 69 *Law & Contemp. Probs.* 47 (2006).

Haiman, Franklyn. *Speech and Law in a Free Society.* Chicago: University of Chicago Press, 1981.

Halliday, Jean. "BP Touts Greenness, Then Asks to Dump Ammonia." *Advertising Age,* Aug. 20, 2007.

Halliday, Jean. "Nissan's Rogue Joins Cast of *Heroes.*" *AdAge.com,* Aug. 29, 2007. http://adage.com/mediaworks/article?article_id=120143.

Hampp, Andrew. "An Ad in Which Boy Gets Girl . . . or Boy." *AdAge.com,* Aug. 6, 2007. http://adage.com/article?article_id=119705.

Hampp, Andrew. "How American Airlines Got a Free Ride in 'Up in the Air.'" *AdAge.com,* Dec. 14, 2009. http://adage.com/print?article_id=141059.

Hampp, Andrew, & Emily Bryson York. "How Miracle Whip, Plenty of Fish Tapped Lady Gaga's 'Telephone.'" *AdAge.com,* Mar. 13, 2010. http://adage .com/madisonandvine/article?article_id=142794.

Hansmann, Henry, & Reinier Kraakman. "The End of History for Corporate Law." 89 *Geo. L.J.* 439 (2000–2001).

Hanson, Jon, & Douglas Kysar. "Taking Behavioralism Seriously." 112 *Harv. L. Rev.* 1420 (1999).

Harris, Gardiner, Benedict Carrey, & Janet Roberts. "Psychiatrists, Troubled Children, and Drug Industry's Role." *N.Y. Times,* May 10, 2007, A1.

Harris, Jennifer L., Jennifer L. Pomeranz, Tim Lobstein, & Kelly D. Brownell. "A Crisis in the Marketplace: How Food Marketing Contributes to Childhood Obesity and What Can Be Done." 30 *Annu Rev. Public Health* 211 (2009).

Hartman, Laura P., Robert S. Rubin, & K. Kathy Dhanda. "The Communication of Corporate Social Responsibility: United States and European Union Multinational Corporations." 74 *J. Bus. Ethics* 373 (2007).

Hartmann, Thom. *Unequal Protection: The Rise of Corporate Dominance and the Theft of Human Rights.* Emmaus, Pa.: Rodale Books, 2002.

Hemsley, Steve. "Who's Responsible?" *PRWeek,* Aug. 12, 2005, 22.

Henry, Neil. "Truth Be Told: Saving the Soul of Journalism." *Chron. Higher Educ.,* May 25, 2007, B11.

Herbert, Bob. "Brutality in Vietnam." *N.Y. Times,* March 28, 1997, A29.

Herbert, Bob. "In America: Nike Blinks." *N.Y. Times,* May 21, 1998, A33.

Herbert, Bob. "Let Nike Stay in the Game." *N.Y. Times,* May 6, 2002, A21.

Hergenhahn, B. R., & Matthew H. Olson. *An Introduction to Theories of Learning.* Upper Saddle River, N.J.: Prentice Hall, 2001.

Herman, Edward S., & Noam Chomsky. *Manufacturing Consent: The Political Economy of Mass Media.* New York: Pantheon, 2002.

Hirschman, Albert O. *Exit, Voice, and Loyalty: Responses to Decline in Firms, Organizations, and States.* Cambridge, Mass.: Harvard University Press, 1970.

Hoch, David, & Robert Franz. "Eco-Porn versus the Constitution: Commercial Speech and the Regulation of Environmental Advertising." 58 *Alb. L. Rev.* 441 (1994).

Hoffman, Claire. "Wal-Mart Warms to a Green Outlook: The Retailer Works Hard to Polish Its Image; Environmental Groups Have Mixed Reviews." *Los Angeles Times,* July 13, 2006.

Hoffman, David A. "The Best Puffery Article Ever." 91 *Iowa L. Rev.* 1395 (2006).

Hoggan, Jim. "Slamming the Climate Skeptic Scam," June 15, 2009 (DeSmog Blog). http://www.desmogblog.com/slamming-the-climate-skeptic-scam.

Holmes, Oliver Wendell. "The Path of Law." 10 *Harv. L. Rev.* 457 (1897).

Horwitz, Morton J. *The Transformation of American Law 1870–1960.* New York: Oxford University Press, 1992.

Howard, John A., & James Hulbert. Report to the U.S. Federal Trade Commission. *Advertising and the Public Interest.* Washington, D.C.: Crain Communications, 1973.

Huxley, Aldous. *Brave New World Revisited.* New York: Harper & Row, 1958.

Ilhen, Øyvind, Betteke van Ruler, & Magnus Fredriksson, eds. *Public Relations and Social Theory: Key Figures and Concepts.* New York & London: Routledge, 2009.

Ingber, Stanley A. "Rediscovering the Communal Worth of Individual Rights: The First Amendment in Institutional Contexts." 69 *Tex. L. Rev.* 1 (1990).

In re Gen. Motors Corp., Anti-Lock Brakes Prods. Liab. Litig. 966 F. Supp. 1525 (E.D. Mo. 1997), *aff'd* 172 F.3d 623 (8th Cir. 1999).

Institute for Policy Studies. "Research Institute Releases Study on Corporate Power on 1st Anniversary of Seattle Protests." http://www.ips-dc.org/reports/top200.htm.

Ives, Nat. "Ad Spending Barely Budged in 2007." *AdAge.com,* Mar. 25, 2008. http://adage.com/print?article_id=125921.

Ives, Nat, & Rich Thomaselli. "Marketing Takes a Beating in Beltway." *Advertising Age,* July 27, 2009, 1, 19.

Ivry, Sara. "Marketers Say They Pay for Play in News Media." *N.Y. Times,* June 26, 2006.

Iyengar, Sheena. *The Art of Choosing.* New York: Hachette Book Group, 2010.

Jansen, Eric. "The Next Bubble: Priming the Markets for Tomorrow's Big Crash." *Harper's Magazine,* Feb. 2008, 39–45.

Jensen, Elizabeth. " 'Sesame' Upgrading Its Address on the Web." *N.Y. Times,* July 15, 2008, E1.

Jofre, Shelly. "Doctoring the Evidence: GlaxoSmithKline Pushes Depression Drug." *CorpWatch,* July 30, 2007. http://corpwatch.org/article.php?id=14606.

John, Deborah Roedder. "Consumer Socialization of Children: A Retrospective Look at Twenty-Five Years of Research." 26 *J. Consumer Res.* 183 (1999).

Johnson, Bradley. "More Ad Spend, Better Economy." *Advertising Age,* Oct. 8, 2007.

Johnson, Bradley. "Spending Fell (Only) 2.7% in '08; The Real Issue: '09." *Advertising Age,* June 22, 2009.

Johnson, Bruce E. H., & Ambika K. Doran. "Amendment XXVIII? Defending Corporate Speech Rights." 58 *S.C. L. Rev.* 855 (2007).

Johnson, Bruce E. H., & Jeffrey L. Fisher. "Why Format, Not Content, Is the Key to Identifying Commercial Speech." 54 *Case W. Res. L. Rev.* 1243 (2004).

Joo, Thomas W. "The Modern Corporation and Campaign Finance: Incorporating Government Analysis into First Amendment Jurisprudence." 79 *Wash. U. L.Q.* 1 (2001).

Mask, Matthew. "Senate Battle over FEC Nominee May Hamper Agency's Ability to Act." *Washington Post,* Oct. 26, 2007, A19.

Kahan, Dan M. "The Cognitively Illiberal State." 60 *Stan. L. Rev.* 115 (2007).

Kahneman, Daniel, Paul Slovik, & Amos Tversky. *Judgment under Uncertainty: Heuristics and Biases.* Cambridge: Cambridge University Press, 1982.

Kahn v. Sullivan. 594 A.2d 48 (Del. 1991).

Kamen, Al. "FEMA Meets the Press, Which Happens to Be—FEMA." *Washington Post,* Oct. 26, 2007.

Kanzer, Adam M., & Cynthia A. Williams. "The Future of Social Reporting Is on the Line." *Bus. Ethics Q.,* Summer 2003. Available at http://www.dominiadvisor.com/advisor/About-Domini/News/Press-Release-Archive/Nike_Kasky_Oped_6_03_cut.htm.

Karnani, Aneel. "Doing Well by Doing Good—Case Study: 'Fair & Lovely' Whitening Cream." 28 *Strategic Mgmt. J.* 1351 (2007).

Kasky v. Nike, Inc. 45 P.3d 243, 247, 27 Cal. 4th 939, 966–67 (2002).

Katzenbach v. McClung. 379 U.S. 294 (1964).

Kilborn, Peter T. "The Five-Bedroom, Six-Figure Rootless Life." *N.Y. Times,* June 1, 2005, A1.

Kilbourne, Jean. *Deadly Persuasion: Why Women and Girls Must Fight the Addictive Power of Advertising.* New York: Free Press, 1999.

Kinsella, Stephan. "Against Intellectual Property." 15 *J. Libertarian Stud.* 1 (2001).

Kirkpatrick, David D. "Lobbyists Get Potent Weapon in Campaign Ruling." *N.Y. Times,* Jan. 22, 2010, A1.

Kirkpatrick, David D. "Tougher Rules Change Game for Lobbyists." *N.Y. Times,* Aug. 7, 2007.

Klaassen, Abbey. "Social Networking Reaches Near Full Penetration among Teens and 'Tweens." *AdAge.com,* June 25, 2007. http://adage.com/digital/article?article_id=118763.

Klaassen, Abbey, & Ira Teinowitz. "Privacy Groups Propose Do-Not-Track List: Demands Would Hinder Marketers' Behavioral-Targeting Practices On-Line." *Advertising Age,* Oct. 30, 2007.

Klick, Jonathan, & Gregory Mitchell. "Government Regulation of Irrationality: Moral and Cognitive Hazards." 90 *Minn. L. Rev.* 1620 (2006).

Klein, Naomi. *No Logo.* New York: Random House, 2000.

Koeppel, Dan. Op-Ed. "Yes, We Will Have No Bananas." *N.Y. Times,* June 18, 2008, A21.

Kreslake, Jennifer M., Jeffrey Farris Wayne, Hillel R. Alpert, Howard K. Koh, & George N. Connelly. "Tobacco Industry Control of Menthol in Cigarettes and Targeting of Adolescents and Young Adults." 98 *Am. J. Pub. Health* 1685 (2008).

Kristula-Green, Michelle. "How to Market to Asia's Masses." *AdAge.com,* Aug. 6, 2007. http://adage.com/print?article_id=119637.

Krugman, Paul. "Enemy of the Planet." *N.Y. Times,* Apr. 17, 2006, A21.

Kysar, Douglas A. "The Consultants' Republic." 121 *Harv. L. Rev.* 2041 (2008) (reviewing Ted Nordhaus & Michael Shellenberger, *Breakthrough: From the Death of Environmentalism to the Politics of Possibility* [New York: Houghton Mifflin, 2007]).

Kysar, Douglas A. "Kids and Cul-de-sacs: *Census 2000* and the Reproduction of Consumer Culture." 87 *Cornell L. Rev.* 853 (2002).

Kysar, Douglas A. "Sustainable Development and Private Global Governance." 83 *Tex. L. Rev.* 2109, 2166 (2008).

La Fetra, Deborah J. "Kick It Up a Notch: First Amendment Protection for Commercial Speech." 54 *Case W. Res. L. Rev.* 1205 (2004).

Lallande, Ann. "Environmental Marketing: The Next Wave." 23 *Marketing & Media Decisions* (vol. 12) 174 (Dec.1988).

Landes, Elisabeth M., & Richard A. Posner. "The Economics of the Baby Shortage." 7 *J. Leg. Studies* 323 (1978).

Lane, Vicki R. "The Impact of Ad Repetition and Ad Content on Consumer Perceptions of Incongruent Extensions." 64 *J. Marketing* 80 (2000).

Lasn, Kalle. *Culture Jam: The Uncooling of America.* New York: Eagle Brook, 1999.

Laufer, William S. *Corporate Bodies and Guilty Minds: The Failure of Corporate Criminal Liability.* Chicago: University of Chicago Press, 2006.

Learmouth, Michael. "Tracking Makes Life Easier for Consumers." *Advertising Age,* July 13, 2009, 3, 25.

Lebron v. Nat'l R.R. Passenger Corp. 513 U.S. 374 (1995).

Ledewitz, Bruce. "Corporate Advertising's Democracy." 12 *B.U. Pub. Int. L.J.* 389 (2003).

Lee, Gia. "Persuasion, Transparency, and Government Speech." 56 *Hastings L.J.* 983 (2005).

Leeds, Jeff. "The New Deal: Band as Brand." *N.Y. Times,* Nov. 11, 2007, Arts & Leisure, 1.

Leighton, Richard J. "Materiality and Puffing in Lanham Act False Advertising Cases: The Proofs, Presumptions, and Pretexts." 94 *Trademark Rep.* 585 (2004).

Lemly, Mark. "The Modern Lanham Act and the Death of Common Sense." 108 *Yale L.J.* 1687 (1999).

Lenzer, Anna. "Fiji Water: Spin the Bottle." *Mother Jones,* Sept./Oct. 2009, 35.

Lerer, Lisa. "Lobbyists Sent 13 Fake Letters to Hill." *Politico* (blog), Aug. 18, 2009. http://www.politico.com/news/stories/0809/26229.html.

Lessig, Lawrence. "Institutional Integrity: *Citizens United* and the Path to a Better Democracy." *Huffington Post,* Jan. 22, 2010. http://www.huffington post.com/lawrence-lessig/institutional-integrity-c_b_433394.html.

Levy, Leonard. *Emergence of a Free Press.* Chicago: Ivan R. Dee, 1985.

Lewis, Anthony. *Freedom for the Thought We Hate: A Biography of the First Amendment.* New York: Basic Books, 2007.

Lichtblau, Eric. "Lawyers Fought U.S. Move to Curb Tobacco Penalty." *N.Y. Times,* June 16, 2005, A1.

Lieberman, Trudy. "The Epidemic." *Colum. Journalism Rev.,* Mar./Apr. 2007, 38–43.

Lindström, Lenart, & Mårten Stenström. "Sweden." In *The European Handbook on Advertising Law,* ed. Lord Campbell of Alloway & Zahd Yaqub. London: Cavendish, 1999.

Lipton, Eric. "FEMA Aide Loses New Job over Fake News Conference." *N.Y. Times,* Oct. 30, 2007, A19.

Lipton, Eric, & Louise Story. "Bid to Root Out Lead Trinkets Falters in U.S." *N.Y. Times,* Aug. 6, 2007.

Litowitz, Douglas. "Are Corporations Evil?" 58 *U. Miami L. Rev.* 811 (2004).

Lobe, Jim. "Majority Still Believe in Iraq's WMD, Al-Qaeda Ties." Inter Press Service, Apr. 22, 2004. http://www.ipsnews.net/interna.asp?idnews=23439.

Lochner v. New York. 198 U.S. 45 (1905).

Locke, John. *Second Treatise on Government: Political Writings of John Locke.* Ed. David Wootton. Indianapolis: Hackett, 2003, 1993 (1689).

Loftus, Elizabeth. "Creating False Memories." *Scientific American,* Sept. 1997, 70–75.

Lohr, Steve. "In Bailout Furor, Wall Street Pay Becomes a Target." *N.Y. Times,* Sept. 24, 2008, A1.

Lohse, Deborah. "Violence Knowingly Marketed to Kids." *San Jose Mercury News,* Sept. 10, 2000, 1A.

Luntz, Frank L. *Words That Work: It's Not What You Say, It's What People Hear.* New York: Hyperion Books, 2007.

Lyman, Rick, & Julian E. Barnes. "The Toy War for Holiday Movies Is a Battle among 3 Heavyweights." *N.Y. Times,* Nov. 12, 2001, C1.

Lyman, Rick, & Stuart Elliot. "Sony Admits It Used Employees as Bogus Fans." *N.Y. Times,* June 16, 2002, B11.

MacKinnon, Catherine A. *Only Words.* Cambridge, Mass.: Harvard University Press, 1993.

Magid, Larry. "Kids Need to Think Critically to Weed Out Unsavory Marketing." *San Jose Mercury News,* Sept 25, 2000, 4F.

Manjoo, Farhad. "Branded." *N.Y. Times,* July 27, 2008.

Mankiw, N. Gregory. "Can A Soda Tax Save Us from Ourselves?" *N.Y. Times,* June 6, 2010, BU 4.

Mann, Ronald J., & Jim Hawkins. "Just Until Payday." 54 *U.C.L.A. L. Rev.* 855 (2007).

Manning, Robert D. *Credit Card Nation: The Consequences of America's Addiction to Credit.* New York: Basic Books, 2000.

Marbury v. Madison. 5 U.S. (1 Cranch) 137 (1803).

Marchand, Roland. *Creating the Corporate Soul: The Rise of Public Relations and Corporate Imagery in American Big Business.* Berkeley: University of California Press, 1998.

Martin, Andrew. "Kellogg to Phase Out Some Food Ads to Children." *N.Y. Times,* June 14, 2007, C1.

Martin, Neale. *Habit: The 95% of Behavior Marketers Ignore.* Upper Saddle River, NJ: FT Press, 2008.

Matthews, Jeff. "This Just In: 'Spin' Becomes 'Lying.' " *Jeff Matthews Is Not Making This Up* (blog), June 19, 2005. http://jeffmatthewsisnotmaking thisup.blogspot.com/2005/06/this-just-in-spin-becomes-lying.html.

McChesney, Robert W. *Rich Media, Poor Democracy.* New York: New Press, 1999.

McClam, Erin. "WorldCom Figures Sentenced." *Tulsa World,* Aug. 6, 2005, E6.

McDonald's Worldwide 2006 Corporate Responsibility Report. http://www.mc donalds.com/corp/values/report/printable.html.

McDougall, Jean, & David Chantry. "The Making of Tomorrow's Consumer." 5(4): *Young Consumers* 8 (2004).

McGarity, Thomas O., & Wendy Elizabeth Wagner. *Bending Science: How Special Interests Corrupt Public Health Research.* Cambridge, Mass.: Harvard University Press, 2008.

McIntyre, Vicki. "*Nike v. Kasky:* Leaving Corporate America Speechless." 30 *Wm. Mitchell L. Rev.* 1531 (2004).

McLean, Bethany, & Peter Elkind. *The Smartest Guys in the Room: The Amazing Rise and the Scandalous Fall of Enron.* New York: Penguin, 2004.

McQuarrie, Edward F., & Barbara J. Phillips. "Indirect Persuasion in Advertising: How Consumers Process Metaphors in Pictures and Words." 34 *J. Advertising* 7 (2007).

Meier, Barry. "Narcotic Maker Guilty of Deceit over Marketing." *N.Y. Times,* May 11, 2007, A1.

Meiklejohn, Alexander. "The First Amendment Is an Absolute." 1961 *Sup. Ct. Rev.* 245 (1961).

Meiklejohn, Alexander. *Free Speech and Its Relation to Self-Government.* New York: Harper Brothers, 1948.

Menand, Louis. *The Metaphysical Club: A Story of Ideas in America.* New York: Farrar, Strauss & Giroux, 2001.

Michaels, David. *Doubt Is Their Product: How Industry's Assault on Science Threatens Your Health.* New York: Oxford University Press, 2008.

Miller, Clyde. *The Process of Persuasion.* New York: Crown, 1946.

Miller, Karen S. *The Voice of Business: Hill and Knowlton and Postwar Public Relations.* Chapel Hill: University of North Carolina Press, 1999.

Miller, Mark Crispin. Introduction to *The Hidden Persuaders,* by Vance Packard. Brooklyn: Ig, 2007.

Miller, Steve. "Coalition Urges FCC to Adopt Product Placement Rules." *Brandweek.com,* June 20, 2008. http://www.brandweek.com/bw/content_dis play/news-and-features/automotive-travel/e3i50d4ccb4056bd834b a90cdf3639ae183.

Miller, Vincent J. *Consuming Religion: Christian Faith and Practice in a Consumer Culture.* New York: Continuum International, 2005.

Milton, John. *Areopagitica.* http://www.guttenberg.org/ebooks/608.

Minow, N., & Craig LaMay. *Abandoned in the Wasteland: Children, Television, and the First Amendment.* New York: Hill & Wang, 1995.

Mishan, Ezra. "Commercial Advertising: A Skeptical View." In *Advertising and Free Speech,* ed. Allen Hyman & M. Bruce Johnson. Lexington, Mass.: Lexington Books, 1977.

Mitchell, Gregory. "Tendencies versus Boundaries: Levels of Generality in Behavioral Law and Economics." 56 *Vand. L. Rev.* 1781 (2003).

Mitchell, Lawrence E. "Cooperation and Constraint in the Modern Corporation: An Inquiry into the Causes of Corporate Immorality." 73 *Tex. L. Rev.* 477 (1995).

Mitchell, Lawrence E. *Corporate Irresponsibility: America's Newest Export.* New Haven, Conn.: Yale University Press, 2001.

Mitchell, Lawrence E. "The Sarbanes-Oxley Act and the Reinvention of Corporate Governance?" 48 *Vill. L. Rev.* 1189 (2003).

Mitchell, Lawrence E., & Theresa A. Gabaldon. "If Only I Had a Heart, or How Can We Identify a Corporate Morality?" 76 *Tul. L. Rev.* 1645 (2002).

Mlodinow, Leonard. *The Drunkard's Walk: How Randomness Rules Our Lives.* New York: Vintage Books, 2008.

Mokhiber, Russell, & Robert Weissman. *Corporate Predators: The Hunt for Mega-Profits and the Attack on Democracy.* Monroe, Me.: Common Courage, 1999.

Monks, Robert A. G. *Corpocracy: How CEOs and the Business Roundtable Hijacked the World's Greatest Wealth Machine—and How to Get It Back.* Hoboken, N.J.: John Wiley & Sons, 2007.

Moore, Elizabeth S., & Richard J. Lutz. "Children, Advertising, and Product Experiences: A Multimethod Inquiry." 27 *J. Consumer Res.* 31 (2000).

Morgenson, Gretchen. "The Quick Buck Just Got Quicker." *N.Y. Times,* Apr. 15, 2009.

Morgenson, Gretchen. "Your Money at Work, Fixing Others' Mistakes." *N.Y. Times,* Sept. 21, 2008, B1, 6.

Morris, Jim. "Worked to Death." *Houston Chronicle,* Oct. 9, 1994, A1.

Morrison, Alan B. "How We Got the Commercial Speech Doctrine: An Originalist's Recollections." 54 *Case W. Res. L. Rev.* 1189 (2004).

Nace, Ted. *Gangs of America: The Rise of Corporate Power and the Disability of Democracy.* San Francisco: Berrett-Koehler, 2003.

Nagourney, Adam, & Carl Hulse. "Republican Election Losses Stir Fall Fears." *N.Y. Times,* May 15, 2008.

National Resource Defense Council. "Historic Hudson River Cleanup to Begin after Years of Delay, but Will General Electric Finish the Job?" news release, March 23, 2007, http://www.nrdc.org/water/pollution/hhudson.asp.

Nayaradou, Maximilien. "Advertising and Economic Growth." Ph.D. diss., University of Paris, 2006. Available at http://www.wfanet.org/documents/3/WFA-UDA_Advertising&Economic_Growth.pdf.

Neff, Jack. "Clorox: Bleach, Charcoal, and . . . Burt's Bees; Company Pays $950 Million for Leading Natural Personal-Care Brand." *Advertising Age,* Oct. 31, 2007.

Neff, Jack. "P&G Rewrites Its Definition of 'Ad Spend.'" *Advertising Age,* Sept. 3, 2007. http://adage.com/article/news/p-grewrites-it-definition-of-ad-spend/120213.

Neff, Jack. "Recall Sheds Light on Pet-Food Industry's Little Secret: Consumers See That Premium, Private-Label Products Can Come from the Same Place." *Advertising Age,* Mar. 20, 2007.

Neff, Jack. "Unilever, P&G War over Which Is Most Ethical." *Advertising Age,* Mar. 3, 2008.

Nelson, Joyce. *Sultans of Sleaze.* Toronto: Between the Lines, 1989.

Neuborne, Burt. "The First Amendment and Governmental Regulation of Capital Markets." 55 *Brook. L. Rev.* 5 (1989).

Neuborne, Burt. "A Rationale for Protecting and Regulating Commercial Speech." 46 *Brook. L. Rev.* 437 (1980).

Neumann Vu, Stacey. "Corporate Criminal Liability: Patchwork Verdicts and the Problem of Locating a Guilty Agent." 104 *Colum. L. Rev.* 459 (2004).

Nike, Inc. v. Kasky. 539 U.S. 654 (2003).

North, Douglas C. "Institutions." 5 *J. Econ. Persp.* 97 (1991).

N.Y. Times. Business Briefs. "Jurors in Trial of Two Tyco Executives End the Week without Completing a Verdict." June 4, 2005, C2.

N.Y. Times. Editorial. "Lobbying from Within." June 17, 2005.

N.Y. Times. Editorial. "Talking about Green (the Other Kind)." Feb. 27, 2008.

N.Y. Times. Editorial. "In TXU's $45 Billion Deal, Many Shades of Green." Feb. 26, 2008 (DealBook Blog).

N.Y. Times Co. v. Sullivan. 376 U.S. 254 (1964).

O'Brien, Kevin J. "Privacy Laws Trip Up Google's Expansion in Parts of Europe." *N.Y. Times*, Nov. 18, 2008, B8.

O'Brien v. U.S. 391 U.S. 367 (1968).

O'Connor-Felman, Marleen. "American Corporate Governance and Children: Investing in Our Future Human Capital during Turbulent Times." 77 *S. Cal. L. Rev.* 1255 (2004).

Ohralik v. Ohio State Bar Association. 436 U.S. 447, 456 (1978).

Oreskes, Naomi, & Erik M. Conway. *Merchants of Doubt.* New York: Bloomsbury Press, 2010.

Olsson, Karen. "Ghostwriting the Law." *Mother Jones*, Sept./Oct. 2002, 17.

Orts, Eric W. "Reflexive Environmental Law." 89 *Nw. U. L. Rev.* 1227 (1995).

Orwell, George. *1984.* London: Harcourt, 1949.

O'Toole, John. *The Trouble with Advertising: A View from the Inside.* New York: Times Books, 1985.

Packard, Vance. *The Hidden Persuaders.* New York: Simon & Schuster, 1957.

Packer, George. "Comment: Name Calling." *New Yorker*, Aug. 8, 2005, 33.

Palazzo, Guido, & Kunal Basu. "The Ethical Backlash of Corporate Branding." 73 *J. Bus. Ethics* 333 (2007).

Parker, Jeffry S., & Raymond A. Atkins. "Did the Corporate Criminal Sentencing Guidelines Matter? Some Preliminary Empirical Observations." 42 *J.L. & Econ.* 423 (1999).

Paulison, R. David. Memo to FEMA employees, Oct. 29, 2007. http://graphic8.nytimes.com/packages/pdf/national/2007/030_FEMA_Paulison_memo.pdf.

PBS. "Bigger than Enron." *Frontline.* PBS television broadcast, June 20, 2002. http://www.pbs.org/wgbh/pages/frontline/shows/regulation/.

PBS. "Merchants of Cool." *Frontline.* PBS television broadcast, Feb. 1, 2001. http://www.pbs.org/wgbh/pages/frontline/shows/cool/view/.

PBS. "The Persuaders." *Frontline.* PBS television broadcast, Nov. 9, 2003. http://www.pbs.org/wgbh/pages/frontline/shows/persuaders/.

Peters, Tom. "The Brand Called You." *Fast Company*, Aug. 31, 1997. http://www.fastcompany.com/magazine/10/brandyou.html.

Peñalver, Eduardo M. "Restoring the Right Constitution?" 116 *Yale L.J.* 732 (2007).

Pfanner, Eric. "At 30,000 Feet, Finding a Captive Audience for Advertising." *N.Y. Times*, Aug. 27, 2007.

Pfanner, Eric. "Cooling Off on Dubious Eco-friendly Claims." *N.Y. Times*, July 18, 2008.

Pfanner, Eric. "Gore to Bring Talk of Green to Ad Festival." *N.Y. Times*, June 18, 2007, C8.

Pfanner, Eric. "No Hunks in the Alcohol Advertisements, Please; We're British." *N.Y. Times*, Aug. 1, 2005, C4.

Piety, Tamara R. "Against Freedom of Commercial Expression." 29 *Cardozo L. Rev.* 2583 (2008).

Piety, Tamara R. "*Citizens United* and the Threat to the Regulatory State." 109 *Mich L. Rev.* First impressions 16 (2010), http://www.michiganlawreview.org/assets/fi/log/piety/pdf.

Piety, Tamara R. "Free Advertising: The Case for Public Relations as Commercial Speech." 10 *Lewis & Clark L. Rev.* 367 (2006).

Piety, Tamara R. "Grounding Nike: Exposing Nike's Quest for a Constitutional Right to Lie." 74 *Temp. L. Rev.* 151 (2004).

Piety, Tamara R. "Market Failure in the Marketplace of Ideas: Commercial Speech and the Problem That Won't Go Away." 41 *Loy. L.A. L. Rev.* 181 (2008).

Piety, Tamara R. "Onslaught: Commercial Speech and Gender Inequality." 60 *Case W. Res. L. Rev.* 47 (2009).

Pittsburgh Press Co. v. Human Relations Comm'n. 423 U.S. 376 (1973).

Plater, Zygmunt J. B. "Law, Media, and Environmental Policy: A Fundamental Link in Sustainable Democratic Governance." 33 *Environmental Affairs* 511 (2006).

Pollack, Andrew, & Duff Wilson. "Former Pfizer Scientist Wins Whistleblower Suit." *N.Y. Times,* Apr. 3, 2010, B3.

Pomeranz, Jennifer L. "Television Marketing to Children Revisited: The Federal Trade Commission Has the Constitutional and Statutory Authority to Regulate." 38 *J.L. Med. & Ethics* 98 (2010).

Posadas de Puerto Rico Associates v. Tourism Co. of Puerto Rico. 478 U.S. 328 (1986).

Posner, Richard. "Bad News." *N.Y. Times Book Review,* July 31, 2005, 1.

Posner, Richard. "Pragmatism versus Purposivism in First Amendment Analysis." 54 *Stan. L. Rev.* 737 (2002).

Posner, Richard. *The Regulation of Advertising by the FTC.* Washington, D.C.: American Enterprise Institute, 1973.

Post, Robert. "Reconciling Theory and Doctrine in First Amendment Jurisprudence." 88 *Cal. L. Rev.* 2353 (2000).

Poynder, John. *Literary Extracts from English and Other Work; Collected during Half a Century: Together with Some Original Matter.* Vol. I. London: John Hatchford & Son, 1844.

Quart, Alissa. *Branded: The Buying and Selling of Teenagers.* New York: Basic Books, 2003.

Rabban, David. *Free Speech in Its Forgotten Years, 1870–1920.* Cambridge: Cambridge University Press, 1997.

Raghubir, Priya, & Joydeep Srivastava. "Monopoly Money: The Effect of Payment Coupling and Form on Spending Behavior." 14 *J. Experimental Psychol.: Applied* 213 (2008).

Rampton, Sheldon, & John Stauber. *Trust Us, We're Experts! How Industry Manipulates Science and Gambles with Your Future*. New York: Jeremy P. Tarcher/Putnam, 2001.

Rapaille, Clotaire. *The Culture Code*. New York: Broadway Books, 2006.

Rapoport, Nancy, & Bala G. Dharan. *Enron: Corporate Fiascos and Their Implications*. New York: Foundation Press, 2004.

Redish, Martin H. "Commercial Speech, First Amendment Intuitionism, and the Twilight Zone of Viewpoint Discrimination." 41 *Loy. L.A. L. Rev.* 67 (2007).

Redish, Martin H. "The First Amendment in the Marketplace: Commercial Speech and the Values of Free Expression." 39 *Geo. Wash. L. Rev.* 429 (1971).

Redish, Martin H. "Self-Realization, Democracy, and Freedom of Expression: A Reply to Professor Baker." 130 *U. Pa. L. Rev.* 678 (1982).

Redish, Martin H. "The Value of Free Speech." 130 *U. Pa. L. Rev.* 591 (1982).

Redish, Martin H., & Howard M. Wasserman. "What's Good for General Motors: Corporate Speech and the Theory of Free Expression." 66 *Geo. Wash. L. Rev.* 235 (1998).

Regan, Milton C., Jr. "Moral Intuitions and Organizational Culture." 51 *St. Louis U. L.J.* 941 (2007).

Renvoisé, Patrick, & Christophe Morin. *Neuromarketing: Is There a "Buy Button" in the Brain? Selling to the Old Brain for Instant Success*. San Francisco: Sales Brain Publishing, 2005.

Rhode, Deborah L. *The Beauty Bias: The Injustice of Appearance in Life and Law*. New York: Oxford University Press, 2010.

Ries, Al, & Laura Ries. *The Fall of Advertising and the Rise of PR*. New York: Harper Business, 2002.

Rich, Frank. "Enron: Patron Saint of Bush's Fake News." *N.Y. Times,* Mar. 20, 2005.

Rich, Frank. *The Greatest Story Ever Sold: The Decline and Fall of Truth from 9/11 to Katrina*. New York: Penguin, 2006.

Rich, Motoko. "Product Placement Deals Make the Leap from Film to Books." *N.Y. Times,* June 16, 2006, C1.

Robbennolt, Paul. "Not Just Smoke and Mirrors: Free Expression and EC Restrictions on Tobacco and Alcohol Advertising." 1992 *U. Chi. Legal F.* 419 (1992).

Roberts, Kevin. *Lovemarks: The Future beyond Brands*. Brooklyn: PowerHouse Books, 2005.

Romano, Roberta. "The Sarbanes-Oxley Act and the Making of Quack Corporate Governance." 114 *Yale L.J.* 1521 (2005).

Rosch, Thomas J. *Responsible Green Marketing*. FTC, 2008 WL 2557919 (2008). Remarks at the American Conference Institute's Regulatory Summit for Advertisers and Marketers, Washington, D.C., June 18, 2008.

Rosenkranz, Nicholas Quinn. "The Subjects of the Constitution." 62 *Stan. L. Rev.* 1209 (2010).

Rovell, Darren. "Investors Fret about Nike's Star Endorsements." *CNBC on MSN Money*, Sept. 22, 2006. http://articles.moneycentral.msn.com/Invest ing/CNBC/TVReports/NikeStarEndorsements.aspx.

Royte, Elizabeth. *Garbage Land: The Secret Trail of Trash.* New York: Little, Brown, 2005.

Rushkoff, Douglas. *Coercion: Why We Listen to What "They" Say.* New York: Riverhead Books, 1999.

Rushkoff, Douglas. "Merchants of Cool." *Frontline.* PBS television broadcast, Feb. 1, 2001. http://www.pbs.org/wgbh/pages/frontline/shows/cool/etc/hunt ing.html.

Rushkoff, Douglas. Introduction to "The Persuaders." *Frontline.* PBS television broadcast, Nov. 9, 2003. http://www.pbs.org/wgbh/pages/frontline/shows/ persuaders/etc/synopsis.html.

Rushton, Michael. "Economic Analysis of Freedom of Expression." 21 *Ga. St. U. L. Rev.* 693 (2005).

Sacharoff, Adriadne K. "Multinationals in Host Countries: Can They Be Held Liable under the Alien Tort Claims Act for Human Rights Violations?" 23 *Brook. J. Int'l L.* 927 (1998).

Sandel, Michael J. "What Money Can't Buy: The Moral Limits of Markets." In *Rethinking Commodification: Cases and Readings in Law and Culture*, ed. Martha M. Ertman & Joan C. Williams. New York: New York University Press, 2005.

Sarbanes-Oxley Act of 2002. Pub. L. No. 107-204, 2002 U.S.C.C.A.N. 116 Stat. 745.

Schauer, Frederick. "The Boundaries of the First Amendment: A Preliminary Exploration of Constitutional Salience." 117 *Harv. L. Rev.* 1765 (2004).

Schauer, Frederick. "Categories and the First Amendment: A Play in Three Acts." 34 *Vand. L. Rev.* 265 (1981).

Schauer, Frederick. "Fear, Risk, and the First Amendment: Unraveling the 'Chilling Effect.'" 58 *B.U. L. Rev.* 685 (1978).

Schauer, Frederick. "Free Speech and the Assumption of Rationality." 36 *Vand. L. Rev.* 199 (1983).

Schauer, Frederick. "Towards an Institutional First Amendment." 89 *Minn. L. Rev.* 1256 (2005).

Schor, Juliet B. *Born to Buy: The Commercialized Child and the New Consumer Culture.* New York: Scribner, 2004.

Schor, Juliet B. *The Overspent American: Why We Want What We Don't Need.* New York: Basic Books, 1998.

Schudson, Michael. *Advertising, the Uneasy Persuasion: The Dubious Impact on American Society.* New York: Basic Books, 1984.

Schwartz, Barry. *The Paradox of Choice.* New York: HarperCollins, 2004.

Seabrook, Andrea. "House Scrutinizes Fake Letters Sent to Congress." NPR, Oct. 30, 2009. http://www.npr.org/templates/story/story.php?storyId=11430 3819.

Segal, David. "A Matter of Opinion?" *N.Y. Times,* July 18, 2009, BU 1, 6.

Segal, David. "Suddenly the Ratings Agencies Don't Seem Untouchable." *N.Y. Times,* May 21, 2010.

Seitel, Fraser, P. *The Practice of Public Relations.* 8th ed. Upper Saddle River, N.J.: Prentice Hall, 2001.

Sennett, Richard. *The Corrosion of Character: The Personal Consequences of Work in the New Capitalism.* New York: W. W. Norton, 2006.

Settle, Robert B., & Pamela L. Alreck. *Why They Buy: American Consumers Inside and Out.* New York: John Wiley & Sons, 1986.

Severson, Kim. "Seduced by Snack? No, Not You." *N.Y. Times,* Oct. 11, 2006.

Sevrens Lyons, Julie. "Donor to Stanford: No Big Oil; University Donation Rescinded over Ad." *San Jose Mercury News,* Mar. 11, 2007.

Sexton, Timothy. "People Are Smart? It Is Time to Sue Ditech for Blatant False Advertising." Associated Content, Sept. 28, 2007. http://www.associatedcontent.com/article/392848/people_are_smart_its_time_to_sue_ditechcom.html?cat=35.

Shahinpoor, Nasrin, & Bernard F. Matt. "The Power of One: Dissent and Organizational Life." 74 *J. Bus. Ethics* 37 (2007).

Shannon, Victoria. "French Court Affirms Auction Site Ruling: Yahoo Faces Deadlines to Block Nazi Items." *Int'l Herald Tribune,* Nov. 21, 2000, 1.

Sharma, Lisa, Stephen P. Teret, & Kelly D. Brownell. "The Food Industry and Self-Regulation: Standards to Promote Success and to Avoid Public Health Failure." 100 *Am. J. Pub. Health* 240 (2010).

Sharper Image Corp. v. Consumers Union of U.S. Inc. 2003 WL 23796370 (Amended Complaint), 2004 WL 2554451 (Order Granting Special Motion to Strike), 2004 WL 2713064 (Order Denying in Part and Continuing in Part Motion to Strike).

Shea, Christopher. "Don't Talk to the Humans: The Crackdown on Social Science Research." *Lingua Franca,* Sept. 2000, 26–34.

Shellenberger, Michael, & Ted Nordhaus. "The Death of Environmentalism: Global Warming Politics in a Post-Environmental World." http://www.thebreakthrough.org/PDF/Death_of_Environmentalism.pdf (2004).

Shiffrin, Steven. "The First Amendment and Economic Regulation: Away from a General Theory of the First Amendment." 78 *Nw. U. L. Rev.* 1212 (1983).

Shiffrin, Steven. *The First Amendment, Democracy, and Romance.* Cambridge, Mass.: Harvard University Press, 1990.

Shimp, Terrence A. *Advertising, Promotion, and Supplemental Aspects of Inte-*

grated Marketing Communications. 6th ed. Mason, Ohio: Thomson / South-Western, 2003.

Shiner, Roger. *Freedom of Commercial Expression*. Oxford: Oxford University Press, 2003.

Shlensky v. Wrigley. 237 N.E.2d 776 (Ill. App. 1968).

Shogren, Elizabeth. "CFL Bulbs Have One Hitch: Toxic Mercury." *All Things Considered*, NPR, Feb. 15, 2007. http://www.npr.org/templates/story/story.php?storyId=7431198.

Siebecker, Michael R. "Building a 'New Institutional' Approach to Corporate Speech." 59 *Ala. L. Rev* 247 (2008).

Simons, Daniel J., & Christopher F. Chabris. "Gorillas in Our Midst: Sustained Inattentional Blindness for Dynamic Events." 28 *Perception* 1059 (1999).

Skover, David M., & Kellye Y. Testy. "Lesbigay Identity as Commodity." 90 *Cal. L. Rev.* 223 (2002).

Slater, Daska. "Public Corporations Shall Take Us Seriously." *N.Y. Times Magazine*, Aug. 12, 2007, SM 22.

Soley, Lawrence. *Censorship, Inc.: The Corporate Threat to Free Speech in the United States*. New York: Monthly Review Press, 2002.

Sorrell v. IMS Health. 131 S.Ct. 2653 (2011).

Southgate, Nick. "Coolhunting with Aristotle." *Int'l J. Market Res.*, Summer 2003, 167–91.

Starkman, Dean. "Boiler Room." *Colum. Journalism Rev.*, Sept./Oct. 2008, 49–53.

Stauber, John, & Sheldon Rampton. *Toxic Sludge Is Good for You: Lies, Damn Lies, and the Public Relations Industry*. Monroe, Me.: Common Courage, 1995.

Steel and Morris v. United Kingdom. 2005-11 Eur. Ct. H.R.

Steinberg, Brian. "Need a Slogan? Ask Your Harshest Critic." *AdAge.com*, July 23, 2008. http://adage.com/print?article_id=129837.

Steinberg, Brian. "Pay-for-Play Wends Its Way Into TV News." *Advertising Age*, July 28, 2008, 4, 32.

Stelter, Brian. "A Network to Make an Environmental Point." *N.Y. Times*, June 2, 2008.

St. Louis Post Dispatch. Editorial. "Credit Cards: Teach Your Children Well." July 15, 2001, B2.

Stone, Brad. "Banks Mine Data and Pitch to Troubled Borrowers." *N.Y. Times*, Oct. 22, 2008, B1.

Strasser, Susan. *Satisfaction Guaranteed: The Making of the American Mass Market*. Washington, D.C.: Smithsonian Books, 1989.

Strugatch, Warren. "L.I . @ Work: When Advertising Mixes Fact and Fiction." *N.Y. Times*, Sept. 8, 2002.

Sullivan, Teresa, Elizabeth Warren, & Jay Lawrence Westbrook. "Less Stigma or More Financial Distress: An Empirical Analysis of the Extraordinary Increase in Bankruptcy Filings." 59 *Stan. L. Rev.* 213 (2006).

Sunstein, Cass R. "Free Speech Now." 59 *U. of Chi. L. Rev.* 255 (1992).

Sunstein, Cass R. "*Lochner*'s Legacy." 87 *Colum. L. Rev.* 873 (1987).

Sun Trust Bank v. Houghton Mifflin Co. 268 F.3d 1257 (11th Cir. 2001).

Suskind, Ron. "Without a Doubt: Faith, Certainty, and the Presidency of George W. Bush." *N.Y. Times Magazine,* Oct. 17, 2004, SM 44.

Sutherland, Max. *Advertising and the Mind of the Consumer: What Works, What Doesn't, and Why.* Crows Nest, Austl.: Allen & Unwin, 1993.

Sydney Morning Herald. Editorial. "Woolworths Blows Away Dodgy Tissues." Aug. 27, 2007.

Szott Moohr, Geraldine. "An Enron Lesson: The Modest Role of the Criminal Law in Preventing Corporate Crime." In *Enron: Corporate Fiascos and Their Implications,* ed. Nancy B. Rapoport & Bala G. Dharan. New York: Foundation Press, 2004.

Taleb, Nassim Nicholas. *The Black Swan: The Impact of the Highly Improbable.* New York: Random House, 2007.

Tan, Emily. "Survey: 'Good Is the New Black.'" *Advertising Age,* July 12, 2007.

Teinowitz, Ira. "FTC Subpoenas Food Advertisers." *Advertising Age,* Aug. 13, 2007, 2.

Teinowitz, Ira. "GM Breaks Up with Big Oil." *Advertising Age,* June 10, 2008, 2.

Teinowitz, Ira. "More Major Food Marketers Establish Kid-Advertising Limits." *Advertising Age,* July 18, 2007, 2.

Thaler, Richard H., & Cass R. Sunstein. *Nudge: Improving Decisions about Health, Wealth, and Happiness.* New Haven, Conn.: Yale University Press, 2008.

This Film Is Not Yet Rated. Directed by Kirby Dick. IFC Films, 2006.

Thomaselli, Rich. "Will Harry and Louise Succeed for the Other Side?" *Advertising Age,* July 27, 2009, 6.

Thompson v. W. States Med. Ctr. 535 U.S. 357 (2002).

TNS Media Intelligence. "TNS Media Intelligence Forecasts 1.7 Percent Increase in U.S. Advertising Spending for 2007." June 12, 2007. http://www.tns global.com/news/news-47bd08cef094a98aad79c2Pubf263eb.aspix.

Trompos, Louis W. Note. "Badwill." 116 *Harv. L. Rev.* 1845 (2003).

Troy, Daniel E. "Advertising: Not 'Low Value' Speech." 16 *Yale J. Reg.* 85 (1999).

Tsai, Robert L. "Fire, Metaphor, and Constitutional Myth-Making." 93 *Geo. L.J.* (2004).

Tushnet, Rebecca. "Copy This Essay: How Fair Use Doctrine Harms Free Speech and How Copying Serves It." 114 *Yale L.J.* 535 (2004).

Twitchell, James B. *Adcult USA.* New York: Columbia University Press, 1996.

Twitchell, James B. *Branded Nation: The Marketing of Megachurch, College Inc., and Museumworld*. New York: Simon & Schuster, 2004.

Tye, Larry. *The Father of Spin: Edward L. Bernays and the Birth of Public Relations*. New York: Henry Holt, 1998.

U.S. v. Lopez. 514 U.S. 549 (1995).

U.S. v. Philip Morris USA, Inc. 449 F. Supp.2d 1 (D.D.C. 2006), aff'd 566 F.3d 1095 (D.C. Cir. 2009), amt. denied, 130 S.Ct. 3501 (2010).

United States v. Purdue Frederick Co. 495 F. Supp.2d 569 (2007).

Up in the Air. Directed by Jason Reitman. Paramount Pictures, 2009.

Urbina, Ian. "School Law Clinics Face a Backlash." *N.Y. Times*, Apr. 3, 2010, A12.

Utset, Manuel A. "Time-Inconsistent Management and the Sarbanes-Oxley Act." 31 *Ohio N.U. L. Rev*. 417 (2005).

Valentine v. Chrestensen. 316 U.S. 52 (1942).

Va. State Bd. of Pharmacy v. Va. Citizens Consumer Council. 425 U.S. 748 (1976).

Vladeck, David C. "The Difficult Case of Direct-to-Consumer Drug Advertising." 41 *Loy. L.A. L. Rev*. 259 (2007).

Vladeck, David C. "Lessons from a Story Untold: *Nike v. Kasky* Reconsidered." 54 *Case W. Res. L. Rev*. 1049 (2004).

Walker, Rob. "The Brand Underground." *N.Y. Times Magazine*, July 30, 2006, SM 28.

Walker, Rob. *Buying In: The Secret Dialog between What We Buy and Who We Are*. New York: Random House, 2008.

Walker, Rob. "Organic Growth: Name Brand? Store Brand? Safeway's Virtue-Food Products Aim to Blur the Line." *N.Y. Times Magazine*, July 13, 2008, SM 22.

Walker, Rob. "Social Currency." *N.Y. Times Magazine*, Nov. 11, 2008, 26.

Walker, Rob. "Water Proof." *N.Y. Times Magazine*, June 1, 2008, 22.

Walsh, John J. "The Supreme Court Should Expand Commercial Speech Protection." *Legal Backgrounder* (online publication of Carter Ledyard & Milburn LLP), Sept. 8, 2000. Available at http://www.clm.com/publication.cfm/ID/90.

Warren, Elizabeth. "The Market for Data: The Changing Role of Social Sciences in Shaping the Law." 2002 *Wis. L. Rev*. 1 (2002).

Warren, Elizabeth. Op-Ed. "Show Me the Money." *N.Y. Times*, Oct. 24, 2005.

Warren, Elizabeth, & Amelia Warren Tyagi. *The Two-Income Trap: Why Middle-Class Mothers and Fathers Are Going Broke*. New York: Perseus Books, 2003.

Washburn, Jennifer. *University Inc.: The Corporate Corruption of Higher Education*. New York: Basic Books, 2005.

Waxman, Henry A. The Lessons of Vioxx—Drug Safety and Sales." 352 *New England J. Medicine* 2576 (2005).

Weever, Patrick. "All the Spin Doctors' News That's Fit to Leak." *Observer*, Nov. 9, 2003, 7.

Wegner, Daniel M. *The Illusion of Conscious Will.* Cambridge, Mass.: Bradford Books / MIT Press, 2002.

Weinstein, James. "Speech Categorization and the Limits of First Amendment Formalism: Lessons from *Nike v. Kasky*." 54 *Case W. Res. L. Rev.* 1091 (2004).

Weisbuch, Robert A. "Branding Isn't a Dirty Word." *Chron. Higher Educ.,* Jan. 26, 2007, C3.

Wells, Christina E. "Reinvigorating Autonomy: Freedom and Responsibility in the Supreme Court's First Amendment Jurisprudence." 32 *Harv. C.R.-C.L. L. Rev.* 159 (1997).

Wells, C. A. Harwell. "The Cycles of Corporate Social Responsibility: An Historical Retrospective for the Twenty-First Century." 51 *Kan. L. Rev.* 77 (2002).

West, Cornel. *The American Evasion of Philosophy: A Genealogy of Pragmatism.* Madison: University of Wisconsin Press, 1989.

Westen, Drew. *The Political Brain: The Role of Emotion in Deciding the Fate of the Nation.* New York: Public Affairs, 2007.

Westen, Tracy. "Government Regulation of Food Marketing to Children: The Federal Trade Commission and the Kid-Vid Controversy." 39 *Loy. L.A. L. Rev.* 79 (2006).

Wheaton, Ken. "Agencies Have a Funny Way of Showing 'Commitment' to Diversity." *AdAge.com,* July 8, 2008. http://adage.com/bigtent/post?article_id= 128219.

White, James Boyd. "Free Speech and Valuable Speech: Silence, Dante, and the 'Marketplace of Ideas.'" 51 *UCLA L. Rev.* 799 (2004).

Whitney v. California. 274 U.S. 357 (1927).

Whitty, Julia. "BP's Deep Secrets." *Mother Jones,* Sept./Oct. 2010, 29.

Whitty, Julia. "The Last Taboo." *Mother Jones,* May/June 2010, 25.

Wilcox, Brian, Dale Kunkel, Joanne Cantor, Peter Dorwick, Susan Linn, & Edward Palmer. *Report of the APA Task Force on Advertising and Children.* Feb. 20, 2004. http://www.apa.org/pi/families/resources/advertising-chil dren.pdf.

Will, George. "The New Adulthood." *Tulsa World,* Nov. 15, 2001, A16.

Williams, Alex. "Buying into the Green Movement." *N.Y. Times,* July 1, 2007, ST 1, 8.

Williams, Alex. "That Buzz in Your Ear May Be Green Noise." *N.Y. Times,* June 15, 2008, ST 1.

Williams, Cynthia A. "Corporate Social Responsibility in an Era of Economic Globalization." 35 *U.C. Davis L. Rev.* 705 (2002).

Williams, Susan H. *Truth, Autonomy, and Speech.* New York: New York University Press, 2004.

Willis, Lauren E. "Decision-Making and the Limits of Disclosure: The Problem of Predatory Lending; Price." 65 *Md. L. Rev.* 707 (2006).

Williston, Samuel. "History of the Law of Business Corporations before 1800." *Harv. L. Rev.* 105 (1888).

Wilson, Timothy D. *Strangers to Ourselves: Discovering the Adaptive Unconscious.* Cambridge, Mass.: Belknap, 2002.

Wilson v. U.S. 221 U.S. 361 (1911).

Winkler, Adam. "Corporate Personhood and the Rights of Corporate Speech." 30 *Seattle U. L. Rev.* 863 (2007).

Wong, Grace. "Kozlowski Gets up to 25 Years." *CNNMoney.com,* Sept. 19, 2005. http://money.cnn.com/2005/09/19/news/newsmakers/kozlowski_sentence/.

Wootton, David. Introduction to *Political Writings of John Locke.* Indianapolis, IN: Hackett, 1993.

York, Emily Bryson. "McNuggets Are Good, but Branded McNuggets Are Even Better," *AdAge.com,* Aug. 8, 2007. http://adage.com/article?article_id=119753.

York, Emily Bryson. "Shopping Aisles at Cutting Edge of Consumer Research and Tech: They Learned It From You; Marketers Working to Better Understand Supermarket Psychology." *Advertising Age,* Mar. 15, 2010, 1, 29.

York, Emily Bryson. "Social Media Allows Giants to Exploit Niche Markets." *Advertising Age,* July 13, 2009, 3.

Zauderer v. Office of Disciplinary Counsel. 471 U.S. 626 (1985).

Zelizer, Julian. "Commentary: When Interest Groups Go Too Far." *CNNPolitics.com,* Aug. 11, 2009. http://www.edition2.cnn.com/2009/POLITICS/08/10/zelizer.town.halls/index.html.

Zmuda, Natalie. "Facebook Turns Focus Group with Splenda Product-Sampling App." *Advertising Age,* July 13, 2009, 18.

Zou, Xi, Kim-Pong Tam, Michael W. Morris, Sau-lai Lee, Ivy Yee-Man Lau, & Chi-yue Chiu. "Culture as Common Sense: Perceived Consensus vs. Personal Beliefs as Mechanisms of Cultural Influence." 97(4) *J. Personality & Soc. Psychol.* 579 (2009).

Index